Edward Gibbon

Memoirs of My Life

Portrait of Edward Gibbon by Sir Joshua Reynolds, painted
in 1779 (see *Letters*, ii, p. 216, n. 5).
(*From the Dalmeny Collection, by permission of Lord Rosebery*)

Edward Gibbon

Memoirs of My Life

edited from the manuscripts

by

Georges A. Bonnard

NELSON

THOMAS NELSON AND SONS LTD
36 Park Street London W1
P.O. Box 336 Apapa Lagos
P.O. Box 25012 Nairobi
77 Coffee Street San Fernando Trinidad

THOMAS NELSON (AUSTRALIA) LTD
597 Little Collins Street Melbourne C1

THOMAS NELSON AND SONS (SOUTH AFRICA) (PROPRIETARY) LTD
P.O. Box 9881 Johannesburg

THOMAS NELSON AND SONS (CANADA) LTD
81 Curlew Drive Don Mills Ontario

THOMAS NELSON AND SONS
Copewood and Davis Streets Camden 3 N.J.

First published 1966
© Georges A. Bonnard 1966
© MSS Sir John Murray, KCVO, DSO

Contents

Illustrations

Preface

What has come to be known as Gibbon's Autobiography was first published in March 1796[1], two years after the historian's death, under the title of MEMOIRS OF MY LIFE AND WRITINGS. It appeared at the beginning of the *Miscellaneous Works of Edward Gibbon, Esq.*, two folio volumes of literary remains and letters selected and edited by his friend and executor John Holroyd, first Earl of Sheffield. In his *Advertisement* Lord Sheffield describes the MEMOIRS as 'a work which Gibbon seems to have projected with peculiar solicitude and attention, and of which he left Six different sketches, all in his own handwriting' and adds: 'From all of them the following Memoirs have been carefully selected, and put together.'

The success of the *Miscellaneous Works*, 'the strong wish repeatedly expressed' that Lord Sheffield should give to the public some more of the unpublished pieces in his possession, induced him to undertake the preparation of a new edition which came out early in 1815, but which was dated 1814. It was issued in two distinct forms. There was, on the one hand, a folio volume containing all the additional matter; to this the owners of the two folios of 1796 were invited to subscribe. On the other hand there was an edition in five 8vo volumes: the first two contained the MEMOIRS and letters, the last three the articles published in 1796 and the additional ones thrown together and arranged in three sections. In his *Advertisement* to this second edition Lord Sheffield says of the MEMOIRS, more explicitly, that 'they were composed and formed from six different Sketches, and from Notes and Memoranda on loose unconnected Papers and Cards, all in Mr Gibbon's Handwriting', and that he 'had taken the opportunity of interweaving several additional Extracts from the same sources'.

---

[1] *A Bibliography of the Works of Edward Gibbon* by J. E. Norton, Oxford University Press, 1940, p. 190.

From the first, the MEMOIRS appear to have been the most popular part of the *Miscellaneous Works*, though the reviewers were not unanimous in their praise, some regretting that the editor had not made a more drastic use of the pruning-knife, while others complained of his having omitted what they supposed might have been of great interest. Although the 1796 edition was at once reprinted at Dublin and Bâle for Irish and Continental readers, in Great Britain itself there was only one reprint, published in 1837[1], complete in one volume of the second, 1814, edition. The MEMOIRS themselves were printed separately in 1827, and again several times in the course of the 19th century. All the editors had to be content with simply reproducing the text of the second edition, and this because access to and use of the material from which it had been compiled was strictly denied to them.

The six sketches, together with a number of letters and other papers by or relating to Gibbon, belonged to the heirs of Lord Sheffield who, by a clause in his will, had 'directed that no further publication of the historian's manuscripts should be made' unless his permission had been given 'by some memorandum written and signed' by him. As, apparently, no such memorandum had ever been found, his son and grandson obeyed his request not to suffer the manuscripts 'to be out of their possession or to be improperly exposed'. It is believed, wrote the third Earl in 1896, 'that no person has ever had access to any of the manuscripts for any literary purpose, excepting the late Dean Milman, who, when editing his well-known edition of the *Decline and Fall*, in 1842, was permitted to inspect the original manuscripts of the Autobiography, on condition of not publishing any new matter'[2].

To the name of Dean Milman, the third Lord Sheffield would probably have added another had he known that his father, the second Lord, had in 1871 lent the box containing

---

[1] *Ibid.*, p. 197.

[2] *Introduction by the Earl of Sheffield* to John Murray's edition of *The Autobiographies* and to R. E. Prothero's edition of the *Private Letters*, both published by Murray in 1896.

all the Gibbon papers to Dr William Alexander Greenhill, M.D., who was practising at Hastings. In the intervals
of a busy and useful life Greenhill pursued various literary
and historical researches[1]. From a letter preserved in the
British Museum it appears that he had been lent the Gibbon
papers for the purpose of sorting and cataloguing them
without being told that they were not to be used for any
literary purpose[2]. In the course of the work he had been
entrusted with, he realized that a new edition of the MEMOIRS
would be amply justified. So on 21 December 1871 he went

[1] For W. A. Greenhill (1814-1894) see *D.N.B.*, xxii (Supplement),
1909. Greenhill's edition of Sir Thomas Browne's *Religio Medici* in the
Golden Treasury series, published in 1881, was frequently reprinted and
long considered authoritative. But to judge from what the latest editor of
Religio Medici says, the edition of Gibbon's *Autobiography* which he contemplated would not have satisfied modern critical standards (see J.-J.
Denonain's edition of *Religio Medici*, Cambridge University Press, 1953,
p. xxxvi).

[2]   Hastings Jan 27 '72
My Lord
   On returning Gibbon's papers I take the opportunity of assuring your
Lordship that I have in every respect endeavoured to carry out your wishes
while they were in my possesssion. Not one of them has ever been out of my
house, (nor indeed out of the box, except when actually being used,) and
not one of them (nor even one sentence of one of them) has been copied.
– As they were sent back two or three days earlier than I had intended, I
was unable to look over all the letters once more, to see that they were
properly arranged, but I hope you will not find many out of their places. I
should have made a fuller catalogue if I had followed my own inclination, but
I hope that what I *have* done will be found useful.
   With respect to some of the other papers I think the Common Place
Books that were taken to pieces for the use of the printer should now be put
together again for their better preservation. And I may add that there [are]
a few of the still unpublished papers which it is almost certain that Gibbon
himself would in some form or other, either wholly or in part, have given to
the world. I allude particularly to his tour in Switzerland, & his list of
authors quoted in his History, (both of which are mentioned by himself) &
also to the short notes & corrections relating to the History, which would
be valuable to any future Editor.
   I have only to thank your Lordship once more for the pleasure you have
afforded me by allowing me to examine the papers at my leisure, & am,
My Lord, Y[r] Lordship's obliged and Obed[t]. Serv[t].
                                                       W. A. Greenhill
R[t] Hon[ble] the Earl of Sheffield
                    (*British Museum, Add. MSS. 34887 ff 378-379*)

to see John Murray, the publisher, and offered to undertake such a new edition. He was ignorant of the clause in the first Lord Sheffield's will, as he had not yet seen Dean Milman's edition of 1839, the first note of which runs: 'The late Lord Sheffield, by a clause in his will, positively prohibited the publication of any more out of the mass of Gibbon's papers in the possession of his family. By the kind favour of the present Lord Sheffield I have been permitted (of course with the distinct understanding that the will of his father should be rigidly respected) to see these six sketches of the life . . . .' Acting on Murray's advice Greenhill went at once to the British Museum where he examined Milman's edition and, on the following day, wrote from Hastings to the publisher, not to withdraw his proposal, but to leave it to him to decide whether he would undertake to publish the new edition[1]. It is probable that Murray informed Lord Sheffield of the proposal he had received. At any rate Lord Sheffield requested Greenhill to return the papers at once, even if his work was not completed. Greenhill, of course, obeyed and so the box of the Gibbon papers was restored to its place in the strong-room of Sheffield Park, somewhat enriched by what the good doctor had been able to do as a cataloguer.

More than twenty years later, as the centenary of Gibbon's

---

[1]
                                        Hastings
                                        Dec. 22. '71
Dear Sir,
    After leaving you yesterday I went to the British Museum, where I saw for the first time Dean Milman's edition of Gibbon's Memoirs in one vol. 1839 (I think). This is altogether fuller than that prefixed to the Decline & Fall, & contains extracts from the Letters & Journals.
    I still think even this edition is capable of improvement, but I am bound to say that it does to a certain extent do away with the necessity of the new edition that I was contemplating. You will judge by the sale of Dean Milman's edition [*published by Murray*] whether my scheme would be likely to be sufficiently popular to induce you to undertake it.
    Let me thank you for the courtesy with which you received my offer, & believe me
                                        Yrs very faithfully
                                        W. A. Greenhill
John Murray Esq[re]
    The editor's thanks are due to Sir John Murray for communicating the above letter to Sir Gavin de Beer and to Sir Gavin himself for making a copy of it.

death was approaching, the Royal Historical Society decided, on the initiative of Frederic Harrison, its vice-president, that this anniversary should be commemorated by a public ceremony and an exhibition of portraits, manuscripts and other relics of the great historian. The third Earl of Sheffield then felt that the time had perhaps come to disregard his grandfather's injunction. 'Whilst persons named in these papers or their children were living,' he wrote, 'whilst the bitter controversies of the last century were still unforgotten, whilst the fame of Edward Gibbon had hardly yet become one of our national glories, it was a matter of good feeling and sound judgment in Lord Sheffield to exercise an editor's discretion in publishing his friend's confession and private thoughts. Now that more than a hundred years have passed since his death, no such considerations have weight or meaning.'[1] Professional friends whom he consulted concurred in his own conclusion that he owed it to the public to give to the world what remains of the historian he possessed. Accordingly he sold the copyright of his Gibbon papers to John Murray, and put them at the disposal of the organizers of the proposed exhibition.

Thus it came about that, for the first time, the public could look at the six sketches, each of which was represented by one or more particularly significant pages.

In his address to the Commemoration meeting on 15 November 1894, Frederic Harrison expressed the hope that the centenary of Gibbon's death would lead to 'a new and exhaustive examination of the larger literary remains of the historian, which . . . have never received any critical review from any eye whatever,' and congratulated the Earl of Sheffield, who was present as president of the Commemoration, for consenting 'to satisfy the curiosity of the reading world with such new and additional publication of these unknown papers as a careful scrutiny shall suggest'. He then proceeded to a detailed criticism of the 1796-1814 editions of the MEMOIRS in the light of the manuscript sketches themselves, which he had been permitted to study. Harrison's address, soon afterwards published by the Royal Historical

[1] *Introduction by the Earl of Sheffield to The Autobiographies. . . , p. viii.*

Society in their *Proceedings of the Gibbon Commemoration*[1], came as a revelation and something of a shock to the learned world. In spite of what the original editor had said in his *Advertisements* no one had suspected the extent of the liberties he had taken with Gibbon's own text.

Before concluding his address, Harrison suggested that 'the British Museum should be urged to obtain what it can of Gibbon's papers and that Lord Sheffield [the third Earl] should give to the public those of the writings which still remained unpublished'. The publication in 1896 of the *Private Letters* and of *The Autobiographies*, the former edited by R. E. Prothero, and the latter by John Murray who gave a faithful reproduction of the sketches in Gibbon's own spelling (but modernized his punctuation and use of capitals), and the acquisition by the British Museum of the original manuscripts in 1895 and 1896[2] proved before long that Harrison's widely supported suggestions had been heard and fortunately acted upon.

The Autobiographies went into a second edition one year after its first publication, but was never reissued after 1897. As John Murray printed the six sketches so as to present a consecutive narrative of Gibbon's life, one might have expected it to supersede the traditional text in the favour of new editors and the reading public. But it had no such influence, at least in Great Britain, and remained only a precious document for specialists of Gibbonian studies. When George Birkbeck Hill, having brought to an end his long labours on Johnson, decided to prepare a new edition of Gibbon's MEMOIRS, he adopted the original text of 1796, merely completing it with the few additions of the second (1814) edition. He thought it sufficient to correct, with the help of John Murray's text, some of Lord Sheffield's obvious misreadings and to record in footnotes a selection of the words and phrases which the first editor had deliberately altered. When Gibbon's *Autobiography* was included in the World's Classics in 1907 and, in 1911, in Everyman's

---

[1] London, Longmans, Green & Co., 1895.
[2] According to a note on the flyleaf of *Add. MSS 34874*, the Sketches were purchased of Lord Sheffield partly on 31 July 1895 and partly on 13 April 1896.

Library, both the Oxford University Press and Messrs
J. M. Dent & Sons reprinted the text of 1814[1]. This continued adherence to Lord Sheffield's text after it had become
known that it hardly gave a proper idea of the author's is
easily accounted for. In the course of a full century it had
been a favourite with the reading public and its undeniable
qualities had often and rightly been extolled. To try to
offer in its place an edition that strictly conformed to modern
critical standards might well, in a way, appear a piece of
impudence, and be given but little attention[2]. These reasons,
however, did not prevent a well-known American scholar,
O. F. Emerson, from giving, two years after the publication
of *The Autobiographies*, a new edition of the MEMOIRS made
up of a selection of the sketches (in John Murray's text).
His selection was partly the same and partly different from
Lord Sheffield's. But what he selected, he printed without
expurgations or textual alterations. The editor, a University
professor, thought of his students rather than of the general
public. His work, and its positive value, remained un-
acknowledged outside University circles.

All the material, with a single exception, from which any
edition of the MEMOIRS must be compiled is contained in one
volume of the Gibbon Papers in the British Museum,
Add. MSS 34874, where are preserved the manuscripts of
Gibbon's six attempts[3] at writing his own life, as well as,
on an untitled loose sheet, a separate version of his introduction to the history of his family. Besides these, Lord

---

[1] Apart from a few accidental alterations.

[2] As George Saintsbury wrote in 1898, 'It has been for three generations
one of the favourite things of its kind . . . and is likely to continue so in the
textus receptus, for which the fussy fidelity of modern literary methods will
probably try in vain to substitute a chaos of rough drafts.' *A Short History
of English Literature*, p. 626.

[3] To call them *sketches* is really misleading: only one of them, E, is a
sketch of Gibbon's life, and it is a complete one; D is a true draft (of E)
and was written as such (see below, pp. xxvi-xxvii); A, B, C and F were
undertaken and, so far as they went, written as definitive texts, but were all
left unfinished. For convenience' sake, however, and because it is traditional since 1796, *sketch* has often been used in the following pages, and so
has *draft* which J. E. Norton preferred.

Sheffield made use of a correspondence card in Gibbon's earlier handwriting, which is now to be found in another volume of the same Papers[1].

After William Alexander Greenhill had examined the sketches, he arranged them in what appeared to him the probable order of their composition, denoting them by the first six letters of the alphabet, A for the earliest and F for the latest, and then drew up a three-page note clearly intended for the catalogue he was making. He attached it to the sketches when he returned the box of Gibbon papers to Lord Sheffield. It was bought with them by the British Museum and there it was bound in the same volume. In the *Catalogue of Additions to the Manuscripts of the British Museum in the years 1894-1899,* London 1901, there is this entry on p. 112: '34874 Vol. 1. Six autobiographical sketches . . . preceded by a short account of them (ff 1-3) by W. A. Greenhill . . . .' When they arrived at the British Museum the sketches seem to have been in the state in which Greenhill had returned them to their owner in January 1872, that is, in batches of loose sheets, some double, most single, and perhaps, at least in one case, in the form of what remained of a note-book, unused pages of which had been torn off[2].

Gibbon had numbered the pages of his successive drafts, the pages of A being numbered 1 to 39, those of B: 1 to 72, those of C: 1 to 41; of the 13 pages of D only the odd ones received their numbers; of the 19 pages of E the last one

---

[1] See below, p. 156, n. 5. The untitled sheet and the card were referred to, rather inaccurately, by Lord Sheffield in the *Advertisement* to his second edition of the *Miscellaneous Works* as 'Notes and Memoranda on loose unconnected Papers and Cards'.

[2] A is followed by a blank sheet of light cardboard of the same 4to size as its pages. This sheet was unnumbered by either Gibbon or the British Museum. It looks like the back cover of a note-book. Its place in the bound volume suggests that it came to the B.M. Library with the batch of A sheets. As all the pages of A are single sheets, with the only exception of pp. 19-20, which are a double sheet and bear clear marks of being the middle pages of a sewn note-book, one is led to the conclusion that Gibbon wrote A in the first thirty-nine pages of a seventy-two-page note-book, the last sixteen blank sheets of which were torn off at some time, possibly to make the suppression of pp. 25-30 easier.

only is numbered, but whether it was by Gibbon himself is doubtful: the writing is Greenhill's rather than Gibbon's; the pages of F are again quite regularly numbered.

In accordance with British Museum practice Gibbon's page-numbers were crossed out in pencil and replaced by a numbering of the folios when the manuscript loose sheets were mounted on guards and bound into a volume. The six sketches with the notes of E and F fill ff 4–127. They are preceded by a flyleaf, unnumbered, with a lock of Gibbon's hair covered by a piece of celluloid pasted on the verso, and Greenhill's descriptive note, three pages written on the recto only and numbered 1–3. The sketches are followed by the independent version of the introduction to a history of the Gibbon family (ff 128-129), a sketch of his life, dated 1 Mars 1781, which Gibbon wrote in French (ff 130-131), a memorandum of subjects to be dealt with in the account of his first stay at Lausanne (f 132), his will and testament of July 1788 (ff 133-134), all these documents being in his own handwriting. The volume ends with some information on the number of students at Oxford and Cambridge in the 18th century sent to Lord Sheffield at his own request (ff 135-136); and it is illustrated with the well-known silhouettes of Gibbon taking snuff on ff 5 and 140.

Concerning the dates of the sketches from which he had compiled his edition of the MEMOIRS, Lord Sheffield did not commit himself to any definite statement. He merely said in the *Advertisement* to the 1796 edition of the *Miscellaneous Works* that it was difficult to ascertain in what order they had been composed. To this statement nothing was added in the second (1814) edition.

Dr Greenhill was the first to date the sketches. His note deserves to be published, which has not been done so far. In fact it seems to have been more or less overlooked or ignored, partly no doubt because its author had not been identified[1]:

---

[1] J. E. Norton refers to Greenhill's note as 'an attached note, said, in the Museum catalogue, to be by Dr Greenwall' (*A Bibliography*, p. 181).

'Six sketches of Gibbon's autobiography, all in his own hand-writing. From a careful examination of all these sketches, and especially of the marginal corrections made by Gibbon himself, it appears probable that they were written in the following order: viz.

A. written 1788, 9, relates to his family.
B.   ,,   '89, '90, ends April '64.
C.   ,,   '90   ,,   Oct, '72.
D.   ,,   '90, '91, ,,   Oct. '72.
E.   ,,   '91,   ,,   July '89.
F.   ,,   '92, '93, ,,   June '53.

'A. 4to. 39 pages (*pp. 25-30 missing*): – called "The Memoirs of the life of Edward Gibbon, with various observations and excursions by himself": – written in his 'fifty-second year', viz. 1788, 9, – and probably before Sketches B and F. – does not get beyond the notice of his family. –
'B. 4to. 72 pages: – called "My own life": – written about two years after seeing Mr Langer, viz. '89, '90, and probably after Sketch A, and before C and F. – history ends April '64. – just before the commencement of his tour in Italy.
'C. fol. 41 pages: – called "Memoirs of the life and writings of Edward Gibbon": – written about three years after seeing Mr Langer, and while Mrs Hester Gibbon was still alive (*she died June '90.*), and probably after Sketch B, and before D: – history ends with his removal to London, Oct. '72. –
'D. fol. 13 pages: – No title: – begins "I was born at Putney," etc.: – probably written after Sketch C, and before E: – history ends with his removal to London, Oct. '72. –
'E. fol. 19 pages of text, and 12 of Notes: – called "My own Life": – dated at the end of the text, "Lausanne, March 2. 1791": – written probably after Sketch D: – history ends with the death of Mr Deyverdun, July '89. – The Notes appear to have been added towards the end of '92 or the beginning of '93, viz. after the abolition of royalty in France, and before the execution of the King. (See Note 48. The passage of the Decline and Fall alluded to in this note is towards the end of Chap. 38. vol. iv. p. 407. ed. 1862.)
'F. fol. 41 pages*. – no title: – begins "My family is origin-

ally derived," etc.: – written 'after the lapse of forty years' since leaving (or residing at) Oxford, viz. '92, '93 – and probably after Sketches A and B: – history ends with his leaving Oxford, June '53. – This is the most copious of all the sketches, and was taken by Lord Sheffield as the basis of his "Memoirs". –

'* with 7 pages of short notes written on paper of a different size and shape.'

Whether Frederic Harrison had seen or paid any attention to Greenhill's note does not appear. In his Commemoration address he spoke of the sketches as 'written apparently at different dates in the five years 1788-1793'. The Catalogue of the commemoration exhibition follows exactly the order and the dating of Greenhill's note, but gives the dates as certain, and not merely probable. John Murray, in his edition of *The Autobiographies* seems to have partly disagreed with Greenhill and the Catalogue: he accepts their dates in the case of A, D and F only, but dates C as 'written about 1788', and leaves undated B and E.

Dissatisfied with the approximate character of the dates assigned to the sketches by the first Lord Sheffield, Frederic Harrison, the Catalogue and John Murray, O. F. Emerson devoted several pages of his introduction to this question of their dates. On the basis of all the evidence he could collect, he concluded that A 'must have been written in the last months of 1788 or the first of 1789', that B 'must have been begun and well under way in the spring of 1789', that C 'was written about the same time as B', but he thought that the weight of evidence was overwhelmingly in favour of placing C before B, because he took B to be 'an elaboration of C'. Likewise he regarded D as an elaboration of E, and assigned both to the winter 1790-1791. He regarded F as 'composed in the early part of 1793'.

Emerson appears, however, to have overlooked some of the evidence in the texts of B and C which helps to date them. In B, Gibbon wrote that John Gibbon's *Introductio ad Latinam Blasoniam* was sent to him 'about two years ago'[1];

---

[1] *The Autobiographies*, p. 108.

this becomes in C 'about three years ago'[1]. Looking back on the *Essai sur l'étude de la littérature,* published in 1761, he wrote: 'at the end of twenty-eight years I may appreciate my juvenile work with the impartiality of a stranger'[2]; he altered this in C to 'in a cool impartial perusal near thirty years after the first effusion'[3]. From these two statements in B and C, it is surely clear that the order B C is the right one, and that Emerson's order C B is mistaken. Two more items may be added in confirmation, though they may not be given the same weight as the first two: in B Gibbon explained that the 14th-century John Gibbon was architect in the service of King Edward III and added in the margin this parenthesis '(the office of an Esquire)' with a clear reference that this addition should be placed after the word 'architect'[4]; in C this parenthesis is duly inserted in the text although Gibbon neglected to put in the second bracket[5]. In B again he introduced the account of his service as an officer in the militia with these words 'I shall describe our marches and counter-marches as they are faithfully recorded in my own journal . . . of the times'[6]; intent on being more concise, he changed this in C to 'With the help of an original journal I could write the history of my . . . campaigns; but . . . they shall be dispatched in a few words'[7].

If there can be no doubt that B preceded C, there is little or even no doubt either that B was written in 1788-1789. In B he says of the annuity settled on him by his father in 1758 that it was 'more valuable thirty years ago'[8] and speaks of his recollections of Paris in January-May 1763 as being 'darkly seen through the medium of five and twenty years'[9]. Of his collaboration with Deyverdun in the *Mémoires littéraires,* which lasted from 1767 to early in 1769, he writes in C that 'at the distance of more than twenty years, it would be impossible for me to ascertain the respective shares of the two associates'[10], which points to 1789.

Emerson's chief reason for putting C before B is that B

[1] *Ibid.,* p. 214.   [2] *Ibid.,* p. 172.
[3] *Ibid.,* p. 256.   [4] *Ibid.,* 107 – MS f 23.
[5] *Ibid.,* p. 213, where the second bracket is wrongly placed – MS f 58ᵛ.
[6] *Ibid.,* p. 184.   [7] *Ibid.,* p. 253.   [8] *Ibid.,* p. 156.
[9] *Ibid.,* p. 199.   [10] *Ibid.,* p. 279.

is 'relatively longer and much more detailed than C, so that . . . C is doubtless the earlier sketch which was then re-written and elaborated into B'. For the same reason he places E, dated at the end 'March 2. 1791' before D. But, while there is some evidence that D was at least partly written in 1790 ('At the distance of thirty-seven years', Gibbon wrote in D, 'I can still remember the melancholy impression of my first arrival at Lausanne'[1] on 30 June 1753), there is nothing in E which can be said to point to 1790 rather than to the early weeks of 1791. Dating his 'establishment at Lausanne' to 27 September 1783, he writes that 'since . . . more than seven years have elapsed'[2]. Further on, speaking of the state of affairs in France: 'Within the last two or three years our tranquillity has been clouded by the disorders of France'[3], where the context shows that he is thinking as much of the financial crisis as of the early events of the Revolution, he may well refer to the two years and four or five months that had passed since he had told Lord Sheffield, in October 1788, how anxious he was at the turn of events in France[4].

There is therefore no reason to change the order of D and E. But the composition of D may not have been inter-rupted before 1791, which would account for Gibbon no longer speaking of the time since the publication of the *Essai* in June 1761 as 'near thirty years'[5], but merely as 'thirty years'[6]. The thirteen pages of D may have been the work of a few weeks at the end of 1790 and of the early days of 1791. The latter part of January and February sufficed to write the nineteen pages of E.

On the basis of the order of the six sketches determined by Greenhill, an attempt may be made at reconstituting – more or less conjecturally, of course – the history of their composition.

---

[1] *Ibid.*, p. 396.   [2] *Ibid.*, p. 328.   [3] *Ibid.*, p. 342.
[4] *The Letters of Edward Gibbon*, edited by J. E. Norton, London, Cassell, 1956, iii, p. 133 (referred to as *Letters* in what follows).
[5] *The Autobiographies*, p. 256.   [6] *Ibid.*, p. 403.

When and why the idea of writing his own life occurred to Gibbon is not known. But it may well be that he was indebted for it to his reading the small Latin treatise on Heraldry published in 1682 by John Gibbon, the Herald, in whom, ignorant as he was of his more remote ancestry, he saw from the first a member of his family, a brother of his great-grandfather Matthew Gibbon. At the end of his little book the Herald had added some notes on his ancestry and career, including among his forbears the Lord High Treasurer whom John Cade, in Shakespeare's *Henry VI, Part II*, condemns to death for having founded a school and caused printing to be used. The right which Gibbon thought he had to claim his descent from a great nobleman, patron and martyr of learning, his fancied kinship with the quaint figure of John Gibbon, Tory pamphleteer as well as Bluemantle pursuivant, the example set by this former Gibbon in recounting his life perhaps suggested the idea of his doing the same one day.

It was late in 1786 or early in 1787 that the *Introductio ad Latinam Blasoniam* was given him by the Duke of Brunswick's librarian, Ernst Theodor Langer, who had found it among the discarded books of the ducal library, and thought it would interest the historian. Langer had stayed at Lausanne as tutor and travelling companion to the duke's eldest son from 1784 to the summer 1786, when he had made Gibbon's acquaintance and got to know him well. In 1787 the duke entrusted him with the education of his second son, and Langer came to Lausanne with his pupil in September. Langer had sent the *Introductio* to Catherine de Sévery with a letter asking her to give it to her great English friend[1]. This must have been between his return to Wolfenbüttel in autumn 1786 and the time when, in the following spring, he planned to return to Lausanne[2]. Gibbon read the *Introductio* on receiving it, but if it aroused his ambition of writing his own life, he felt that he must put it off until his great work

[1] This letter is quoted, but without a date, in W. de Sévery's *La Vie de Société dans le Pays de Vaud à la fin du dix-huitième siècle*, Lausanne and Paris, 1912, ii, p. 8.

[2] See P. Zimmerman's article on E. T. Langer in *Zeitschrift des Harz-vereins für Geschichte und Alterthumskunde*, 1884, pp. 41-42.

was off his hands, as he was then giving his whole time
to bringing it to an end. To the mornings, his 'usual period
of study', he was now frequently adding the evenings: 'by
this extraordinary industry which I never practised before,
and to which I hope never to be again reduced I see the
last part of my history growing apace under my hands'[1],
he wrote to Lord Sheffield on 20 January 1787. To his
publisher who wanted him to correct a new 8vo edition
of the first three volumes of the *Decline and Fall*, he had
already answered that at a moment when he was 'straining
every nerve to conclude' his labours, he could spare no time
for such work[2].

When in July 1787 he made ready to take the manuscript
of the last volumes to his publisher and printer in London,
he also took with him the *Introductio*, ostensibly to show it
to Lord Sheffield and his stepmother[3], secretly because he
was determined to use the opportunity of his stay in England
to make sure that its author really was, as he believed, his
great-great-uncle. Seeing his three volumes through the
press, visiting his friends and relatives filled his time so well
that it was not until May 1788 that he could begin his researches into the history of his family. He went to the College
of Arms, got into touch with one of the heralds, John
Charles Brooke, who promised to help him and to whom
he wrote twice in June, stating that his chief ambition was
to connect himself 'with the Herald John Gibbon, both on
account of his original character and to appropriate all that
he says of his own kindred and descent'[4]. At the time
Brooke could not supply him with anything that he did not
already know[5] and he returned to Lausanne still feeling that
he must be connected with the author of the *Introductio*
though the proof had not been found. Brooke, however,
continued his investigations and actually made sure that the
herald and the historian of the Roman Empire belonged to
different branches of the Kentish Gibbons. This information
he imparted to Lord Sheffield who did not realize the interest it had for his friend and neglected to pass it on to him[6].

---

[1] *Letters*, iii, pp. 59-60.   [2] *Ibid.*, p. 55.   [3] *Ibid.*, p. 82.
[4] *Ibid.*, p. 114.   [5] *Ibid.*, p. 110, n. 3.   [6] *Add. MSS 34887*, f 48.

For the next four years, Gibbon stuck to his conviction.

Back at Lausanne at the end of July 1788, he was delighted to be 'free to enjoy all the pleasure of study . . . no longer chained to the regular performance of a laborious task'[1]. His October letter to Lord Sheffield gives a pleasant picture of his freedom from actual work: 'After having been so long chained to the oar in a splendid galley indeed, I freely and fairly enjoy my liberty . . . range without controul over the wide expanse of my library, converse, as my fancy prompts me with poets and historians, philosophers and orators of every age and language, and often indulge my meditations in the invention and arrangement of mighty works which I shall probably never find time or application to execute.'[2] Among these mighty works (is he not ironical at his own expense?), the invention and arrangement of which fed his meditations in this autumn of 1788 there was surely the story of his own life. For it was before the end of the year or early in 1789 that he started writing it, less than two years since he had first read John Gibbon's *Introductio*, 'in the fifty-second year of my age'.

He believed that the story of his life and career was all arranged in his mind and that there only remained to write it down. So he took a note-book of seventy-two pages, similar to those he had used, years earlier, for his Journals[3] and filled its first page with the full title he had decided upon, composing it in the most careful and elaborate manner[4]. He repeated it in a shortened form on the upper part of his third page and started on his Chapter I with a summary of what he meant it to contain. But in the course of his composition, after three paragraphs of Introduction (one to explain his purpose in writing his memoirs, one to justify his beginning with a history of his family, and one to relate how he had come to know so much about it), fifteen pages[5] of family history, thirteen devoted to his grandfather and father, he suddenly deviated from his plan in the summary and, instead of passing on to his birth and

---

[1] *Letters*, iii, p. 125.   [2] *Ibid.*, p. 131.
[3] See above, p. xiv, n. 2.   [4] See below, p. xxxvi.
[5] The pages referred to are those numbered by Gibbon himself.

infancy, wrote at length about his two aunts, Catherine and Hester Gibbon, and Hester's life-companion and spiritual director, William Law. He had thus reached his page 39 when he stopped. Why? Did he suddenly realize that he had yielded to the temptation of adding new matter to a chapter carefully planned in advance? Did he feel that he was running the risk of being much too long? After writing nearly forty pages, he had not yet begun to deal with the better half of the subjects to which he meant to devote his first chapter. Whatever his reasons, he decided to put aside what he had done and start again on different lines.

Between his first and his second attempt there was but a short interval. In A he had written that he had received the *Introductio* 'not two years since'; this becomes in B 'about two years ago'. Coming, further on in B, to his present opinion of his *Essai* published in June 1761, he dates it 'at the end of twenty-eight years', that is, in the late spring 1789. He continued his work steadily but was interrupted by the news of the death at Aix-les-Bains, on 4 July, of George Deyverdun. In the following months there was no possibility for Gibbon to give his mind to his Memoirs. But he had filled seventy-two pages, taking the narrative down to his departure from Lausanne on his Italian tour in April 1764. He had reduced the thirty-nine pages[1] of his first attempt to a mere five, his introduction was now limited to one paragraph only, the first of A, which he had completed by giving at once the reasons and examples which he had first meant to reserve for his last chapter (did he now feel less confident of ever reaching this final chapter?)[2]; the early history of his family was summed up in about two pages; not quite two sufficed him to give the main facts about his grandfather, the Actons and his aunts; one was enough for his parents; he then dwelt at some length on his many diseases as an infant and a child, his early schooling and reading (pages 7-14), his year at Oxford and his conversion

[1] The size of the 4to pages of B is exactly the same as that of the pages of A; but, by using a smaller hand, Gibbon managed to include some more lines in each page of B.

[2] His entitling B simply 'My own life', his not dividing it into chapters, may also be due to his lack of confidence.

(14–19), pursuing his account to 1764. This long narrative was not divided into chapters, as though such a division had better be introduced when the end had been reached.

Had he not been compelled, by the death of his friend, the rearrangement of his life and a long absence from his library at La Grotte, to lay down his pen, there is no reason why he should not have proceeded in the same leisurely pace and narrated the last twenty-five years of his life as he had the first twenty-seven.

On 19 November 1789, after staying five or six weeks with the de Séverys at Rolle, he returned to Lausanne in the best of health and, a few days later, wrote to his stepmother: she may 'possibly hear that Mr Gibbon has undertook some new history', but 'be persuaded that . . . after his weighty quartos, he now reads and writes for his own amusement though I will not answer for what those amusements may one day produce'[1]. He had probably taken up his second attempt and was considering what he would do with it. Rereading it, he was dissatisfied with the order in which some subjects had been dealt with, thought it overlong and altogether in need of correction. So he resolved to write it all over again. Frederic Harrison thought that 'it was not at all clear that the historian had the other drafts before him whilst composing any one'[2]. But a close comparison of the texts of B and C proves beyond doubt that he kept his second draft under his eyes while writing his third, and very often contented himself with simply copying what he had already written.

As regards the arrangement of his matter, he preserved the same order as in B as far as his return from his Lausanne exile; but, instead of dealing with his *Essai* first and his time in the militia second, he now began with a much shortened survey of his military service, and followed it with an account of the composition and publication of the *Essai*, its reception and his mature judgment of it, and then of his literary studies and projects when under arms. For his three months in Paris (1763) and his year at Lausanne

[1] *Letters*, iii, p. 176.
[2] *Proceedings of the Gibbon Commemoration*, p. 27.

(1763-1764), he reverted to the order of B, and then continued beyond B until 1772 when, two years after his father's
death, he let Buriton and settled in London. C is much
shorter than B. It covers in twenty-eight pages the ground
covered by B in seventy-two, or, taking into account the
larger size of the paper he was now using, we may say that
he reduced the seventy-two pages of B to thirty-seven pages
of the same size. This reduction was obtained by the radical
suppression of several topics and the drastic shortening of
most of the others. This of course entailed the sacrifice of
much matter of biographical interest, but gave him some
room to add a few facts[1]. From a literary standpoint, C is
unquestionably better than B. Not only is its composition
more satisfactory, and is it free from matter devoid of
biographical interest, but throughout his rewriting Gibbon
was intent on correcting his style, so that a comparison of
C with B would be most rewarding to anyone studying his
art as a writer.

The time taken in writing his third attempt may not have
been more than a few weeks. Begun late in November 1789
it was perhaps finished by the middle of January 1790.
Another ten pages and he reached the end of his second
Section for, on coming, in his new narrative, to his return
to England in 1758, he had decided[2] to revert to his original
plan, divide it into what he now preferred to call Sections,
and give a distinct Section to his life from 1758 to his
father's death in 1770. He could now start on the third,
which was to treat of his life in London when he turned all
his energies to the composition of the *Decline and Fall*. Of
this new chapter he had written two pages in what reads
like a comfortable mood, making work easy and pleasant,
and he was beginning a third page (the 41st of C) when
he stopped as though his fingers refused to hold his pen.
What had happened? Three months later, he wrote to Lord
Sheffield: 'On the ninth of February I was seized by such a

---

[1] See Appendix I, 14-20.
[2] The second Section begins on a new page headed *Section ii* (MS f 66ᵛ);
so does the third section (f 78) headed *Section iii*, but there is no heading
to the first section.

fit of the Gout as I had never known . . . With some vicissitudes of better and worse I have groaned between two and
three months; the debility has survived the pain, and
though now easy, I am carried about in my chair'[1]. How long
was it before he could resume the composition of his Memoirs?
On 7 August, he was gradually recovering, but still felt
very weak[2]. In September he accepted an invitation to
spend part of the autumn at Rolle whither he went on
5 October. He also had an invitation to Coppet and was
there for a few days in November. Back in his Lausanne
home, rendered still more agreeable by various arrangements made during his absence, he felt well enough to contemplate the composition of a supplementary volume to his
great history[3].

The resumption of his Memoirs was now possible. He
was surely anxious to bring them to an end, but his experience of previous interruptions made him chary of too
ambitious a plan. Even shortened as they were in their last
form (C), to complete them on the same lines would require
at least fifty more pages. So instead of going on with C, he
decided to try to write a much more compendious narrative
of his life and see what he could do. This fourth attempt he
looked upon as a mere experiment, started it without a title,
and neglected his usual systematic numbering of his pages.
In a few days, in only thirteen pages, he had succeeded in
covering all his life to 1770, that is, the first two sections or
thirty-nine pages of C. He had omitted some topics altogether, barely mentioned a number of others, and reduced
each of the remaining ones to a few lines; for the first time
he added some dates in the margin, but not systematically.
This experiment[4] made him realize that he could easily

---

[1] *Letters*, iii, p. 191.   [2] *Ibid.*, p. 197.   [3] *Ibid.*, pp. 209-210.
[4] Concluding a paragraph on the work he had done in the fifteen years
between the publication of the *Essai* and the first volume of the *History*
(1761-1776), Gibbon wrote in D (MS f 85ᵛ – M 412): 'These various
studies were productive of many remarks and memorials, and in this supplement I may perhaps introduce a Critical dissertation on the miraculous
darkness of the Passion.' What did he mean by 'this supplement'? His
fourth attempt at writing his Memoirs cannot be described as a supplement
to any of his previous attempts. Had the idea that he might turn it into a
real supplement, including various topics which he had so far left out,

complete a short but precise survey of the main events of his career, leaving some at least of the interesting matter which he omitted for notes to be written later, and he started at once on a fifth attempt. But this time he saw quite clearly what he had to do. So in four or five weeks E was completed to his satisfaction and he could note, with relief, the date on which he had reached the end of his task, 2 March 1791. In nineteen pages it was done. The thirteen pages of D had been compressed to four only, and in fifteen more he had found ample room to deal with the twenty years of his life which were most worth remembering. The new text was not divided into chapters; it was not long enough for such a division; but each event or subject, duly dated in the margin, had a distinct paragraph to itself, which gives E the appearance of annals, but the appearance only, for the narrative flows on in a smooth and regular course. Could it be that his relief found expression in the great ball, 'a magnificent entertainment', which he gave on 29 March to all the best company of Lausanne?[1]

There were still the notes which he had decided were to be added to his memoirs, now modestly entitled 'My own life'. They fill thirteen pages (MS ff 97-102 recto). They contain many accurate references, many quotations and must have cost Gibbon a good deal of work. Still, they need not have taken him more than two or three months[2]. They were probably all finished when Lord Sheffield arrived with

suddenly occurred to him? However that may be, he did not pursue it. He wrote two more pages on his father's death and the change in his circumstances and then put D aside.

[1] *Letters* iii, pp. 217 and 219.

[2] The Notes to E are dated by Greenhill (see above, p. xvi) 'end of 1792 or beginning of 1793' on account of Note 48 in which Gibbon says of Louis XVI that 'he *is* a great reader of English books', but speaks of him as 'the *late* King of France'. Royalty was legally suspended by the Legislative Assembly on 10 August 1792 and abolished by the Convention in September. But in fact, since Varennes, i.e. since June 1791, if not earlier, it would have been natural for Gibbon to refer to Louis XVI as 'the late King of France' (see his letters of 1 July 1791: 'The Royal animal is again caught', and of 15 December 1789: 'Their king brought a captive to Paris', *Letters*, iii, pp. 132, 184). There is confirmation of 1791 as the date of the E notes in note 34, where he speaks of his *Vindication*, published in January 1779, 'at the distance of twelve years'.

his family at La Grotte at the end of July 1791 on a two months' visit to his friend. Neither in conversation during his year in England (1787-1788), nor in any of his letters to Lord Sheffield, had Gibbon made the slightest allusion to the Memoirs for which he had tried to collect information in the last months of his stay at Sheffield Park, and on which he had been working from time to time ever since the end of 1788. But at Lausanne he told him once at least of his intention to write the story of his own life, as though he had never written one line of it. Sheffield showed genuine interest and encouraged him. After his friend's departure, Gibbon realized that there was a risk that his secret might be revealed. So, at the end of his letter of December 1791, he wrote: 'I have much revolved the plan of the Memoirs I once mentioned, and as you do not think it ridiculous I believe I shall make the attempt; if I can please myself I am confident of not displeasing: but let this be a profound secret between us: people must not be prepared to laugh: they must be taken by surprize.'[1]

'I shall make the attempt' may be taken as evidence, if not of his already being at work on his Memoirs again, at least of his having decided to try once more to please himself. What he had last written was all very well, but it was a mere sketch and it left out far too many things to deserve to be considered as real memoirs. He must return to his original plan, enter into far more particulars than in E, and make use of his first three attempts, but take care not to be drawn away from his main purpose by all kinds of side-issues, and he must now divide the work into chapters. Without bothering to begin with a title – his first pages would be a rewriting of A, and the A titles might suffice when the time came, if it ever did, to send his manuscript to the printer – he simply headed his first page CHAPTER I and, discarding any introduction, started straight away with the history of his family, making large use of his first draft. Besides the folio sheets of strong white paper he was using for his text, he had taken some quarto leaves of light bluish paper which he folded into narrow pages. On these,

---

[1] *Ibid.*, p. 240.

while writing, he jotted down references and mementoes
which he would later on expand into proper notes. He had
probably completed his first chapter and passed on to the
second when, by mere accident, he happened to read, in the
Gentleman's Magazine for August 1788, an article signed
N.S. which made it perfectly clear that he did not belong to
the same branch of the Gibbons as the Herald. He at once
realized that he must renounce his fond desire of ever
connecting himself with him, and that his first chapter had
to be partly altered. But first he must get into touch with
the man who had signed himself N.S. and obtain more information from him. So he wrote immediately – it was the
24th of February 1792 – to John Nichols, the editor of the
magazine, asking for the name of the author of the article[1].
In the meantime he would go on whenever he could. A
month's stay at the Neckers' Geneva house in March kept
him away from his library, but in April there was nothing
that interfered with his work. He had asked Lord Sheffield
to lend him his letters of former years, which might be of
use in the composition of his memoirs. A batch of fourteen
letters of 1777-1779 was brought to him in May by the
governess of the children of Lord Sheffield's elder daughter
who was passing through Lausanne on her way to Geneva.
Gibbon acknowledged their delivery into his own hands,
but said he now doubted 'they would be of much service to
him' as 'the work appears far more difficult in the execution
than in the idea'. He added: 'as I am now taking my leave
for some time of my library, I shall not make much progress
in the Memoirs . . . till I am on English ground'[2]. As no
answer had come from the editor of the *Gentleman's Magazine*
he begs his friend in the same letter of 30 May to call upon
Nichols and inquire whether his February letter had ever
been received. His request being apparently disregarded by
Lord Sheffield, he repeated it in September, and a fortnight
later asked his publisher to help him to find out who N.S.
could possibly be. So it is evident that he was still intent on
correcting his first chapter. He had been hoping and planning
to go to England in the early autumn of 1792, but when the

---

[1] *Ibid.*, p. 246.   [2] *Ibid.*, p. 264.

moment approached to start travelling, he was too frightened
by what was happening in France and he put it off 'to another year'[1].

The following months were anything but favourable for
work, as can be realized by reading his letters, and it is not
surprising that on 6 January 1793, he wrote: 'Of the *Memoirs*
little has been done and with that little I am not satisfied:
they must be postponed till a mature season, and I much
doubt whether the book and the author can ever see the
light at the same time.'[2] To this Lord Sheffield replied on
23 January: 'I shall never consent to your dropping the
Memoirs. Keep that work always going; but you should
decide whether the book and the author are to see the light
together, because it might be differently filled up according
to that decision.'[3] This may well have encouraged Gibbon
to persist in their composition. At any rate, considering the
'little has been done' of his January letter, he is unlikely to
have written the whole of his second and third chapters in
1792. Part of it probably belongs to the early months of
1793, in spite of his spending some time at Rolle in the
latter fortnight of January and again at the end of February,
staying with the Neckers, to whom the de Séverys had lent
their house at his suggestion[4], and although the death of
M. de Sévery and Gibbon's deep and active sympathy with
the mourners robbed him of some of the time that he would
otherwise have spent in his library. However that may be,
his two letters to John Nichols[5] in January and April make
it clear that he was still anxious to rewrite his first chapter.
And when, on 26 April, the news of Lady Sheffield's death
at last reached him and he decided at once to go and stay
with his friend in grief, only regretting 'the few days that
must be lost in some necessary preparations'[6], he took care
to take with him all he had written of the Memoirs, not
merely the new version on which he was at work, but the
five previous drafts as well; he certainly meant to go on
with it, as is proved by his doing all he could, as soon as he

---

[1] *Ibid.*, p. 267.
[2] *Ibid.*, p. 312.
[3] *Private Letters*, ed. by R. E. Prothero, ii, p. 366.
[4] *Letters*, iii, p. 277.
[5] *Ibid.*, pp. 314–315 and 323–324.
[6] *Ibid.*, p. 328.

was in England, to discover at last who N.S. was and endeavouring to add to the information he possessed on his ancestors. But illness and death overtook him before he could add anything to his last attempt at writing his Memoirs or even correct their first chapter.

The present edition of Gibbon's MEMOIRS is built on the same general lines as Lord Sheffield's. It contains a consecutive narrative of the life of the historian, written by himself.

It begins with a general Introduction in which Gibbon explains his purpose and justifies himself for undertaking to write his own life; this is made up of the first paragraphs of A and B, the latter completing the former.

Chapter I opens with Gibbon's vindication of his resolve to write a history of his family as a preamble to his own life; there are two versions of this vindication, one (MS ff 128-129) more developed, the other (in A) shorter. Both are given.

There follow the whole[1] of F (Chapters I, II, III); B from where F stops (1753) in Chapters IV, V and part of VI; C from where B stops (1764) in Chapter VI, latter part, and Chapter VII, earlier part; E from where C stops (1770) in Chapters VII and VIII[2].

[1] With the exception of the passage referred to on p. 27, n. 2.

[2] Here is a synopsis of the composition of the text of the MEMOIRS in the present edition:

	Sketch	Add. MSS 34874 Folios	*The Autobiographies* ed. John Murray
Introduction	A	6-6^v	pp. 353-354
	B	22-22^v	104-105
	Loose sheet	128-129	417-419
Chapter I	A	6^v-7	354-355
	F	103-108^v	1-27
Chapter II	F	109-116	28-61
Chapter III	F	116-123	62-95
Chapter IV	B	31-39	129-154
Chapter V	B	39-54	154-197
Chapter VI	B	55-57^v	198-210
	C	72^v-77^v	265-288
Chapter VII	C	78-79	288-292
	E	88^v-92	306-327
Notes	E	98^v-101	Footnotes 27-48
Chapter VIII	E	92-96	327-349
Notes	E	101-102	Footnotes 49-74

There are, therefore, left out: the whole of A, the first twenty pages or so of B, the first twenty-eight pages or so of C, the whole of D and the first five pages or so of E, these omitted parts containing, roughly speaking, nothing which is not found, either in more or less the same words, or more fully and more detailed in the corresponding pages of B, C and F. However, there are in these omitted parts passages of biographical interest or great literary value: these are placed in the textual notes if short enough, or in Appendix I if too long.

The text is as accurate a reproduction of Gibbon's own manuscripts as printing permits. Spelling, capitalization and punctuation throughout are Gibbon's own. Words and syllables which he undoubtedly meant, but failed, to write are placed between square brackets. Gibbon did not use commas or full stops at the end of a line; passing from one line to the next was to his eyes or ear a sufficient break; in some places, the reader might be disturbed by the absence of a comma and one has there been added, also between square brackets.

The division into Chapters was certainly Gibbon's original and final decision: the first page of A is headed Chapter I, C is divided into three sections, F into three chapters. The very fact that there is no such division in B may prove it to have been undertaken as a draft. D and E are much too short for any sub-division.

There have also been left out of the text Gibbon's notes to F, mere jottings of references and mementoes. The most interesting of them, however, have been given and explained in the EDITOR'S NOTES. His notes to E, on the other hand, fully and carefully written out as they are, could not have been left out. Notes 27-48 form an inter-chapter between Chapters VII and VIII. Notes 49-74 are placed after Chapter VIII. To insert them, or some of them at least, in the text of E, as Lord Sheffield did, is really to destroy the perfect composition of E. To turn them into footnotes is to disregard Gibbon's preference so clearly expressed in note 64 (see below, p. 194).

My thanks are due to Sir John Murray who kindly allowed me to make repeated use of the Gibbon manuscripts in the British Museum, to the Trustees of the British Museum for permission to reproduce some selected pages from the manuscript in facsimile, to the Keeper and Staff of the Department of Manuscripts for their unfailing help and courtesy, to Dr H. P. Morrison, President of Thomas Nelson & Sons Ltd. and Sir Gavin de Beer who first proposed, and jointly insisted on, my undertaking a new edition of Gibbon's MEMOIRS, and constantly encouraged me in the long labours it entailed.

G. A. BONNARD

List of Abbreviations
used in the Textual Notes

The following TEXT, as is shown by the Synopsis on p. xxxi, is made up of the whole of the sixth (F) attempt Gibbon made at writing his MEMOIRS, completed by parts of the first (A), second (B), third (C) and fifth (E). In each case it is a faithful reproduction of the author's own text such as he left it after revision.

In the Textual Notes at the foot of the page are recorded: under *I* the words, phrases, clauses and sentences which Gibbon had written first and then cancelled or corrected, as well as those he added when revising what he had written, either soon after completing his sentence, paragraph or page(s), or later[1]:

Under *II* all the alterations (words changed; order of words, clauses and sentences modified; omissions; additions; etc.) for which the editor (Lord Sheffield) of the first edition (1796) must be held responsible but not his alterations of Gibbon's spelling (except in the case of proper names), use of hyphens, manner of giving dates, use of *an* before *h*, and punctuation:

Under *III* all changes to the 1796 text carried out in the second (1814) edition of the *Miscellaneous Works*.

I may therefore be read 'Gibbon had written first . . . *or* added'; *II* 'Lord Sheffield[2] in 1796 altered into (or omitted or added, *as the case may be*)'; *III* 'Lord Sheffield in 1814 . . .'.

References to the Textual Notes are placed (*a*) immediately after any word or phrase which was altered, (*b*) in front of words, passages, paragraphs, pages even (as specified in the Textual Note itself) which were omitted, (*c*) at an equal distance of two words between which an addition was made.

Passages quoted in the notes are usually located by a reference to both the folio of the manuscript and the page in John Murray's edition of *The Autobiographies*.

MS = British Museum *Add. MSS* 34874   *f* = folio
M = Murray's edition   n = note   om = omitted   *ff* = folios

[1] Cancellations which Gibbon made in the course of writing (a word being deleted and another written immediately after) are not recorded as they cannot be distinguished from the choice of the most suitable word or phrase, a choice which the writer is continually making, but of which no visible trace remains.

[2] Or Lord Sheffield's editorial committee. See J. E. Norton, *op. cit.*, pp. 183-184.

The Memoirs
of
the Life
of
Edward Gibbon
with
various observations and excursions

by himself

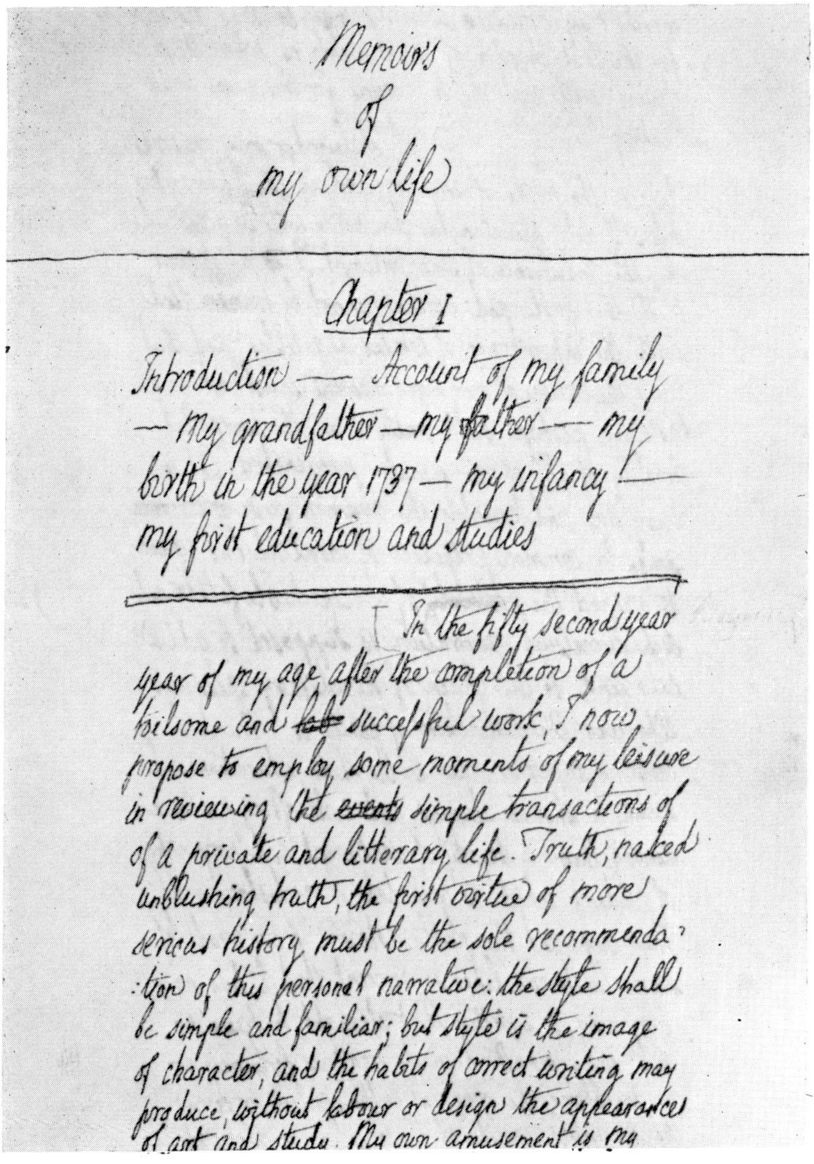

Memoirs
of
my own life

Chapter I

Introduction — Account of my family
— my grandfather — my father — my
birth in the year 1737 — my infancy —
my first education and studies

In the fifty second year
year of my age after the completion of a
toilsome and ~~but~~ successful work, I now
propose to employ some moments of my leisure
in reviewing the ~~events~~ simple transactions of
of a private and litterary life. Truth, naked
unblushing truth, the first virtue of more
serious history, must be the sole recommendation of this personal narrative: the style shall
be simple and familiar; but style is the image
of character, and the habits of correct writing may
produce, without labour or design the appearances
of art and study. My own amusement is my

Plate I. First page of the text of A, numbered 3 by G
MS *f* 6

My own Life

A sincere and simple, ~~little the~~ narrative of my own life, ~~which I have resolved to attempt~~, may amuse some of my leisure hours but it will expose me and perhaps with justice to the imputation of vanity. Yet I may ~~presume~~ from the experience of past, and of the present times, that the public ~~curiosity~~ is always ~~desirous~~ curious to know the men who have left behind them any image of their minds: the most scanty accounts are compiled with diligence and perused with eagerness; and the student of every class may derive a lesson or an example from the lives most similar to his own. The author of an important and successful work may hope without presumption that he is not totally indifferent to his numerous readers: my name may hereafter be placed among the thousand articles of a Biographia Britannica: and I must be conscious that no one is so well qualified as myself to describe the ~~the~~ series of my thoughts and actions. The authority of my masters, of the grave Thuanus, and the philosophic Hume might be sufficient to justify my design: but it would not be difficult to produce a long list of ancients and moderns, who, in various forms have exhibited their own portraits: Such portraits are often the most interesting, and sometimes, the only interesting, parts of their writings; and, if they be sincere we seldom complain of the minuteness or pro: :lixity of these personal memorials. The lives of the younger Pliny, of Petrarch and of Erasmus are expressed in ~~the Collection~~ the Epistles which they themselves have given to the World: the Essays of Montagne and Sir William Temple bring us home to the houses and bosoms of the authors. We smile without contempt at the head: :strong passions of Benvenuto Cellini, and the gay follies of Colley Cibber. The confessions of S.t Austin

I judge
both

Plate II.   First page of B, numbered 1 by G
MS f 22

Introduction[1]

6   [2]IN the fifty second year of my age, after the completion of a toilsome[3] and successful work, I now propose to employ some moments of my leisure in reviewing the simple transactions of a private and litterary life. Truth, naked unblushing truth, the first virtue of more serious history must be the sole recommendation of this personal narrative: the style shall be simple and familiar; but style is the image of character, and the habits of correct writing may produce, without labour or design the appearance of art and study.

6ᵛ   My own amusement is my | motive and will be my reward; and, if these sheets are communicated to some discreet and indulgent friends, they will be secreted from the public eye till the author shall be removed beyond the reach of criticism or ridicule. [4]The reasons and examples which may furnish some Apology will be reserved for the last chapter of these Memoirs, when the order of time will lead me to account for this vain undertaking.

22   [5]A sincere and simple narrative of my own life[6] may amuse some of my leisure hours but it will expose[7] me, and perhaps with justice to the imputation of vanity. Yet[8] I may judge[9] from the experience both[10] of past, and of the present,

---

[1] *As can be seen from plate I, the text of A is headed* CHAPTER I *and preceded by a summary of the matter which Gibbon proposed to treat in it. But he never completed his first chapter. The present editor has therefore left out the summary, preserving only its first word 'Introduction'. He has also transferred the heading to page 3 so as to bring out clearly the distinction between Gibbon's general introduction to his* MEMOIRS *from his introduction to the history of his family.*
[2] *This paragraph, the first of A, is a general introduction to the* MEMOIRS: *Gibbon explains and justifies his undertaking. Of the other drafts, B alone has a similar, but more developed, introduction which is given in the second paragraph (see below, note 5).*   [3] II arduous   [4] *II om this last sentence of the paragraph.*   [5] *This second paragraph is the first one of B. II placed it in his fourth one after a sentence from A to which he linked it by a spurious* Yet   [6] *I* The narrative of my own life, which I have resolved to attempt   [7] *II* subject
[8] *II om* Yet *and added* however *after* judge   [9] *I* presume   [10] *I added* both *in the margin.*

1

times, that [1] the public is[2] always curious to *know* the men
who have left behind them any image of their minds: the
most scanty accounts [3] are compiled with diligence and
perused with eagerness; and the student of every class may
derive a lesson or an example from the lives most similar to
his own. [4] The author of an important and successful work
may hope without presumption that he is not totally indifferent to his numerous readers: my name may hereafter
be placed among the thousand articles of a Biographia
Britannica: and I must be conscious that no one is so well
qualified as myself to describe the series of my thoughts and
actions. The authority of my masters, of the grave Thuanus,
and the philosophic Hume might be sufficient to justify my
design: but it would not be difficult to produce a long list of
ancients and moderns, who, in various forms have exhibited
their own portraits. Such portraits are often the most interesting, and sometimes, the only interesting, parts of their
writings; and, if they be sincere, we seldom complain of the
minuteness or prolixity of these personal memorials. The
lives of the younger Pliny, of Petrarch and of Erasmus are
expressed in the Epistles which they themselves have given
to the World: the Essays of Montagne and Sir William
Temple bring us home to the houses and bosoms of the
authors: we smile without contempt at the headstrong
passions of Benvenuto Cellini, and the gay follies of Colley
Cibber. The confessions of S! Austin | and Rousseau disclose 22ᵛ
the secrets of the human heart: the Commentaries of the
learned Huet have survived his Evangelical demonstration;
and the Memoirs of Goldoni are more truly dramatic than
his Italian comedies. The Heretic and the Churchman are
strongly marked in the characters and fortunes of Whiston
and Bishop Newton; and even the dullness of Michael de
Marolles and Antony Wood acquires some value from the
faithful representation of men and manners. That I am the
equal or superior of[5] some of these Biographers [6] the efforts [7]
of modesty or affectation cannot force me to dissemble.

---

[1] *I* the public curiosity is always desirous to know   [2] *II* the public are
[3] *II added* of such men   [4] *II om this sentence down to* readers   [5] *II* am
equal or superior to   [6] *II om* Biographers   [7] *II* effects

Chapter I

128 [1] A lively desire of knowing and recording our ancestors so generally prevails, that it must depend on the influence of some common principle in the minds of men. Our imagination is always active to enlarge the narrow circle in which Nature has confined us. Fifty or an hundred years may be alotted to an individual; but we stretch forwards[2] beyond death with such hopes as Religion and Philosophy will suggest[3], and we fill up the silent vacancy that precedes our birth by associating ourselves to the authors of our existence. We seem to have lived in the persons of our forefathers: it is the labour and reward[4] of Vanity to extend the term of this ideal longevity; and few there are who can sincerely despise in others, an advantage, of which they are secretly ambitious to partake. The knowledge of our own family from a remote period will be always esteemed as an abstract pre-eminence since it can never be promiscuously enjoyed[5], but the longest series of peasants and mechanics would not afford much gratification to the pride of their descendant. We wish to discover our ancestors, but we wish to discover them, possessed of ample fortunes, adorned with honourable titles, and holding an eminent rank in the class of hereditary nobles,

128ᵛ which has been | maintained for the wisest and most beneficial

---

[1] *After writing the first paragraph of A, Gibbon went on with another in which he justifies his purpose of giving first a history of his family. This initial justification has no parallel in the five other drafts. But, at some time or other, he wrote an independent version of it on a double sheet of small size which is bound with the drafts in the MS (ff 128-9). This independent version is given in the first two paragraphs of CHAPTER I. The A version follows – II composed the text of his second paragraph out of this independent version by freely altering Gibbon's order of its sentences: after the first one* A lively desire . . . minds of men. *he put 1. the beginning of the fourth* We seem to have lived . . . longevity; *2. the second and third* Our imagination . . . of our existence. *3. the first of the second paragraph* Our calmer . . . worthy race: *4. the last of the first paragraph* The Satirist . . . of mankind.—*III added part of what II had left out of the first paragraph* Few there are . . . political society.   [2] *II* step forward
[3] *I* afford   [4] *I* gratification   [5] *I* enjoyed by the multitude

3

purposes, in almost every climate of the Globe, and in almost every form of political society. If any of these have been conspicuous[1] above their equals by personal merit and glorious atchievments, the generous feelings of the heart will sympathize in an alliance with such characters: nor does the man exist who would not peruse with warmer curiosity the life of an hero from whom his name and blood[2] were lineally derived. The Satirist may laugh, the Philosopher may preach: but reason herself will respect the prejudices and habits which have been consecrated by the experience of mankind.

[3] Our calmer judgement will rather tend to moderate than to suppress the pride of an ancient and worthy race: but in the estimate of honour we should learn to value the gifts of Nature above those of fortune; to esteem in our ancestors the qualities that best promote the interest[4] of Society, and to pronounce the descendant of a King less truly noble, than the offspring of a man of Genius whose writings will instruct or delight the latest posterity. The family of Confucius is in my opinion the most illustrious in the World. After a painful ascent of eight or ten Centuries, our Barons and Princes of Europe are lost in the darkness of the middle age[5]: but in the vast equality of the Empire of China the posterity of Confucius has[6] maintained above two thousand | two hundred 129 years its[7] peaceful honours and perpetual succession; and[8] the Chief of the family is still revered by the Sovereign and the people, as the living[9] image of the wisest of mankind. The nobility of the Spencers has been illustrated and enriched by the trophies of Marlborough; but I exhort them to consider the *Faery Queen* as the most precious jewel of their coronet

> Nor less praise-worthy are the ladies three
> The honour of that noble familie
> Of which I meanest boast myself to be.

---

[1] *I* distinguished   [2] *I* blood even   [3] *II made of these two lines* Our calmer . . . race *the fifth sentence of his second paragraph* (*see p. 3, n. 1*) [4] *II* interests   [5] *II* ages   [6] *II* have   [7] *II* their   [8] *II om* and [9] *II* lively

[1] Our immortal Fielding was of a[2] younger branch of the Earls of Denbigh who draw their origin from the Counts of Habsburgh, the lineal descendants of Eltrico, in the seventh Century Duke of Alsace. Far different have been the fortunes of the English and German divisions of the family of Habsburgh. The former, the Knights and Sheriffs of Leicestershire have slowly risen to the dignity of a peerage: the latter the Emperors of Germany, and Kings of Spain have threatened the liberty of the old and invaded the treasures of the new World. The successors of Charles the fifth may disdain their [3] brethren of England: but the Romance of Tom Jones, that exquisite picture of human manners will outlive the palace of the Escurial and the Imperial Eagle of the house of Austria.

6ᵛ   [4] A Philosopher may reasonably despise the pride of ancestry; and if the philosopher himself be a plebeian, his own pride will be gratified by the indulgence of such contempt. It is an obvious truth that parts and virtue cannot be transmitted with the inheritance of estates and titles; and that even the claim of our legal descent must rest on a basis not perhaps sufficiently firm, the unspotted chastity of *all* our female progenitors. Yet in every age and country the common sense or common prejudice of mankind has agreed to respect the son[5] of a respectable father, and each successive generation is supposed to add a new link to the chain of hereditary splendour. Wherever the distinction of birth is allowed to form a superior order in the state, education and example should always, and will often, produce among them a dignity of sentiment, and propriety of conduct which is

---

[1] *II om the end of the paragraph, III restored it.*   [2] *III the*   [3] *I humble*
[4] *This and the next paragraph are the A version of Gibbon's introduction to the history of his family. – II om the first three sentences* A Philosopher . . . *here-ditary splendour, began his third paragraph with the fourth and fifth sentences* Wherever the distinction . . . *honours of its name, then, leaving out the sixth* In the study . . . *or a city, went on with part of the seventh* For my own part . . . *filial love, to which he added the beginning of the sixth* In the study . . . *to ourselves. There he inserted part of the second paragraph of the separate version of Gibbon's introduction* but in the estimate . . . *their coronet. – III added the end of the paragraph and, as a footnote to* Faery Queen, *the quotation from Colin Clout, the reference to which is given as* Spencer, Colin Clout, &c. *v. 538.*   [5] *I posterity*

guarded from dishonour by their own, and the public, esteem. If we read of some illustrious line, so ancient that it has no beginning, so worthy that it ought to have no end, we sympathize in its various fortunes; nor can we blame the generous enthusiasm, or even the harmless vanity of those who are associated[1] | to the honours of its name. In the study[2] 7 of past events our curiosity is stimulated by the immediate or indirect reference to ourselves; within its own precincts a local history is always popular[3]; and the connection of a family is more dear and intimate [4]than that of a Kingdom, a province or a city. For my own part, could I draw my pedigree from a General, a statesman, or a celebrated author, I should study their lives or their writings with the diligence of filial love, and I suspect that from this casual relation some emotions of pleasure, shall I say of vanity, might arise in my breast. Yet I will add that I should take more delight in their personal merit, than in the memory of their titles or possessions; that I should be more affected by litterary than by martial fame: and that I would rather descend from Cicero than from Marius, from Chaucer than from one of the first Companions of the Garter. [5]The family of Confucius is in my opinion the noblest upon Earth. Seventy *authentic* Generations have elapsed from that Philosopher to the present Chief of his posterity; who reckons one hundred and thirty five degrees from the Emperor Hoang-ti, the father, as it is believed, of an illustrious line which has now flourished in China four thousand four hundred and twenty five years. I have exposed my private feelings, as I shall always do, without scruple or reserve—Let every reader whether noble or plebeian, examine his own conscience on the same subject.

That these sentiments are just or at least natural I am the more[6] inclined to believe, since I do not feel myself[7] interested in the cause, since[8] I can derive from *my* ancestors neither glory nor shame.

---

[1] *II* allied   [2] *II* investigation   [3] *I* entertained (*?entertaining*)   [4] *I added* than that of a Kingdom . . . or a city *in the margin.*   [5] *I added this sentence and the next two down to* reserve *in the margin.*   [6] *II om* the more   [7] *III* I am the more inclined to believe, as I am not myself   [8] *II* for

103 [1] My family is originally derived from the County of Kent, [2] whose inhabitants have maintained from the earliest antiquity a provincial character of civility, courage and freedom. The southern district [3] of the Country, which borders on Sussex and the sea was formerly overspread with the great forest Anderida, and even now retains the denomination of the *Weald* or Woodland. In this district and in the hundred and parish of Rolvenden, the Gibbons were possessed of lands in the year one thousand three hundred and twenty six; and the elder branch of the family, without much encrease or diminution of property, still adheres to its native soil. Fourteen years after the first appearance of his name John Gibbon is recorded as the *Marmorarius* or Architect of King Edward the third; the strong and stately castle of Queenborough, which guarded the entrance of the Medway was a monument of his skill; and the grant of an hereditary toll on the passage from Sandwich to Stonar in the Isle of Thanet is the reward of no vulgar artist. In the visitations of the Heralds the Gibbons are frequently mentioned: they held the rank of Esquire in an age when that title was less promiscuously assumed: one of them under[4] the reign of Queen Elizabeth was Captain of the militia of Kent; and a free school in the neighbouring town of Benenden proclaims the charity and opulence of its founder. But time or their own obscurity has cast a veil of oblivion over the virtues and vices of my Kentish ancestors: their character or station confined them

103v to the labours and pleasures of a rural | life: nor is it in my power to follow the advice of the poet in an enquiry after a name

> Go! search it there, where to be born, and dye
> Of rich and poor makes all the history.

So recent is the institution of our parish registers. In the beginning of the seventeenth century a younger branch of the Gibbons of Rolvenden migrated from the Country to the city, and from this branch I do not blush to descend. The Law requires some abilities; the Church imposes some

---

[1] *From here to p. 67 the text is that of F.* [2] *II om two lines from here* *to* and freedom. [3] *II om* of the Country [4] *III* in

restraints, and before our army and navy, our Civil establishments and Indian[1] Empire, had opened so many paths of
fortune, the mercantile profession was more frequently
chosen by youths of a liberal race and education who aspired
to create their own independence. Our most respectable
families have not disdained the Counting-house or even the
shop: their names are enrolled in the livery and companies of
London: and in England as well as in the Italian common-
wealths, Heralds have been compelled to declare, that
Gentility is not degraded by the exercise of trade.

The armorial ensigns which in the times of Chivalry
adorned the crest and shield of the soldier are now become
an empty decoration which every man who has money to
build a carriage may paint according to his fancy, on the
pannels. My family arms are the same which were borne by
the Gibbons of Kent in an age when the College of Heralds
religiously guarded the distinctions of blood and name; *a
Lyon, rampant, gardant, between three scallop-shells, Argent on
a field Azure.* I should not however have been tempted to
blazon my coat of arms, [2]the most useless of all coats, were
it not connected with a whimsical anecdote About the reign
of James the first the three harmless scallop-shells were
changed by Edmund Gibbon Esq[re] into three *Ogresses* or female cannibals with the[3] design of stigmatizing three Ladies,
his kinswomen who had provoked him by an unjust law-suit.
But this singular mode of revenge, for which he obtained the
sanction of Sir William Segar King at arms, soon expired
with its author; and on his own monument in the Temple
Church, the Monsters vanish, and the three scallop-shells
resume their proper and hereditary place.

Our alliances by marriage, it is not disgraceful to mention.
[4]Blue-mantle Poursuivant who will soon be introduced to
the reader's acquaintance enumerates the Phillips de la Weld[5]
in Tenterden, the Whetnals of East-Peckham, the Edgars
of Suffolk, the Cromers, the Bercleys of Beauston, the
Hextalls, the Ellenbriggs, the Calverleys, the Whetnalls of
Cheshire—modestly checking his pen lest he should seem to

[1] *II* India   [2] *II om* the most useless of all coats   [3] *II a*   [4] *II om*
twenty lines from here down to Lord Mayors of London.   [5] *I* of the Weald

indulge the pride of pedigree: nam genus et proavos &c. As such pride would be ridiculous, it would be scarcely less ridiculous to disclaim it; and I shall simply observe that the Gibbons have been immediately or remotely connected with several worthy families of the old Gentry of England. The Memoirs of the Count de Grammont, a favourite book of every man and woman of taste immortalize the Whetnalls or Whitnells of Peckham; 'la blanche Whitnell et le triste Peckham'. But the insipid charms of the Lady, and the dreary 104 solitude of the mansion were | sometimes enlivened by Hamilton and love: and had not *our* alliance preceded *her* marriage I should be less confident of my descent from the Whetnalls of Peckham. The Cromers in the fifteenth century were twice Sheriffs of Kent and twice Lord Mayors of London. But the chief honour of my ancestry is James Fiens Baron Say and Seale and Lord High Treasurer of England in the reign of Henry the sixth; from whom by the Phelips, the Whetnalls and the Cromers I am lineally descended in the eleventh degree. His dismission and imprisonment in the Tower were insufficient to appease the popular clamour; and the Treasurer with his son in law Cromer was beheaded (1450) after a mock tryal by the Kentish insurgents. The black list of his offences, as it is exhibited in Shakespeare, displays the ignorance and envy of a plebeian tyrant. Besides the vague reproaches of selling Maine and Normandy to the Dauphin, the Treasurer is specially accused of luxury for riding on a foot-cloth, and of treason for speaking French, the language of our enemies. 'Thou has[t] most traiterously corrupted the youth of the 'Realm (says Jack Cade to the unfortunate Lord), in erecting 'a grammar school: and whereas before, our fore-fathers 'had no other books than the score and the tally, thou hast 'caused printing to be used; and, contrary to the King, his 'Crown, and dignity, thou hast built a paper-mill. It will be 'proved to thy face, that thou hast men about thee, who 'usually talk of a noun, and a verb, and such abominable 'words as no Christian ear can endure to hear.' Our dramatic Poet is generally more attentive to character than to history; and I much fear that the art of printing was not

introduced into England till several years after Lord Say's
death: but of some of these meritorious crimes I should hope
to find my ancestor guilty; and a man of letters may be
proud of his descent from a[1] Patron and martyr of learning.

In the beginning of the last Century, Robert Gibbon Esq[re]
of Rolvenden in Kent who died in 1618[2] had a son of the
same name of Robert who settled in London in trade[3] and
became a member of the Cloth-workers Company. His wife
was a daughter of the Edgars, who flourished above[4] four
hundred years in the County of Suffolk, and produced an
eminent and wealthy Serjeant at law, Sir Gregory Edgar in
the reign of Henry the seventh. Of the sons of Robert
Gibbon who died in 1643, Matthew did not aspire above the
station of a linnen-draper in Leadenhall street [5] in the Parish
of St Andrews, but John has given [6] the Public some curious
Memorials of his existence, his character and his family. He
was born [7] the third of November in the year 1629; his education was liberal at a grammar-school, and afterwards in
Jesus College at Cambridge, and he celebrates the retired
content which he enjoyed at Allesborough in Worcestershire
in the house of Thomas Lord Coventry where John Gibbon
was[8] employed as [9] domestic tutor, the same office which Mr
Hobbes exercised[10] in the Devonshire family. But the spirit
of my kinsman soon emerged[11] into more active life: he
visited foreign countries as a soldier and a traveller, acquired
the knowledge of the French and Spanish languages, passed
some time | in the isle of Jersey, crossed the Atlantic, and 104ᵛ
resided upwards of a twelfmonth (1659) in the rising Colony
of Virginia. In this remote province his taste or rather
passion for Heraldry found a singular gratification at a War
dance of the native Indians As they moved in measured steps
brandishing their Tamahawks his curious eye contemplated
their little shields of bark, and their naked bodies which
were painted with the colours and symbols of his favourite

---

[1] *I the*   [2] *I added* who died in 1618 *in the margin.*   [3] *II om* in trade
[4] *II* about   [5] *II om* in the Parish of St Andrews   [6] *II added* to   [7] *II
added* on   [8] *III* where he was   [9] *II added* a   [10] *I* tutor while Mr
Hobbes exercised the same office in – *III om the end of the sentence from*
the same office   [11] *II* immerged

science. 'At which [1] I exceedingly wondered; and concluded
'that Heraldry was ingrafted *naturally* into the sense of
'humane race. If so, it deserves a greater esteem than now-
'a-days is put upon it.' His return to England, after the
restoration, was soon followed by his marriage, his settlement in an house in St Catherine's cloyster near the Tower
which devolved to my grandfather, and his introduction into
the Heralds College (in 1671)[2] by the style and title of Blue
mantle Poursuivant at arms. In this office he enjoyed near
fifty years the rare felicity of uniting in the same pursuit his
duty and inclination: his name is remembered in the College
and many of his letters are still preserved. Several of the
most respectable characters of the age Sir William Dugdale,
Mr Ashmole, Dr John Betts, and Dr Nehemiah Grew were
his friends; and in the society of such men, John Gibbon may
be recorded without disgrace as the member of an Astro-
logical Club. The study of hereditary honours is favourable
to the Royal prerogative; and my kinsman, like most of his
family was a high Tory [3] in Church and State. In the latter
end of the reign of Charles the second, his pen was exercised
in the cause of the Duke of York: the Republican faction he
most cordially detested; and as each animal is conscious of
its proper arms, the Herald's revenge was emblazoned on
a most Diabolical scutcheon. But the triumph of the Whig
Government checked the preferment of Blue-Mantle; and
he was even suspended from his office till his tongue could
learn to pronounce the oath of abjuration. His life was prolonged to the age of ninety; and in the expectation of the
inevitable though uncertain hour, he wishes to preserve the
blessings of health competence and virtue. In the year 1682
he published at London his *Introductio ad Latinam Blasoniam*,
an original attempt which Camden had desiderated to define
in the[4] Roman idiom the terms and attributes of a Gothic
institution. [5] His manner is quaint and affected; his order is
confused: but he displays some wit, more reading, and still
more enthusiasm; and if an enthusiast be often absurd, he is

[1] *III added* (says he)   [2] *I added this date in the margin.*   [3] *II added*
both   [4] *II* a   [5] *II inserted here a passage from A* (MS f 7ᵛ). *See Appendix I, 1, ll. 7-17.*

never languid. An English text is perpetually interspersed with Latin sentences in prose and verse; but in his own poetry he claims an exemption from the laws of prosody. Amidst a profusion of Genealogical knowledge my kinsman could not be forgetful of his own name; and to him I am indebted for almost the whole of my[1] information concerning the Gibbon family. From this small work, a duodecimo of one hundred and sixty five pages the Author expected immortal fame; and at the conclusion of his labour, he sings in a strain of self-exultation

> Usque huc corrigitur Romana Blasonia per me
> Verborumque dehinc barbara forma cadat
> Hic liber in meritum si forsitan incidet usum
> Testis rite meae sedulitatis erit. | 105
> Quicquid agat Zoilus, ventura fatebitur aetas
> Artis quod fueram non Clypearis inops.

Such are the hopes of authors! In the failure of those hopes, John Gibbon has not been the first of his profession, and very possibly may not be the last of his name.

His brother Matthew Gibbon the [2]linnen draper of [2]Leadenhall Street had one daughter and two sons, my grandfather Edward who was born in the year 1666, and Thomas afterwards Dean of Carlisle. According to the mercantile creed that the best book is a profitable ledger the writings of John the Herald would be much less precious than those of his nephew Edward: but an author professes at least to write for the public benefit; and the slow balance of trade can only be pleasing to those persons[3] to whom it is advantageous. The successful industry of my grandfather raised him above the level of his immediate ancestors; he appears to have launched into various and extensive dealings: even his opinions were subordinate to his interest and I find him in Flanders cloathing King William's troops; while he would have contracted with more pleasure, though not, perhaps at a cheaper rate, for the service of King James. During his residence abroad, his concerns at home were managed by his mother Hester an active and notable woman.

---

[1] *III om* of my   [2] *II om* linnen *and* of Leadenhall street   [3] *II* can be pleasing to those persons only

Her second husband was a widower of the name of Acton: they united the children of their first nuptials: after his marriage with the daughter of Richard Acton Goldsmith in Leadenhall street, he gave his own sister to Sir Whitmore Acton of Aldenham; and I am thus connected by a triple alliance with that ancient and loyal family of Shropshire Baronets. It consisted about that time of seven brothers all of Gigantic stature; one of whom a pygmy of six feet two inches, confessed himself the last and [1] least of the seven: adding in the true spirit of party, that such men were not born since the Revolution. Under the Tory administration of the four last [2] years of Queen Anne (1710-1714), Mr Edward Gibbon was appointed one of the Commissioners of the [3] Customs; he sat at that board with Prior, but the merchant was better qualified for his station than the poet; since Lord Bolingbroke has been heard to declare, that he never conversed with a man who more clearly understood the commerce and finances of England. In the year 1716 he was elected one of the Directors of the South-sea company; and his books exhibited the proof, that before his acceptance of this fatal office, he had acquired an independent fortune of sixty thousand pounds.

But his fortune was overwhelmed in the shipwreck of the year twenty, and the labours of thirty years were blasted in a single day. Of the use or abuse of the South-sea scheme, of the guilt or innocence of my grandfather and his brother-Directors, I am neither a competent nor a disinterested Judge. Yet the equity of modern times must condemn the violent and arbitrary proceedings which would have disgraced the cause of Justice, and would render injustice still more odious. No sooner had the nation awakened from its Golden dream, than a popular and even a parliamentary clamour demanded their victims: but it was acknowledged on all sides that the South-sea Directors | however guilty could not be touched by any known laws of the land. The speech of Lord Molesworth, the author of the state of Denmark may show the temper or rather the intemperance of

105ᵛ

---

[1] *II added* the [2] *III* last four [3] *I* Customs; a place which he was well qualified to fill; since Lord

the House of Commons. 'Extraordinary crimes (exclaimed 'that ardent Whig) call aloud for extraordinary remedies. 'The Roman lawgivers had not foreseen the possible ex-'istence of a parricide. But as soon as the first monster 'appeared he was sewed in a sack, and cast headlong into the 'river; and I shall be content to inflict the same treatment on 'the authors of our present ruin.' His motion was not literally adopted; but a bill of pains and penalties was introduced, a retroactive statute to punish the offences which did not exist at the time they were committed. Such a pernicious violation of liberty and law can only be excused by[1] the most imperious necessity: nor could it be defended on this occasion by the plea of impending danger, or useful example. The Legislature restrained the persons of the Directors, imposed an exorbitant security for their appearance, and marked their characters with a prævious note of ignominy: they were compelled to deliver upon oath the strict value of their estates, and were disabled from making any transfer or, alienation of any part of their property. Against a bill of pains and penalties it is the common right of every subject to be heard by his counsel at the bar: they prayed to be heard their prayer was refused; and their oppressors who required no evidence would listen to no defence. It had been at first proposed that one eighth of their respective estates should be allowed for the future support of the Directors: but it was speciously urged, that in the various shades of opulence and guilt, such an equal[2] proportion would be too light for many and for some might possibly be too heavy. The character and conduct of each man were separately weighed: but instead of the calm solemnity of a judicial enquiry, the fortune and honour of three and thirty Englishmen were made the topic of hasty conversation, the sport of a lawless majority: and the basest member of the committee, by a malicious word or a silent vote might indulge his general spleen, or personal animosity. Injury was aggravated by insult; and insult was embittered by pleasantry. Allowances of twenty pounds or one shilling were facetiously moved. A vague report that a Director had formerly been concerned

---

[1] *II* can be excused only by   [2] *II* unequal

in *another* project by which some unknown persons had lost
their money, was admitted as a proof of his actual guilt. One
man was ruined because he had dropt a foolish speech, that
his horses should feed upon gold; another because he was
grown so proud, that, one day, at the Treasury he had
refused a civil answer to persons much above him. All were
condemned, absent and unheard in arbitrary fines and for-
feitures which swept away the greatest part of their substance.
Such bold oppression can scarcely be shielded by the omnipotence of Parliament: and, yet, it may be seriously questioned whether the Judges of the South-sea Directors were
106 the true and legal representatives | of their country. The
first Parliament of George the first had been chosen (1715)
for three years: the term had elapsed: their trust was expired; and the four additional years (1718-1722) during
which they continued to sit, were derived not from the
people, but from themselves; from the strong measure of the
septennial bill, which can only be paraleled by *il serrar di
Consiglio* of the Venetian history. Yet candour will own that
to the same Parliament every Englishman is deeply indebted: the septennial act, so vicious in its origin, has been
sanctioned by time, experience and the national consent: its
first operation secured the house of Hanover on the throne,
and its permanent influence maintains the peace and stability
of Government. As often as a repeal has been moved in the
house of Commons, I have given in its defence a clear and
conscientious vote.

My grandfather could not expect to be treated with more
lenity than his companions. His Tory principles and connections rendered him obnoxious to the ruling powers: his
name is reported in a suspicious secret; and his well-known
abilities could not plead the excuse of ignorance or error.
In the first proceedings against the South-sea Directors, Mr
Gibbon is one of the few who were taken in[1] custody; and in
the final sentence the measure of his fine proclaims him
eminently guilty. The total estimate which he delivered on
oath to the house of commons amounted to one hundred
and six thousand five hundred and forty three pounds, five

[1] *II* into

shillings and six pence exclusive of antecedent settlements. Two different allowances of fifteen, and of ten, thousand pounds were moved for Mr Gibbon: but on the question being put it was carried without a division for the smaller sum; [1]and as a Philosopher, I *should* mention, without a sigh the irreparable loss of above ninety six thousand pounds of which, in a single moment, and by an arbitrary vote I have been ultimately deprived. The provision reserved for his wife could not be very considerable; but the valuable gift which he afterwards received from his friend and companion Mr Francis Acton was understood in the family to be the restitution of an honourable trust. Against irresistible rapine the use of fraud is almost legitimate: in the dextrous anticipation of a conveyance some fragments of property might escape: debts of honour will not be annulled by any positive law; and the frequent imposition of oaths had enlarged and fortified the Jacobite conscience. On these ruins, with the skill and credit of which Parliament had not been able to despoil him, my grandfather, at a mature age erected the edifice of a new fortune: the labours of sixteen years were amply rewarded, and I have reason to believe that the second Temple[2] was not much inferior to the first. [3]A large stock of money was vested in the funds, and in trade: and his warehouses at Cadiz were replenished with naval stores for which he had contracted to supply the Court of Madrid[4]. | 106v But[5] he had realized a very considerable property in Sussex, Hampshire, Buckinghamshire, and the New-River Company: and had acquired a spacious house with gardens and lands at Putney in Surry, where he resided in decent hospitality. [6]His portraits represent a stern and sensible countenance: his children trembled in his presence; tradition informs me that the independent visitors, who might have smiled at his anger were awed by his frown; and as he was the richest, or wisest or oldest of his neighbours, he soon became the oracle and the tyrant of a petty Kingdom. His own wrongs had not

---

[1] *II om thirteen lines from here down to* Jacobite conscience.   [2] *II* structure
[3] *II om this sentence.*   [4] *I had added here* but which were perfidiously seized on the breaking out of the Spanish War.   [5] *II om* But   [6] *II om ten lines from here down to* prudently omitted.

reconciled him to the house of Hanover; his wishes might be expressed in some harmless toasts: but he was disqualified from all public trust; and in the daily devotions of the family the name of the King, for whom they prayed, was prudently omitted. My grandfather[1] died at Putney[2] in December 1736, at the age of seventy; [3] leaving Edward his only son and two daughters Hester and Catherine.

My father Edward Gibbon was born in October 1707: at the age of thirteen he could scarcely feel that he was disinherited by act of parliament; and as he advanced towards manhood new prospects of fortune opened on[4] his view. A parent is most attentive to supply in his children the deficiencies of which he is conscious in himself: my grandfather's knowledge was derived from a strong understanding and the experience of the ways of men: but my father enjoyed the benefits of a liberal education, as a scholar and a Gentleman. At Westminster school, and afterwards at Emanuel College in Cambridge, he passed through a regular course of Academical discipline; and the care of his learning and morals was entrusted to his private Tutor the celebrated[5] Mr William Law. But the mind of a Saint is above or below the present World; and while the pupil proceeded on his travels, the tutor remained at Putney the much-honoured friend and spiritual director of the whole family. My father resided some time at Paris to acquire the fashionable exercises; and, as his temper was warm and social, he indulged in those pleasures for which the strictness of his former education had given him a keener relish. He afterwards visited several provinces of France; but his excursions were neither long nor remote, and the slender knowledge which he had gained of the French language was gradually obliterated. His passage through Besançon is marked by a singular consequence in the chain of human events. In a dangerous illness Mr Gibbon was attended at his own request by one of his kinsmen of the name of Acton, the

[1] *II* He   [2] *II om* at Putney   [3] *For the end of this paragraph, II substituted the corresponding passage of B (see Appendix I, 10), adding to it the F passage on Law (see below, pp. 21-23) and concluding with a brief sentence from C (see below, p. 23, n. 1).*   [4] *II* to   [5] *II* same *owing to the passage on Law coming first.*

younger brother of a younger brother, who had applied himself to the study of Physic. During the slow recovery of his
patient, the Physician himself was attacked by the malady
of love: he married his mistress, renounced his country and
religion, settled at Besançon, and became the father of three
sons the eldest of whom General Acton is conspicuous in
Europe as the principal minister of the King of the two
Sicilies. By an uncle whom another stroke | of fortune had 107
transplanted to Leghorn, he was educated in the naval
service of the Emperor; and his valour and conduct in the
command of the Tuscan frigates protected the retreat of the
Spaniards from Algiers. On my father's return to England he
was chosen, at[1] the general election of 1734 to serve in
Parliament for the borough of Petersfield, a burgage tenure
of which my grandfather possessed a weighty share, till he
alienated I know not why, such important property. [2] Prejudice and society connected his son with the Tories,[3] or as they
were pleased to style themselves, the Country Gentlemen:
with them he gave many a vote, with them he drank many
a bottle. Without acquiring the fame of an orator or statesman he eagerly joyned in the great opposition, which, after
a seven years chase, hunted down Sir Robert Walpole: and
in the pursuit of an unpopular minister, he gratified a
private revenge against the oppressor of his family in the
South-sea persecution.

[4] The union to which I owe my birth was a marriage of
inclination and esteem. Mr James Porten a Merchant of
London resided with his family at Putney in a house adjoining
to the bridge and Church-yard, where I have passed many
happy hours of my childhood. Of his son Stanier, and of a
daughter, Catherine who preserved her maiden name I shall
hereafter speak: another daughter married Mr Darrel of
Richmond and her two sons are opulent and worthy; the
youngest and handsomest of the three sisters was Judith my
mother. In the society of Putney the two families lived in

---

[1] *II* in   [2] *II added here a few words from E* (*MS f* 87 – *M 294*): In the
opposition to Sir Robert Walpole and the Pelhams   [3] *II added here from
the same page of E this parenthesis:* – shall I say Jacobites?   [4] *II om four
pages from here down to* acquaintance with the Saint. (*p. 21*).

friendly and frequent intercourse: the familiar habits of the young people improved into a tender attachment: and their mutual affection, according to the difference of the sexes, was ardently professed and modestly acknowledged. These sentiments were justified by a more perfect knowledge of each other: my father's constancy was neither chilled by absence nor dissolved by pleasure: and after his return from his travels and his election into Parliament, he seriously resolved to unite himself for ever with the object of his choice.

> Notitiam primosque gradus vicinia fecit:
> Tempore crevit amor, tædæ quoque jure coïssent;
> Sed vetuere patres. Quod non potuere vetare
> Ex æquo captis ardebant mentibus ambo

Such is the beginning of a love tale at Babylon or at Putney. On the present occasion however the opposition of the two fathers was not equally strenuous or sincere. The slender fortunes and dubious credit of Mr Porten would have been pleased with such an alliance: but he was provoked by a sense of honour to imitate the reluctance of his wealthy and ambitious neighbour. The usual consequences ensued: harsh threats and tender protestations frowns and sighs; the seclusion of the Lady, the despair of the Lover; clandestine correspondence and stolen interviews. At the distance of forty years my aunt Catherine Porten could relate with pleasure the innocent artifices which she practised to second or screen her beloved sister: and I have found among my father's papers many letters of both parties that breathe a spirit of constancy and love. All their acquaintance, the whole neighbourhood of Putney was favourable to their wishes; 107ᵛ my | paternal grandfather yielded a tardy and ungracious consent; and as soon as the marriage ceremony had been performed the young couple was received into his house on the hard terms of implicit obedience and a precarious maintenance. Yet such were the charms and talents of my mother, with such soft dexterity did she follow and lead the morose humour of the old Tyrant, that in a few months she became his favourite. Could he have embraced the first child of which she was pregnant at the time of his decease, it is probable that a Will executed in anger would have been cancelled by affection; and that he would have moderated the shares of his two daughters, whom, in resentment to his son he had enriched beyond the measure of female inheritance.

Of my two wealthy aunts on the father's side, Hester persevered in a life of celibacy, while Catherine became the wife of Mr Edward Elliston, a Captain in the service of the East-India Company, whom my grandfather styles his nephew in his Will. Both Mr and Mrs Elliston were dead before the date of my birth, or at least of my memory; and their only daughter and heiress will be mentioned in her proper place. These two Ladies are described by Mr Law under the names of Flavia and Miranda, the Pagan and the Christian sister: The sins of Flavia, which excluded her from the hope of salvation, may not appear to our carnal apprehension of so black a dye. Her temper was gay and lively: she followed the fashion in her dress, and indulged her taste for company and public amusements: but her expence was regulated by œconomy: she practised the decencies of Religion, nor is she accused of neglecting the essential duties of a wife or a mother. The sanctity of her sister the original or the copy of Miranda was indeed of an higher cast. By austere pennance Mrs Hester Gibbon laboured to attone for the faults of her youth, for the profane vanities into which she had been led or driven by authority and example. But no sooner was she mistress of her own actions and plentiful fortune than the pious virgin abandoned for ever the house of a brother from whom she was alienated by the interest of this World and of the next. With her spiritual guide, and a widow lady of the name of Hutchinson, she retired to a small habitation at Cliffe in Northamptonshire, where she lived almost half a Century, surviving many years the loss of her two friends. It is not my design to enumerate or extenuate the Christian virtues of Miranda as they are described by Mr Law. Her charity even in its excess commands our respect. Her fortune (says the historian[)] is divided between herself 'and several *other* poor people; and 'she has only her part of relief from it.' The sick and lame,

young children and aged persons were the first objects of
her benevolence: but she seldom refused to give alms to a
common beggar: 'and instead (I resume Mr Law's words)
'of driving him away as a cheat, because she does not know
'him, she relieves because he *is* a stranger, and unknown to
108 'her. | Excepting her victuals she never spent ten pounds a
'year upon herself. If you was to see her you would wonder
'what poor body it was, that was so surprizingly neat and
'clean. She eats and drinks only for the sake of living; and
'with so regular an abstinence, that every meal is an exercise
'of self denial, and she humbles her body every time that she
'is forced to feed it.' Her only study was the Bible with
some legends and books of piety which she read with
implicit faith: she prayed five times each day; and, as singing,
according to the Serious Call, is an indispensable part of
devotion, she rehearsed the psalms and hymns of thanks-
giving, which she now, perhaps, may chant in a full chorus
of Saints and Angels. Such is the portrait and such was the
life of that holy Virgin who by Gods was Miranda called,
and by men Mrs Hester Gibbon. Of the pains and pleasures
of a spiritual life *I* am ill-qualified to speak; yet I am inclined
to believe that her lot, even on earth has not been unhappy.
Her pennance was voluntary, and, in her own eyes, meritorious; her time was filled by regular occupations; and
instead of the insignificance of an old maid, she was surrounded by dependents poor and abject as they were, who
implored her bounty, and imbibed her lessons. In the course
of these Memoirs I shall not forget to introduce[1] my personal acquaintance with the Saint.

At an advanced age, about the year 1761 Mr Law died in
the[2] house, [3] I may not say in the arms, of his beloved Miranda. In our family he has[4] left the reputation of a worthy
and pious man, who believed all that he professed and practised all that he enjoyned. The character of a Nonjuror which
he maintained to the last is a sufficient evidence of his
principles in Church and state, and the sacrifice of interest
to conscience will be always respectable. His Theological

---

[1] *I added* to introduce *in the margin.*   [2] *II* her   [3] *II om the end of the
sentence.*   [4] *II* had

writings which our domestic connection has tempted me to peruse, preserve an imperfect sort of life, and I can pronounce with more confidence and knowledge on the merits of the author. His last compositions are darkly tinctured with[1] the incomprehensible visions of Jacob Behmen and his discourse on the absolute unlawfullness of stage-entertainments is sometimes quoted for a ridiculous intemperance of sentiment and language. 'The actors and 'spectators must all be damned: the play-house is the porch 'of Hell, the place of the Devil's abode, where he holds his 'filthy court of evil spirits: a play is the Devil's triumph; a 'sacrifice performed to his glory, as much as in the Heathen 'temples of Bacchus or Venus &c &c.' But these sallies of Religious phrenzy must not extinguish the praise which is due to Mr William Law as a wit and a scholar. His argument, on topics of less absurdity is specious and acute, his manner is lively, his style forcible and clear; and had not his vigourous mind been clouded by enthusiasm, he might be ranked with the most agreable and ingenious writers of the times. While the Bangorian controversy was a fashionable[2] theme he entered the lists on the subject of Christ's Kingdom, and the authority of the Priesthood: against the plain account of the sacrament of the Lord's supper he resumed the combat with Bishop Hoadley, the object of Whig Idolatry | and Tory 108ᵛ abhorrence, and at every weapon of attack and defence the Nonjuror, on the ground which is common to both, approves himself at least equal to the Prelate. On the appearance of the fable of the Bees he drew his pen against the licentious doctrine that private vices are public benefits, and morality as well as Religion must joyn in his applause. Mr Law's master-work, the *Serious Call* is still read as a popular and powerful book of devotion. His precepts are rigid, but they are founded on the Gospel: his satire is sharp, but it is drawn from the knowledge of human life; and many of his portraits are not unworthy of the pen of La Bruyere. If he finds a spark of piety in his reader's mind he will soon kindle it to a flame, and a Philosopher must allow, that he exposes with equal severity and truth, the strange contradiction

[1] *II* by   [2] *I* popular

between the faith and practise of the Christian World.[1]
[2] Hell-fire, and eternal damnation are darted from every page
of the book: and it is indeed somewhat whimsical that the
Fanatics who most vehemently inculcate the love of God,
should be those who despoil him of every amiable attribute.

[1] *II added here a brief sentence from C (MS f 59ᵛ – M 216):* Under the
names of Flavia and Miranda he has described my two aunts, the Heathen
and the Christian sister *adding* admirably *before* described   [2] *II om this last
sentence.*

Chapter II

[1] I was born at Putney in Surry, the twenty seventh of April. 109 OS, the eighth of May. N.S. in the year one thousand seven hundred and thirty seven, within a twelfmonth of my father's marriage with Judith Porten his first wife. From my birth I have enjoyed the right of Primogeniture; but I was succeeded by five brothers and one sister, all of whom were snatched away in their infancy. [2]They died so young and I was myself so young at the time of their deaths, that I could not then feel, nor can I now estimate, their loss, the importance of which could only have been ascertained by future contingencies. The shares of fortune to which younger children are reduced by our English laws, would have been sufficient however to oppress my inheritance; and the compensation[3] of their friendship must have depended on the uncertain event of character and conduct, on the affinity or opposition of our reciprocal sentiments. My five brothers, whose names may be found in the Parish register of Putney, I shall not pretend to lament: but from my childhood to the present hour I have deeply and sincerely regretted my sister; whose life was somewhat prolonged, and whom I remember to have seen an amiable infant. The relation of a brother and a sister, especially if they do not marry, appears to me of a very singular nature. It is a familiar and tender friendship with a female, much about our own age; an affection, perhaps softened by the secret influence of sex, but pure

---

[1] *II substituted for this first sentence the corresponding sentence from B (MS f 22ᵛ – M 105):* I was born at Putney in the County of Surrey, the twenty seventh of April. OS. (the eighth of May NS) in the year one thousand seven hundred and thirty seven; the first child of the marriage of Edward Gibbon Esqʳᵉ and of Judith Porten. – *omitted from it the parenthesis, and added the B sentence which follows immediately:* My lot might have been that of a slave, a savage or a peasant; nor can I reflect without pleasure on the bounty of Nature, which cast my birth in a free and civilized country, in an age of science and Philosophy, in a family of honourable rank and decently endowed with the gifts of fortune. [2] *II om ten lines from here down to* reciprocal sentiments.   [3] *I* value

MEMOIRS OF MY LIFE

from any mixture of sensual desire, the sole species of Platonic love that can be indulged with truth and without danger.

[1] About four months before the birth of their eldest son my parents were delivered from a state of servitude, and my father inherited a considerable estate, which was magnified in his own eyes by flattery and hope. The prospect of Spanish gold from our naval contract with the Court of

109v Madrid | was suddenly overclouded about three years after my grandfather's decease. The public faith had been pledged for the security of the English merchants: their effects were seized (in 1740,) on the first hostilities between the two nations. After the return of peace (in 1749 and 1763) the Contractors or their representatives demanded the restitution of their property with a large claim[2] of damages and interest. But the Catholic Kings absolve themselves from the engagements of their predecessors: the helpless strangers were referred by the ministers to the Judges, and from the Judges to the Ministers, and this antiquated debt has melted away[3] in oblivion and despair. Such a stroke could not have been averted by any foresight or care: but the arts of industry were not devolved from the father to the son, and several undertakings which had been profitable in the hands of the merchant became barren or adverse in those of the Gentleman. At the general election of 1741 Mr Gibbon and Mr Delmé stood an expensive and successful contest[4] against Mr Dummer and Mr Henly, afterwards Lord Chancellor and Earl of Northington. The Whig candidates had a majority of the resident voters; but the corporation was firm in the Tory interest: a sudden creation of one hundred and seventy new freemen turned the scale; and a supply was readily obtained of respectable Volunteers who flocked from all parts of England to support the cause of their political friends. The new Parliament opened with the victory of an opposition which was fortified by strong clamour and strange coalitions. From the event of the first divisions, Sir Robert Walpole perceived that he could no longer lead a Majority

---

[1] II om *twenty-one lines from here down to* of the Gentleman.   [2] I addition
[3] I been finally lost   [4] II added at Southampton

in the house of Commons, and prudently[1] resigned after a reign[2] of one and twenty years the sceptre[3] of the state (1742). But the fall of an unpopular Minister was not succeeded, according to general expectation, by a millennium of happiness and virtue: some Courtiers lost their places, some patriots lost their characters[,] Lord Orford's offences vanished with his power, and, after a short vibration, the Pelham government was fixed on the old basis of the Whig Aristocracy. In the year 1745 the throne, and the constitution were attacked by a rebellion which does not reflect much honour on the national spirit: since the English friends of the Pretender wanted courage to joyn his standard, and his enemies (the bulk of the people) allowed him to advance into the heart of the Kingdom. Without daring, perhaps without desiring to aid the rebels, my father invariably adhered to the Tory opposition: in the most critical season he accepted for the service of the party[4], the office of Alderman in the city of London: but the duties were so repugnant to his inclination and habits, that he resigned his Gown at the end of a few months. The second parliament, in which he sate was præmaturely dissolved (1747): and as he was unable or unwilling to maintain a second contest for Southampton, the life of the Senator expired in that dissolution.

[5] At home my father possessed the inestimable treasure of an amiable and affectionate wife, the constant object, during a twelve years marriage of his tenderness and esteem. My mother's portraits convey some idea of her beauty: the elegance of her manners has been | attested by surviving 110 friends; and my aunt Porten could descant for hours on the talents and virtues of her amiable sister. A domestic life would have been the choice, and the felicity of my mother: but she vainly attempted to check with a silken rein the passions of an independent husband. The World was open before him: his spirit was lively[6], his appearance splendid, his aspect chearful, his address polite: he gracefully moved in the highest circles of society, and I have heard him boast

---

[1] *I added* prudently *in the margin.*   [2] *II* dominion   [3] *II* guidance
[4] *I added* for the service of the party *in the margin.*   [5] *II om two paragraphs from here down to* age of puberty (*p. 27, last line*).   [6] *I* social

that he was the only member of opposition admitted into the old Club at White's where the first names of the Country were often rejected. Yet such was the pleasing flexibility of his temper that he could accommodate himself with ease and almost with indifference to every class[1]; to a meeting of Lords or farmers, of Citizens or Foxhunters: and without being admired as a wit, Mr Gibbon was every where beloved as companion and esteemed as a man. But in the pursuit of pleasure, his happiness, alas! and his fortune were gradually injured. Œconomy was superseded by fashion: his income proved inadequate to his expence: his house at Putney in the neighbourhood of London acquired the dangerous fame of hospitable entertainment: against the more dangerous temptation of play he was not invulnerable; and large sums were silently precipitated into that bottomless pit. Few minds have sufficient ressources to support the weight of idleness: and had he continued to walk in the path of mercantile industry my father might have been a happier and his son would be a richer man.

Of these public and private scenes and of the first years of my own life, I must be indebted not to memory but to 110v information; | [2] and I strive without much success to recollect the persons and objects which might appear at the time most forcibly to affect me. The local scenery of my education is however before my eyes: my father's contest for Southampton when I must have been between three and four years old, and my childish revenge in shouting, after being whipt, the names[3] of his opponents is the first event that I seem to remember: but even that belief may be illusive, and I may only repeat the hearsay of a riper season. In the entire period of ten or twelve[4] years from our birth, our pains and pleasures, our actions and designs are remotely connected[5] with our present mode of existence: and according to a just computation we should begin to reckon our life from the age of puberty.

[1] *I* of mankind   [2] *There follows here in F a fairly long digression (MS f 110-110ᵛ, l. 27 – M 32-34) in which G, after quoting 'Paradise Lost', viii 253-273, opposes the actual growth of the infant to Milton's description of the birth or awakening of Adam.*   [3] *I wrote* names *twice.*   [4] *I* twelve or fourteen
[5] *I* designs have scarcely any connection

The death of a new-born child before that of its parents may seem an unnatural, but it is strictly a probable, event: since of any given number, the greater part are extinguished before their ninth year, before they possess the faculties of the mind or body. Without accusing the profuse waste or imperfect workmanship of Nature, I shall only observe that this unfavourable chance was multiplied against my infant existence. So feeble was my constitution, so precarious my life, that, in the baptism of each of[1] my brothers, my father's prudence successively repeated my Christian name of Edward, that in case of the departure of the eldest son, this patronymic appellation might be still perpetuated in the family.

—— Uno avulso non deficit alter.

To preserve and to rear so frail a being, the most tender assiduity was scarcely sufficient, and my mother's attention was somewhat diverted by her frequent pregnancies, by an exclusive passion for her husband, and by the dissipation | of 111 the World in which his taste and authority obliged her to mingle. But the maternal office was supplied by my aunt, Mrs Catherine Porten, at whose name I feel a tear of gratitude trickling down my cheek. A life of celibacy transferred her vacant affection to her sister's first child: my weakness excited her pity: her attachment was fortified by labour and success, and if there are[2] any, as I trust there are some who rejoyce that I live, to that dear and excellent woman they must hold themselves indebted. Many anxious and solitary days did she consume in the patient tryal of every mode of relief and amusement. Many wakeful nights did she sit by my bedside in trembling expectation that each hour would be my last. [3]My poor aunt has often told me with tears in her eyes, how I was nearly starved by a nurse that had lost her milk: how long she herself was apprehensive lest my crazy frame, which is now of common shape should remain for ever crooked and deformed. From one dangerous malady, the small-pox, I was indeed rescued by the practise

---

[1] *II om* each of   [2] *II be*   [3] *II om fifteen lines from here down to* would be omitted.

of inoculation which had been recently introduced into England, and was still opposed by medical, Religious, and even political prejudice. But it is only against the small pox that a preservative has been found: I was successively afflicted by lethargies and feavers; by opposite tendencies to a consumptive and a dropsical habit; by a contraction of my nerves, a fistula in my eye, and the bite of a dog most vehemently suspected of madness: and in the list of my sufferings from my birth to the age of puberty few physical ills would be omitted. [1] From Sir Hans Sloane and Dr Mead, to Ward and the Chevalier Taylor every practitioner was called to my aid: the fees of Doctors were swelled by the bills of Apothecaries and Surgeons: there was a time when I swallowed more Physic than food; and my body is still marked with the indelible scars of lancets, issues and caustics. Of the various and frequent disorders of my childhood my own recollection is dark; nor do I wish to expatiate on so disgusting a topic. I will not follow the vain example of Cardinal Quirini who has filled half a volume of his memoirs with medical consultations on his particular case; nor shall I imitate the naked frankness of Montagne, who exposes all the symptoms of his malady, and the operation of each dose of physic on his nerves and bowels. It may not however be useless to observe that in this early period, the care of my mind was too frequently neglected for that of my health: compassion always suggested an excuse for the indulgence of the master, or the idleness of the pupil: and the chain of my education was broken as often as I was recalled from the school of learning to the bed of sickness.

As soon as the use of speech had prepared my infant

---

[1] *II turned the fifteen lines from here down to* this early period *into an entirely different text which he obtained by altering the sentence order, adding words of his own, omitting about ten lines, and replacing two more by words taken from D. His text is as follows:* 'Of the various and frequent disorders of my childhood my own recollection is dark: nor do I wish to expatiate on so disgusting a topic [*fourth sentence of the F text*]. Suffice it to say that while [*II's own addition*] every practitioner from Sloane and Ward to the Chevalier Taylor, was successively summoned to torture or relieve me [*words taken from D (MS f 80^v – M 392) where, however, G had written* Sloane and Mead to Ward and the Chevalier Taylor] the care of my mind . . .

reason for the admission of knowledge, I was taught the arts of reading writing and vulgar[1] Arithmetic. So remote is the date so vague is the memory of their origin in myself, that were not the error corrected by Analogy I should be tempted to conceive them as innate. [2] In the improved state of society in which I have the good fortune to exist these attainments are so generally diffused | that they no longer 111v constitute the liberal distinctions of Scholars and Gentlemen. The operations of writing and reading must seem on an abstract view to require the labour of Genius; to transform articulate sounds into visible signs by the swift and almost spontaneous motion of the hand; to render visible signs into articulate sounds by the voluntary and rapid utterance of the voice. Yet experience has proved that these operations of such apparent difficulty, when they are taught to all may be learned by all, and that the meanest capacity in the most tender age is not inadequate to the task. Between the sister arts there exists however a material difference, the one is connected with mental intelligence, the other with manual dexterity. The excellence of reading, if the vocal organ be not defective, the propriety of the cadence, the tones, and the pauses is always in just proportion to the knowledge, taste and feelings of the reader. But an illiterate scribe may delineate a correct and elegant copy of penmanship: while the sense and style of the Philosopher or poet, are most awkwardly scrawled in such ill-formed and irregular characters, that the authors themselves, after a short interval, will be incapable of deciphering them. My own writing is of a middle cast, legible rather than fair: but I may observe that age and long practise which are often productive of negligence have rather improved than corrupted my hand. The science of numbers, the third element of our primitive[3] education, may be esteemed the best scale to measure the degrees of the human understanding: a child or a peasant performs with ease and assurance the four first rules of arithmetic; the profound mysteries of Algebra are reserved for the disciples of Newton and Bernouilli. In my childhood I was praised for

[1] *II om* vulgar   [2] *II om thirty-two lines from here down to* Bernouilli.
[3] *I* young

the readiness with which I could multiply and divide by
memory alone two sums of several figures: such praise encouraged my growing talent; and had I persevered in this
line of application, I might have acquired some fame in
Mathematical studies.

After this prævious institution at home or at a day-school
at Putney, I was delivered at the age of seven (April 1744) [1]
into the hands of Mr John Kirkby who exercised about
eighteen months the office of my domestic Tutor. His own
words which I shall here transcribe, inspire in his favour, a
sentiment of pity and esteem 'During my abode in my
'native County of Cumberland, in quality of an indigent
'Curate, I used now-and-then, in a summer, when the
'pleasantness of the season invited, to take a solitary walk
'to the sea-shore, which lies about two miles from the town
'where I lived. Here I would amuse myself one while in
'viewing at large, the agreable prospect which surrounded
'me; and another while, (confining my sight to nearer
'objects) in admiring the vast variety of beautiful shells,
'thrown upon the beach, some of the choicest of which I
'always picked up to divert my little-ones upon my return.
'One time among the rest taking such a journey in my head,
'I sat down upon the declivity of the beach, with my face to
'the sea, which was now come up within a few yards of my
'feet: when immediately the sad thoughts [2] of the wretched
'condition of my family, and the unsuccessfulness of all en-
112 'deavours to amend it, came crowding | into my mind, which
'drove me into a deep melancholy and ever and anon forced
'tears from my eyes.' Distress at last forced him to leave the
country, his learning and virtue introduced him to my
father, and at Putney he might have found at least a temporary shelter, had not an act of indiscretion again driven
him into the World. One day, reading prayers in the parish
Church he most unluckily forgot the name of King George:
his patron, a loyal subject, dismissed him with some reluctance and a decent reward; and *how* the poor man ended
his days I have never been able to learn. Mr John Kirkby

---

[1] *I* in the seventh year of my age (1743) – *II om the parenthesis.*   [2] *II*
thought

is the author of two small Volumes, the Life of Automathes
(London 1745), and an English and Latin Grammar (London 1746), which as a testimony of gratitude he dedicated
(Nov. 5. 1745) to my father. The books are before me:
from them the pupil may judge the præceptor and, upon the
whole the[1] judgement will not be unfavourable. The Grammar is executed with accuracy and skill, and I know not
whether any better existed at the time in our language:
but the life of Automathes aspires to the honours of a Philosophical fiction. It is the story of a youth the son of a ship-
wrecked exile[2], who lives alone on a desert island from infancy to the age of manhood. A Hind is his nurse: he inherits
a cottage with many useful and curious instruments; some
ideas remain of the education of his two first years, some
arts are borrowed from the beavers of a neighbouring lake,
some truths are revealed in supernatural visions. With these
helps and his own industry Automathes becomes a self taught
though speechless philosopher, who had investigated with
success his own mind, the Natural World, the abstract
sciences, and the great principles of morality and Religion.
The author is not entitled to the merit of invention since
he has blended the English story of Robinson Crusoe with
the Arabian romance of Hai Ebn Yokhdan which he might[3]
read in the Latin version of Pocock. In the Automathes I
cannot praise either the depth of thought or elegance of
style, but the book is not devoid of entertainment or instruction; and, among several interesting passages, I would
select the discovery of fire which produces by accidental mischief the discovery of conscience. A man who had thought so
much on the subjects of language and education was surely
no ordinary præceptor: my childish years and his hasty departure prevented me from enjoying the full benefit of his
lessons: but they enlarged my knowledge of Arithmetic and
left[4] a clear impression of the English and Latin Rudiments.

In my ninth year (January 1746) in a lucid interval of
comparative health, my father adopted the convenient and
customary mode of English education: and I was sent to

---

[1] *II* his   [2] *I added* the son of a ship-wrecked exile *in the margin.*   [3] *II*
added have   [4] *II added* me

Kingston upon Thames to a school of about seventy boys which was kept by Dr Woodson[1] and his assistants. Every time I have since passed over Putney Common I have always noticed the spot where my mother, as we drove along in the coach, admonished me that I was now going into the World, and must[2] learn to think and act for myself. The expression may appear ludicrous; yet there is not in the course of life a more remarkable change than the removal of a child from the luxury and freedom of a wealthy house to the frugal diet,
112ᵛ and strict subordination of a school | from the tenderness of parents, and the obsequiousness of servants to the rude familiarity of his equals, the inso[le]nt tyranny of his seniors, and the rod, perhaps, of a cruel and capricious pædagogue. Such hardships may steel the mind and body against the injuries of fortune: but my timid reserve was astonished by the crowd and tumult of the school; the want of strength and activity disqualified me for the sports of the play-field; nor have I forgot how often in the year forty six I was reviled and buffeted for the sins of my Tory ancestors. By the common methods of discipline, at the expence of many tears and some blood, I purchased the knowledge of the Latin syntax: and not long since I was possessed of the dirty volumes of Phædrus and Cornelius Nepos which I painfully construed and darkly understood. The choice of these authors is not injudicious. The *lives* of Cornelius Nepos, the friend of Atticus and Cicero, are composed in the style of the purest age: his simplicity is elegant, his brevity copious: he exhibits a series of men and manners; and with such illustrations, as every pedant is not indeed qualified to give, this Classic biographer may initiate a young Student in the history of Greece and Rome. The use of fables or apologues has been approved in every age from ancient India to modern Europe: they convey in familiar images the truths of morality and prudence; and the most childish understanding (I advert to the scruples of Rousseau) will not suppose either that beasts *do* speak, or that men *may* lye. A fable represents the genuine characters of animals, and a skillful

---

[1] *II* Wooddeson   [2] much *in MS – II* must (*so also Emerson*) *– M preferred to correct* had much to learn

master might extract from Pliny and Buffon some pleasing lessons of Natural history, a science well adapted to the taste and capacity of children. The Latinity of Phædrus is not exempt from an alloy[1] of the Silver age; but his manner is concise, terse, and sententious: the Thracian slave discreetly breathes the spirit of a freeman: and when the text is sound, the style is perspicuous. But his fables, after a long oblivion were first published by Peter Pithou from a corrupt manuscript: the labours of fifty Editors confess the defects of the copy, as well as the value of the original; and a schoolboy may have been whipt for misapprehending a passage, which Bentley could not restore, and which Burman could not explain.

My studies were too frequently interrupted by sickness; and after a real or nominal residence at Kingston school of near two years, I was finally recalled (December 1747) by my mother's death, which was occasioned, in her thirty eighth year, by the consequences of her last labour. [2]As I had seldom enjoyed the smiles of maternal tenderness she was rather the object of my respect than of my love: some natural tears were soon wiped: I was too young to feel the importance of my loss; and the image of her person and conversation is faintly imprinted in my memory. The affectionate heart of my aunt Catherine Porten bewailed a sister and a friend, but my poor father was inconsolable: and the transport of grief seemed to threaten his life or his reason. I can never forget the scene of our first interview, some weeks after the fatal event; the awful silence, the room hung with black | the mid-day tapers, his sighs and tears; his praises 113 of my mother a saint in heaven, his solemn adjuration that I would cherish her memory, and imitate her virtues; and the fervour with which he kissed and blessed me as the sole surviving pledge of their loves. The storm of passion insensibly subsided into calmer melancholy: [3]but he persevered in the use of mourning much beyond the term which has been fixed by decency and custom. Three years after my mother's death, his situation is described by Mr Mallet who

---

[1] *I* a taint   [2] *II om three lines from here down to* soon wiped: [3] *II om twenty-two lines from here down to* happier air.

then resided at Putney, and with whose family my father had formed a very intimate connection. In a pleasing little composition entitled the *Wedding-day*, Cupid and Hymen undertake the office of inviting some chosen friends to celebrate the ninth anniversary (October 2: 1750) of the poet's nuptials. Cupid flies eastward to London.

> His brother too, with sober cheer,
> For the same end did westward steer:
> But first a pensive love forlorn,
> Who three long weeping years has borne
> His torch revers'd, and all around,
> Where once it flam'd with cypress bound,
> Sent off, to call a neighbouring friend,
> On whom the mournful train attend:
> And bid him, this one day at least,
> For such a pair, at such a feast,
> Strip off the sable vest, and wear
> His once-gay look, and happier air.

At a convivial meeting of his friends, Mr Gibbon might affect or enjoy a gleam of chearfulness: but his plan of happiness was for ever destroyed, and after the loss of his companion, he was left alone in a world of which the business and pleasure[1] were to him irksome or insipid. After some unsuccessful tryals he renounced the tumult of London and the hospitality of Putney, and buried himself [2]in the rural or rather rustic solitude of Buriton from which during several years he seldom emerged. [3]It must not however be dissembled that the sorrowful widower was urged to this resolution by the growing perplexity of his affairs. His fortune was impaired: his debts had multiplied, and as long as his son was a minor, he could not disengage his estate from the legal fetters of an entail. Had my mother lived, he must soon have retired into the country, with more comfort indeed, but without the credit of a pious and disinterested motive. Shall I presume to add, that a secret inconstancy, which always adhered to his disposition might impell him at once to sink the man of fashion in the character and occupations of a Hampshire farmer.

---

[1] *II* pleasures   [2] *I* in a rural solitude from which   [3] *II om twelve lines from here down to* Hampshire farmer.

As far back as I can remember the house, near Putney bridge and church yard, of my maternal grandfather, appears in the light of my proper and native home. It was there that I was allowed to spend the greatest part of my time, in sickness or in health, during my school-vacations and my parents residence in London, and finally after my mother's death. Three months after that event, in the spring of 1748, the commercial ruin of her father Mr James Porten was accomplished and declared: he suddenly absconded[1]: but as his effects | were not sold, nor the house evacuated till the 113ᵛ Christmas following, I enjoyed during the whole year the society of my aunt without much consciousness of her impending fate. I feel a melancholy pleasure in commemorating[2] my obligations to that excellent woman, Mrs Catherine Porten, the true mother of my mind as well as of my health. Her natural good sense was improved by the perusal of the best books in the English language; and if her reason was sometimes clouded by prejudice, her sentiments were never disguised by hypocrisy or affectation. Her indulgent tenderness, the frankness of her temper, and my innate rising curiosity soon removed all distance between us: like friends of an equal age we freely conversed on every topic, familiar or abstruse: and it was her delight and reward to observe the first shoots of my young ideas. Pain and languor were often soothed by the voice of instruction and amusement: and to her kind lessons I ascribe my early and invincible love of reading, which I would not exchange for the treasures of India. I should perhaps be astonished were it possible to ascertain the date at which a favourite tale, was engraved by frequent repetition in my memory; the cavern of the winds, the palace of Felicity, and the fatal moment at the end of three months or centuries, when Prince Adolphus is overtaked by Time, who had worn out so many pair of wings in the pursuit. Before I left Kingston school, I was well acquainted with Pope's Homer, and the Arabian Nights-entertainments, two books which will always please by the moving picture of human manners and specious miracles[3].

---

[1] *III om* he suddenly absconded: but   [2] *II* repeating   [3] *II inserted here*
two lines from B (MS f 27 – M 118): nor was I then capable of discerning that

The [1] verses of Pope accustomed my ear to the sound of poetic harmony: in the death of Hector and the shipwreck of Ulysses I tasted the new emotions of terror and pity, and seriously disputed with my aunt on the vices and virtues of the Heroes of the Trojan War. From Pope's Homer to Dryden's Virgil was an easy transition: but I know not how, from some fault in the author, the translator or the reader, the pious Æneas did not so forcibly seize on my imagination, and I derived more pleasure from Ovid's Metamorphoses, especially in the fall of Phaeton, and the speeches of Ajax and Ulysses. My grandfather's flight unlocked the door of a tolerable library, and I turned over many English pages of Poetry and romance, of history and travels. Where a title attracted my eye, without fear or awe I snatched the volume from the shelf, and Mrs Porten, who indulged herself in moral and religious speculation[2], was more prone to encourage than to check, a curiosity above the strength of a boy. This year 1748, the twelfth of my age I shall note as the most propitious to the growth of my intellectual stature.

[3] After such satisfaction, as could be given to his creditors, the relicks of my grandfather's fortune afforded a bare annuity for his own maintenance: and his daughter, my worthy aunt, who had already passed her fortieth year was left naked and[4] destitute. [5] Her more wealthy relations were not *absolutely* without bowels: but her noble spirit scorned a life of obligation and dependence; and after revolving several schemes, she preferred the humble industry of keeping a boarding-house for Westminster school, where she laboriously earned a competence for her old age. This singular opportunity of blending the advantages of private and public education decided my father: after | the Christmas holydays, in January 1749, I accompanied Mrs Porten to her new house in College street, and was immediately entered in the school, of which Dr John Nicoll was at [that] time Head-master. At first I was alone: but my aunt's resolu-

114

Pope's translation is a portrait endowed with every merit, except likeness to the original, *replacing* except *by* by excepting that of   [1] *I* sonorous
[2] *II* speculations   [3] *II om this line to* creditors   [4] *II om* naked and
[5] *II om this line to* bowels: but

tion was praised: her character was esteemed: her friends were numerous and active: in the course of some years she became the mother of forty or fifty boys, for the most part of family and fortune; and as her primitive habitation was too narrow, she built and occupied a spacious mansion in Dean's Yard. I shall always be ready to joyn in the common opinion, that our public schools, which have produced so many eminent characters are the best adapted to the Genius and constitution of the English people. A boy of spirit may acquire a prævious and practical experience of the World, and his playfellows [1] may be the future friends of his heart or his interest. In a free intercourse with his equals the habits of truth, fortitude and prudence will insensibly be matured: birth and riches are measured by the standard of personal merit; and the mimic scene of a rebellion has [2] displayed in their true colours the ministers and patriots of the rising generation. Our seminaries of learning do not exactly correspond with the precept of a Spartan king [3] 'that the child 'should be instructed in the arts which will be useful to the 'man' since a finished scholar may emerge from the head of Westminster or Eaton in total ignorance of the business and conversation of English Gentlemen in the latter end of the eighteenth century. But these schools may assume the merit of teaching all that they pretend to teach, the Latin and Greek languages: they deposit in the hands of a disciple the keys of two valuable chests; nor can he complain if they are afterwards lost or neglected by his own fault. The necessity of leading in equal ranks so many unequal powers of capacity and application will prolong to eight or ten years the juvenile studies which might be dispatched in half that time by the skillful master of a single pupil. Yet even the repetition of exercise and discipline contributes to fix in a vacant mind the verbal science of grammar and prosody: and the private or voluntary student who possesses the sense and spirit of the Classics, may offend by a false quantity the scrupulous ear of a well-flogged Critic. For myself I must be content with a very small share of the civil and litterary fruits of a

[1] *I* may one day become the friends of his heart and interest   [2] *I* sometimes   [3] *I* of an ancient sage

public school: in the space of two years (1749, 1750) interrupted by danger and debility I painfully climbed into the third form: and my riper age was left to acquire the beauties of the Latin, and the rudiments of the Greek, tongue. Instead of audaciously mingling in the sports, the quarrels, and the connections of our little World, I was still cherished at home under the maternal wing of my aunt; and my removal from Westminster long preceded the approach of manhood. [1] In our domestic society I formed however an[2] intimate acquaintance with a young nobleman of my own age, and vainly flattered myself that our sentiments would prove as lasting as they seemed to be mutual. On my return from abroad his coldness repelled such faint advances as my pride allowed me to make, and in our different walks of life, we gradually became strangers to each other. Yet his private character[3], for Lord H. has never affected a public name leaves[4] me no room to accuse the propriety and merit of my early choice.

114ᵛ The violence and variety of my complaints which had excused my frequent absence from Westminster school, at length engaged Mrs Porten, with the advice of physicians to conduct me to Bath: at the end of the Michaelmas vacation (1750) she quitted me with reluctance, and I remained several months under the care of a trusty maid-servant. A strange nervous affection which alternately contracted my legs, and produced without any visible symptoms the most excruciating pain was ineffectually opposed by the various methods of bathing and pumping. From Bath I was transported to Winchester to the house of a physician, and after the failure of his medical skill we had again recourse to the virtues of the Bath waters. During the intervals of these fits, I moved with my father to Buriton and Putney, and a short unsuccessful tryal was attempted to renew my attendance at Westminster school. But my infirmities could not be reconciled with the hours and discipline of a public seminary: and instead of a domestic tutor, who might have watched the favourable moments, and gently advanced the progress of

---

[1] *II om ten lines from here to the end of the paragraph.*   [2] *I one*   [3] *I and conduct*   [4] *I leave*

my learning, my father was too easily content with such occasional teachers as the different places of my residence could supply. I was never forced, and seldom was I persuaded to admit these lessons: yet I read with a Clergyman at Bath some odes of Horace, and several episodes of Virgil which gave me an imperfect and transient enjoyment of the Latin Poets. It might now be apprehended that I should continue for life an illiterate cripple: but as I approached my sixteenth year, Nature displayed in my favour her mysterious energies; my constitution was fortified and fixed: and my disorders, instead of growing with my growth and strengthening with[1] my strength, most wonderfully vanished. I have never possessed or abused the insolence of health: but since that time few persons have been more exempt from real or imaginary ills: and till I am admonished by the Gout, the reader shall[2] no more be troubled with the history of any[3] bodily complaints. My unexpected recovery again encouraged the hope of my education: and I was placed at Esher in Surrey, in the house of the Reverend Mr Philip Francis, in a pleasant spot which promised to unite the various benefits of air, exercise, and study (January, 1752). [4] Mr Francis was recommended, I believe by the Mallets, as a scholar and a wit: his two tragedies have been coldly received, but his version of Demosthenes, which I have not seen, supposes some knowledge of Greek litterature, and he had executed with success and applause the arduous task of a compleat translation of Horace in English verse. Besides a young Gentleman whose name I do not remember, our family consisted only of myself, and his son, who has since been conspicuous in the supreme council of India, from whence he is returned to England with an ample fortune. It was stipulated that his father should always confine himself to a small number; and with so able a præceptor, in this private academy, the time which I had lost might have been

---

[1] *I wrote* with *twice* (*end of a line, beginning of the next*).　　[2] *II* will
[3] *II* my　　[4] *II om twenty lines from here down to* indignantly rescued: but *and inserted instead four lines from* C (*MS f 61 – M 222*): the translator of Horace might have taught me to relish the Latin poets, had not my friends discovered in a few weeks that he preferred the pleasures of London to the instruction of his pupils.

speedily retrieved. But the experience of a few weeks was sufficient to discover that Mr Francis's spirit was too lively for his profession: and while he indulged himself in the pleasures of London, his pupils were left idle at Esher in the custody of a Dutch Usher, of low manners and con-

115 temptible learning. From such | careless or unworthy hands I was indignantly rescued: but my father's perplexity [1] rather than his prudence was urged to embrace a singular and desperate measure. Without preparation or delay he carried me to Oxford; and I was matriculated in the University, as a Gentleman Commoner of Magdalen College before I [2] accomplished the fifteenth year of my age (April. 3. 1752).

The curiosity which had been implanted in my infant mind was still alive and active: but my reason was not sufficiently informed to understand the value, or to lament the loss, of three precious years from my entrance at Westminster to my admission at Oxford. Instead of repining at my long and frequent confinement to the chamber or the couch, I secretly rejoyced in those infirmities which delivered me from the exercises of the school and the society of my equals. As often as I was tolerably exempt from danger and pain, reading, free desultory reading, was the employment and comfort of my solitary hours: at Westminster my aunt sought only to amuse and indulge me; in my stations at Bath and Winchester, at Buriton and Putney a false compassion respected my sufferings, and I was allowed without controul or advice to gratify the wanderings of an unripe taste. My indiscriminate appetite subsided by degrees in the *Historic* line: and, since Philosophy has exploded all innate ideas and natural propensities, I must ascribe this choice to the assiduous perusal of the Universal history as the octavo Volumes successively appeared. This unequal work, and a treatise of Hearne, the *Ductor Historicus*, referred and introduced me to the Greek and Roman historians to as many at least as were accessible to an English reader. All that I could find were greedily devoured from Littlebury's lame Herodotus, and Spelman's valuable Xenophon, to the

[1] *II added* at this time   [2] *II added* had

pompous folios of Gordon's Tacitus, and a ragged Procopius of the beginning of the last Century. The cheap acquisition of so much knowledge confirmed my dislike to the study of languages, and I argued with Mrs Porten, that, were I master of Greek and Latin I must interpret to myself in English the thoughts of the Original, and that such extemporary versions must be inferior to the elaborate translations of professed scholars; a silly sophism, which could not easily be confuted by a person ignorant of any other language than her own. From the ancient, I leaped to the modern World: many crude lumps of Speed, Rapin, Mezeray, Davila, Machiavel, Father Paul, Bower &c. passed through me like so many novels, and I swallowed[1] with the same voracious appetite the descriptions of India and China, of Mexico and Peru. [2]Our family collection was decently furnished: the circulating libraries of London and Bath afforded rich treasures[3]: I borrowed many books, and some I contrived to purchase from my scanty allowance. My father's friends who visited the boy were astonished at finding him surrounded with a heap of folios, of whose titles *they* were ignorant and on whose contents *he* could pertinently discourse.

My first introduction to the Historic scenes, which have since engaged so many years | of my life must be ascribed to 115ᵛ an accident. In the summer of 1751 I accompanied my father on a visit to Mr Hoare's in Wiltshire: but I was less delighted with the beauties of Stourhead, than with discovering in the library a common book, the continuation of Echard's Roman history which is indeed executed with more skill and taste than the prævious work: to me the reigns of the successors of Constantine were absolutely new; and I was immersed in the passage of the Goths over the Danube when the summons of the dinner-bell reluctantly dragged me from my intellectual feast. This transient glance served rather to irritate than to appease my curiosity, and no sooner was I returned to Bath, than[4] I procured the second and third Volumes of Howell's history of the World, which exhibit

---

[1] *II* devoured   [2] *II om seven lines from here to the end of the paragraph.*
[3] *I* a rich treasures (*added* s *but forgot to cancel* a).   [4] *II* as soon as I returned to Bath I procured

the Byzantine period on a larger scale. Mahomet and his
Saracens soon fixed my attention: and some instinct of
criticism directed me to the genuine sources. Simon Ockley,
an original in every sense, first opened my eyes, and I was
led from one book to another till I had ranged round the
circle of Oriental history. Before I was sixteen I had exhausted all that could be learned in English, of the Arabs and
Persians, the Tartars and Turks, and the same ardour urged
me to guess at the French of d'Herbelot, and to construe the
barbarous Latin of Pocock's *Abulpharagius*[1]. Such vague and
multifarious reading could not teach me to think, to write
or to act; and the only principle that darted a ray of light
into the indigested Chaos was an early and rational application to the order of time and place. The maps of Cellarius
and Wells imprinted in my mind the picture of ancient
Geography: from Strauchius[2] I imbibed the elements of
Chronology: the tables of Helvicus and Anderson, the
annals of Usher and Prideaux distinguished the connection
of events, and I[3] engraved the multitude of names and dates
in a clear and indelible series. But in the discussion of the
first ages I overleaped the bounds of modesty and use. In
my childish balance I presumed to weigh the systems of
Scaliger and Petavius, of Marsham and Newton which I
could seldom study in the originals; [4]the Dynasties of Assyria
and Egypt were my top and cricket-ball: and my sleep has
been disturbed by the difficulty of reconciling the Septuagint
with the Hebrew computation. I arrived at Oxford with a
stock of erudition that might have puzzled a Doctor, and a
degree of ignorance of which a school boy would have been
ashamed.

At the conclusion of this first period of my life, I am
tempted to enter a protest against the trite and lavish praise
of the happiness of our boyish years, which is echoed with
so much affectation in the World. That happiness I have
never known; that time I have never regretted, and were my
poor aunt still alive she would bear testimony to the early
and constant uniformity of my sentiments. It will indeed be

[1] *II* Abulfaragius   [2] *II* Stranchius   [3] *II om* I   [4] *II om this line to*
cricket-ball

replied, that *I* am not a competent Judge: that pleasure is
incompatible with pain, that joy is excluded from sickness;
and that the felicity of a school boy consists in the perpetual
motion of thoughtless and playful agility, in which I was
never qualified to excell. My name, it is most true, could
never | be enrolled among the sprightly race, the idle 116
progeny of Eton or Westminster, [1] who delight to cleave the
water with pliant arm, to urge the flying ball, and to chace
the speed of the rolling circle. But I would ask the warmest
and most active Hero of the play field, whether he can
seriously compare his childish with his manly enjoyments;
whether he does not feel, as the most precious attribute of
his existence, the vigorous maturity of sensual and spiritual
powers, which Nature has reserved for the age of puberty.
A state of happiness arising[2] only from the want of foresight
and reflection shall[3] never provoke my envy; such degenerate
taste would tend to sink us in the scale of beings from a man
to a child, a dog, and an oyster; till we had reached the confines of brute matter, which cannot suffer, because it cannot
feel. The poet may gaily describe the short hours of recrea-
tion; but he forgets the daily tedious labours of the school,
which is approached each morning with anxious and reluctant steps. [4]Degrees of misery are proportioned to the
mind, rather than to the object; parva leves capiunt animos:
and few men, in the tryals of life, have experienced a more
painful sensation, than the poor school-boy, with an imperfect task, who trembles on the eve of the black Monday.
A school is the cavern of fear and sorrow: the mobility of
the captive youths is chained to a book and a desk: an
inflexible master commands their attention, which, every
moment, is impatient to escape: they labour, like the soldiers
of Persia, under the scourge; and their education is nearly
finished before they can apprehend the sense or utility of
the harsh lessons, which they are forced to repeat. Such

---

[1] *To G's prose paraphrase II substituted Gray's lines 25, 26 and 30 of his
'Ode on a Distant Prospect of Eton College', leaving out line 29 'To chase the
rolling circle's speed' and replacing in line 25* 'now delight' *by* 'might delight', *and in line 26* 'thy glassy wave' *by* 'the glassy wave'.   [2] *I* which
arises   [3] *I* will   [4] *II om seventeen lines from here to the end of the
chapter.*

blind and absolute dependence may be necessary, but can never be delightful: Freedom is the first wish of our heart; freedom is the first blessing of our nature: and, unless we bind ourselves with the voluntary chains of interest or passion, we advance in freedom as we advance in years.

Chapter III

A traveller who visits Oxford or Cambridge is surprized and edified by the apparent order and tranquillity that prevail in the seats of the English muses. In the most celebrated Universities of Holland, Germany and Italy, the students, who swarm from different countries are loosely dispersed in private lodgings at the houses of the burghers: they dress according to their fancy and fortune: and, in the intemperate quarrels of youth and wine, their *swords*, though less frequently than of old, are sometimes stained with each other's blood. The use of arms is banished from our English Universities: the uniform habit of the Academics, the square cap, and black gown is adapted to the civil and even clerical profession: and from the Doctor in Divinity to the undergraduate, the degrees of learning and age are externally distinguished. Instead of being scattered in a town, the students of Oxford and Cambridge are united in Colleges: their maintenance is provided at their own expence, or that of the founders; and the stated hours of the hall and chappel represent the discipline of a regular, and, as it were, a Religious community. The eyes of the traveller are attracted by the size or beauty of the public edifices; and the principal colleges appear to be so many palaces which a liberal nation has erected and endowed for the habitation of Science. My own introduction to the University of Oxford forms a new æra in my life, and at the distance of forty years I still remember my first emotions of surprize and satisfaction. In my fifteenth year, I felt myself suddenly raised from a boy to a man: the persons whom I respected as my superiors in age and Academical rank entertained me with every mark of attention | and civility; and my vanity was flattered by 117 the velvet Cap and silk gown which discriminate[1] a Gentleman-Commoner from a plebeian student. A decent allowance, more money than a school-boy had ever seen, was at my

[1] *II* distinguish

Chapter III

A traveller who visits Oxford
or Cambridge is surprized and edified by the apparent
order and tranquillity that prevail in the seats of the English
muses. In the most celebrated Universities of Holland, Germany
and Italy, the students, who swarm from different countries
are loosely dispersed in private lodgings at the houses of
the burghers: they dress according to their fancy and fortune:
and in the intemperate quarrels of youth and wine, their
swords, though less frequently than of old, are sometimes
stained with each other's ~~brothers~~ blood. The use of arms
is banished from our English Universities: the uniform
habit of the Academics, the square cap, and black gown is
adapted to the civil and even clerical profession: and from
the Doctor in Divinity to the under-graduate the degrees
of learning and age are externally distinguished. Instead
of being scattered in a town, the students of Oxford and
Cambridge are united in Colleges: their maintenance
is provided at their own expence or that of the founders;
and the stated hours of the hall and ~~the~~ chappel re-
:present the discipline of a regular, and, as it were, a
Religious community. The eyes of the traveller are at-
:tracted by the size or beauty of the public edifices;
and the principal colleges appear to be so many ~~st~~
palaces which a liberal nation has erected and en:
:dowed for the habitation of Science. My own introduc-
:tion to the University of Oxford forms a new æra
in my life; and at the distance of ~~four~~ forty years
I still remember my first emotions of surprize and
satisfaction. ~~At the~~ In my fifteenth year, I felt my:
:self suddenly raised from a boy to a man: the persons
whom I respected as my superiors in age and Academi:
:cal rank entertained me with every mark of attention

Plate III. First page of Chapter III of F, numbered 28 by G
MS *f* 116ᵛ

own disposal, and I might command, among the tradesmen of Oxford, an indefinite and dangerous latitude of credit. A key was delivered into my hands which gave me the free use of a numerous and learned library: my apartment consisted of three elegant and well furnished rooms in the new building, a stately pile, of Magdalen College: and the adjacent walks, had they been frequented by Plato's disciples, might have been compared to the Attic shade on the banks of the Ilissus. Such was the fair prospect of my entrance (April 3: 1752) into the University of Oxford.

A venerable prelate, whose taste and erudition must reflect honour on the society in which they were formed has drawn a very interesting picture of his Academical life. 'I 'was educated (says Bishop Lowth[)] in the UNIVERSITY OF 'OXFORD. I enjoyed all the advantages both public and private, 'which that famous seat of learning so largely affords. I spent 'many years in that illustrious Society, in a well-regulated 'course of useful discipline and studies; and in the agreable 'and improving commerce of Gentlemen and of Scholars: 'in a society where emulation without envy, ambition with- 'out jealousy, contention without animosity incited industry, 'and awakened genius: where a liberal pursuit of knowledge, 'and a genuine freedom of thought was raised encouraged 'and pushed forward by example, by commendation, and by 'authority. I breathed the same atmosphere, that the 'HOOKERS, the CHILLINGWORTHS, and the LOCKES, had breathed 'before: whose benevolence and humanity were as extensive 'as their vast Genius and comprehensive knowledge, who 'always treated their adversaries with civility, and respect, 'who made candour, moderation, and liberal judgement as 'much the rule and law as the subject of their discourse.— 'And do you reproach me with my education in This place, 'and with my relation to This most respectable Body; 'which I shall always esteem my greatest advantage, and 'my highest honour?' I transcribe with pleasure this eloquent passage, without examining what benefits or what rewards were derived by Hooker, or Chillingworth or Locke from their Academical institution, without enquiring whether in this angry controversy the spirit of Lowth himself is purified

from the intolerant zeal, which Warburton had ascribed to
the Genius of the place. [1] The expression of gratitude is a
virtue and a pleasure: a liberal mind will delight to cherish
and celebrate the memory of its parents, and the teachers of
science are the parents of the mind. I applaud the filial piety
which it is impossible for me to imitate: since I must not
confess an imaginary debt to assume the merit of a just or
generous retribution. To the University of Oxford *I* acknowledge no obligation, and she will as chearfully renounce me
for a son, as I am willing to disclaim her for a mother. I
spent fourteen months at Magdalen College: they proved
the fourteen months the most idle and unprofitable of my
whole life: the reader will pronounce between the school
and | the scholar: but I cannot affect to believe that Nature 117ᵛ
had disqualified me for all litterary pursuits. The specious
and ready excuse of my tender age, imperfect preparation,
and hasty departure may doubtless be alleged, nor do I wish
to defraud such excuses of their proper weight. Yet in my
sixteenth year I was not devoid of capacity or application;
even my childish reading had displayed an early though blind
propensity for books; and the shallow flood might have been
taught to flow in a deep channel, and a clear stream. In the
discipline of a well-constituted Academy, under the guidance
of skillful and vigilant professors, I should gradually have
risen from translations to originals, from the Latin to the
Greek Classics, from dead languages to living science: my
hours would have been occupied by useful and agreable
studies: the wanderings of fancy would have been restrained,
and I should have escaped the temptations of idleness which
finally precipitated my departure from Oxford.

Perhaps, in a separate annotation I may coolly examine
the fabulous and real antiquities of our sister-Universities,
a question which has kindled such fierce and foolish disputes
among their fanatic sons. In the mean while, it will be acknowledged that these venerable bodies are sufficiently old

---

[1] *II inserted here a sentence from B (MS f 29 – M 123):* It may indeed be observed that the Atmosphere of Oxford did not agree with Mr Locke's constitution, and that the Philosopher justly despised the Academical bigots
who expelled his person, and condemned his principles.

to partake of all the prejudices and infirmities of age. The schools of Oxford and Cambridge were founded in a dark age of false and barbarous science; and they are still tainted with the vices of their origin. Their primitive discipline was adapted to the education of priests and monks; and the gover[n]ment still remains in the hands of the Clergy, an order of men, whose manners are remote from the present World, and whose eyes are dazzled by the light of Philosophy. The legal incorporation of these societies by the charters of Popes and Kings had given them a monopoly of the public instruction; and the spirit of monopolists is narrow, lazy and oppressive: their work is more costly and less productive than that of independent artists; and the new improvements so eagerly grasped by the competition of freedom, are admitted with slow and sullen reluctance in those proud corporations, above the fear of a rival, and below the confession of an error. We may scarcely hope that any reformation will be a voluntary act, and so deeply are they rooted in law and prejudice that even the omnipotence of Parliament would shrink from an enquiry into the state and abuses of the two Universities.

The use of Academical degrees, as old as the thirteenth century, is visibly borrowed from the mechanic corporations in which an apprentice, after serving his time, obtains a testimonial of his skill, and a licence to practise his trade and mystery. It is not my design to depreciate those honours which could never gratify or disappoint my ambition: and I should applaud the institution, if the degrees of Batchelor or licentiate were bestowed as the reward of manly and successful study: if the name and rank of Doctor or Master were strictly reserved for the professors of science who have approved their title to the public esteem. [1] The mysterious | faculty of Theology must not be scanned by a profane eye, the cloak[2] of reason sits awkwardly on our fashionable Divines and in the Ecclesiastical studies of the fathers and councils their modesty will yield to the Catholic universities. Our English civilians and canonists have never been famous:

118

---

[1] *II om twenty-three lines from here down to the end of the paragraph.*   [2] *I a* shadow

their real business is confined to a small circle; and the double jurisprudence of Rome is overwhelmed by the enormous profession of common lawyers, who, in the pursuit of honours and riches disdain the mock majesty of our *budge* Doctors. We are justly proud of the skill and learning of our physicians: their skill is acquired in the practise of the hospitals: they seek their learning in London, in Scotland, or on the continent; and few patients would trust their pulse to a medical student, if he had passed the fourteen years of his noviciate at Oxford or Cambridge, whose degrees however, are exclusively admitted in the Royal College. The *Arts* are supposed to include the liberal knowledge of Philosophy and litterature: but I am informed that some tattered shreds of the old Logic and Metaphysics compose the exercises for a Batchelor and Master's degree; and that modern improvements[1], instead of introducing a more rational tryal, have[1] only served to relax the forms which are now the object of general contempt.

In all the Universities of Europe except[2] our own, the languages and sciences are distributed among a numerous list of effective professors: the students, according to their taste, their calling, and their diligence apply themselves to the proper masters, and in the annual repetition of public and private lectures, these masters are assiduously employed. Our curiosity may enquire what number of professors has been instituted at Oxford (for I shall now confine myself to my own University)? by whom are they appointed, and what may be the probable chances of merit or incapacity? how many are stationed to the three faculties, and how many are left for the liberal Arts? what is the form, and what the substance of their lessons? But all these questions are silenced by one short and singular answer. 'That, in the 'University of Oxford, the greater part of the public professors 'have for these many years, given up altogether even the 'pretence of teaching' Incredible as the fact may appear I must rest my belief on the positive and impartial evidence of a Philosopher[3] who had himself resided at Oxford. Dr Adam

---

[1] *I* Improvement . . . has   [2] *II* excepting   [3] *For* a Philosopher *II* substituted, from C (*MS f 62 – M 225*), a master of moral and political wisdom

Smith assigns as the cause of their indolence, that, instead of being paid by voluntary contributions which would urge them to encrease the number, and to deserve the gratitude, of their pupils, the Oxford professors are secure in the enjoyment of a fixed stipend, without the necessity of labour, or the apprehension of controul. It has indeed been observed, nor is the observation absurd, that except[1] in experimental sciences, which demand a costly apparatus and a dextrous hand, the many valuable treatises that have been published on every subject of learning may now supersede the ancient mode of oral instruction. Were this principle true in its utmost latitude, I should only infer that the offices and salaries which are become useless ought, without delay to be abolished. But there still remains a material difference between a book and a professor: the hour of the lecture en-

118ᵛ forces attendance: | attention is fixed by the presence, the voice, and the occasional questions of the teacher: the most idle will carry something away; and the more diligent will compare the instructions which they have heard in the school, with the volumes which they peruse in their chamber. The advice of a skillful professor will adapt a course of reading to every mind and every situation; [2] his learning will remove difficulties, and solve objections: his authority will discover, admonish, and at last chastise the negligence of his disciples; and his vigilant enquiries will ascertain the steps of their litterary progress. Whatsoever[3] science he professes, he may illustrate in a series of discourses, composed in the leisure of his closet, pronounced on public occasions and finally delivered to the press. I observe with pleasure, that in the University of Oxford, Dr Lowth, with equal eloquence and erudition, has executed this task, in his incomparable *Prælections* on the poetry of the Hebrews.

The College of St Mary Magdalen [4](it is vulgarly pronounced Maudlin) was founded in the fifteenth Century by a[5] Bishop of Winchester; and now consists of a President, forty fellows, and a number of inferior students. It is esteemed one of the largest and most wealthy of our Aca-

---

[1] *II* excepting   [2] *II om this line to* objections: [3] *II* Whatever   [4] *II om this parenthesis.*   [5] *II* Wainfleet,

demical corporations, which may be compared to the Benedictine Abbeys of Catholic countries: and I have loosely heard that the estates belonging to Magdalen College, which are leased by those indulgent landlords at small quit-rents and occasional fines, might be raised, in the hands of private avarice, to an annual revenue of near[1] thirty thousand pounds. Our Colleges are supposed to be schools of science as well as of education: nor is it unreasonable to expect that a body of litterary men, addicted[2] to a life of celibacy, exempt from the care of their own subsistence, and amply provided with books, should devote their leisure to the prosecution of study, and that some effects[3] of their studies should be [4]manifested to the World. The shelves of their library groan under the weight of the Benedictine folios, of the editions of the fathers, and the Collections of the middle ages, which have issued from the single Abbey of St Germain des Préz[5] at Paris. A composition of Genius must be the offspring of one[6] mind: but such works of industry as may be divided among many hands, and must be continued during many years are the peculiar province of a laborious community. If I enquire into the manufactures of the monks at Magdalen, if I extend the enquiry to the other Colleges of Oxford and Cambridge, a silent blush, or a scornful frown, will be the only reply. The fellows or monks of my time were decent easy men who supinely enjoyed the gifts of the founder: their days were filled by a series of uniform employments; [7]the Chappel and the Hall, the Coffee house, and the common room, till they retired, weary, and well-satisfied, to a long slumber. From the toil of reading or thinking, or writing they had absolved their conscience, and the first shoots of learning and ingenuity withered on the ground without yielding any fruit[8] to the owners or the public. [9]The only student was a young fellow, (a future Bishop) who was deeply immersed in the follies of the Hutchinsonian system: the only author was an

---

[1] *II* nearly   [2] *II* devoted   [3] *I* fruits   [4] *I* given to the public. [5] *II* de Préz   [6] *I* a single   [7] *I* a long breakfast at no early hour, the chappel, the dinner in the Hall, their regular walk, afternoon prayers, the Coffee-house, the evening assembly in the common room, till   [8] *II* fruits [9] *II om five lines from here to* Great Britain.

119 half-starved Chaplain, Ballard was his name | who begged subscriptions for some Memoirs concerning the learned ladies of Great-Britain. As a Gentleman-Commoner I was [1] admitted to the society of the fellows, and fondly expected that some questions of litterature would be the amusing and instructive topics of their discourse. Their conversation stagnated in a round of College business, Tory politics, personal stories[2] and private scandal: their dull and deep potations excused the brisk intemperance of Youth; and their constitutional toasts were not expressive of the most lively loyalty for the house of Hanover. A general election was now approaching: the great Oxfordshire contest already blazed with all the malevolence of party-zeal: Magdalen College was devoutly attached to the Old interest; and the names of Wenman and Dashwood were more frequently pronounced than those of Cicero and Chrysostom. The example of the senior fellows could not inspire the under-graduates with a liberal spirit a[3] studious emulation: and I cannot describe, as I never knew, the discipline of the[4] College. Some duties may possibly have been imposed on the poor scholars, whose ambition aspired to the peaceful honours of a fellowship (ascribi quietis ordinibus . . . Deorum): but no independent members were admitted, below the rank of a Gentleman-Commoner; and our velvet cap was the cap of liberty. A tradition prevailed that some of our predecessors had spoken Latin declamations in the Hall, but of this ancient custom no vestige remained: the obvious methods of public exercises and examinations were totally unknown; and I have never heard that either the President or the Society interfered in the private œconomy of the Tutors and their pupills.

The silence of the Oxford professors, which deprives the Youth of public instruction is imperfectly supplied by the Tutors as they are styled of the several colleges. Instead of confining themselves to a single science which had satisfied the ambition of Burman or Bernouilli, they teach or promise to teach either History or Mathematics, or ancient litterature or moral philosophy; and as it is possible that they may be

[1] *I* sometimes   [2] *II* anecdotes   [3] *II* or   [4] *I* Magdalen. – *II om* the

defective in all, it is highly probable that of some they will be ignorant. They are paid indeed by private contributions; but their appointment depends on the head of the house: their diligence is voluntary, and will consequently be languid, while the pupills themselves and[1] their parents are not indulged in the liberty of choice or change. The first Tutor into whose hands I was resigned, appears to have been one of the best of the tribe: Dr Waldegrave was a learned and pious man, of a mild disposition, strict morals and abstemious life, who seldom mingled in the politics or the jollity of the College. But his knowledge of the World was confined to the University; his learning was of the last, rather than[2] the present age, his temper was indolent; his faculties, which were not of the first rate, had been relaxed by the climate; and he was satisfied, like his fellows with the slight and superficial discharge of an important trust. As soon as my tutor had sounded the insufficiency of his disciple in school-learning he proposed that we should read every morning from ten to eleven the comedies of Terence: the sum of my improvement in the University of Oxford is confined to three or four Latin plays; and even the study of an elegant Classic which might have been illustrated by a comparision of ancient and modern theatres was reduced to a dry and literal interpretation of the Author's text During the first weeks I constantly attended these | lessons in my 119^v tutor's room; but as they appeared equally devoid of profit and pleasure, I was once tempted to try the experiment of a formal apology. The apology was accepted with a smile: I repeated the offence with less ceremony, the excuse was admitted with the same indulgence: the slightest motive of lazyness or indisposition, the most trifling avocation at home or abroad was allowed as a worthy impediment nor did my tutor appear conscious of my absence or neglect. Had the hour of lecture been constantly filled, a single hour was a small portion of my Academic leisure. No plan of study was recommended for my use: no exercises were prescribed for his inspection; and at the most precious season of Youth whole days and weeks were suffered to elapse without labour

[1] *II* or   [2] *II added* of

or amusement, without advice or account. I should have
listened to the voice of reason and of my tutor: his mild
behaviour had gained my confidence: I preferred his society
to that of the younger students; and in our evening walks
to the top of Heddington hill we freely conversed on a variety
of subjects. Since the days of Pocock and Hyde, Oriental
learning has always been the pride of Oxford, and I once
expressed an inclination to study Arabic. His prudence discouraged this childish fancy: but he neglected the fair
occasion of directing the ardour of a curious mind. During
my absence in the summer vacation, Dr Waldegrave accepted a college living at Washington in Sussex, and on my
return I no longer found him at Oxford. From that time I
have lost sight of my first tutor: but at the end of thirty
years (1781) he was still alive; and the practise of exercise
and temperance had entitled him to an healthy old-age.

The long recess between the Trinity and Michaelmas
terms empties the Colleges of Oxford as well as the courts
of Westminster. I spent at my father'[s] house at Buriton
in Hampshire the two months of August and September[1],
which, in the year 1752 were curtailed, to my great surprize,
of eleven days, by the alteration of the style. It is whimsical
enough that as soon as I left Magdalen college my taste for
books began to revive, but it was the same blind and boyish
taste for the pursuit of exotic history. Unprovided with
original learning, unformed in the habits of thinking, un-
skilled in the arts of composition, I resolved—to write a
book. The title of this first Essay, *the Age of Sesostris* was
perhaps suggested by Voltaire's Age of Lewis XIV which
was new and popular, but my sole object was to investigate
the probable date of the life and reign of the Conqueror of
Asia. I was then enamoured of Sir John Marsham's Canon
Chronicus, an elaborate work of whose merits and defects I
was not yet qualified to judge. According to his specious,
though narrow plan, I settled my Hero about the time of
Solomon, in the tenth Century before the Christian Æra. It
was therefore incumbent on me, unless I would adopt Sir
Isaac Newton's shorter Chronology, to remove a formidable

[1] *II om the end of this sentence from* ,which, in the year

objection; and my solution, for a youth of fifteen is not devoid of ingenuity. In his version of the sacred books, Manetho the High priest has identified Sethosis or Sesostris with the elder brother of Danaus who landed in Greece, according to the Parian marble fifteen hundred and ten years before Christ. But in my supposition the High-priest is guilty of a voluntary error; flattery is the prolific parent of falsehood, [1] and falsehood, I will now add, is not incompatible with the sacerdotal | Character. Manetho's history of Egypt 120 is dedicated to Ptolemy Philadelphus who derived a fabulous or illegitimate pedigree from the Macedonian Kings of the race of Hercules: Danaus is the ancestor of Hercules; and after the failure of the elder branch his descendants the Ptolemies are the sole representatives of the Royal family and may claim by inheritance the kingdom which they hold by conquest. Such were my juvenile discoveries; at a riper age I no longer presume to connect the Greek, the Jewish, and the Egyptian antiquities which are lost in a distant cloud: nor is this the only instance, in which the belief and knowledge of the child are superseded by the more rational ignorance of the man. During my stay at Buriton, my infant labour was diligently prosecuted without much interruption from company or country-diversions: and I already heard the music of public applause. [2] The discovery of my own weakness was the first symptom of taste: on my return to Oxford, the Age of Sesostris was wisely relinquished; but the imperfect sheets remained twenty years at the bottom of a drawer, till in a general clearance of papers (November 1772) they were committed to the flames.

After the departure of Dr Waldegrave, I was transferred with the rest of his live stock to a senior fellow[3], whose literary and moral[4] character did not command the respect of the College. Dr Winchester[5] well remembered that he had a salary to receive, and only forgot that he had a duty to

---

[1] *II om the end of this sentence from* and falsehood   [2] *I ended this paragraph thus* . . . applause. But on my return to Oxford, in the beginning of October (1752), I nodded to the Genius of the place, and gently relapsed into my former lethargy.   [3] *II with his other pupils to his academic heir*   [4] *II om* and moral   [5] *II* Dr. ****

perform. Instead of guiding the studies and watching over the behaviour of his disciple[1], I was never summoned to attend even the ceremony of a lecture; and except[2] one voluntary visit to his rooms, during the eight months of his titular office, the tutor and pupill lived in the same College as strangers to each other. The want of experience, of advice, and of occupation soon betrayed me into some improprieties of conduct, ill-chosen company, late hours and inconsiderate expence. My growing debts might be secret; but my frequent absence was visible and scandalous: and a tour to Bath, a visit into Buckinghamshire, and four excursions to London in the same winter, were costly and dangerous frolicks. They were indeed without a meaning, as without an excuse: the irksomeness of a cloystered life repeatedly tempted me to wander: but my chief pleasure was that of travelling; and I was too young and bashful, to enjoy like a manly Oxonian in town, the [3] taverns and bagnios of Covent Garden. In all these excursions, I eloped from Oxford; I returned to College; in a few days I eloped again, as if I had been an independent stranger in a hired lodging[4], without once hearing the voice of admonition, without once feeling the hand of controul. Yet my time was lost, my expences were multiplied, my behaviour abroad was unknown; folly as well as vice should have awakened the attention of my superiors, and my tender years would have justified a more than ordinary degree of restraint and discipline.

It might at least be expected that an Ecclesiastical school should inculcate the orthodox principles[5] of Religion. But our venerable Mother had contrived to unite the opposite extremes of bigotry and indifference: an heretic or unbeliever was a monster in her eyes; but she was always, or often, or sometimes, remiss in the spiritual education of her own children. According to the statutes of the University, every student, before he is matriculated, must subscribe his assent to the thirty nine articles of the Church of England, which are signed by more than read, and read by more than believe

---

[1] *I* pupill   [2] *II* excepting   [3] *II ended this sentence thus: . . .* town, the pleasures of London.   [4] *I added* in a hired lodging *in the margin.*
[5] *I* system

them. My insufficient age excused me however from the immediate performance of this legal ceremony: and the Vice-Chancellor directed | me to return, so[1] soon as I should have 120ᵛ accomplished my fifteenth year; recommending me in the mean while to the instruction of my College. My College forgot to instruct: I forgot to return, and was myself forgotten by the first Magistrate of the University. Without a single lecture, either public or private, either Christian or protestant, without any Academical subscription, without any episcopal confirmation, I was left, by the dim light of my Catechism, to grope my way to the Chappel and communion-table, where I was admitted, without a question how far, or by what means I might be qualified to receive the sacrament. Such almost incredible neglect was productive of the worst mischiefs. From my childhood I had been fond of Religious disputation: my poor aunt has been often puzzled by my objections to[2] the mysteries which she strove to believe; nor had the elastic spring been totally broken by the weight of the Atmosphere of Oxford. The blind activity of idleness urged me to advance without armour into the dangerous mazes of controversy, and at the age of sixteen I bewildered myself in the errors of the Church of Rome.

The progress of my conversion may tend to illustrate, at least the history of my own mind. It was not long since Dʳ Middleton's free Enquiry had sounded an alarm in the Theological World: much ink and much gall had been spilt in the defence of the primitive miracles; and the two dullest [3] of their champions were crowned with Academic honours by the University of Oxford. The name of Middleton was unpopular; and his proscription very naturally tempted[4] me to peruse his writings and those of his antagonists. His bold criticism, which approaches the precipice of infidelity produced on my mind a singular effect; and had I persevered in the communion of Rome I should now apply to my own fortune the prediction of the Sibyll,

—— —— —— —— Via prima salutis
Quod minimum[5] reris, Graiâ pandetur ab Urbe.

---

[1] II as   [2] II om my objections to   [3] I had added and most angry of
[4] II led   [5] II minime

The elegance of style and freedom of argument were repelled by a[1] shield of prejudice. I still revered the characters[2], or rather the names, of the Saints and fathers whom Dr Middleton exposes, nor could he destroy my implicit belief, that the gift of miraculous powers was continued in the Church during the first four or five Centuries of Christianity. But I was unable to resist the weight of historical evidence, that within the same period, most of the leading doctrines of Popery were already introduced in Theory and practise: nor was my conclusion absurd, that Miracles are the test of truth, and that the Church must be orthodox and pure, which was so often approved by the visible interposition of the Deity. The marvellous tales, which are so boldly attested by the Basils and Chrysostoms, the Austins and Jeroms, compelled me to embrace the superior merits of Celibacy, the institution of the monastic life, the use of the sign of the cross, of holy oil, and even of images, the invocation of Saints, the worship of relicks, the rudiments of purgatory in prayers for the dead, and the tremendous mystery of the sacrifice of the body and blood of Christ, which insensibly swelled into the prodigy of Transubstantiation. In these dispositions, and already more than half a convert, I formed an unlucky intimacy with a young
121 Gentleman of | our College whose name I shall spare[3]. With a character less resolute Mr ———[4] had imbibed the same Religious opinions, and some Popish books, I know not through what channel, were conveyed into his possession. I read, I applauded, I believed: the English translations of two famous works of Bossuet, Bishop of Meaux, the Exposition of the Catholic doctrine, and the history of the Protestant variations, atchieved my conversion, and I surely fell by a noble hand. I have since examined the originals with a more discerning eye, and shall not hesitate to pronounce that Bossuet is indeed a master of all the weapons of controversy. In the Exposition, a specious Apology, the Orator assumes, with consummate art, the tone of candour and simplicity: and the ten-horned Monster is transformed, at his magic

---

[1] *II* the   [2] *II* character   [3] *III om* whose name I shall spare.
[4] *III* Molesworth

touch[,] into the milk-white hind, who must be loved as soon
as she is seen. In the history, a bold and well-aimed attack,
he displays with an happy mixture of narrative and argument, the faults and follies, the changes and contradictions
of our first Reformers; whose Variations, (as he dextrously
contends), are the mark of heretical[1] error, while the perpetual Unity of the Catholic Church is the sign and test of
infallible truth. To my actual[2] feelings it seems incredible
that I could[3] ever believe that I believed in Transubstan[tia]-
tion! But my conqueror oppressed me with the sacramental
words 'Hoc est corpus meum', and dashed against each other
the figurative half-meanings of the Protestant sects: every
objection was resolved into Omnipotence; and after repeating
at St Mary's, the Athanasian creed, I humbly acquiesced in
the Mystery of the real presence.

> To take up half on trust, and half to try,
> Name it not faith, but bungling bigotry.
> Both knave and fool the merchant we may call
> To pay great sums and to compound the small
> For who would break with Heaven, and would not
>   break for all?

No sooner had I settled my new Religion, than I resolved to
profess myself a Catholic: Youth is sincere and impetuous;
and a momentary glow of Enthusiasm had raised me above
all temporal considerations.

By the keen protestants, who would gladly retaliate the
example of persecution, a clamour [is raised][4] of the encrease
of popery: and they are always loud to declaim against the
toleration of priests and Jesuits who pervert so many of his
Majesty's subjects from their Religion and Allegiance. On
the present occasion the fall of one, or more, of her sons,
directed this clamour against the University: and it was
confidently affirmed that Popish missionaries were suffered,
under various disguises to introduce themselves into the Colleges of Oxford. But the love of truth and[5] justice enjoyns[6]
me to declare, that as far as relates to myself, this assertion
is false, and that I never conversed with a priest or even

---

[1] *II* historical   [2] *II* present   [3] *II* should   [4] *II added* is raised
[5] *II om* the love of truth and   [6] *II* obliges

with a papist, till my resolution, from books, was absolutely fixed. In my last excursion to London, I addressed myself to [1] a Roman Catholic bookseller in Russell-street Covent Garden, who recommended me to a priest of whose name and order I am at present ignorant. In our first interview, he soon discovered that persuasion was needless; after sounding the motives and merits of my conversion, he consented to admit me into the pale of the Church: and at his feet on the eighth of June, 1753, I solemnly, though privately abjured
121ᵛ the errors of heresy. The seduction of an English | Youth of family and fortune was an act of as much danger as glory; but he bravely overlooked the danger of which I was not then sufficiently informed. 'Where a person is reconciled to the see of Rome, or procures others to be reconciled, the offence (says Blackstone [)] amounts to High-treason.' And if the humanity of the age would prevent the execution of this sanguinary statute there were other laws, of a less odious cast, which condemned the priest to perpetual imprisonment, and transferred the proselyte's estate to his nearest relation. An elaborate controversial Epistle approved by my director, and addressed to my father, announced and justified the step which I had taken. My father was neither a bigot nor a philosopher; but his affection deplored the loss of an only son; and his good sense was astonished at my strange departure from the Religion of my Country. In the first sally of passion, he divulged a secret, which prudence might have suppressed: and the gates of Magdalen College were for ever shut against my return. Many years afterwards when the name of Gibbon was become as notorious as that of Middleton, it was industriously whispered at Oxford that the historian had formerly 'turned Papist': my character stood exposed to the reproach of inconstancy; and this invidious topic would have been handled without mercy by my opponents, could they have separated my cause from that of the University. For my own part I am proud of an honest sacrifice of interest to conscience; I can never blush if[2] my tender mind was entangled in the sophistry that[3] seduced the acute and manly understandings

[1] *II added* Mr. Lewis *from C* (*MS f 62ᵛ – M 227*).   [2] *I that*   [3] *I which*

of CHILLINGWORTH and BAYLE [1], who afterwards emerged from superstition to scepticism.

While Charles the first governed England, and was himself governed by a Catholic Queen, it cannot be denied that the Missionaries of Rome laboured with impunity and success in the Court, the country, and even the Universities. One of the sheep,

> —— Whom the grim Wolf, with privy paw
> Daily devours apace, and nothing said,

is Mr William Chillingworth, master of arts, and fellow of Trinity College[2], who, at the ripe age of twenty eight years was persuaded to elope from Oxford to the English[3] seminary of[4] Douay in Flanders. Some disputes with Fisher, a subtle Jesuit might first awaken him from the prejudices of education, but he yielded to his own victorious argument 'That 'there must be somewhere an infallible judge and that the 'Church of Rome is the only Christian society, which either 'does or can pretend to that character'. After a short tryal of a few months Mr Chillingworth was again tormented by religious scruples[5]: he returned home, resumed his studies, unravelled his mistakes, and delivered his mind from the yoke of authority and superstition. His new creed was built on the principle that the Bible is our sole[6] judge, and private reason our sole interpreter: and he ably maintains this principle in the 'Religion of a protestant', a book (1634)[7] which, after startling the Doctors of Oxford, is still esteemed the most solid defence of the Reformation. The learning the virtue, the recent merits of the author entitled him to[8] fair preferment, but the slave had now broke his fetters, and the more he weighed, the less was he disposed to subscribe[9] the thirty nine articles of the Church of England. In a private letter he declares, with all the energy of language, that he could not subscribe[9] them, without subscribing[9] his own damnation, and that if ever, he should depart from this[10] | immoveable resolution, he would allow his friends to think him   122

[1] *I added the end of this sentence from* , who afterwards *in the margin.*   [2] *II added* , Oxford   [3] *II om* English   [4] *II at*   [5] *I was tormented by his own spirit*   [6] *I only*   [7] *II om this date.*   [8] *II added* a   [9] *II added* to   [10] *II* his

a madman or an atheist. As the letter is without a date, we cannot ascertain the number of weeks or months that elapsed between this passionate abhorrence, and the Salisbury register which is still extant. 'Ego Gulielmus Chillingworth '. . . omnibus hisce articulis et singulis in iisdem contentis, 'volens et ex animo subscribo, et consensum meum iisdem 'præbeo. 20 die Julii 1638.' But, alas! the Chancellor and prebandary of Sarum soon deviated from his own subscription; as he more deeply scrutinized the article of the Trinity, neither Scripture nor the primitive fathers, could long uphold his orthodox belief, 'and he could not but confess, that the 'doctrine of Arius is either a truth, or at least no damnable 'heresy' From this middle region of the air, the descent of his reason would naturally rest on the firmer ground of the Socinians: and, if we may credit a doubtful story, and the popular opinion, his anxious enquiries at last subsided in Philosophic indifference. So conspicuous however were the candour of his Nature, and the innocence of his heart, that this apparent levity did not affect the reputation of Chillingworth. His frequent changes proceeded from too nice an inquisition into truth. His doubts grew out of himself, he assisted them with all the strength of his reason: he was then too hard for himself: but finding as little quiet and repose in those victories, he quickly recovered by a new appeal to his own judgement; so that in all his sallies and retreats, he was, in fact, his own convert.

Bayle was the son of a Calvinist minister in a remote province of[1] France at the foot of the Pyrenees. For the benefit of education, the Protestants were tempted to risk their children in the Catholic Universities; and in the twenty second year of his age young Bayle was seduced by the arts and arguments of the Jesuits of Tholouse. He remained about seventeen months (19th March 1669—19th August 1670) in their hands, a voluntary captive; and a letter to his parents, which the new convert composed or subscribed (15th April 1670) is darkly tinged with the spirit of Popery. But Nature had designed him to think as he pleased and to speak as he thought: his piety was offended by the ex-

1 *III* in

cessive worship of creatures; and the study of physics convinced him of the impossibility of Transubstan[tia]tion, which is abundantly refuted by the testimony of our senses. His return to the communion of a falling sect was a bold and disinterested step, that exposed him to the rigour of the laws, and a speedy flight to Geneva protected him from the resentment of his spiritual tyrants, unconscious as they were of the full value of the prize which they had lost. Had Bayle adhered to the Catholic Church, had he embraced the Ecclesiastical profession, the Genius and favour of such a proselyte might have aspired to wealth and honours in his native country: but the Hypocrite would[1] have found less happiness in the comforts of a benefice, or the dignity of a mitre than he enjoyed at Rotterdam, in a private state of exile, indigence, and freedom. Without a country, or a patron or a prejudice, he claimed the liberty, and subsisted by the labours of his pen: the inequality of his voluminous works is explained and excused by his alternately writing for himself, for the booksellers, and for posterity, and if a severe critic would reduce him to a single folio, that relick, like the books of the Sybill would become still more valuable. A calm and lofty spectator of the Religious tempest, the Philosopher of Rotterdam condemned | with equal firmness 122ᵛ the persecution of Lewis xiv[2]; and the Republican maxims of the Calvinists; their vain prophecies and the intolerant bigotry which sometimes vexed his solitary retreat. In reviewing the controversies of the times, he turned against each other, the arguments of the disputants: successively wielding the arms of the Catholics and protestants, he proves that neither the way of authority, nor the way of examination can afford the multitude any test of Religious truth; and dextrously concludes, that custom and education must be the sole grounds of popular belief. The ancient paradox of Plutarch, that Atheism is less pernicious than superstition acquires a tenfold vigour when it is adorned with the colours of his wit, and pointed with the acuteness of his logic. His critical Dictionary is a vast repository of facts and opinions; and he balances the *false* Religions in his

[1] *I* but he would   [2] *II* Lewis the Fourteenth

sceptical scales, till the opposite quantities, (if I may use the language of Algebra) annihilate each other. The wonderful power, which he so boldly exercised of assembling doubts and objections had tempted him, jocosely to assume the title of the νεφεληγερετα Ζευς, the cloud-compelling Jove; and in a conversation with the ingenious Abbé, (afterwards Cardinal) de Polignac, he freely disclosed his universal Pyrrhonism 'I am most truly (said Bayle) a protestant; for I protest indifferently against all Systems, and all Sects.'

The Academical resentment, which I may possibly have provoked will prudently spare this plain narrative of my studies, or rather of my idleness; and of the unfortunate event which shortened the term of my residence at Oxford. But it may be suggested that my father was unluckly in the choice of a society, and the chance of a tutor. It will perhaps be asserted, that in the lapse of forty years many improvements have taken place in the College and ¹ the University. I am not unwilling to believe that some Tutors might have been found more active than Dr Waldegrave, and less contemptible than Dr Winchester². ³ About the same time, and in the same walk a Bentham was still treading in the footsteps of a Burton, whose maxims he had adopted and whose life he has published. The Biographer indeed preferred the school-logic to the new Philosophy, Burgersdicius to Locke; and the Hero appears in his own writings a stiff and conceited Pedant. Yet even these men, according to the measure of their capacity, might be diligent, and useful; and it is recorded of Burton that he taught his pupills what he knew, some Latin, some Greek, some Ethics and Metaphysics, referring them to proper masters for the languages, and sciences of which he was ignorant. At a more recent period many students have been attracted by the merit and reputation of Sir William Scott, then a tutor in University College, and now conspicuous in the profession of the Civil law: my personal acquaintance with that Gentleman has inspired me with a just esteem for his abilities and knowledge; and I am assured that his Lectures on history would compose, were

---

¹ *II added in* he was ignorant.   ² *II Dr.* ****   ³ *III om twelve lines from here down to*

they given to the public, a most valuable treatise. Under the auspices of the [1]present Archbishop of York, D[r] Markham, himself an eminent scholar, a more regular discipline has been introduced, as I am told at Christ-Church: a course of Classical and philosophical studies is proposed and even pursued in that numerous seminary: Learning has been made a duty, a pleasure and even a fashion; and several young Gentlemen | who[2] do honour to the College in which 123 they have been educated. According to the Will of the Donor the profits[3] of the second part of Lord Clarendon's history has been applied to the establishment of a riding school, that the polite exercises might be taught, I know not with what success in the University. The Vinerian professorship is of far more serious importance; the laws of his country are the first science of an Englishman of rank and fortune, who is called to be a Magistrate, and may hope to be a Legislator. This judicious institution was coldly entertained by the graver Doctors, who complained, I have heard the complaint, that it would take the young people from their books: but Mr Viner's benefaction is not un-profitable since it has at least produced the excellent commentaries of Sir William Blackstone. [4]The manners and opinions of our Universities must follow at a distance the progressive motion of the age; and some prejudices, which reason could not subdue, have been slowly obliterated by time. The last generation of Jacobites is extinct: 'the right Divine of Kings to govern wrong' is now exploded even at Oxford: and the[5] remains of Tory principles are rather salutary than hurtful, at a time when the Constitution has nothing to fear from the prerogative of the Crown, and can only be injured by popular innovation. But the inveterate evils which are derived from their birth and character must still cleave to our Ecclesiastical corporations: the fashion of the present day is not propitious, in England, to discipline

---

[1] *II om ten words from here to* scholar, *replacing them by* late Deans   [2] *II om* who, *left undeleted by* G who *had first written* whos, *having perhaps intended something like* whose careers, *but deleted the* s *without noticing that his sentence, as it stood, was incorrect.*   [3] *II* profit   [4] *II om twenty-one lines from here to the end of the chapter, i.e. to the end of F.*   [5] *I* some

and œconomy; and even the exceptionable[1] mode of foreign education has been lately preferred by the highest and most respectable authority in the Kingdom. I shall only add that Cambridge appears to have been less deeply infected than her sister with the vices of the Cloyster: her loyalty to the house of Hanover is of a more early date; and the name and philosophy of her immortal Newton were first honoured in his native[2] Academy.[3]

[1] *I* preposterous   [2] *I* own   [3] *Here ends G's sixth and last attempt (F) at writing his Memoirs.*

Chapter IV[1]

No sooner was my reason subdued than I resolved to ap- 31
prove my faith by my works and to enter without delay into
the pale of the Church of Rome. .[2]. . In the sacrifice of | this 31ᵛ
world to the next, I might affect the glory of a Confessor:
but I must freely acknowledge that the sincere change of my
speculative opinions was not inflamed by any lively sense of
devotion or enthusiasm; and that in the giddyness of my age
I had not seriously weighed the temporal consequences of
this rash step. The intelligence which I imparted to my father
in an elaborate controversial Epistle struck him with astonishment and grief: he was neither a bigot nor a philosopher;
but his affection deplored the loss of an only son, and his
good-sense could not understand or excuse my strange departure from the Religion of my Country. After carrying me
to Putney to the house of his friend Mr Mallet, by whose
philosophy I was rather scandalized than reclaimed, it was necessary[3] to form a new plan of education, and to devise some
method, which, if possible might effect the cure of my spiritual malady.[4] The gates of Oxford were shut against my return; in every part of England I might be accessible to the
seductions of my new friends, and after much debate it was
determined from the advice and personal experience of Mr
Eliot (now Lord Eliot) to fix me during some years at Lausanne in Switzerland. Mr Frey a Swiss Gentleman of Basil
undertook the conduct of the journey: we left London the 19ᵗʰ
of June, crossed the sea from Dover to Calais, travelled post[5]
through several provinces of France by the direct road of
Sᵗ Quentin, Rheims, Langres and Besançon and arrived

---

[1] *This heading is the present editor's. Chapter IV gives the text of B (MS
ff 31-39 – M 129-154).* [2] *The next two sentences, which are almost identical
with the two corresponding sentences of F:* In my last excursion . . . the errors
of heresy. *(see above, p. 61, ll. 2-10) have been omitted.* [3] *Beginning his
use of B with this sentence, II added here* for my father *to make it intelligible.*
[4] *II om two lines from here to* my new friends, and [5] *II passed*

68

the 30ᵗʰ of June at Lausanne, where I was immediately settled under the roof and tuition of Mr Pavilliard a Calvinist Minister.

The first marks of my father's displeasure rather astonished than afflicted me: when he threatened to banish and disown and disinherit a rebellious son, I cherished a secret hope that he would not be able or willing to effect his menaces, and the pride of conscience encouraged me to sustain the honourable and important part which I was now acting. My spirits were raised and kept alive by the rapid motion of the[1] journey, the new and various scenes of the continent, and the civility of Mr Frey, a man of sense and[2] who was not ignorant of books or the World. But after he had resigned me into Pavilliard's hands, and I was fixed in my new habitation, I had leisure to contemplate the strange and melancholy prospect[3]. My first complaint arose from my ignorance of the language. | In my childhood I had once studied the French Grammar, and I could imperfectly understand the easy prose of a familiar subject. But when I was thus suddenly cast on a foreign land I found myself deprived of the use of speech and of hearing; and during some weeks, incapable not only of enjoying the pleasures of conversation, but even of asking or answering a question in the common intercourse of life. To an homebred Englishman every object every custom was offensive, but the native of any country might have been disgusted with the general aspect of his lodging and entertainment. [4] The minister's wife Madame Pavilliard governed our domestic œconomy: I now speak of her without resentment, but in sober truth she was ugly, dirty, proud, ill-tempered and covetous. [5] Our hours, of twelve for dinner, of seven for supper were arbitrary, though inconvenient customs: the appetite of a young man might have overlooked the badness of the materials and cookery, but his appetite was far from being satisfied with the scantiness of our daily meals, and more than one sense was offended by the appearance of the table which during eight successive days was regularly covered with the same

32

---

[1] *II* my   [2] *II om* and   [3] *II added* before me.   [4] *II om ten lines from here down to* the same linnen.   [5] *I added this sentence down to* customs *in the margin.*

linnen. I had now exchanged my elegant apartment in
Magdalen-College for a narrow gloomy street the most
unfrequented of an unhandsome town; for an old inconvenient
house, and for a small chamber ill-contrived and ill-furnished,
which on the approach of winter instead of a companionable
fire must be warmed by the dull invisible heat of a stove.
From a man I was again degraded[1] to the dependence of a
school-boy: Mr Pavilliard managed my expences which had
been reduced to a diminutive scale[2]: I received a small monthly
allowance for my pocket money; and helpless and awkward
as I have ever been, I no longer enjoyed the indispensable[3]
comfort of a servant. My condition seemed as destitute of
hope as it was devoid of pleasure: I was separated for an
indefinite, which appeared an infinite, term, from my native
Country; and I had lost all connection with my Catholic
friends. I have since reflected with surprize, that as the
Romish Clergy of every part of Europe maintain a close
correspondence with each other, they never attempted, [4] by
letters or messages, to rescue me from the hands of the
heretics, or at least to confirm my zeal and constancy in the
profession of the faith—Such was my first introduction to
Lausanne, a place where I spent near[5] five years with pleasure
and profit[6], which I afterwards revisited[7] without compulsion,
and which I have finally selected as the most grateful retreat
for the decline of my life.

But it is the peculiar felicity of youth, that the most un-
pleasing objects and events seldom make a deep or lasting
impression[8]. At the flexible age of sixteen I soon learned to
endure and gradually to adopt the new forms of arbitrary
manners: the real hardships of my situation, the [9]house, the
table | and the mistress were alleviated[10] by time;[11] and to 32ᵛ
this coarse and scanty fare I am perhaps indebted for the
establishment of my constitution. Had I been sent abroad in

[1] *I* reduced　[2] *II* state　[3] *I* invaluable　[4] *I* either　[5] *II* nearly
[6] *I added* with pleasure and profit *in the margin.*　[7] *I* to which I afterwards returned　[8] *II added here*　; it forgets the past, enjoys the present
and anticipates the future – *words taken from C (MS f 63ᵛ – M 231) where
the sentence begins* The lively and flexible character of youth　[9] *II om*　, the
house, the table and the mistress　[10] *II* alienated　[11] *II om the end of this
sentence from here to* my constitution

a more splendid style such as the fortune and bounty of my father might have supplied, I might have returned home with the same stock of language and science as[1] our countrymen usually import from the continent. An exile and a prisoner as I was, their example betrayed me into some irregularities of wine, of play and of idle excursions: but I soon felt the impossibility of associating with them on equal terms, and after the departure of my first acquaintance I held a cold and civil correspondence with their successors. This seclusion from English society was attended with the most solid benefits. In the *pays de Vaud* the French language is used with less imperfection than in most of the distant provinces of France; in Pavilliard's family, necessity compelled me to listen and to speak; and if I was at first disheartened by the apparent slowness, in a few months, I was astonished by the rapidity, of my progress. My pronunciation was formed by the constant repetition of the same sounds; the variety of words and idioms, the rules of grammar and distinctions of genders were impressed in my memory: ease and freedom were obtained by practise, correctness and elegance by labour; and before I was recalled home, French, in which I spontaneously thought was more familiar than English to my ear, my tongue and my pen. The first effect of this opening [2] knowledge was the revival of my love of reading, which had been chilled at Oxford, and I soon turned over without much choice almost all the French books in my tutor's library. Even these amusements were productive of real[3] advantage: my taste and judgement were now somewhat riper; I was introduced to a new mode of style and litterature: by the comparison of manners and opinions my views were enlarged, my prejudices were corrected, and a copious voluntary abstract of the *Histoire de l'Eglise et de l'Empire* by le Sueur may be placed in a middle line between my childish and my manly[4] studies. As soon as I was able to converse with the natives, I began to feel some satisfaction in their company: my awkward timidity was polished and emboldened, and, I frequented for the first time assemblies of men and women. The acquaintance of the Pavilliards

[1] *II* which   [2] *I* of my   [3] *I* some   [4] *I* rational

prepared me by degrees for more elegant society: I was
received with kindness and indulgence in the best families[1] of
Lausanne and it was in one of these, that I formed an
intimate lasting[2] connection with Mr Deyverdun a young
man of an amiable temper and excellent understanding. In
the arts[3] of fencing and | dancing, small indeed was my 33
proficiency, and some expensive[4] months were idly wasted
in the riding-school. My unfitness to bodily exercise reconciled me to a sedentary life, and the horse the favourite of
my countrymen never contributed to the pleasures of my
youth.

My obligations to the lessons of Mr Pavilliard, gratitude
will not suffer me to forget: [5]but truth compels me to own,
that my best præceptor was not himself eminent for genius
or learning. Even the real measure of his talents was under-
rated in the public opinion: the soft credulity of his temper
exposed him to frequent imposition; and his want of eloquence and memory in the pulpit disqualified him for the
most popular duty of his office. But he was endowed with a
clear head and a warm heart: his innate benevolence had
asswaged the spirit of the Church; he was rational because
he was moderate: in the course of his studies he had acquired a just though superficial knowledge of most branches
of litterature, by long practice he was skilled in the arts of
teaching; and he laboured with assiduous patience to know
the character, gain the affection and open the mind of his
English pupil. As soon as we began to understand each
other, he gently led me [6] into the path of instruction: I consented with pleasure that a portion of the morning-hours,
should be consecrated to a plan of modern history and
Geography, and to the critical[7] perusal of the French and
Latin Classics, and at each step I felt myself invigorated by
the habits of application and method. [8] The principles of

---

[1] *I cancelled* houses *and replaced it by* families of Lausanne *written in the margin.*   [2] *I added* lasting *in the margin. – II* intimate and lasting   [3] *I exercises*   [4] *II om* expensive   [5] *II om seven lines from here down to* his
office. But   [6] *II added here* , from a blind and undistinguishing love of reading, *– words taken from C (MS f 63ᵛ – M 230) where G, however, has* the blind
[7] *I added* critical *in the margin.*   [8] *II added here these two sentences:*
His prudence repressed and dissembled some youthful sallies: and as soon as

philosophy were associated with the examples of taste, and by a singular chance the book as well as the man which contributed the most effectually to my education, has a stronger claim on my gratitude than on my admiration. Mr de Crousaz the adversary of Bayle and Pope is not distinguished by lively fancy or profound reflexion, and even in his own country at the end of a few years, his name and writings are almost obliterated. But his philosophy had been formed in the school of Locke, his Divinity in that of Limborch and Le Clerc; in a long and laborious life several generations of pupils were taught to think and even to write, his lessons rescued the Academy of Lausanne from Calvinistic prejudice, and he had the rare merit of diffusing a more liberal spirit among the Clergy and people of the Pays de Vaud. His System of logic which in the last editions has swelled to six tedious and prolix volumes, may be praised as a clear and methodical abridgement of the art of reasoning from our[1] simple ideas to the most complex operations of the
33ᵛ human understanding. This system I studied, and | meditated and abstracted, till I have[2] obtained the free command of an universal instrument which I soon presumed to exercise on my catholic opinions. Pavilliard was not unmindful that his first task his most important duty was to reclaim me from the errors of Popery: the intermixture of sects has rendered the Swiss Clergy acute and learned on the topics of controversy; and I have some of his letters in which he celebrates the dexterity of his attack, and my gradual concessions after a firm and well-managed defence. I was willing and I am now willing to allow him an handsome[3] share of the honour of my conversion: yet I must observe that it was principally effected by my private reflexions, and I still remember my solitary transport at the discovery of a philosophical argument against the doctrine of transubstan[tia]tion: *that* the text of scripture which seems to inculcate the real presence

I was confirmed in the habits of industry and temperance, he gave the reins into my own hands. His favourable report of my behaviour and progress gradually obtained some latitude of action and expence, and he wished to alleviate the hardships of my lodging and entertainment. – *sentences taken from C (MS f 63ᵛ – M 230) where I had added* from my father *after* obtained
[1] *I* the   [2] *II om* have   [3] *I* ample

is attested only by a single sense, our sight; while the real presence itself is disproved by three of our senses, the sight, the touch and the taste. The various articles of the Romish creed disappeared like a dream, and, after a full conviction, on Christmas day 1754, I received the sacrament in the Church of Lausanne. It was here that I suspended my Religious enquiries, acquiescing with implicit belief in the [1] tenets and mysteries which are[2] adopted by the general consent of Catholics and Protestants[3].

Such, from my arrival at Lausanne during the first eighteen or twenty months (July 1753–March 1755) were my useful studies, the foundation of all my future improvements. [4]But in the life of every man of letters, there is an æra, a level from whence he soars with his own wings to his proper height, and the most important part of his education is that which he bestows on himself. My worthy tutor had the good-sense and modesty to discern how far he could be useful: as soon as he felt that I advanced beyond his speed and measure he wisely left me to my Genius; and the hours of lesson were soon lost in the voluntary labour of the whole morning, and sometimes of the whole day. The desire of prolonging my time gradually confirmed the salutary habit of early rising to which I have always adhered with some regard to seasons and situations: but it is happy for my eyes and my health, that my temperate ardour has never been seduced to trespass on the hours of the night. During the last three years of my residence at Lausanne I may assume the merit of serious and solid application, but I am tempted to distinguish the last eight months of the year 1755 as the period of the most extraordinary diligence and rapid progress. In my French and Latin translations I adopted an excellent method | which from my own success 34 I would recommend to the imitation of students. I chose some

---

[1] *I* protestant   [2] *I* were   [3] *I* consent of the Christian World.   [4] *For this sentence II substituted the corresponding sentences from C (MS f 63ᵛ – M 231)* Every man, who rises above the common level, has received two educations, the first from his teachers, the second more personal and important from himself. He will not, like the fanatics of the last age, define the moment of grace; but he cannot forget the aera of his life, in which his mind has expanded to its proper form and dimensions.

Classic writer, such as Cicero and Vertot the most approved for purity and elegance of style. I translated for instance an Epistle of Cicero into French, and after throwing it aside till the words and phrases were obliterated from my memory, I re-translated my French into such Latin as I could find, and then compared each sentence of my imperfect version with the ease, the grace, the propriety of the Roman orator[1]. A similar experiment was made on some[2] pages of the Revolutions of Vertot; I turned them into Latin, re-turned them after a sufficient interval into my own French, and again scrutinized the resemblance or dissimilitude of the copy and the original. By degrees I was less ashamed, by degrees I was more satisfied with myself, and I persevered in the practice of these double translations, which filled several books, till I had acquired the knowledge of both idioms, and the command at least of a correct style. This useful exercise of writing was accompanied and succeeded by the more pleasing occupation of reading the best authors. [3] Dr Middleton's history which I then appreciated above its true value naturally directed me to the writings of Cicero. The most perfect editions, that of Olivet which may adorn the shelves of the rich, that of Ernesti which should lye on the table of the learned were not [4] in my power[5] For the familiar Epistles I used the text and English Commentary of Bishop Ross: but my general Edition was that of Verbruggius[6] published at Amsterdam in two large Volumes in folio with an indifferent choice of various notes. I read with application and pleasure *all* the Epistles, *all* the Orations, and the most important treatises of Rhetoric and Philosophy, and as I read, I applauded the observation of Quintilian that every student may judge of his own proficiency by the satisfaction which he receives from the Roman Orator. [7] Cicero in Latin and Xenophon in Greek are indeed the two ancients whom I would first propose to a liberal scholar, not only for the merit

---

[1] *I* of the original   [2] *II* several   [3] *II added here this sentence* The perusal of the Roman Classics was at once my exercise and reward. – *taken from* C (*MS f 63ᵛ – M 232*).   [4] *I* then   [5] *III* within my reach.   [6] *II* Verburgius   [7] *II added here* I tasted the beauties of language, I breathed the spirit of freedom, and I imbibed from his precepts and examples the public and private sense of a man. – *a sentence taken from* C (*MS f 64 – M 232-3*).

of their style and sentiments but for the admirable lessons which may be applied almost to every situation of public and private life. Cicero's Epistles may in particular afford the models of every form of correspondence from the careless effusions of tenderness and friendship to the well-guarded declaration of discreet and dignified resentment. | After 34ᵛ finishing, this great Author, a library of eloquence and reason I formed a more extensive plan of reviewing the Latin Classics under the four divisions of 1 Historians, 2 Poets, 3 Orators and 4 Philosophers in a Chronological series from the days of Plautus and Salust to the decline of the language and Empire of Rome: and this plan in the last twenty seven months of my residence at Lausanne (January 1756–April 1758), I *nearly* accomplished. Nor was this review however rapid, either hasty or superficial. I indulged myself in a second, and even a third perusal of Terence, Virgil, Horace, Tacitus &c and studied to imbibe the sense and spirit most congenial to my own. I never suffered a difficult or corrupt[1] passage to escape till I had viewed it in every light of which it was susceptible: though often disappointed, I always consulted the most learned or ingenious[2] commentators, Torrentius and Dacier on Horace, Catrou and Servius on Virgil, Lipsius on Tacitus, Meziriac on Ovid[3] &c; and in the ardour of my enquiries I [4] embraced a large circle of historical and critical erudition. My abstracts of each book were made in the French language: my observations often branched into particular Essays, and I can still read without contempt a dissertation of eight folio pages on eight lines (287-294) of the fourth Georgic of Virgil. Mr. Deyverdun my friend[5], whose name will be frequently repeated had joined with equal zeal, though not with equal perseverance in the same undertaking. To him every thought, every composition was instantly communicated; with him I enjoyed the benefits of a free conversation on the topics of our common studies.

But it is scarcely possible for a mind endowed with any

---

[1] *I added* or corrupt *in the margin.*   [2] *I* the most approved   [3] *I added* Meziriac on Ovid *in the margin.*   [4] *I* often, *corrected into* sometimes, *this being cancelled.*   [5] *I added* my friend *in the margin.*

active curiosity to be long conversant with the Latin Classics without aspiring to know the Greek originals whom they celebrate as their masters, and of whom they so warmly recommend the study and imitation.

—— Vos exemplaria Graeca
Nocturnâ versate manû, versate diurnâ.

It was now that I regretted the early years which had been wasted in sickness, or idleness, or more[1] idle reading, that I condemned the perverse method of our school-masters who, by first teaching the mother-language might descend with so much ease and perspicuity to the origin and etymology of a derivative idiom. In the nineteenth year of my age I determined to supply this defect, and the lessons of Pavilliard again contributed to smooth the entrance of the way, the Greek Alphabet, the grammar and the pronunciation

35 according to the French accent. [2]As he | possessed only such a stock as was requisite for an Ecclesiastic, our first book was St John's Gospel, and [we] should probably have construed the whole of the new testament had I not represented the absurdity of adhering to the corrupt dialect of the Hellenist Jews. At my earnest request we presumed to open the Iliad; and I had the pleasure of beholding, though darkly and through a glass, the true image of Homer whom I had long since admired in an English dress. After my tutor conscious of his inability[3] had left me to myself I worked my way through abont half the Iliad, and afterwards interpreted alone[4] a large portion of Xenophon and Herodotus. But my ardour destitute of aid and emulation was gradually cooled, and, from the barren task of searching words in a lexicon, I withdrew to the free and familiar conversation of Virgil and Tacitus. Yet in my residence at Lausanne I had laid a solid foundation, which enabled me in a more propitious season to prosecute the study of Grecian litterature.

From a blind idea of the usefullness of such abstract science, my father had been desirous and even pressing that I should devote some time to the Mathematics, nor could I

[1] *II* mere　　[2] *II om five lines from here down to* Hellenist Jews.　　[3] *II om* conscious of his inability　　[4] *I* to myself

MML H

refuse to comply with so reasonable a wish. During two winters I attended the private lectures of Mr de Traytorrens who explained the Elements of Algebra and Geometry as far as the Conic sections of the Marquis de l'Hopital and appeared satisfied with my diligence and improvement. But as my childish propensity for numbers and calculations was totally extinct, I was content to receive the passive impression of my professor's lectures, without any active exercise of my own powers: as soon as I understood the principles, I relinquished for ever the pursuit of the Mathematics; nor can I lament that I desisted before my mind was hardened by the habit of rigid demonstration so destructive of the finer feelings of moral evidence which must however determine the actions and opinions of our lives. I listened with more pleasure to the proposal of studying the law of Nature and Nations, which was taught in the Academy of Lausanne by Mr Vicat a professor of some learning and reputation. But instead of attending his public or private course, I preferred, in my closet, the lessons of his masters and my own reason. Without being disgusted by the pedantry of[1] Grotius or the prolixity | of[2] Puffendorf, I studied in their writings the 35ᵛ duties of a man, the rights of a Citizen, the theory of Justice (it is alas! a theory) and the laws of peace and war which have had some influence on the practise of modern Europe. My fatigues were alleviated by the good sense of their commentator Barbeyrac: Locke's treatise of Government instructed me in the[3] knowledge of Whig principles, which are rather founded in reason than experience; but my delight was in the frequent perusal of Montesquieu whose energy of style, and boldness of hypothesis were powerful to awaken and stimulate the Genius of the Age. The logic of de Crousaz had prepared me to engage with his master Locke and his antagonist Bayle, of whom the former may be used as a bridle and the latter as a [spur][4] to the curiosity of a young philosopher. According to the nature of their respective

[1] *II om* the pedantry of   [2] *II om* the prolixity of   [3] *I* in Locke's . . .
I was introduced to the   [4] *G has here* bridle *which he corrected when writing*
C the former of whom may be applied as a spur and the latter as a bridle to
. . . (*MS ff 64-64ᵛ – M 234*). – *II* spur

works the schools of argument and objection I carefully went through the Essay on human understanding, and occasionally consulted the most interesting articles of the Philosophic dictionary. In the infancy of my reason I turned over as an idle amusement the most serious and important treatise[s]: in its maturity the most trifling performance could exercise my taste or judgement; and more than once I have been led by a novel into a deep and instructive train of thinking. But I cannot forbear to mention three particular books, since they may have remotely contributed to form the historian of the Roman Empire. 1 From the provincial letters of Pascal which, almost every year I have perused with new pleasure, I learned to manage the weapon of grave and temperate irony even on subjects of Ecclesiastical solemnity. 2. The life of Julian by the Abbé de la Bleterie, first introduced me to the man and the times: and I should be glad to recover my first essay on the truth of the miracle which stopped the re-building of the temple of Jerusalem. 3. In Giannone's Civil history of Naples, I observed with a critical eye the progress and abuse of Sacerdotal power, and the Revolutions of [1] Italy in the darker ages. This various reading which I now con-ducted with skill and[2] discretion was digested according to the precept and model of Mr Locke into a large Common-place book, a practice however which I do not strenuously recommend. The action of the pen will doubtless imprint an idea on the mind as well as on the paper: but | I much question whether the benefits of this laborious method are adequate to the waste of time; and I must agree with Dr Johnson (Idler N° 74) 'that what is twice read is commonly better remembered than what is transcribed.'

36

During two years, if I forget some boyish excursions of a day or a week, I was fixed at Lausanne but at the end of the third summer, my father consented that I should make the tour of Switzerland with Pavilliard, and our short absence of one month (September 21^{rst}–October 20th, 1755) was a reward and relaxation of my assiduous studies. The fashion of climbing the mountains, and viewing[3] the *Glaciers* had not yet been introduced by foreign travellers who seek the

[1] *I* Rome and   [2] *II om* skill and   [3] *II* reviewing

sublime beauties of Nature. But the political face of the
Country is not less diversified by the forms and spirit of so
many various Republics from the jealous government of[1] the
few to the licentious freedom of the *many*: I contemplated
with pleasure the new prospects of men and manners;
though my conversation with the natives would have been
more free and instructive, had I possessed the German, as
well as the French language. We passed through most of
the principal towns of[2] Switzerland, Neufchâtel, Bienne,
Soleurre, Arau, Baden, Zurich, Basil, and Bern: in every
place we visited the Churches, arsenals, libraries and all the
most eminent persons; and after my return, I digested my
notes in fourteen or fifteen sheets of a French journal, which
I dispatched to my father as a proof that my time and his
money had not been mispent. Had I found this journal
among his papers, I might be tempted to select some
passages; but I will not transcribe the printed accounts; and
it may be sufficient to notice a remarkable spot, which left a
deep and lasting impression on my memory. From Zurich
we proceeded on a pilgrimage [3] not of devotion, but of
curiosity to the Benedictine Abbey of Einsidlen, more commonly styled our Lady of the Hermits. I was astonished by
the profuse ostentation of riches in the poorest corner of
Europe: amidst a savage scene of woods and mountains, a
palace appears to have been erected by Magic; and it *was*
erected by the potent magic of Religion. A crowd of palmers
and votaries was prostrate before the Altar; the title and
worship of the Mother of God provoked my indignation;
and the lively naked image of superstition suggested to me,
as in the same place it had done to Zuinglius, the most
pressing argument | for the reformation of the Church. 36ᵛ
About two years after this tour, I passed at Geneva an useful
and agreable month, but this excursion, and some short
visits in the Pays de Vaud did not materially interrupt my
studious and sedentary life at Lausanne.

My thirst of improvement and the languid state of science
at Lausanne soon prompted me to solicit a litterary corres-

---

[1] *I* from the jealousy of   [2] *II* of – *III* in.   [3] *II om six words from here*
to curiosity

pondence with several men of learning whom I had not an opportunity of personally consulting. 1. In the perusal of Livy (xxx. 44) I had been stopped by a sentence in a speech of Hannibal, which cannot be reconciled by any torture with his character or argument. The commentators dissemble or confess their perplexity: it occurred to me that the change of a single letter by substituting *Otio* instead of *Odio* might restore a clear and consistent sense; but I wished to weigh my emendation in scales less partial than my own. I addressed myself to Mr Crevier, the successor of Rollin and a Professor in the University of Paris, who had [1] published a large and valuable Edition of Livy: his answer was speedy and polite; he praised my ingenuity and adopted my conjecture, [2] which I must still applaud as easy and happy. 2. I maintained a Latin correspondence, at first anonymous and afterwards in my own name with Professor Breitinger of Zurich, the learned Editor of a Septuagint Bible: in our frequent letters we discussed many questions of antiquity, many passages of the Latin Classics. I proposed my interpretations and amendments[3]: his censures, for he did not spare my boldness of conjecture, were sharp and strong; and I was encouraged by the consciousness of my strength, when I could stand in free debate against a Critic of such eminence and erudition. 3. I corresponded on similar topics with the celebrated Professor, Matthew Gesner of the University of Gottingen, and he accepted as courteously as the two former, the invitation of an unknown Youth. But his abilities might possibly be decayed; his elaborate letters were feeble and prolix; and when I asked his proper direction, the vain old man covered half a sheet of paper with the foolish enumeration of his titles and offices. 4. These professors of Paris, Zurich and Gottingen were strangers whom I presumed to address on the credit of their name but Mr Allamand, Minister at Bex was my personal friend with whom I maintained a more
37 free and interesting correspondence. He was a master of | language[,] of science, and above all of dispute: and his [4] acute and flexible logic could support with equal address and

---

[1] *I* lately   [2] *II om the end of this sentence.*   [3] *I* corrections   [4] *I* strong

perhaps with equal indifference the adverse sides of every possible question. His spirit was active but his pen had been indolent. Mr Allamand had exposed himself to much scandal and reproach by an anonymous letter (1745)[1] to the Protestants of France; in which he labours to persuade them that *public* worship is the exclusive right and duty of the State, and that their numerous assemblies of dissenters and rebels are[2] not authorized by the law or the Gospel. His style is animated, his arguments are[3] specious; and if the papist may seem to lurk under the mask of a protestant, the philosopher is concealed under the disguise of a papist. After some tryals in France and Holland which were defeated by his fortune or his character, a Genius that might have enlightened, or deluded the World was buried in a Country-living unknown to fame and discontented with mankind 'Est sacrificulus in 'pago et rusticos decipit' As often as private or Ecclesiastical business called him to Lausanne, I enjoyed the pleasure and benefit of his conversation, and we were mutually flattered by our attention to each other. Our correspondence in his absence chiefly turned on Locke's Metaphysics which he attacked and I defended, the origin of ideas, the principles of evidence, and the doctrine of liberty.

> And found no end, in wandering mazes lost

By fencing with so skillful a master, I acquired some dexterity in the use of my philosophic weapons: but I was still the slave of education and prejudice; he had some measures to keep; and I much suspect that he never shewed me the true colours of his secret scepticism.

Before I was recalled from Switzerland I had the satisfaction of seeing the most extraordinary man of the age, a poet, an historian, a Philosopher; who has filled thirty quartos of prose and verse with his various productions often excellent and always entertaining: need I add the name of Voltaire? After forfeiting by his own misconduct the friendship of the first of Kings, he retired at the age of sixty with a plentiful fortune to a free and beautiful country, and resided two winters (1757 and 1758) in the | town or 37ᵛ

---

[1] *I added this date in the margin.*   [2] *II* were   [3] *II om* are

neighbourhood of Lausanne. My desire of beholding Voltaire, whom I then rated above his real magnitude was easily gratified: he received me with civility as an English youth; but I cannot boast of any peculiar notice[1] or distinction 'Virgilium vidi tantum'. The Ode which he composed on his first arrival on the banks of the Leman Lake:

O Maison d'Aristippe! O Jardin d'Epicure! &c

had been imparted as a secret to the Gentleman by whom I was introduced: he allowed me to read it twice; I knew it by heart; and as my discretion was not equal to my memory, the author was soon displeased by the circulation of a copy. In writing this trivial anecdote I wished to observe whether my memory was impaired and I have the comfort of finding that every line of the poem is still engraved in fresh and indelible characters. The highest gratification which I derived from Voltaire's residence at Lausanne was the uncommon circumstance of hearing a great poet declaim[2] his own productions on the stage. He had formed a troop[3] of Gentlemen and Ladies, some of whom were not destitute of talents: a decent theatre was framed at Monrepos a country-house at the end of a suburb: dresses and scenes were provided at the expence of the actors; and the author directed the rehearsals with the zeal and attention of paternal love. In two successive winters his tragedies of Zayre, Alzire, Zulime, and his sentimental comedy of the Enfant prodigue were played at the Theatre of Monrepos, [4] but it was not without much reluctance and ill-humour that the envious bard allowed the representation of the Iphigenie of Racine. The parts of the young and fair were distorted by his fat and ugly niece Madame Denys who could not, like our admirable Pritchard, make the spectators forget the defects of her age and[5] person. For himself Voltair reserved[6] the characters best adapted to his years, Lusignan, Alvaréz, Benassar, Euphemon; his declamation was fashioned to the pomp and cadence of the old stage and he expressed the enthusiasm of poetry, rather than the feelings of Nature. My

[1] *I* favour   [2] *I* rehearse   [3] *II* company   [4] *II om five lines from here down to* age and person.   [5] *I added* age and *in the margin.*   [6] *II* represented

ardour which soon became conspicuous seldom failed of procuring me a ticket: the habits of pleasure fortified my taste for the French theatre: and that taste has perhaps abated my idolatry for the Gigantic Genius of Shakespeare which is inculcated from our infancy as the first duty of an Englishman. The wit and philosophy of Voltaire his table and theatre refined in a visible degree the manners of Lausanne, and however addicted to study, I enjoyed my share of the amusements of Society. After the representa- tions[1] of Monrepos I sometimes supped with the Actors: I was now familiar in some, and | acquainted in many houses; 38 and my evenings were generally devoted to cards and con- versation either in private parties or numerous assemblies.

I hesitate from the apprehension of ridicule, when I approach the delicate subject of my early love. By this word I do not mean the polite attention, the gallantry without hope or design which has originated from[2] the spirit of chivalry, and is interwoven with the texture of French manners. [3] I do not confine myself to the grosser appetite which our pride may affect to disdain, because it has been implanted by Nature in the whole animal creation 'Amor omnibus idem' The discovery of a sixth sense, the first consciousness of manhood is a very interesting moment of our lives: but it less properly belongs to the memoirs of an individual, than to the natural history of the species. I understand by this passion the union of desire, friendship and tenderness, which is inflamed by a single female, which prefers her to the rest of her sex, and which seeks her pos- session as the supreme or the sole happiness of our being. I need not blush at recollecting the object of my choice, and though my love was disappointed of success, I am rather proud, that I was once capable of feeling such[4] a pure and exalted sentiment. The personal attractions of Mademoiselle Susanne[5] Curchod were embellished by the virtues and talents of the mind. Her fortune was humble but her family was respectable: her mother [6] a native of France had preferred

---

[1] *II* representation   [2] *II* in   [3] *II om seven lines from here down to history of the species.*   [4] *I added* such *in the margin.*   [5] *II* Susan
[6] *I had added here* a woman of spirit and beauty

her religion to her country: the profession of her father did not extinguish the moderation and philosophy of his temper: and he lived content with a small salary and laborious duty in the obscure lot of Minister of Crassy, in the mountains that separate the pays de Vaud from the County of Burgundy. In the solitude of a sequestered village he bestowed a liberal and even learned education on his only daughter; she surpassed his hopes by her proficiency in the sciences and languages; and in her short visits to some relations at Lausanne, the wit and[1] beauty, and erudition[2] of Mademoiselle Curchod were the theme of universal applause. The report of such a prodigy awakened my[3] curiosity; I saw and loved. I found her learned without pedantry, lively in conversation, pure in sentiment, and elegant in manners; and the first sudden emotion was fortified by the habits and knowledge of a more familiar acquaintance. She permitted me to make her two or three visits at her father's house: I passed some happy days[4] in the mountains of Burgundy: and her parents honourably encouraged a[5] connection [6]which might raise their daughter above want and dependence. In a calm retirement the gay vanity of youth no longer fluttered in her bosom: she listened to the voice of truth and passion: and I 38ᵛ might presume to hope that I had made some | impression on a virtuous heart. At Crassy, and Lausanne I indulged my dream of felicity: but on my return to England I soon discovered that my father would not hear of this strange alliance, and that without his consent I was myself destitute and helpless. After a painful struggle I yielded to my fate: [7]the remedies of absence and time were at length effectual; and my love subsided in friendship and esteem. The minister of Crassy soon afterwards died; his stipend died with him:

[1] *II* the wit, the beauty   [2] *I* knowledge   [3] *by* in MS – *II* my   [4] *II added* there   [5] *II* the   [6] *II om the end of the sentence from* which might
[7] *For this line II substituted the famous passage in C (MS f 65ᵛ – M 239)* I sighed as a lover: I obeyed as a son: my wound was insensibly healed by time, absence, and the habits of a new life; and my cure was accelerated by a faithful report of the tranquillity and chearfulness of the Lady herself. *G had written first . . .* accelerated by time, and absence; and against the dangers of a serious attachment, my heart has been steeled by the image of that amiable woman. *He then cancelled the first and as well as the end of his sentence from* and against *replacing it by the new ending, written in the margin.*

his daughter retired to Geneva where, by teaching young ladies she earned a hard subsistence for herself and her mother: but in her lowest distress she maintained a spotless reputation and a dignified behaviour. [1] The Dutchess of Grafton (now Lady Ossory) has often told me that she had nearly engaged Mademoiselle Curchod as a Governess, and her declining a life of servitude was most probably blamed by the wisdom of her short-sighted friends. A rich banker of Paris, a citizen of Geneva had the good-fortune, and good sense to discover and possess this inestimable treasure: and in the capital of taste and luxury, she resisted the temptations of wealth as she had sustained the hardships of indigence. The Genius of her husband has exalted him to the most conspicuous station in Europe: in every change of prosperity and disgrace he has reclined on the bosom of a faithful friend; and Mademoiselle Curchod is now the wife of Mr Necker the Minister and perhaps the Legislator of the French Monarchy.

[2]Such as I am in Genius or learning or in manners, I owe my creation to Lausanne: it was in that school, that the statue was discovered in the block of marble; and my own religious folly, my father's blind resolution produced the effects of the most deliberate wisdom. One mischief however and in the eyes of my countrymen[3] a serious and irreparable mischief was derived from the success of my Swiss[4] education: I had ceased to be an Englishman. At the flexible period of youth, from the age of sixteen to twenty one[5], my opinions, habits and sentiments were cast in a foreign mould; the faint and distant remembrance of England was almost obliterated; my native language was grown less familiar; and I should have chearfully accepted the offer of a moderate independent[6] fortune on the terms of perpetual exile. By the good sense and temper of Pavilliard my yoke was insensibly lightened: he left me master of my time and actions: but he could

---

[1] *II om this sentence.*   [2] *For this sentence II substituted a passage from C (MS f 65ᵛ – M 239-240) without, however, giving it in full (See Appendix I, 16)*   [3] *II in their eyes – a change called for by the insertion of the C passage which ends* poverty and pride estranged me from my countrymen.   [4] *I added* Swiss *in the margin.*   [5] *I added* from the age of sixteen to twenty one *in the margin.*   [6] *I added* independent *in the margin.*

neither change my situation, nor encrease my allowance, and
39 with the progress | of my years and reason I impatiently
sighed for the moment of my deliverance. At length in the
spring of the year one thousand seven hundred and fifty eight
my father signified his permission and his pleasure that I
should immediately return home. We were then in the
midst of a war: the resentment of the French at our taking
their ships without a declaration had rendered that polite
nation somewhat peevish and difficult: they denied a passage
to English travellers; and the road through Germany was
circuitous, toilsome[1], and perhaps in the neighbourhood of
the armies exposed to some danger. In this perplexity two
Swiss officers of my acquaintance in the Dutch service, who
were returning to their garrisons offered to conduct me
through France as one of their companions; nor did we
sufficiently reflect that my borrowed name and regimentals
might have been considered in case of a discovery in a very
serious light. I took my leave of Lausanne on the 11th of
April 1758 with a mixture of joy and regret, in the firm
resolution of revisiting as a man, the persons and places
which had been so dear to my youth. We travelled slowly
but pleasantly in a hired coach over the hills of Franche-
comté and the fertile province of Lorraine, and passed
without accident or enquiry through several fortified towns
of the French frontier: from thence we entered the wild
Ardennes of the Austrian dutchy of Luxemburgh, and after
crossing the Meuse at Liege, we traversed the heaths of
Brabant, and reached on the fifteenth day our Dutch garrison
of Bois le Duc. In our passage through Nancy, my eye was
gratified by the aspect of a regular and beautiful City, the
work of Stanislaus, who after the storms of Polish royalty
reposed in the love and gratitude of his new subjects of
Lorraine. In our halt at Maestricht I visited Mr de Beaufort
a learned Critic who was known to me by his specious arguments against the five first Centuries of the Roman history.
After dropping my regimental companions I stepped aside
to visit Rotterdam and the Hague. I wished to have observed
a country, the monument of freedom and industry: but my

[1] *I* fatiguing

days were numbered, and a longer delay would have been ungraceful: I hastened to embark at the Brill, landed the next day at Harwich and proceeded to London where my father awaited my arrival. The whole term of my first absence from England was four years, ten months, and fifteen days.

Chapter V[1]

^{39ᵛ} In the prayers of the Church our personal concerns are judiciously reduced to the threefold distinction of *mind, body* and *estate*. The sentiments of the mind excite and exercise our social sympathy: the review of my moral and litterary character is the most interesting to myself and to the public; and I may expatiate without reproach on my private studies since they have produced the public writings which can alone entitle me to the esteem and friendship of my readers. [2] The pains and pleasures of the body how important soever to ourselves are an indelicate topic of conversation . . . The experience of the World inculcates a discreet reserve on the subject of our [3] estate; and we soon learn that a free disclosure of our riches or poverty, would provoke the malice of envy, or encourage the insolence of contempt. [4] Yet I am tempted to glance in a few words on the state of my private circumstances, as I am persuaded that had I been more indigent or more wealthy, I should not have possessed the leisure or the perseverance to prepare and execute my voluminous history. My father's impatience for my return to England was not wholly of the desinterested kind. I have already hinted that he had been impoverished by his two sisters, and that his gay character and mode of life were less adapted to the acquisition than the expenditure of wealth. A large and legitimate debt for the supply of naval stores was lost by the injustice of the Court of Spain: His elegant hospitality at Putney [5] exceeded the measure of his income; the honour of being chosen a Member of the Old club at White's had been dearly paid, and a more pernicious species of gaming, the

---

[1] *This heading is again the present editor's. Chapter V contains the next fifteen ff of B (MS ff 39-54 - M 154-197).*   [2] *II om three sentences from here; of these the first only is kept in the present text, while are left out the second and third which G made use of almost word for word when writing F. See above, p. 29, ll. 18-23.* I will not follow the vain example . . . on his nerves and bowels. [3] *II added here* person and   [4] *II om fifty lines from here down to the end of the paragraph.*   [5] *I* had

contest for Southampton exhausted his sickly finances. His
retirement into Hampshire on my mother's death was
coloured by a pious motive; some years of solitude allowed
him to breathe; but it was only by his son's majority that
he could be restored to the command of an entailed estate.
The time of my recall had been so nicely computed that I
arrived in London three days before I was of age: the
priests and the altar had been prepared, and the victim was
unconscious of the impending stroke. | According to the 40
forms and fictions of our law I levied a fine and suffered a
recovery: the entail was cut off: a sum of ten thousand
pounds was raised on mort[g]age for my father's use: and
he repaid the obligation by settling on me an annuity for
life of three hundred pounds a year. My submission at the
time was blind and almost involuntary; but it has been
justified by duty and interest to my cooler thoughts; and I
could only regret, that the receipt of some appropriated fund
was not given into my own hands. My annuity, though
somewhat more valuable thirty years ago, was however inadequate to the style of a young Englishman of fashion in
the most wealthy Metropolis of Europe: but I was rich in
my indifference or more properly my aversion for the active
and costly pleasures of my age and country. Some arrears,
[1] especially my bookseller's bill, were occasionally discharged;
and the extraordinaries of my travels into France and Italy
amounted, by prævious agreement, to the sum of twelve
hundred pounds. But the ordinary scale of my expence was
proportioned to my ordinary revenue; my desires were
regulated by temper as much as by philosophy; and as soon
as my purse was empty I had the courage to retire into
Hampshire, where I found in my father's house a liberal
maintenance, and in my own studies an inexhaustible source
of amusement. With a credit which might have been largely
abused, I may assume the singular merit, that I never lost,
or borrowed twenty pounds in the twelve years which
elapsed between my return from Switzerland and my father's
death.

The only person in England whom I was impatient to see

[1] *I* more

was [1] my aunt Porten, the affectionate guardian of my tender years. I hastened to her house in College street Westminster, and the evening was spent in the effusions of joy and confidence. It was not without some awe and apprehension, that I approached the presence of my father. My infancy, to speak the truth, had been neglected at home: the severity of his look and language at our last parting still dwelt on my memory; nor could I form any notion of *his* character, or *my* probable reception. They were both more agreable than I could expect. The domestic discipline of our ancestors has been relaxed by the philosophy and softness of the age: and if my father remembered that *he* had trembled before a stern parent, it was only to adopt with his own son an opposite mode of behaviour. He received me as a man and a friend:

40ᵛ all constraint was banished | at our first interview, and we ever afterwards [2] continued on the same terms of easy and equal politeness: he applauded the success of my education; every word and action was expressive of the most cordial affection; and our lives would have passed without a cloud, if his œconomy had been equal to his fortune, or if his fortune had been equal to his desires [3]. During my absence he had married his second wife Miss Dorothea Patton, who was introduced to me with the most unfavourable prejudice: I considered his second marriage as an act of displeasure, [4] and the rival [5] who had usurped my mother's bed appeared in the light of a personal and domestic enemy. I will not say that I was apprehensive of the bowl or dagger, or that I had then weighed the sentence of Euripides—

$$Εχθρα γαρ επιουσα μητρυια τεκνοις$$
$$Τοις προσθ' εχιδνης ουδεν ηπιοτερα.$$

But I well knew that the *odium novercale* was proverbial in the language of antiquity; the Latin poets always couple with

---

[1] *I* that kind and sensible woman, *this being cancelled and replaced by the* affectionate guardian of my tender years *written in the margin.*   [2] *I added* ever afterwards *in the margin.*   [3] *I* wishes   [4] *II om ten lines from here down to* injusta noverca *and replaced them by a short sentence from C (MS f 66ᵛ – M 242)* and I was disposed to hate the rival of my mother   [5] *I* woman

the name of stepmother, the hateful epithets of *crudelis, saeva, scelerata*; and on the road I had often repeated the line of Virgil

Est mihi namque domi pater, est injusta noverca.

But the injustice was in my own fancy; and the imaginary monster was an amiable and deserving woman. I could not be mistaken in the first view of her understanding her knowledge, and the elegant spirit of her conversation: her polite welcome, and her assiduous care to study and gratify my wishes announced at least that the surface would be smooth: and my suspicions of art and falsehood were gradually dispelled by the full discovery of her warm and exquisite sensibility. After some reserve on my side our minds associated in confidence and friendship, and as Mrs Gibbon had neither children nor the hopes of children, we more easily adopted the tender names and genuine characters of mother and of son. By the indulgence of these parents I was left at liberty to consult my taste or reason in the choice of place of company, and of amusements, and my excursions were only bounded by[1] the limits of the island and the measure of my income. Some faint efforts were made to procure me an[2] employment of Secretary to a foreign Embassy: and I listened to a scheme which would again have transported me to the Continent. Mrs Gibbon with seeming wisdom, exhorted me to take chambers in the Temple, and devote my leisure to the study of the Law. I cannot repent of having neglected her advice: few men | without the spur 41 of necessity have resolution to force their way through the thorns and thickets of that gloomy labyrinth. Nature had not endowed me with the bold and ready eloquence which makes itself heard amidst the tumult of the bar

Vincentem strepitus, et natum rebus agendis.[3]

and I should probably have been diverted from the labours of litterature without acquiring the fame or fortune of a successful pleader. I had no need to call to my aid the regular duties of a profession: every day every hour was agreably filled: nor have I known like so many of my countrymen, the tediousness of an idle life.

[1] *II* bounded only by   [2] *II* the   [3] *II om this quotation.*

Of the two years (May 1758–May 1760) between my return to England and the embodying [1] the Hampshire militia, I passed about nine months in London and the remainder in the country. The metropolis affords many amusements which are open to all: it is itself an astonishing and perpetual spectacle to the curious eye; and each taste, each sense may be gratified by the variety of objects that[2] will occur in the long circuit of a morning walk. I assiduously frequented the Theatres at a very prosperous[3] æra of the stage, when a constellation of excellent actors both in tragedy and comedy was eclipsed by the meridian brightness of Garrick, in the maturity of his judgement, and vigour of his performance. The pleasures of a town life, [4]the daily round from the tavern to the play, from the play to the coffee-house, from the coffee-house to the —[5] are within the reach of every man who is regardless of his health his money and his company. By the contagion of example I was sometimes seduced: but the better habits which I had formed at Lausanne induced me to seek a more elegant and rational society: and if my search was less easy and successful than I might have hoped I shall at present impute the failure to the disadvantages of my situation and character. Had the rank and fortune of my parents given them an annual establishment in London, their own house would have introduced me to a numerous and polite circle of acquaintance. But my father's taste had always preferred[6] the highest and the lowest company, for which he was equally qualified; and after a twelve years retirement he was no longer in the memory of the great with whom he had associated. I found myself a stranger in the midst of a vast and unknown city, and at my entrance into life[7], I was reduced to some dull family parties, and some scattered connections which were not such as I should have chosen for myself. The most useful friends of my father were the
41ᵛ Mallets: they received me with civility and kindness | at first on his account, and afterwards on my own; and (if I may use Lord Chesterfield's word[8]) I was soon *domesticated* in their

---

[1] *II added* of   [2] *II* which   [3] *II* propitious   [4] *II om two lines from here to* to the   [5] *In* C (*MS f* 67 – *M* 244) *the sentence ends* to the Bagnio   [6] *I* But the life of my father had been spent in   [7] *I* the World   [8] *II* words

MML I

house. Mr Mallet, a name among the English poets, is praised by an unforgiving enemy for the ease and elegance of his conversation, and whatsoever might be the defects of[1] his wife, she[2] was not destitute of wit or learning. By his assistance I was introduced to Lady Hervey, the mother of the present Earl of Bristol: her age and infirmities confined her at home: her dinners were select; in the evening her house was open to the best company of both sexes and all nations; nor was I displeased at her preference and even[3] affectation of the manners the language and the litterature of France. But my progress in the English World was in general left to my own efforts and those efforts were languid and slow. I had not been endowed by art or Nature with those happy gifts of confidence and address which unlock every door, and every bosom[4]; nor would it be reasonable to complain of the just consequences of my sickly childhood, foreign education, and reserved temper. While coaches were rattling through Bond Street, I have passed many a solitary evening in my lodging with my books: my studies were sometimes interrupted by a sigh which I breathed towards Lausanne; and on the approach of spring I withdrew without reluctance from the noisy and expensive[5] scene of crowds without company, and dissipation without pleasure. In each of the twenty five years of my acquaintance with London (1758-1783) the prospect gradually brightened: and this unfavourable picture most properly belongs to the first period after my return from Switzerland.

My father's residence in Hampshire where I have passed many light, and some heavy, hours was at Buriton near Petersfield, one mile from the Portsmouth road, and at the easy distance of fifty eight miles from London. An old mansion, in a state of decay had been converted into the fashion and convenience of a modern house; and if strangers had nothing to see, the inhabitants had little to desire. The spot was not happily chosen at the end of the village and the bottom of the hill: but the aspect of[6] the adjacent grounds

---

[1] *II om* whatsoever might be the defects   [2] *II om* , she   [3] *II om* even
[4] *I added* which unlock . . . bosom *in the margin.*   [5] *II* extensive   [6] *I added* the aspect of *in the margin.*

was[1] various and chearful: the downs commanded a noble prospect, and the long hanging woods in sight of the house could not perhaps have been improved by art or expence. 42 My father kept in his own hands, the whole of his[2] estate | and even rented some additional land: and whatsoever might be the balance of profit and loss, the farm supplied him with amusement and plenty. The produce maintained a number of men and horses, which were[3] multiplied by the inter-mixture of domestic and rural servants; and in the intervals of labour, the favourite team, an handsome set of bays or greys was harnessed to the coach. The œconomy of the house was regulated by the taste and prudence of Mrs Gibbon; she prided herself in the elegance of her occasional dinners; and from the uncleanly avarice of Madame Pavilliard, I was suddenly transported to the daily neatness and luxury of an English table. Our immediate neighbourhood was rare and rustic; but from the verge of our hills as far as Chichester and Goodwood, the western district of Sussex was interspersed with noble seats and hospitable families; with whom we culti-vated a friendly, and might have enjoyed a very frequent, inter-course. As my stay at Buriton was always voluntary, I was received and dismissed with smiles: but the comforts of my retirement did not depend on the ordinary pleasures of the Country. My father could never inspire me with his love[4] and knowledge of farming: [5] When he galloped away on[6] a fleet hunter to follow the Duke of Richmond's fox hounds, I saw him depart[7] without a wish to join in the sport; and in the command of an ample manour, I valued the supply of the kitchen much more than the exercise of the field. I never handled a gun, I seldom mounted an horse; and my philo-sophic walks were soon terminated by a shady bench where I was long detained by the sedentary amusement[8] of reading or meditation. At home I occupied a pleasant and spacious apartment; the library on the same floor was soon considered as my peculiar domain; and I might say with truth that I

[1] *I* were   [2] *II* the   [3] *I* His attendants – *this was cancelled and replaced by* The produce . . . horses, which *written in the margin. See editor's note to p. 95.*   [4] *I* taste   [5] *II om five lines from here to* of the field.   [6] *I* he mounted   [7] *I* gallop away   [8] *I* occupation

was never less alone than when by myself. My sole complaint, which I piously suppressed, arose from the kind
restraint imposed on the freedom of my time. By the habit
of early rising I always secured a sacred portion of the day,
and many scattered moments were stolen and employed by
my studious industry. But the family-hours of breakfast,
of dinner, of tea and of supper were regular and long: after
breakfast Mrs Gibbon expected my company in her dressing-
room: after tea my father claimed my conversation and the
perusal of the newspapers; and in the midst of an interesting
work, | I was often called down to receive the visit of some 42ᵛ
idle neighbours. Their dinners and visits required in due
season a similar return, and I dreaded the period of the full-
moon which was usually reserved for our more distant excursions. I could not refuse attending my father, in the
summer of 1759 to the races at Stockbridge, Reading, and
Odiham[1], where he had entered an horse for the hunter's[2]
plate; and I was not displeased with the sight of our Olympic
games, the beauty of the spot, the fleetness of the horses,
and the gay tumult of the numerous spectators. As soon as
the Militia business was agitated many days were tediously
consumed in meetings of Deputy-Lieutenants at Petersfield,
Alton and Winchester. In the close of the same year 1759,
Sir Simeon (then Mr) Stewart attempted an unsuccessful
contest for the county of Southampton against Mr Legge,
Chancellor of the Exchequer: a well known contest in which
Lord Bute's influence was first exerted and censured. Our
canvass at Portsmouth and Gosport lasted several days: but
the interruption of my studies was compensated in some
degree by the spectacle of English manners, and the acquisition of some practical knowledge.

   If in a more domestic or more dissipated scene my application was somewhat relaxed, the love of knowledge was
inflamed and gratified by the command of books, and I
compared the poverty of Lausanne with the plenty of
London. My father's study[3] at Buriton, was[4] stuffed with
much trash of the last age, with much High-church Divinity
and politics which have long since gone to their proper

---

¹ *II* Odiam   ² *III* hunters'   ³ *I* The Study library   ⁴ *I* though

place: yet it contained some valuable Editions of the Classics and the fathers, the choice as it should seem of Mr Law; and many English publications of the times had been occasionally added. From this slender beginning I have gradually formed a numerous and Select library, the foundation of my works and the best comfort of my life both at home and abroad. On the receipt of the first quarter a large share of my allowance was appropriated to my litterary wants: I cannot forget the joy with which I exchanged a bank-note of twenty pounds for the twenty volumes of the Memoirs of the Academy of Inscriptions; nor would it have been easy by any other expenditure of the same sum to have procured so large and lasting a fund of rational amusement. At a time when I most assiduously frequented this school of ancient litterature[1] | I thus expressed my opinion of a learned and various Collection, which since the year 1759 has been doubled in magnitude though not equally[2] in merit. 'Une de 'ces sociétés qui ont mieux immortalisé Louis XIV qu'une 'ambition souvent pernicieuse aux hommes, commençoit deja 'ces recherches qui reunissent la justesse de l'esprit, l'aménité 'et l'erudition: où l'on voit tant de decouvertes, et quel- 'quefois, ce qui ne céde qu'à peine aux decouvertes, une '*ignorance* modeste et *savante*.' The review of my library must be reserved for the period of its maturity: but in this place I may allow myself to observe that I am not conscious of having ever bought a book from a motive of ostentation, that every volume before it was deposited on the shelf was either read or sufficiently examined, and that I soon adopted the tolerating maxim of the elder Pliny, nullum esse librum tam malum ut non ex aliquâ parte prodesset. I could not yet find leisure or courage to renew the pursuit of the Greek language except[3] by reading the lessons of the old and new testament every Sunday when I attended the family to Church. The series of my Latin authors was less strenuously compleated; but the acquisition by inheritance or purchase of the best editions of Cicero, Quintilian, Livy, Tacitus, Ovid &c afforded a fair opportunity[4] which I seldom neglected. I persevered in the useful method of abstracts and observa-

43

---

[1] *I* learning   [2] *II om* equally   [3] *II* excepting   [4] *II* prospect

tions[1] and a single example may suffice of a note which had almost swelled into a work. The solution of a passage of Livy (xxxviii 38) involved me in the dry and dark treatises of Greaves, Arbuthnot, Hooper, Bernard, Eisenschmidt Gronovius, La Barre, Freret &c, and in my French Essay (C. xx) I ridiculously send the reader to my own *manuscript* remarks on the weights, coins, and measures of the ancients, which were abruptly terminated by the Militia drum.

As I am now entering on a more ample field of society and study, I can only hope to avoid a vain and prolix garrulity by overlooking the vulgar crowd of my acquaintance, and confining myself to such intimate friends, among books and men, as are best entitled to my notice, by their own merit and reputation, or by the deep impression which they have left on my mind. Yet I will embrace this occasion of recommending to the young student a practise which about this time I adopted myself[2]. After glancing my eye over the design and order of a new book, I suspended the perusal till I had finished the task of self-examination, till I had | re- 43v volved in a solitary walk all that I knew, or believed or had thought on the subject of the whole work, or of some particular chapter. I was then qualified to discern how much the author added to my original stock; and [3] I was sometimes satisfied by the agreement, I was sometimes armed by the opposition of our ideas. The favourite companions of my leisure were our English writers since the Revolution: they breathe the spirit of reason and liberty, and they most seasonably contributed to restore the purity of my own language which had been corrupted by the long use of a foreign Idiom. By the judicious advice of Mr Mallet I was directed to the writings of Swift and Addison: wit and simplicity are their common attributes: but the style of Swift is supported by manly original vigour; that of Addison is adorned by the [4] female graces of elegance and mildness; [5] and the contrast of too coarse or too thin a texture is visible even in the defects of these celebrated authors. The old reproach that no British altars had been raised to the muse

---

[1] *I* notes   [2] *II* I myself adopted   [3] *II added* if   [4] *I* more   [5] *II om* the end of the sentence from here.

of history, was recently disproved by the first performances of Robertson and Hume, the Histories of Scotland and of the Stuarts. I will assume the presumption to say[1] that I was not unworthy to read them: nor will I disguise my different feelings in the repeated perusals. The perfect composition, the nervous language, the well-turned periods of Dr Robertson inflamed me to the ambitious hope, that I might one day tread in his footsteps: the calm philosophy, the careless inimitable beauties of his friend and rival often forced me to close the volume, with a mixed sensation of delight and despair.

The design of my first work the Essay on the study of litterature was suggested by a refinement of vanity, the desire of justifying and praising the object of a favourite pursuit. In France, to which my ideas were confined, the learning and language of Greece and Rome were neglected by a philosophic age. The guardian of those studies the Academy of Inscriptions was degraded to the lowest[2] rank among the three Royal societies of Paris: the new appellation of *Erudits* was contemptuously applied to the successors of Lipsius and Casaubon; and I was provoked to hear (see Mr d'Alembert's Discours preliminaire à l'Encyclopedie) that the exercise of the memory, their sole merit, had been superseded by the nobler faculties of the imagination | and the judgement. I was ambitious of proving by my own example as well as by my precepts that all the faculties of the mind may be exercised and displayed by [the] study of ancient litterature; I began to select and adorn the various proofs and illustrations which had offered themselves in reading the classics, and the first pages or chapters of my Essay were composed before my departure from Lausanne. The hurry of the journey and of the first weeks of my English life suspended all thoughts of serious application: but my object was ever before my eyes, and no more than ten days from the first to the eleventh of July were suffered to elapse after my summer establishment at Buriton. My Essay was finished in about six weeks, and as soon as a fair copy had been transcribed by one of the French prisoners at Petersfield

44

[1] *II* of saying   [2] *I* third

I looked round for a critic and a¹ judge of my first performance.
A writer can seldom be content with the doubtful recompense
of solitary approbation, but a youth ignorant of the World
and of himself must desire to weigh his talents in some scales
less partial than his own: my conduct was natural my motive
laudable, my choice of Dᴿ Maty judicious and fortunate. By
descent and education, Dᴿ Maty, though born in Holland
might be considered as a Frenchman, but he was fixed in
London by the practice of physic, and an office in the British
Musæum. His reputation was justly founded on the eighteen
Volumes of the *Journal Britannique* which he had supported
almost alone with perseverance and success. This humble
though useful labour which had once been dignified by the
Genius of Bayle and the learning of Le Clerc was not dis-
graced by the taste, the knowledge and the judgement of
Maty: he exhibits a candid and pleasing view of the state of
litterature in England during a period of six years (January
1750–December 1755); and far different from his angry son,
he handles the rod of criticism with the tenderness and
reluctance of a parent. The author of the Journal Britannique
sometimes aspires to the character of a Poet and philosopher:
his style is pure and elegant, and in his virtues or even ² his
defects he may be ranked as one of the last disciples of the
school of Fontenelle. His answer to my first letter was
prompt and polite: after a careful examination he returned
my Manuscript with some animadversion and much applause,
and when I visited London, in the ensuing winter, we dis-
cussed | the design and execution in several free and familiar 44ᵛ
conversations. In a short excursion to Buriton, I reviewed
my Essay according to his friendly advice, and after sup-
pressing a third, adding a third and altering a third, I con-
summated my first labour by a short preface, which is dated
February 3ᵈ 1759. Yet I still shrunk from the press with the
terrors of virgin-modesty: the Manuscript was safely
deposited in my desk; and as my attention was engaged by
new objects, the delay might have been prolonged till I
had fulfilled the precept of Horace, [']nonumque prematur in
annum'. Father Sirmond, a learned Jesuit, was still more

¹ *II om a*   ² *II added* in

rigid, since he advised a young friend to expect the mature age of fifty before he gave himself or his writings to the public (Olivet. Histoire de l'Academie Françoise Tom ii p. 143). The counsel was singular, but it is still more singular that it should have been approved by the example of the author. Sirmond was himself fifty five years of age when he published (in 1614) his first work an Edition of Sidonius Apollinaris with many valuable annotations. (See his life before the great Edition of his works in five Volumes in[1] folio. Paris 1696 e Typographiâ Regiâ.)

Two years elapsed in silence: but in the spring of 1761, I yielded to the authority of a parent, and complyed like a pious son with the wish of my own heart. My private resolves were influenced by the state of Europe. About this time the Belligerent powers had made and accepted overtures of peace: our English plenipotentiaries were named to assist at the Congress of Augsbourg which never met; I wished to attend them as a Gentleman or a secretary, and my father fondly believed that the proof of some litterary talents might introduce me to public notice and second the recommendations of my friends. After a last revisal [2] I consulted with Mr Mallet and Dr Maty who approved the design and promoted the execution. Mr Mallet after hearing me read my manuscript, received it from my hands and delivered it into those of Becket, with whom he made an agreement in my name: an easy agreement; I required only a certain number of copies, and without transferring my property, I devolved on the bookseller the charges and profits of the Edition. | Dr Maty undertook in my absence to correct the sheets: he inserted without my knowledge an elegant and flattering Epistle to the Author: which is composed however with so much art that in case of a defeat, his favourable report might have been ascribed to the indulgence of a friend for the rash attempt of a *young, English, Gentleman*. The work was printed and published under the title of *Essai sur l'etude de la litterature à Londres chez T. Becket et P. A. de Hondt 1761*, in a small Volume in duodecimo. My dedication to my father, a proper and pious address was composed the 28th of

45

---

[1] *II om* in   [2] *I* and some improvements

May[1]: D[r] Maty's letter is dated the 16th of June; and I received the first copy June the 23[d] at Alresford two days before I marched with the Hampshire militia. Some weeks afterwards, on the same ground I presented my book to the late Duke of York who breakfasted in Colonel Pitt's tent, [2] and as the regiment was just returned from a field day, the author appeared before his Royal Highness, somewhat disordered with sweat and dust, in the Cap, dress, and acoutrements of a Captain of Grenadiers. By my father's direction and Mallet's advice, a number of copies were given to several of their acquaintance and my own; to the Duke of Richmond, the Marquis of Caernarvon, the Earls of Litchfield, Waldegrave, Egremont, Shelburne, Bute, Hardwicke, Bath, Granville, and Chesterfield, Lady Hervey, Sir Joseph Yorke, Sir Matthew Fetherstone, Messieurs Walpole, Scott, Wray &c: two books were sent to the Count de Caylus, and the Dutchess d'Aiguillon at Paris; I had reserved twenty [3] for my friends at Lausanne, as the first fruits of my education and a grateful token of my remembrance: and on all these persons I levied an unavoidable tax of civility and compliment. It is not surprising that a work of which the style and sentiments were so totally foreign should have been more successful abroad than at home. I was delighted by the copious extracts, the warm commendations, and the flattering predictions of the Journals of France and Holland: and the next year (1762), a new Edition (I believe at Geneva) extended the fame or at least the circulation of the work. In England it was received with cold indifference, little read and speedily forgotten: a small impression was slowly dispersed; the bookseller murmured, and the author (had his feelings been more exquisite[)] might have wept over the blunders and the[4] baldness of the English translation. The publication of my history fifteen years afterwards revived the memory of my first performance, and the Essay

---

[1] *I added* My dedication . . . of May *in the margin.*   [2] *II om ten lines from here down to* Scott, Wray &c *and for them substituted a sentence from C:* According to my father's and Mallet's directions, my litterary gifts were distributed to several eminent characters in England and France (*MS f 70ᵛ – M 255*), *altering, however, its beginning into* By my father's direction and Mallet's advice, many literary gifts   [3] *II added* copies   [4] *II om* the

was eagerly sought in the shops. But I refused the permission
45ᵛ which Becket solicited of reprinting it; the public | curiosity
was imperfectly satisfied by a pyrated copy of the booksellers
of Dublin; and when a copy of the original edition has been
discovered in a sale, the primitive value of half a crown has
risen to the fanciful price of a Guinea or thirty shillings. [1] Such
is the power of a name.

I have expatiated on [2]the loss of my litterary maidenhead;
a memorable æra in the life of a student, when he ventures
to reveal the measure of his mind. His hopes and fears are
multiplied by the idea of self-importance, and he believes
for a while, that the eyes of mankind are fixed on his person
and performance. Whatsoever[3] may be my present reputation
it no longer rests on the merit of this first Essay, and at the
end of twenty eight years, I may appreciate my juvenile
work, with the impartiality, and almost with the indifference
of a stranger. In his answer to Lady Hervey, the Count de
Caylus admires or affects to admire 'les livres sans nombre
'que Mr Gibbon a lûs et très bien lus' But alas my stock of
erudition at that time was scanty and superficial; and if I
allow myself the liberty of naming the Greek masters, my
genuine and personal acquaintance was confined to the Latin
Classics. The most serious defect of my Essay is a kind of
obscurity and abruptness which allways fatigues, and may
often elude the attention of the reader. Instead of a precise
and proper definition, [4] the title itself, the sense of the word
Litterature is loosely and variously applied: a number of
remarks, and examples historical, critical, philosophical are
heaped on each other without method or connection, and if
we except some introductory pages, all the remaining
chapters might indifferently be reversed or transposed. The
obscurity of many passages is often affected, brevis esse
laboro, obscurus fio, the desire of expressing, perhaps a
common idea, with sententious and oracular brevity: alas
how fatal has been the imitation of Montesquieu! But this
obscurity sometimes proceeds from a mixture of light and

---

[1] *II om this sentence.*   [2] *For* loss . . . maidenhead *II substituted* petty circumstances and period of my first publication (*which is not G's*).   [3] *II* Whatever   [4] *II replaced the comma by* of

darkness in the author's mind, from a partial ray which strikes upon an angle, instead of spreading itself over the surface of an object. After this fair confession I shall presume to say that the Essay does credit to a young writer of two and twenty years of age, who had read with taste, who thinks with freedom, and who writes in a foreign language with spirit and elegance. The defence of[1] the early history of Rome and the new Chronology of Sir Isaac Newton form a specious argument. | The patriotic and political design of 46 the Georgics is happily conceived; and any probable conjecture which tends to raise the dignity of the poet and the poem deserves to be adopted without a rigid scrutiny. Some dawning[2] of a philosophic spirit enlightens the general remarks on the study of history and of man. I am not displeased with the enquiry into the origin and nature of the Gods of Polytheism. [3] In a riper season of judgement and knowledge, I am tempted to review the curious question whether these fabulous Deities were mortal men or allegorical beings: perhaps the two systems might be blended in one; perhaps the distance[4] between them is in a great measure verbal and apparent. In the rapid course of this narrative I have only time to scatter two or three hasty observations. *That* in the perusal of Homer, a naturalist would pronounce his Gods and men to be of the same species since they were capable of engendering together a fruitful progeny. *That* before the Reformation St Francis and the Virgin Mary had almost attained a similar Apotheosis; and that the Saints and Angels so different in their origin were worshipped with the same rites by the same nations. *That* the current of superstition and science flowed from India to Egypt from Egypt to Greece and Italy; and that the incarnations of the Cœlestial Deities so darkly shadowed in our fragments of Egyptian Theology are copiously explained in the sacred books of the Hindoos: Fifteen centuries before Christ, the great Osiris the invisible agent of the Universe was born or manifested at Thebes in Bœotia under the name of Bacchus; the idea of Bishen is a metaphysical abstraction, the ad-

---

[1] *I* observations on   [2] *II* dawnings   [3] *II om twenty-five lines from here down to* Delhi   [4] *I* difference

ventures of Kishen his perfect image are those of a man who lived and died about five thousand years ago in the neighbourhood of Delhi—Upon the whole I may apply to the first labour of my pen the speech of a far superior[1] Artist when he surveyed the first productions of his pencil. After viewing some portraits which he had painted in his youth, my friend Sir Joshua Reynolds acknowledged to me, that he was rather humbled than flattered by the comparison with his present works; and that after so[2] much time and study he had conceived his improvement to be much greater than he found it to have been.

At Lausanne I composed the first chapters of my Essay 46ᵛ in French, the familiar language | of my conversation and studies, in which it was easier for me to write than in my mother-tongue. After my return to England I continued the same practise without any affectation or design of repudiating (as Dʳ Bentley would say[)] my vernacular idiom. But I should have escaped some Anti-gallican clamour had I been content with the more natural character of an English author; I should have been more consistent had I rejected Mallet's foolish[3] advice of prefixing an English dedication to a French book; a confusion of tongues which[4] seemed to accuse the ignorance of my patron. The use of a foreign dialect might be excused by the hope of being employed as a negociator, by the desire of being generally understood on the continent; but my true motive was doubtless the ambition of new and singular fame, an Englishman claiming a place among the writers of France. The Latin tongue had been consecrated by the service of the Church; it was refined by the imitation of the ancients: and in the xvᵗʰ and xviᵗʰ Centuries the scholars of Europe enjoyed the advantage which they have gradually resigned of conversing and writing in a common and learned idiom. As that idiom was no longer in any country the vulgar speech, they all stood on a level with each other: yet a citizen of old Rome might have smiled at the best Latinity of the Germans and Britons, and we may learn from the *Ciceronianus* of Erasmus how difficult it was

---

[1] *I* greater   [2] so so *in MS (end of a line, beginning of the next)*   [3] *II om* foolish   [4] *II* that

found to steer a middle course between pedantry and barbarism. The Romans themselves had sometimes attempted a more perilous task, of writing in a living language, and appealing to the taste and judgement of the natives. The vanity of Tully was doubly interested in the *Greek* memoirs[1] of his own Consulship; and if he modestly supposes that some Latinisms might be detected in his style, he is confident of his own skill in the art of Isocrates and Aristotle and he requests his friend Atticus to disperse the copies of his work at Athens and in the other cities of Greece (ad Atticum. I. 19 ii. 1) But it must not be forgot that, from infancy to manhood, Cicero and his contemporaries had read and declaimed and composed with equal diligence in both lang[u]ages, and | [2] that he was not allowed to frequent a Latin 47 school till he had imbibed the lessons of the Greek Grammarians and Rhetoricians. In modern times the language of France has been diffused by the merit of her writers, the social manners of the natives, the influence of the Monarchy, and the exile of the protestants: several foreigners have seized the opportunity of speaking to Europe in this common dialect[3], and Germany may plead the authority of Leibnitz and Frederic, of the first of her philosophers, and the greatest of her Kings. The just pride and laudable prejudice of England has restrained this communication of idioms; and of all the nations on this side of the Alps my countrymen are the least practised and least perfect in the exercise of the French tongue. By Sir William Temple and Lord Chesterfield it was only used on occasions of civility and business and their printed letters will not be quoted as models of composition. Lord Bolingbroke may have published in French a sketch of his reflections on exile: but [his] reputation now reposes on the address of Voltaire, 'Docte sermones utriusque linguae' and by his English dedication to Queen Caroline, and his Essay on Epic poetry, it should seem that Voltaire himself wished to deserve a return of the same compliment. The exception of Count Hamilton cannot fairly be urged; though an Irishman by birth, he was educated in France from his childhood: yet I *am* surprised that a long residence

[1] *I* which he composed   [2] *I* and   [3] *I* this general idiom

in England, and the habits of domestic conversation did not affect the ease and purity of his inimitable style; and I regret the omission of his English verses which might have afforded an amusing object of comparison. I might therefore assume the primus ego in patriam meam[1] &c; but with what success I have explored this untrodden path must be left to the decision of my French readers. Dr Maty who might himself be questioned as a foreigner has secured his retreat at my expence 'Je ne crois pas que vous vous piquiez 'd'etre moins facile à reconnoître pour un Anglois que 'Lucullus pour un Romain' My friends at Paris have been more indulgent: they received me as a countryman, or at least as a provincial, but they were friends and Parisians. The defects which Maty insinuates 'Ces traits saillans, ces 'figures hardies, ce sacrifice de la regle au sentiment, et de 'la cadence à la force' | are the faults of the youth rather than of the stranger: and after the long and laborious exercise of my own language, I am conscious that my French style has been ripened and improved.

I have already hinted that the publication of my Essay was delayed till I had embraced[2] the military profession. I shall now amuse myself with the recollection of an active scene which bears no affinity to any other period of my studious and social life. [3] From the general idea of a militia I shall descend to the Militia of England in the war before the last; to the state of the Regiment in which I served, and to the influence of that service on my personal situation and character.

The defence of the state may be imposed on the body of the people, or it may be delegated to a select number of mercenaries: the exercise of arms may be an occasional duty or a separate trade; and it is this difference which forms the distinction between a militia and a standing army. Since the union of England and Scotland the public safety has never been attacked and has seldom been threatened by a foreign invader; but the sea was long the sole safeguard of

47[v]

---

[1] *II om* meam   [2] *I assumed*   [3] *II om G's digression, which begins here, on the general idea of a militia and the Militia in England in the Seven Years' war (pp. 107-111).*

our isle. If the reign of the Tudors or the Stuarts was often
signalized by the valour of our Soldiers and sailors, they
were dismissed at the end of the campaign or the expedition
for which they had been levied. The nati[o]nal spirit at home
had subsided in the peaceful occupations of trade, manufactures[1] and husbandry, and if the obsolete forms of a militia
were preserved, their discipline in the last age was less the
object of confidence than of ridicule.

> The country rings around with loud alarms,
> And raw in fields, the rude Militia swarms:
> Mouths without hands maintained at vast expence
> In peace a charge, in war a weak defence.
> Stout once a month they march, a blust'ring band,
> And ever but in times of need at hand.
> This was the morn when issuing on the guard,
> Drawn up in rank and file they stood prepar'd
> Of seeming arms to make a short essay;
> Then hasten to be drunk, the business of the day.

The impotence of such unworthy[2] soldiers was supplied from
the æra of the restoration by the establishment of a[3] body of
mercenaries: the conclusion of each war encreased the num-
bers that were kept on foot, and | although their progress 48
was checked by the jealousy of opposition[4], time and necessity
reconciled, or at least accustomed, a free country[5] to the
annual perpetuity of a standing army. The zeal of our
patriots, both in, and out of, Parliament (I cannot add both
in, and out of, office) complained that the sword had been
stolen from the hands of the people. They appealed to the
victorious example of the Greeks and Romans among whom
every citizen was a soldier; and they applauded the happiness
and independence of Switzerland which, in the midst of the
great monarchies of Europe is sufficiently defended by a
constitutional and effective militia. But their enthusiasm
overlooked the modern changes in the art of war, and the
insuperable difference of government and manners. The
liberty of the Swiss is maintained by the concurrence of
political causes: the superior discipline of their militia arises
from the numerous intermixture of Officers and soldiers

---

[1] *I added* manufactures *in the margin.*   [2] *I* disgraceful   [3] *I* an encreasing   [4] *I* parliament   [5] *I* people

whose youth has been trained in foreign service; and the annual exercise of a few days is the *sole* tax which is imposed on a martial people consisting for the most part of shepherds and husbandmen. In the primitive ages of Greece and Rome[1], a war was determined by a battle, and a battle was decided by the personal qualities of strength, courage and dexterity which every citizen derived from his domestic education. The public quarrel was his own: he had himself voted in the assembly of the people; and the private passions of the majority had pronounced the general decree of the Republic. On the event of the contest each freeman had staked his fortune and family, his liberty and [2] life: and if the enemy prevailed he must expect to share in the common calamity of the ruin or servitude of his native city. By such irresisitible motives were the first Greeks and Romans summoned to the field: but when the art was improved, when the war was protracted, their militia was transformed into a standing army, or their freedom was oppressed by the more regular forces of an ambitious neighbour.

Two disgraceful events the progress in the year forty five of some naked highlanders, the invitation of the Hessians and Hanoverians in fifty six had betrayed and insulted the weakness of an unarmed people. The country-Gentlemen of England unanimously demanded the establishment of a militia: a patriot was expected

> Otia qui rumpet patriae, residesque movebit
> —— in arma viros.

48ᵛ and the merit of the plan or at least of the execution | was assumed by Mr Pitt who was then in the full splendour of his popularity and power. In the new model the choice of the officers was founded on the most cons[ti]tutional principle since they were all obliged, from the Colonel to the Ensign to prove a certain qualification, to give a landed security to the country, which entrusted them for her defence with the use of arms. But in the first steps of this institution the legislators of the Militia despaired of imitating the practise

---

[1] *I* In the first ages of ancient freedom   [2] *I* his liberty/and liberty and life *in MS* (*end of a line, beginning of the next*).

of Switzerland. Instead of summoning to the standard *all* the inhabitants of the Kingdom who were not disabled by age, or excused by some indispensable avocation they directed that a moderate proportion should be chosen by lot for the term of three years, at the end of which their places were to be supplied by a new and similar ballot. Every man who was drawn had the option of serving in person, of finding a substitute or of paying ten pounds; and in a country already burthened, this honourable duty was degraded into an additional tax. It is reported that the subjects of Queen Elizabeth amounted to 1.172,674 men able to bear arms (Hume's History of England Vol V p 482 of the last octavo Edition); and if in the war before the last many active and vigorous hands were employed in the fleet and army, the difference must have been amply compensated by the general encrease of population, and we may[1] smile at this might [y] effort which reduced the national defence to the puny establishmen[t] of thirty two thousand men. The Sunday afternoons had first been appointed for their exercise, but superstition clamoured against the profanation of the sabbath, and a useful day was substracted from the labour of the week. Whatever was the day such rare and superficial practise could never have entitled them to the character of soldiers. But the King was invested with the power of calling the Militia into actual service on the event or the danger of rebellion or invasion; and in the year 1759 the British islands were seriously threatened by the armaments of France. At this crisis the national spirit most gloriously disproved the charge of effeminacy which, in a popular Estimate had been imputed to the times; a martial enthusiasm seemed to have pervaded the land, and a constitutional army was formed under the command of the nobility and gentry of England. After the naval victory of Sir | 49 Edward Hawke (November 20th 1759) the danger no longer subsisted; yet instead of disbanding the first regiments of militia, the remainder was embodied the ensuing year, and public unanimity applauded their illegal continuance in the field till the end of the War. In this new mode of

[1] *I* must

service they were subject like the regulars to martial law: they received the same advantages of pay and cloathing, and the families, at least of the principals were maintained at the charge of the parish. At a distance from their respective counties, these provincial corps were stationed, and removed, and encamped by the command of the Secretary at War; the officers and men were trained in the habits of subordination[1] nor is it surprizing that some regiments[2] should have assumed the discipline and appearance of veteran troops. With the skill they soon imbibed the spirit of mercenaries, the character of a militia was lost; and, under that specious name, the crown had acquired a second army more costly and less useful than the first—The most beneficial effect of this institution was to eradicate among the Country gentlemen the relicks of Tory or rather of Jacobite prejudice. The accession of a British King reconciled them to the government and even to the court: but they have been since accused of transferring their passive loyalty from the Stuarts to the family[3] of Brunswick; [4] and I have heard Mr Burke exclaim in the house of Commons 'They have changed the Idol, but they have preserved the Idolatry!'

[5] By the general ardour of the times, my father, a new Cincinnatus, was drawn from the plough: his authority and advice prevailed on me to relinquish my studies: a general meeting was held at Winchester; and before we knew the consequences of an irretrievable step, we accepted (June 12th 1759) our respective commissions of Major and Captain in the South battalion of the Hampshire. The proportion of the County of Southampton had been fixed at nine hundred, and sixty men who were divided into the two regiments of the North and South, each consisting of eight companies. By the special exemption of the isle of Wight *we* lost a company; our Colonel resigned, and we were reduced to the

---

[1] *I added* the officers . . . subordination *in the margin*   [2] *I* of them   [3] *I* house   [4] *II made use of this last sentence of the paragraph changing its beginning into* in the language of Mr. Burke (*see below, note 5*).   [5] *For the B account of G's service in the militia (from here to p. 115, first paragraph), II substituted the shorter C account (MS ff 69ᵛ-70 – M 252-254), shortening it by leaving out two passages, bracketed in M, but adding to its second sentence the Burke quotation (see above, note 4).*

legal definition of an independent battalion, of a Lieutenant
Colonel Commandant (Sir Thomas Worsley Baronet) a
Major, five Captains, seven lieutenants, seven Ensigns,
twenty one Serjeants, fourteen drummers, and | four hundred 49ᵛ
and twenty rank and file. I will not renew our prolix and
passionate dispute with the Duke of Bolton our Lord
Lieutenant, which at that time appeared to me an object of
the most serious importance: by the interpretation of an act
of parliament we contested his right of naming himself
Colonel of the two Battalions; after the final decision of the
Attorney-general, and Secretary at War, his poor revenge
was confined to the use and abuse of his power in the choice
of an Adjutant, and the promotion of officers. In the year
1759 our ballot was slowly compleated, and as the fear of an
invasion passed away we began to hope, my father and
myself that our campaigns would extend no farther than
Petersfield and Alton the seat of our particular companies.
We were undeceived by the King's sign manual for our
embodying which was issued May 10ᵗʰ 1760: it was too
late to retreat: it was too soon to repent: the Battalion, on
the 4ᵗʰ of June assembled at Winchester, from whence in
about a fortnight we were removed at our own request for
the benefit of a foreign education. In a new raised Militia
the neighbourhood of home was always[1] found inconvenient
to the Officers and mischievous to the men.

The battalion continued in actual service above two years
and a half from May 10.1760 to December 23.1762. In this
period of a military life, I have neither sieges nor battles to
relate; but, like my brother Major Sturgeon, I shall describe
our marches and counter-marches as they are faithfully
recorded in my own journal or commentary of the times.
i Our first and most agreable station was at Blandford in
Dorsetshire where we enjoyed about two months (June 17–
August 23) the beauty of the country, the hospitality of the
neighbouring gentlemen, the novelty of command, and
exercise, and the consciousness of our daily and rapid improvements. ii From this school we were led against the
enemy, a body of French three thousand two hundred[2]

---

[1] *I added* always *in the margin.*   [2] *I added* two hundred *in the margin.*

strong who had occupied Portchester castle near Portsmouth: It must not indeed be dissembled that our enemies were naked unarmed prisoners, the object of pity rather than of terror; their misery was somewhat alleviated by public and private bounty; but their sufferings exhibited the evils of war, and their noisy spirits the character of the nation. During the months of September, October and November 1760 we performed this disagreable duty by large detach-

50 ments of a | Captain, four subalterns, and two hundred and thirty men at first from Hilsea-barracks, and afterwards from our quarters at Tichfield and Fareham. The barracks, within the Portsmouth lines are a square of low ill built huts in a damp and dreary situation: On this unwholesome spot we lost many men by feavers and the small-pox; and our dispute with the Duke of Bolton, which produced a series of arrests, memorials and court-martials was not less pernicious to the discipline than to the peace of the regiment. iii. Rejoycing in our escape from this sink of distemper and discord, we performed with alacrity a long march (December 1-11) to Cranbrook in the weald of Kent, where we had been sent to guard eighteen hundred French prisoners at Sissinghurst. The inconceivable dirtyness of the season, the country and the spot aggravated the hardships of a duty too heavy for our numbers: but these hardships were of short duration, and before the end of the month we were relieved by the interest of our Tory friends under the new reign. iv At Dover, in the space of five[1] months we began to breathe (December 27.1760–May 31.1761): for the men the quarters were healthy and plentiful, and our dull leisure was enlivened by the society of the fourteenth Regiment in the castle, and some sea parties in the spring. Our persecutions were at an end; the command was settled; we smiled at our own prowess, as we exercised each morning in sight of the French coast; and before we left Dover we had recovered the union and discipline which we possessed at our departure from Blandford: v. In the summer of 1761 a camp was formed near Winchester in which we solicited and obtained a place. Our March from Dover to Alton in Hampshire was a pleasant

[1] *I* three

walk (June 1-12): I was appointed Captain of the new company of Grenadiers, and with proper cloathing and accoutrements we assumed somewhat of the appearance of regular troops. The four months (June 25–October 21) of this encampment were the most splendid and useful period of our military life. Our establishment amounted to near five thousand men, the thirty fourth regiment of foot, and six militia corps, the Wiltshire, Dorsetshire, South-Hampshire, Berkshire and the North and South Gloucestershire. The regulars were satisfied with their ideal pre-eminence; the Glocestershire, Berkshire and Dorsetshire approached by successive steps the superior merit of the Wiltshire | the 50ᵛ pride and pattern[1] of the Militia, an active steady well-appointed regiment of eight hundred men, which had been formed by the strict and skillful discipline of their Colonel Lord Bruce. At our entrance into camp *we* were indisputably the last and worst: but we were excited by a generous shame

> Extremos pudeat rediisse ———

and such was our indefatigable labour, that in the general reviews, the South Hampshire were rather a credit than a disgrace to the line. A friendly emulation, ready to teach and eager to learn, assisted our mutual progress: but the great evolutions, the exercise of acting and moving as an army which constitutes the best lessons of a camp never entered the thoughts of the Earl of Effingham our drowzy General. vi. The Devizes, our winter quarters during four months, (October 23.1761–February 28.1762) are a[2] populous town full of disorder and disease: the men who were allowed to work earned too much money; and their drunken quarrels with the townsmen, and Colonel Barré's black musqueteers were painfully repressed by the sharp sentences of one and twenty Court-martials. The Devizes afforded however a great number of fine young recruits whom we enlisted from the Regimental stock-purse without much regard to the forms or the spirit of the Militia laws. vii After a short march and halt at Salisbury we paid a second visit of ten

---

[1] *I added* and pattern *in the margin.*   [2] *I first wrote* are a, *crossed it out and wrote* is which he deleted to write *are a again.*

weeks (March 9–May 31[)] to our old friends at Blandford where in that garden of England we again experienced[1] the warm and constant hospitality of the natives. The spring was favourable to our military exercise, and the Dorsetshire Gentlemen who had cherished our infancy now applauded a Regiment, in appearance and discipline, not inferior to their own. viii. The necessity of discharging a great number of men whose term of three years was expired forbade our encampment in the summer of 1762, and the colours were stationed at Southampton in[2] the last six or seven months (June–December) of our actual service. But after so long an indulgence we could not complain, that during many of the first and last weeks of this period, a detachment almost equal to the whole was required to guard the French prisoners at Forton and Fareham. The operation of the ballot was slow and tedious. In the months of August and September our life at Southampton was indeed gay and busy: the battalion had been renewed in youth and vigour; and so rapid was the improvement, | that, had the militia lasted another year we should not have yielded to the most perfect of our brethren. The preliminaries of peace and the suspension of arms determined our fate: we were dismissed with the thanks of the King and parliament; and on the 23ᵈ of December 1762, the companies were disembodyed at their respective[3] homes. The officers, possessed of property, rejoyced in their freedom; those who had none lamented the loss of their pay and profession: but it was found by experience that the greatest part of the men were rather civilized than corrupted by the habits of military subordination.

51

[4] A young mind, unless it be of a cold and languid temper, is dazzled even by the play of arms; and in the first sallies of my enthusiasm I had seriously wished and tryed to embrace the regular profession of a soldier. This military feaver was cooled by the enjoyment of our mimic Bellona, who gradually unveiled her naked deformity. How often did I sigh for my

[1] *I* where we again enjoyed the beauty of the country, the garden of England, and the warm   [2] *I* during   [3] *I* separate   [4] *For the first seventeen lines of this paragraph down to* principal support *II substituted the corresponding C passage* (MS f 71ᵛ – M 260).

true situation of a private gentleman and a man of letter[s]:
how often did I repeat the complaint of Cicero 'Clitellæ bovi
'sunt impositæ. Est incredibile quam me negotii tædat . . .
'Ille cursus animi et industriæ meæ præclarâ operâ cessat.
'Lucem, *libros*, urbem, domum, vos desidero Sed feram ut
'potero, sit modo annuum; Si prorogatur, actum est' From
a service without danger, I might indeed have retired without disgrace; but as often as I hinted a wish of resigning, my
fetters were rivetted by my father's authority the entreaties
of Sir Thomas Worsley, and some regard for the welfare of
a corps of which I was the principal support. [1] My proper
province was the care of my own, and afterwards of the
Grenadier, company: but, with the rank of first captain, I
possessed the confidence, and supplied the place, of the
Colonel and Major. In their presence or in their absence I
acted as the commanding officer: every memorial and letter
relative to our disputes was the work of my pen: the detach-
ments or court-martials of any delicacy or importance were
my extraordinary duties: and to supersede the Duke of
Bolton's Adjutant I always exercised the Battalion in the
field. Sir Thomas Worsley was an easy good-humoured man
fond of the table and of his bed: our conferences were marked
by every stroke of the midnight and morning hours, and the
same drum which invited him to rest has often summoned
me to the parade. His example encouraged the daily practise
of hard and even excessive drinking which has sown in my
constitution the seeds of the gout: [2] the loss of so | many busy 51ᵛ
and idle hours was not compensated by any elegant pleasure;
and my temper was insensibly soured by the society of our
rustic officers, [3] who were alike deficient in the knowledge of
scholars, and the manners of gentlemen. In every state there
exists however[4] a balance of good and evil. The habits of a
sedentary life were usefully broken by the duties of an active
profession: in the healthful[5] exercise of the field I hunted
with a battalion instead of a pack; and at that time I was

---

[1] *II om sixteen lines from here down to* seeds of the gout   [2] *Of the end of this
paragraph, II made a distinct paragraph which he put first, immediately after
the C account of G's militia service.*   [3] *II om the end of this sentence.*   [4] *I
But in every state there is*   [5] *I added* healthful *in the margin.*

ready at any hour of the day or night, to fly from quarters to London from London to quarters on the slightest call of private or regimental business. But my principal obligation to the militia was the making me an Englishman and a soldier. After my foreign education, with my reserved temper, I should long have continued a stranger in[1] my native country had I not been shaken in this various scene of new faces and new friends: had not experience forced me to feel the characters of our leading men, the state of parties, the forms of office and the operation of our civil and military system. In this peaceful service I imbibed the rudiments of the language and science of tactics which opened a new field of study and observation. I diligently read and meditated the *Memoires militaires*[2] of Quintus Icilius (Mr Guichardt) the only writer who has united the merits of a professor and a veteran. The discipline and evolutions of a modern battalion gave me a clearer notion of the Phalanx and the Legion, and the Captain of the Hampshire grenadiers (the reader may smile) has not been useless to the historian of the Roman Empire.

When I complain of the loss of time, justice to myself and to the Militia must throw the greatest part of that reproach on the first seven or eight months while I was obliged to learn as well as to teach. The dissipation of Blandford, and the disputes of Portsmouth consumed the hours which were not employed in the field; and amid the perpetual hurry of an Inn, a barrack or a guard-room, all litterary ideas were banished from my mind. After this long fast, the longest which I have ever known, I once more tasted at Dover the pleasures of reading and thinking, and the hungry appetite with which I opened a volume of Tully's philosophical works is still present to my memory. The last review of my Essay before its publication had prompted me to | investigate the 52 *Nature of the Gods*: my enquiries led me to the Histoire Critique du Manicheisme of Beausobre who discusses many deep questions of Pagan and Christian Theology: and from this rich treasury of facts and opinions I deduced my own consequences[3] beyond the holy circle of the Author. After

[1] *III* to   [2] *I* works   [3] *I* opinions

this recovery, I never relapsed into indolence, and my example might prove that in the life most adverse to study some hours may be stolen, some minutes may be snatched: amidst the tumult of Winchester camp I sometimes thought and read in my tent; in the more settled quarters of the Devizes, Blandford, and Southampton, I always secured a separate lodging and the necessary books, and in the summer of 1762, while the new militia was raising I enjoyed at Buriton two or three months of litterary repose. In forming a new plan of study I [1] hesitated between the Mathematics and the Greek language, both of which I had neglected since my return from Lausanne. I consulted a learned and friendly Mathematician, Mr George Scott, a pupil of de Moivre, and his map of a country which I have never explored may perhaps be more serviceable to others. As soon as I had given the preference to Greek, the example of Scaliger and my own reason determined me on the choice of Homer, the Father of poetry, and the bible of the ancients: but Scaliger ran through the Iliad in one and twenty days, and I was not dissatisfied with my own diligence for performing the same labour in an equal number of weeks. After the first difficulties were surmounted, the language of Nature and harmony soon became easy and familiar, and each day I sailed on the Ocean with a brisker gale and a more steady course.

> Ἐν δ' ανεμος πρησεν μεσον ἱστιον, αμφι δε κυμα
> Στειρῃ πορφυρεον μεγαλ' ιαχε, νηος ιουσης:
> Ἡ δ' εθεεν κατα κυμα διαπρησσουσα κελευθα.

In the study of a poet, who has since become the most intimate of my friends, I successively applied many passages and fragments of Greek writers; and among these I shall notice a life of Homer in the Opuscula Mythologica of Gale, several books of the Geography of Strabo, and the entire treatise of Longinus which, from the title and the style is equally worthy of the epithet of *Sublime*. My grammatical skill was improved, my vocabulary was enlarged; and in the militia, I acquired a just and indelible knowledge of the first

[1] *I* long

52ᵛ of languages. On every march | in every journey, Horace was always in my pocket and often in my hand: but I should not mention his two critical Epistles, the amusement of a morning, had they not been accompanied by the elaborate commentary of Dʳ Hurd now Bishop of Worcester. On the interesting subjects of composition and imitation of Epic and Dramatic poetry, I presumed to think for myself, and fifty[1] close written pages in folio could scarcely comprize my full and free discussion of the sense of the master and the pedantry of the servant.

After his oracle Dʳ Johnson, my friend Sir Joshua Reynolds denies all original Genius, any natural propensity of the mind to one art or science rather than another. Without engaging in a metaphysical or rather verbal dispute, I *know* by experience that from my early youth, I aspired to the character of an historian. While I served in the Militia, before and after the publication of my Essay, this idea ripened in my mind; nor can I paint in more lively colours the feelings of the moment, than by transcribing[2] some passages, under their respective dates from a Journal which I kept at that time.

Buriton. April 14. 1761

(in a short excursion from Dover).

'Having thought of several subjects for an historical com-
'position, I chose the expedition of Charles viii of France
'into Italy. I read two Memoirs of Mr de Foncemagne in
'the Academy of Inscription[s] (Tom xvii p 539-607) and
'abstracted them. I likewise finished this day a dissertation,
'in which I examine the right of Charles viii to the crown of
'Naples, and the rival claims of the houses of Anjou and
'Arragon. It consists of ten folio pages besides large notes.'

[1] *II* thirty   [2] *In transcribing from his Journal the following extracts,*
G freely altered their text as can be ascertained by comparing it with that of
Journal A.

Buriton. August 4. 1761

(in a week's excursion from Winchester Camp)

'After having long revolved subjects for my intended
'historical Essay, I renounced my first thought of the ex-
'pedition of Charles viii as too remote from us, and rather
'an introduction to great events than great and important in
'itself. I successively chose and rejected the Crusade of
'Richard the first, the Barons Wars against John and
'Henry iii, the history of Edward the black Prince, the lives
'and comparison of Henry V, and the Emperor Titus; the
'life of Sir Philip Sidney, or[1] of the Marquis of Montrose At
'length I have fixed on Sir Walter Raleigh for my | Hero. 53
'His eventful story is varied by the characters of the soldier
'and sailor, the courtier and historian, and it may afford such
'a fund of materials as I desire which have not yet been
'properly manufactured. At present I cannot attempt the
'execution of this work. Free leisure and the opportunity of
'consulting many books both printed and manuscript are as
'necessary as they are impossible to be attained in my present
'way of life. However to acquire a general insight into my
'subject and ressources, I read the life of Sir Walter Raleigh
'by Dr Birch, his copious article in the General Dictionary
'by the same hand, and the reigns of Queen Elizabeth and
'James the first in Hume's History of England.[']

Buriton. January 1762.

(In a month's absence from the Devizes)

'During this interval of repose I again turned my thoughts
'to Sir Walter Raleigh, and looked more closely into my
'materials. I read the two volumes in quarto of the Bacon
'papers published by Dr Birch, the Fragmenta Regalia of
'Sir Robert Naunton, Mallet's life of Lord Bacon and the
'political treatises[2] of that great man in the first Volume of
'his works with many of his letters in the second, Sir William
'Monson's Naval tracts, and the elaborate life of Sir Walter
'Raleigh which Mr Oldys has prefixed to the best edition of

---

[1] *II* and that   [2] *I* works

'his history of the World. My subject opens upon me and in
'general improves on[1] a nearer prospect.[']

Buriton. July 26. 1762
(During my summer residence)

'I am afraid of being reduced to drop my Hero: but my
'[time] has not however been lost in the research of his
'story and of a memorable æra of our English annals. The
'life of Sir Walter Raleigh by Oldys is a very poor per-
'formance; a servile panegyric or flat Apology, tediously
'minute, and composed in a dull and affected style. Yet the
'author was a man of diligence and learning who had read
'every thing relative to his object[2], and whose ample collec-
'tions are arranged with perspicuity and method. Except[3]
'some anecdotes lately revealed in the Sidney and Bacon
'paper[s] I know not what I should be able to add. My
'ambition (exclusive of the uncertain merit of style and
'sentiment) must be confined to the hope of giving a good
'abridgement of Oldys. I have even the disappointment of
53v 'finding | some parts of this copious work very dry and
'barren; and these parts are unluckily some of the most
'characteristic; Raleigh's Colony of Virginia, his quarrels
'with Essex, the true secret of his conspiracy and above all
'the detail of his private life the most essential and important
'to a Biographer. My best ressource would be in the circum-
'jacent history of the times, and perhaps in some digressions
'artfully introduced, like the fortunes of the Peripatetic
'philosophy in the portrait of Lord Bacon. But the reigns of
'Elizabeth and James i are the period[4] of English history
'which has[5] been the most variously illustrated: and what
'new lights could I reflect on a subject which has exercised
'the accurate industry of *Birch*, the lively and curious acute-
'ness of *Walpole*, the critical spirit of *Hurd*, the vigorous
'sense of *Mallet* and *Robertson*, and the impartial philosophy
'of *Hume*. Could I even surmount these obstacles, I should
'shrink with terror from the modern history of England,
'where every character is a problem and every reader a

[1] *II* upon   [2] *II* subject   [3] *II* Excepting   [4] *II* periods   [5] *II* have

'friend or an enemy: where a writer is supposed to hoist a
'flag of party, and is devoted to damnation by the adverse
'faction. Such would be *my* reception at home: and abroad
'the historian of Raleigh must encounter an indifference far
'more bitter than censure or reproach. The events of his life
'are interesting: but his character is ambiguous, his actions
'are obscure, his writings are English, and his fame is[1] con-
'fined to the narrow limits of our language and our island.
'I must embrace a safer and more extensive theme.

'There is one which I should prefer to all others, *The*
'*history of the liberty of the Swiss*, of that independence
'which a brave people rescued from the house of Austria,
'defended against a Dauphin of France, and finally sealed
'with the blood of Charles of Burgundy. From such a theme,
'so full of public spirit, of military glory, of examples of
'virtue, of lessons of government the dullest stranger would
'catch fire: what might not *I* hope, whose talents, whatsoever
'they may be, would be inflamed by[2] the zeal of patriotism.
'But the materials of this history are inaccessible to me, fast
'locked in the obscurity of an old barbarous German dialect
'of which I am totally ignorant, and which I cannot resolve
'to learn for this sole and peculiar purpose.

'I have another subject in view which is the contrast of
'the former history: the one a poor, warlike, virtuous Re-
'public which emerges into | glory and freedom; the other 54
'a Commonwealth, soft, opulent and corrupt, which by just
'degrees is precipitated from the abuse, to the loss, of her
'liberty: both lessons are perhaps equally instructive. This
'second subject is, *The history of the Republic of Florence under*
'*the house of Medicis*: a period of one hundred and fifty years
'which rises or descends from the dregs of the Florentine
'democracy to the title and dominion of Cosmo de Medicis
'in the Grand-Dutchy of Tuscany. I might deduce a chain
'of revolutions not unworthy of the pen of Vertot: singular
'men and singular events; the Medicis four times expelled,
'and as often recalled, and the Genius of freedom reluctantly
'yielding to the arms of Charles V, and the policy of Cosmo.
'The character and fate of Savanarola, and the revival of arts

[1] *I* must be   [2] *II* with

'and letters in Italy will be essentially connected with the
'elevation of the family and the fall of the Republic. The
'Medicis (stirps quasi fataliter nata ad instauranda vel
'fovenda studia. Lipsius ad Germanos et Gallos. Epist. vii)
'were illustrated by the patronage of learning, and en-
'thusiasm was the most formidable weapon of their adver-
'saries—On this splendid subject I shall most probably fix;
'but *when*, or *where* or *how* will it be executed? I behold in
'a dark and doubtful perspective.

'Res altâ terrâ, et caligine mersas.'

Chapter VI[1]

The youthful habits of the language and manners of France had left in my mind an ardent desire of revisiting the continent on a larger and more liberal plan. According to the law of custom and perhaps of reason, foreign travel compleats the education of an[2] English Gentleman: my father had consented to my wish, but I was detained above four years by my rash engagement in the militia. I eagerly grasped the first moments of freedom: three or four weeks in Hampshire and London were employed in the preparations of my journey and the farewell visits of friendship and civility: my last act in town was to applaud Mallet's new tragedy of Elvira; a post-chaise conveyed me to Dover, the packet to Boulogne, and such was my diligence, that I reached Paris on the 28th of January 1763, only thirty six days after the disbanding of the Militia. Two or three years were loosely defined for the term of my absence; and I was left at liberty to spend that time in such places, and in such a manner as was most agreable to my taste and judgement.

In this first visit I passed three months and a half (January 54ᵛ 28–May 9) at Paris[3] and a much longer space might have been agreably filled without any intercourse with the natives. At home we are content to move in the daily round of pleasure and business; and a scene which is always present is supposed to be within our knowledge or at least within our power. But in a foreign country, curiosity is our business and our pleasure; and the traveller conscious of his ignorance and covetous of his time, is diligent in the search and the view of every object that can deserve his attention. I devoted many hours of the morning to the circuit of Paris and the neighbourhood, to the visit of churches, and palaces, con-

---

[1] *Chapter VI gives the end of B (MS ff 54-57 – M 198-210) to my Italian journey (p. 132); followed by the latter part of C, Section ii (MS ff 72-77 – M 265-288). The heading is again the present editor's.*   [2] *I a young*
[3] *II om at Paris*

spicuous by their architecture, to the royal manufactures, collections of books and pictures and all the various treasures of art, of learning, and of luxury. An Englishman may hear without reluctance that in these curious and costly articles Paris is superior to London, since the opulence of the French capital arises from the defects of its government and Religion. In the absence of Louis xiv and his successors, the Louvre has been left unfinished: but the millions which have been lavished on the sands of Versailles and the morass of Marli[1] could not be supplied by the legal allowance of a British King. The splendour of the French nobles is confined to their town-residence: that of the English is more usefully distributed in their country-seats: and we should be astonished at our own riches, if the labours of architecture, the spoils of Italy and Greece which are now scattered from Inverary to Wilton were accumulated in a few streets between Marybone and Westminster. All superfluous ornament is rejected by the cold frugality of the Protestants; but the Catholic superstition which is always the enemy of reason is often the parent of taste[2]: the wealthy communities of priests and monks expend their revenues in stately edifices, and the parish Church of St Sulpice one of the noblest structures in Paris was built and adorned by the private industry of a late Curate[3]. In this outset and still more in the sequel of my tour, my eye was amused; but the pleasing vision cannot be fixed by the pen: the particular images are darkly seen through the medium of five and twenty years, and the narrative of my life must not degenerate into a book of travels.

55   But the principal end of my journey was to enjoy the society of a polished[4] and amiable people in whose favour I was strongly prejudiced; and to converse with some authors, whose conversation as I fondly imagined, must be far more pleasing and instructive than their writings. The moment was happily chosen. At the close of a successful war, the British[5] name was respected on the continent:

   —— Clarum et venerabile nomen
   Gentibus —— ——

[1] *I added* and the morass of Marli *in the margin.*   [2] *II* of the arts
[3] *II* curé   [4] *I* an highly-polished   [5] *I* English

our opinions, our fashions, even our games were adopted in France: a ray of national glory illuminated each individual, and every Englishman was supposed to be born a patriot and a philosopher. For myself I carried a personal recommendation: my name and my Essay were already known; the compliment of writing[1] in the French language entitled me to some returns of civility and gratitude. I was considered as a man of letters, or rather as a gentleman[2] who wrote for his[3] amusement:[4] my appearance, dress and equipage distinguished me from the tribe of authors who even at Paris, are secretly envied and despised by those who possess the advantages of birth [and] fortune. Before my departure I had obtained from the Duke de Nivernois, Lady Hervey, the Mallets, Mr Walpole &c many letters of recommendation to their private or litterary friends. Of these epistles the reception and success was[5] determined by the character and situation of the persons by whom and to whom they were addressed: the seed was sometimes cast on a barren rock, and it sometimes multiplied an hundred fold in the production of new shoots, spreading branches and exquisite fruit. But upon the whole I had reason to praise the national urbanity which from the court has diffused its gentle influence to the shop, the cottage and the schools. Of the men of Genius of the age, Montesquieu and Fontenelle were no more; Voltaire resided on his own estate near Geneva; Rousseau in the preceding year had been driven from his hermitage of Montmorency, and I blush at my neglecting[6] to seek, in this journey the acquaintance of Buffon. Among the men of letters whom I saw, d'Alembert and Diderot held the foremost rank, in merit, or, at least, in fame:[7] these two associates were the elements of water and fire; but the eruption was clouded with smoke and the stream though devoid of grace was limpid and copious. I shall content myself with enumerating the well-known names of the | Count 55ᵛ de Caylus, of the Abbés[8] de la Bleterie, Barthelemy, Raynal,

---

[1] *II* having written   [2] *II om* or rather as a gentleman   [3] *II om* his
[4] *II om three lines from here to* fortune.   [5] *II* were   [6] *II* having neglected   [7] *II om three lines from here to* copious.   [8] *II* Abbé

Arnaud, of Messieurs de la Condamine, Duclos[1][,] de Ste Palaye, de Bougainville, Caperonnier, de Guignes, Suard, &c without attempting to discriminate the shades of their characters, or the degrees of our connection. Alone in a morning visit I commonly found the wits[2] and authors of Paris less vain and more reasonable than in the circles of their equals, with whom they mingle in the houses of the rich. Four days in the[3] week I had a place without invitation at the hospitable tables of Mesdames Geoffrin and du Bocage, of the celebrated Helvetius, and of the Baron d'Olbach: In these *Symposia* the pleasures of the table were improved by lively and liberal conversation; the company was select, though various and voluntary, [4] and each unbidden guest might mutter [5] a proud[6], and[7] ungrateful sentence

Αυτοματοι δ'αγαθοι δειλων επι δαιτας ιασιν

Yet I was often disgusted with the capricious tyranny of Madame Geoffrin, nor could I approve the intolerant zeal of the philosophers and Encyclopædists the friends of d'Olbach and Helvetius: they laughed at the scepticism of Hume, preached the tenets of Atheism with the bigotry of dogmatists, and damned all believers with ridicule and contempt. The society of Madame du Bocage was more soft and moderate than that of her rivals; and the evening conversations of Mr de Foncemagne were supported by the good sense and learning of the principal members of the Academy of inscriptions. The Opera and the Italians I occasionally visited: but the French theatre both in tragedy and comedy was my daily and favourite amusement. Two famous actresses then divided the public applause: for my own part I preferred the consummate art of the Clairon, to the intemperate sallies of the Dumesnil which were extolled by her admirers as the genuine voice of nature and passion. [8] I have reserved for the last the most pleasing connection which I formed at Paris, the acquisition of a female friend

---

[1] *II* du Clos   [2] *II* artists   [3] *II* a   [4] *II om nine lines from here down to* ridicule and contempt.   [5] *I* had he understood Greek   [6] *I added* a proud *in the margin.*   [7] *I* an   [8] *II om twenty-two lines from here down to* her frailties

by whom I was sure of being received every evening with
the smile of confidence and joy. I delivered a letter from
Mrs Mallet to Madame Bontems who had distinguished
herself by a translation of Thomson's Seasons into | French 56
prose: at our first interview we felt a sympathy which
banished all reserve, and opened our bosoms to each other.
In every light, in every attitude, Madame B was a sensible
and amiable Companion; an author careless of litterary
honours, a devotee untainted with Religious gall. She managed a small income with elegant œconomy: her apartment
on the Quai des Theatins commanded the river, the bridges,
and the Louvre; her familiar suppers were adorned with
freedom and taste; and I attended her in my carriage to the
houses of her acquaintance, to the sermons of the most popular preachers, and in [1] pleasant excursions to St Denys, S^t
Germain, and Versailles. In the middle season of life, her
beauty was still an object of desire: the Marquis de Mirabeau,
a celebrated name, was neither her first nor her last lover; but
if her heart was tender, if her passions were warm, a veil of
decency was cast over her frailties—Fourteen weeks insensibly stole away: but had I been rich and independent I should
have prolonged and perhaps have fixed my residence at Paris.

Between the expensive style of Paris and of Italy, it was
prudent to interpose some months of tranquil simplicity;
and at the thoughts of Lausanne, I again lived in the pleasures
and studies of my early youth. Shaping my course through
Dijon and Besançon in the last of which places I was kindly
entertained by my cousin Acton, I arrived in the month of
May 1763 on the banks of the Leman lake. It had been my
intention to pass the Alps in the autumn: but such are the
simple attractions of the place that the annual circle was
almost revolved[2] before my departure from Lausanne in the
ensuing spring. An absence of five years had not made much
alteration in manners or even in persons: my old friends of
both sexes hailed my voluntary return, the most genuine
proof of my attachment: they had been flattered by the
present of my book, the produce of their soil, and the good

---

[1] *I* some   [2] *II* that the year had almost expired

Pavilliard shed tears of joy as he embraced a pupil [1] with whose success his vanity as well as friendship might be delighted. To my old list I added some new acquaintance, [2] who in my former residence had not been on the spot, or in my way, and among the strangers I shall distinguish Prince Lewis of Wirtemberg the brother of the reigning Duke at whose country-house near Lausanne I frequently dined. A wandering meteor and at length a falling star, his light and

56v ambitious | spirit had successively dropt from the firmament[3] of Prussia of France and of Austria; and his faults which he styled his misfortunes had driven him into philosophic exile in the Pays de Vaud. He could now moralize on the vanity of the World, the equality of mankind and the happiness of a private station: his address was affable and polite, and as he had shone in courts and armies, his memory could supply, and his eloquence could adorn a copious fund of interesting anecdotes. His first enthusiasm was that of charity and agriculture, but the Sage gradually lapsed in the Saint, and Prince Lewis of Wirtemberg is now buried in an hermitage near Mayence in the last stage of mystic devotion. By some Ecclesiastical quarrel Voltaire had been provoked to withdraw himself from Lausanne[4]: but the theatre which he had founded, the Actors whom he had formed survived the loss of their master; and recent from Paris I assisted[5] with pleasure at the representation of several tragedies and comedies. I shall not descend to specify particular names and characters; but I cannot forget a private institution which will display the innocent freedom of Swiss manners. My favourite society, had assumed from the age of its members the proud denomination of the spring (*la societé du printemps*). It consisted of fifteen or twenty young unmarried Ladies[6] of genteel, though not of the very first, families; the eldest perhaps about twenty, all agreable,

---

[1] *For the end of this sentence II substituted a line taken from C (MS f 72 – M 264):* whose litterary merit he might fairly impute to his own labours.
[2] *II om this line to* in my way   [3] *I* horizon   [4] *II added here a passage taken from C (MS f 72ᵛ – M 265):* and retire to his castle at Ferney, where I again visited the poet and the actor, without seeking his more intimate acquaintance, to which I might now have pleaded a better title.   [5] *II* attended   [6] *I* twenty girls

several handsome and two or three of exquisite beauty. At each others houses they assembled almost every day: without the controul or even the presence of a mother or an aunt, they were trusted to their own prudence among a crowd of young men of every nation in Europe. They laughed, they sung, they danced, they played at cards, they acted comedies; but in the midst of this careless gayety, they respected themselves, and were respected by the men: the invisible line between liberty and licentiousness was never transgressed by a gesture, a word or a look, and their virgin-chastity was never sullied by the breath of scandal or suspicion[1]. After tasting[2] the luxury of England and Paris[3], I could not have returned with patience[4] to the [5] table and table-cloth[6] of Madame Pavilliard, nor was her husband offended that I now entered myself as a *pensionaire* or boarder in the more[7] elegant house of Mr de Mesery, which may be entitled to a short remembrance, as it has stood | above twenty years, 57 perhaps, without a paralel in Europe. The house in which we lodged was spacious and convenient in the best street, and commanding from behind a noble prospect over the country and the lake. Our table was served with neatness and plenty: the boarders were[8] numerous[9]; we had the liberty of inviting any guests at a stated price; and in the summer the scene was occasionally transferred to a pleasant Villa about a league from Lausanne. The characters of the[10] master and mistress were happily suited to each other and to their situation. At the age of seventy five Madame de Mesery who has survived her husband is still a graceful, I had almost said a handsome woman: she was alike qualified to preside in her kitchen and her drawing room, and such was the equal propriety of her conduct that of two or three hundred foreigners, none ever failed in respect, none could complain of her neglect and none could ever boast of her favour. Mesery himself of the noble family of de Crousaz, was a

---

[1] *II added here a few words taken from C (MS f 72° – M 265):* a singular institution, expressive of the innocent simplicity of Swiss manners!   [2] *II having tasted*   [3] *I* the habits of luxury in England and at Paris   [4] *II satisfaction*   [5] *II added* coarse and homely   [6] *II om* and table-cloth   [7] *II om* more   [8] *I* ordinary company was   [9] *II* select   [10] *II om* the

of the pencil. I have received, for the last a colour which
borders on a vice; the flexible temper which can assimilate
itself to every tone of society from the court to the cottage; the
happy flow of spirits which can amuse and be amused in
every company and situation. With the ready use of national
and provincial idiom, the traveller should unite the pleasing
aspect and decent familiarity which makes every stranger an
acquaintance; and the art of conversing with ignorance and
dullness on some topic of local or professional information.
The benefits of foreign travel will correspond with the
degrees of their various qualifications: but in this sketch
of ideal perfection those to whom I am known will not accuse
me of framing my own panegyric.— Yet the historian of the
decline and fall must not forget his time or expence, since
it was the view of Italy and Rome which determined the
choice of the subject. In my Journal the place and moment of
conception are recorded; the fifteenth of October 1764, at first in the
close of evening, as I sat musing in the Church of the Zocco-
:lante or Franciscan fryars, while they were singing Vespers
in the Temple of Jupiter on the ruins of the Capitol. But my
original plan was circumscribed to the decay of the City
rather than of the Empire: and, though my reading and
reflections began to point towards that object some years
elapsed, and several avocations intervened before I was
seriously engaged in the execution of that laborious work.
                    I had not totally renounced
the southern provinces of France: but the letters which
I found at Lyons were expressive of some impatience,
the measure of absence and expence was filled; Rome and
Italy had satiated my curious appetite, and the excessive
heat of the weather decided the sage resolution of tur-
:ning my face to the north and ... the peaceful retreat
of my family and books. After an happy fortnight, I
tore myself from the embraces of Paris, embarked at
Calais, again landed at Dover, after an interval of two
years and five months and hastily drove through the
summer dust and solitude of London. On the 25th of June
1769 1765, I reached the general mansion of my parents to
whom I was endeared by my long absence and too cheerful submission

*advantage of an inde
:pendent fortune and
the

*I was now ready to
seek / return.*

Plate IV. Lower part of a page of C, numbered 30 by G
MS f 73ᵛ
showing Lord Sheffield's pencil corrections

man of the World, a jovial companion, whose easy manners and natural sallies maintained the chearfulness of his house. His wit could laugh at his own ignorance: he disguised by an air of profusion a strict attention to his interest; and in the exercise of a mean trade[1], he appeared like a nobleman who spent his fortune, and entertained his friends. In this agreable family[2] I resided near eleven months (May 1763–April 1764); [3]but the habits of the militia and the example of my countrymen betrayed me into some riotous acts of intemperance; and before my departure, I had deservedly forfeited the public opinion which had been acquired by the virtues of my better days. Yet in this second visit to Lausanne, among a crowd of my English companions, I knew and esteemed Mr Holroyd [4]late Captain in the Royal Forresters and our mutual attachment was renewed and fortified in the subsequent stages of our Italian journey. Our lives are in the power of chance, and a slight variation, on either side, in time or place might have deprived me of a friend, whose activity in the ardour of youth was always prompted by a benevolent heart, and directed by a strong understanding.

If my studies at Paris had been confined to the study of the World three or four months would not have been unprofitably[5] spent. My visits, however superficial to the cabinet of medals and the public libraries opened a new field of enquiry, and the view of so many Manuscripts of different ages and characters induced me to consult the two great 57v Benedictine | Works, the *Diplomatica* of Mabillon, and the *Palæographica* of Montfaucon. I studied the theory, without attaining the practise of the art: nor should I complain of the intricacy of Greek abbreviations and Gothic alphabets since every day, in a familiar language, I am at a loss to decypher the Hieroglyphics of a female note. In a tranquil scene which revived the memory of my first studies idleness would have been less pardonable: the public libraries of Lausanne and Geneva liberally supplied me with books, and if many hours were lost in dissipation many more were

---

[1] *II* and in this situation   [2] *II* society   [3] *II om four lines from here to* better days.   [4] *For* late Captain . . . Forresters *II substituted* (now Lord Sheffield);   [5] *I* fruitlessly

employed in litterary labour. In the country, Horace and
Virgil, Juvenal and Ovid were my assiduous companions:
but in town I formed and executed a plan of study for the use
of my Transalpine expedition: the topography of old Rome,
the ancient Geography of Italy and the science of Medals.
1. I diligently read almost always with my[1] pen in my hand
the elaborate treatises of Nardini, Donatus &c which fill the
fourth Volume of the Roman Antiquities of Grævius. 2. I
next undertook and finished the *Italia Antiqua* of Cluverius,
a learned native of Prussia who had measured on foot every
spot, and has compiled and digested every passage of the
ancient writers. These passages in Greek or Latin [2] I perused
in the text of Cluverius in two folio Volumes: but I separately
read the descriptions of Italy by Strabo, Pliny and Pom-
ponius Mela, the Catalogues of the Epic poets, the Itineraries
of Wesseling's Antoninus, and the coasting Voyage of
Rutilius Numatianus; and I studied two kindred subjects in
the Mesures Itineraires of d'Anville and the copious work
of Bergier, *Histoire des grands Chemins de l'Empire Romain*.
From these materials I formed a table of roads and distances
reduced to our English measure; filled a folio common-place
book with my collections and remarks on the Geography of
Italy, and inserted in my journal many long and learned
notes on the *Insulae* and populousness of Rome, the Social
War, the passage of the Alps by Hannibal &c. 3. After
glancing my eye over Addison's agreable Dialogues, I more
seriously read the great work of Ezechiel Spanheim de
præstantia et usû Numismatum, and applied with him the
medals of the Kings and Emperors, the families and colonies
to the illustration of ancient history—And thus was I armed
for my Italian journey. | [3] Perhaps I might boast that few 72ᵛ
travellers more compleatly armed and instructed have ever
followed[4] the footsteps of Hannibal. As soon as the return
of Spring had unlocked the mountains, I departed from
Lausanne (April 18.1764) with an English companion (Mr,
afterwards Sir William, Guise) whose partnership divided
and alleviated the expences of the Journey.

---

[1] *II* a   [2] *II added* authors   [3] *From here the text is that of C. II did not
make use of these first two sentences.*   [4] *I trod in*

I shall advance with rapid brevity in the narrative of my Italian tour[1], in which somewhat more than a year (April 1764–May 1765) was agreably employed. Content with tracing my line of march and slightly touching on my personal feelings I shall wave the minute investigation of the scenes [2] which have been viewed by thousands and described by hundreds of our modern travellers. ROME is the great object of our pilgrimage and I The Journey. ii. The residence, and iii The return will form the most proper and perspicuous division. I. I climbed Mount Cenis and descended into the plain of Piedmont, not on the back of an Elephant; but on a light osier seat in the hands of the dextrous and intrepid chairmen of the Alps. The architecture and government of Turin presented the same aspect of tame and tiresome uniformity: but the Court was regulated with decent and splendid œconomy; and I was introduced to his Sardinian Majesty, Charles Emanuel, who after the incomparable Frederic, held the second rank (proximus, longo tamen intervallo) among the Kings of Europe. The size and populousness of Milan could not surprize an inhabitant of London: the Dome or Cathedral is an unfinished monument of Gothic superstition and wealth: but the fancy is amused by a visit to the Boromean islands, an enchanted palace a work of the fairies in the midst of a lake encompassed with 73 mountains and far removed from the haunts of men. | I was less amused by the marble palaces of Genoa, than by the recent memorials of her deliverance (in December 1746) from the Austrian tyranny: and I took a military survey of every scene of action within the inclosure of her double walls. My steps were detained at Parma and Modena by the precious relicks of the Farnese and Este collections: but, alas! the far greater part had been already transported by inheritance or purchase to Naples and Dresden. By the road of Bologna and the Apenine I at last reached Florence, where I reposed from June to September during the heat of the summer months. In the gallery, and especially in the *Tribune*, I first acknowledged, at the feet of the Venus of Medicis, that the chissel may dispute the pre-eminence with the pencil,

---

[1] *II* narrative of this tour   [2] *I* and objects

a truth in the fine arts, which cannot, on this side of the Alps be felt or understood. At home I had taken some lessons of Italian: on the spot I read with a learned native the Classics of the Tuscan idiom: but the shortness of my time, and the use of the French language prevented my acquiring any facility of speaking: and I was a silent spectator in the conversations of our envoy Sir Horace Mann whose most serious business was that of entertaining the English at his hospitable table. After leaving Florence I compared the solitude of Pisa with the industry of Lucca and Leghorn, and continued my journey through Sienna to Rome, where I arrived in the beginning of October. ii. My temper is not very susceptible of enthusiasm, and the enthusiasm which I do not feel I have ever scorned to affect. But at the distance of twenty five years I can neither forget nor express the strong emotions which agitated my mind as I first approached and entered the *eternal City*. After a sleepless night I trod with a lofty step the ruins of the Forum; each memorable spot where Romulus *stood*, or Tully spoke, or Caesar fell was at once present to my eye[1]; and several days of intoxication were lost or enjoyed before I could descend to a cool and minute investigation. My guide was Mr Byers a Scotch antiquary of experience and taste; but in the daily labour of eighteen weeks the powers of attention were sometimes fatigued, till I was myself qualified in a last review to select and study the capital works of ancient and modern art. Six weeks were borrowed for my tour of Naples, the most populous of cities relative to its size, whose luxurious inhabitants seem to dwell on the confines of paradise and hell-fire. I was presented to the boy-King by our new Envoy Sir William Hamilton who, wisely diverting his correspondence from the Secretary of State to the Royal society, and British Museum has elucidated a country of such inestimable value to the Naturalist and Antiquarian. On my return, I fondly embraced for the last time the miracles of Rome; but I departed without kissing the feet[2] of Rezzonico (Clement xiii[)], who neither possessed the wit of his predecessor Lambertini, nor the virtue[3] of his successor Ganganelli.

[1] *I* and fancy   [2] *III* foot   [3] *II* virtues

iii. In my pilgrimage from Rome to Loretto, I again crossed the Apennine; from the coast of the Adriatic I traversed a fruitful and populous country which would[1] alone disprove the paradox of Montesquieu that modern Italy is a desert[2]. Without adopting the exclusive prejudice of the natives I sincerely admired[3] the paintings of the Bologna school. I hastened to escape from the sad solitude of Ferrara, which in the age of Cæsar was still more desolate The spectacle of Venice afforded some hours of astonishment and some days of disgust[4]: the university of Padua is a dying taper: but Verona still boasts her amphitheatre, and his native Vicenza is adorned by the classic architecture of Palladio. The road of Lombardy and Piedmont (did Montesquieu find them without inhabitants?) led me back to Milan, Turin, and the passage of Mount Cenis, where I again crossed the Alps in my way to Lyons.

The use of foreign travel has been often debated as a general question; but the conclusion must be finally applied 73ᵛ to the character and circumstances | of each individual. With the education of boys, *where*, or *how* they may pass over some juvenile years with the least mischief to themselves or others, I have no concern. But after supposing the prævious and indispensable requisites of age, judgement, a competent knowledge of men and books, and a freedom from domestic prejudices, I will briefly describe the qualifications which I deem most essential to a traveller. He should be endowed with an active indefatigable vigour of mind and body, which can seize every mode of conveyance, and support with a careless smile every hardship of the road, the weather or the Inn. [5] I must stimulate him with a restless curiosity, impatient of ease, covetous of time and fearless of danger; which drives him forth at any hour of the day or night, to brave the flood, to climb the mountain, or to fathom the mine on the most doubtful promise of entertainment or instruction The arts of common life are not studied in the closet; with

---

[1] *II* could   [2] *I added* that modern Italy is a desert *in the margin.*   [3] *II* admire   [4] *II om* and some days of disgust   [5] *II om twenty-five lines from here down to* professional information – *M tacitly corrected* I must stimulate *into* It must stimulate. *Is this correction necessary?*

a copious stock of classical and historical learning, my traveller must blend the practical knowledge of husbandry and manufactures; he should be a Chymist, a botanist, and a master of mechanics. A musical ear will multiply the pleasures of his Italian tour: but a correct and exquisite eye, which commands the landskip of a country, discerns the merits of a picture, and measures the proportions of a building is more closely connected with the finer feelings of the mind[1], and the fleeting image should[2] be fixed and realized by the dexterity of the pencil. I have reserved for the last a virtue which borders on a vice; the flexible temper which can assimilate itself to every tone of society from the court to the cottage; the happy flow of spirits which can amuse and be amused in every company and situation. With the advantage of an independent fortune and the ready[3] use of national and provincial idioms, the traveller should unite the pleasing aspect and decent familiarity, which makes every stranger an acquaintance; and the art of conversing with ignorance and dullness on some topic of local or professional information. The benefits of foreign travel will correspond with the degrees of these various[4] qualifications: but in this sketch of ideal perfection[5] those to whom I am known will not accuse me of framing my own panegyric[6].—[7] Yet the historian of the decline and fall must not regret his time or expence, since it was the view of Italy and Rome which determined the choice of the subject. In my Journal the place and moment of conception are recorded; the fifteenth of October 1764, in the close of evening, as I sat musing in the Church of the Zoccolanti or Franciscan fryars, while they were singing Vespers in the Temple of Jupiter on the ruins of the Capitol. But my original plan was circumscribed to the decay of the City, rather than of the Empire: and, though my reading and reflections began to point towards the[8] object, some years

---

[1] *I* imagination　　　[2] *M* shall　　　[3] *I added* advantage . . . ready *in the margin*
[4] *II om* various　　　[5] *II om* of ideal perfection　　　[6] panygeric *in MS*　　　[7] *For this C account of G's first conception of his History, II substituted the corresponding E passage (MS f 88 – M 302)*: It was at Rome on the fifteenth of October 1764, as I sat musing amidst the ruins of the Capitol while the barefooted fryars were singing Vespers in the temple of Jupiter, that the idea of writing the decline and fall of the City first started to my mind.　　　[8] *II* that

elapsed, and several avocations intervened before I was
seriously engaged in the execution of that laborious work.

I had not totally renounced the southern provinces of
France: but the letters which I found at Lyons were expressive of some impatience, [1]the measure of absence and
expence was filled; Rome and Italy had satiated my curious
appetite, [2]and the excessive heat of the weather decided the
sage resolution of turning my face to the north, and seeking
the peaceful retreat of my family and books. After an happy
fortnight, I tore myself from the embraces of Paris[3], embarked at Calais, again landed at Dover, after an interval of
two years and five months, and hastily drove through the summer dust and solitude of London. On the 25th of June 1765 I
[4]reached the rural mansion of my parents to whom I was
endeared by my long absence and chearful submission.

74   [5]After my first (1758) and my second return to England
(1765) the forms of the pictures were nearly the same: but
the colours had been darkened by time; and the five years
and a half between my travels and my father's death (1770)
are the portion of my life which I passed with the least
enjoyment, and which I remember with the least satisfaction.
[6]I have nothing to change (for there was not any change) in
the annual distribution of my summers and winters, between
my domestic residence in Hampshire, and a casual lodging
at the west end of the town; though, once, from the tryal of
some months I was tempted to substitute the tranquil dissipation of Bath instead of the smoke, the expence and the
tumult of the Metropolis, fumum, et opes, strepitumque
Romæ. Every spring I attended the monthly meeting and
exercise of the militia at Southampton; and by the resignation of my father and the death of Sir Thomas Worsley I
was successively promoted to the rank of Major, and
Lieutenant Colonel-Commandant. [7]Under the care (may I

---

[1] *II om eight words from here to* filled   [2] *II om two lines from here to*
seeking, *replacing them by* and I was now ready to return to   [3] *For* tore
. . . embraces of *II substituted* reluctantly left   [4] *II replaced these last
two lines of the paragraph by* arrived at my father's house.   [5] *II om the
first three lines of this paragraph to* by time *and joined the end of the sentence
immediately to the previous paragraph.*   [6] *II om seven lines from here to*
Romæ.   [7] *II om four lines from here to* subordination:

presume to say?) of a veteran officer, the south Battalion of the Hampshire militia acquired the degree of skill and discipline which was compatible with the brevity of time and the looseness of peaceful subordination: but I was each year more disgusted with the Inn, the wine, the company, and the tiresome repetition of annual attendance and daily exercise. At home, the œconomy of the family and farm still maintained the same creditable appearance. [1] I was received, entertained and dismissed with similar kindness and indulgence: my connection with Mrs Gibbon was mellowed into a warm and solid attachment: my growing years abolished the distance that might yet remain between a parent and a son, and my behaviour satisfied[2] my father, who was proud of the success, however imperfect in his own lifetime, of my litterary talents. Our solitude was soon, and often, enlivened by the visit of the friend of my youth, Mr Deyverdun, whose absence from Lausanne I had sincerely lamented. About three years after my first departure he had migrated[3] from his native lake to the banks of the Oder in Germany. The res angusta domi, the waste of a decent patrimony by an improvident father, obliged him, like many of his countrymen to confide in his own industry: and he was entrusted with the education of a young prince, the grandson of the Margrave of Schwedt[4] of the Royal family of Prussia. Our friendship was never cooled: our correspondence was sometimes interrupted: but I rather wished than hoped to obtain Mr Deyverdun for the companion of my Italian tour. An unhappy though honourable passion drove him from his German court: and the attractions of hope and curiosity were fortified by the expectation of my speedy return to England: [5] I was allowed to offer him the hospitality of the house: during four successive summers he passed several weeks or months at Buriton, and our free conversations on every topic that could interest the heart or understanding would have reconciled me to a desert or a prison. In the winter months of London my sphere of knowledge and action was somewhat enlarged by the many new acquaintance which I had con-

---

[1] *II om this sentence to* indulgence: [2] *I* was satisfactory to   [3] *II* emigrated   [4] *II* Schavedt   [5] *II om this line.*

tracted in the Militia and abroad: and I must regret as more than an acquaintance Mr Godfrey Clarke of Derbyshire an amiable and worthy young man who was snatched away by an untimely death. A weekly convivial meeting was instituted[1] by myself and my fellow[2] travellers under the name of the Roman club; [3]and I was soon ballotted into Boodle's (the school of virtue, as the Earl of Shelburne had first named it) where I found the daily ressource of excellent dinners, 74.v mixed | [4] company and moderate play. I must own, however, with a blush, that my virtues of temperance and sobriety had not compleatly recovered themselves from the wounds of the militia, that my connections were much less among women, than men; and that these men, though far from contemptible in rank and fortune, were not of the first eminence in the litterary or political World.

The renewal, or perhaps the improvement, of my English life was embittered by the alteration of my own feelings. At the age of twenty one, I was in my proper station of a youth, delivered from the yoke of education, and delighted with the comparative state of liberty and affluence: my filial obedience was natural and easy; and in the gay prospect of futurity, my ambition did not extend beyond the enjoyment of my books, my leisure[5], and my patrimonial estate[6], undisturbed[7] by the cares of a family and the duties of a profession. But in the militia I was armed with power, in my travels I was exempt from controul; and as I approached, as I gradually transcended[8] my thirtieth year, I began to feel the desire of being master in my own house. The most gentle authority will sometimes frown without reason, the most chearful submission will sometimes murmur without cause; and such is the law of our imperfect nature, that we must either command or obey, that our personal liberty is supported by the obsequiousness[9] of our own dependents. While so many of my acquaintance were married, or in parliament, or advanc-

---

[1] *II* established   [2] *II* and other   [3] *From here, II om the end of the paragraph.*   [4] *I* mixed   [5] *I* enjoyment of myself, my books and my leisure
[6] *I added* and my patrimonial estate *in the margin.*   [7] undisburbed *in MS*
[8] *II* passed   [9] *I* our personal independence requires the service and complyance

ing with a rapid step in the various roads of honours[1] and fortune, I stood, alone, immoveable and insignificant; for after the monthly meeting of 1770 I had even withdrawn myself from the militia by the resignation of an empty and barren commission. My temper is not susceptible of envy, and the view of successful merit has always excited my warmest applause. [2]A matrimonial alliance[3] has ever been the object of my terror rather than of my wishes. I was not very strongly pressed by my family or my passions to propagate the name and race of the Gibbons, and if some reasonable temptations occurred in the neighbourhood, the vague idea never proceeded to the length of a serious negociation. The miseries of a vacant life were never known to a man, whose hours were insufficient for the inexhaustible pleasures of study. But I lamented, that at the proper age, I had not embraced the lucrative pursuits of the law or of trade, the chances of civil office or India adventure, or even the fat slumbers of the Church; and my repentance became more lively as the loss of time was more irretrievable. Experience shewed me the use of grafting my private consequence on the importance of a great professional body; the benefits of those firm connections, which are cemented by hope and interest, by gratitude and emulation, by the mutual exchange of services and favours. From the emoluments of a profession I might have derived an ample fortune or a competent income; instead of being stinted to the same narrow allowance to be encreased only by an event which I sincerely deprecated. The progress and the knowledge of our domestic disorders aggravated my anxiety, and I began to apprehend that I might be left in my old age without the fruits either of industry or inheritance.

In the first summer after my return, whilst I enjoyed at Buriton, the society of my friend Deyverdun, our daily conversations expatiated over the field of ancient and modern litterature, and we freely discussed my studies, my first Essay, and my future projects. The decline and fall of Rome, I still contemplated at | an awful distance: but the two 75 historical designs which had balanced my choice were sub-

---

[1] *II* honour   [2] *II om six lines from here to* negotiation.   [3] *I* connection

mitted to his taste; and in the paralel between the revolutions of Florence and Switzerland our common partiality for a country, which was *his* by birth and *mine* by adoption, inclined the scale in favour of the latter. According to the plan, which was soon conceived and digested, I embraced a period of two hundred years from the association of the three peasants of the Alps to the plenitude and prosperity[1] of the Helvetic body in the sixteenth Century. I should have described the deliverance and victory of the Swiss who have never shed the blood of their tyrants, but in a field of battle; the laws and manners of the confederate states; the splendid trophies of the Austrian, Burgundian, and Italian wars; and the wisdom of a nation, who[2] after some sallies of martial adventure has been content to guard the blessings of peace with the sword of freedom

> ———Manus hæc inimica tyrannis
> Ense petit placidam sub libertate quietem.

My judgement as well as my enthusiasm was satisfied with the glorious theme; and the assistance of Deyverdun seemed to remove an insuperable obstacle. The French or Latin memorials, of which I was not ignorant, are inconsiderable in number and weight; but in the perfect acquaintance of my friend with the German language, I found the key of a more valuable collection. The most necessary books were procured: he translated for my use the[3] folio Volume of Schilling, a copious and contemporary relation of the war of Burgundy; we read and marked the most interesting parts of the great chronicle of Tschudi; and by his labour or that of an inferior assistant, large extracts were made from the history of Lauffer, and the Dictionary of Leu[4]. Yet such was the distance and delay that two years elapsed in these preparatory steps; and it was late in the third summer (1767) before I entered with these slender materials on the more agreable task of composition. A specimen of my history, the first book, was read the following winter in a litterary society of foreigners in London: and as the author was unknown, I listened without observation, to the free strictures and unfavourable

---

[1] *I* peace   [2] *II which*   [3] *I* a   [4] *II* Lew

sentence of my judges. The momentary sensation was painful; but their condemnation was ratified by my cooler thoughts; I delivered my imperfect sheets to the flames; and for ever renounced a design in which some expence, much labour, and more time had been so vainly consumed. I cannot [1] regret the loss of a slight and superficial Essay: for such the work must have been in the hands of a stranger, uninformed by the scholars and statesmen, [2] remote from the libraries and archives, of the Swiss Republics. My ancient habits, and the presence of Deyverdun encouraged me to write in French, for the Continent of Europe: but I was conscious myself, that my style, above prose and below poetry, degenerated into a verbose and turgid declamation. Perhaps I may impute the failure to the injudicious choice of a foreign language. Perhaps I may suspect that the language itself is ill adapted to sustain the vigour and dignity of an important narrative. But if France, so rich in litterary merit, had produced a great original historian, his Genius would have formed and fixed the idiom to the proper tone, the peculiar mode of historical eloquence.

It was in search of some liberal and lucrative employment that my friend Deyverdun had visited England: his remittances from home were scanty and precarious: my purse was always open but it was often empty, and I bitterly felt the want of riches | and power, which might have enabled me to 75ᵛ correct the errors of his fortune. His wishes and qualifications solicited the station of the travelling governor of some wealthy pupill: but every vacancy provoked so many eager candidates, that for a long time I struggled without success; nor was it till after much application that I could even place him as a clerk in the office of the Secretary of state. In a residence of several years, he never acquired the just pronunciation and familiar use of the English tongue: but he read our most difficult authors with ease and taste: his critical knowledge of our language and poetry [3] was such as few foreigners have possessed; and few of our countrymen could enjoy the Theatre of Shakespeare and Garrick with more exquisite feeling, and discernment. The consciousness of his

[1] *I* much   [2] *II added* and   [3] *I* litterature

own strength, and the assurance of my aid emboldened him to imitate the example of Dr Maty, whose *Journal Britannique* was esteemed and regretted; and to improve his model by uniting with the transactions of litterature, a philosophic view of the arts and manners of the British nation. Our Journal for the year 1767, under the title of *Memoires Litteraires de la Grande Bretagne,* was soon finished and sent to the press. For the first article, Lord Lyttleton's[1] history of Henry ii, I must own myself responsible: but the public has ratified my judgement of that voluminous work, in which sense and learning are not illuminated by a ray of Genius. The next specimen was the choice of my friend, *the Bath Guide,* a light and whimsical performance of local and even verbal pleasantry. I started at the attempt: he smiled at my fears: his courage was justified by success; and a master of both languages will applaud the curious felicity with which he has transfused into French prose the spirit, and even [2] humour, of the English verse. It is not my wish to deny, how deeply I was interested in these Memoirs; of which I need not surely be ashamed; but at the distance of more than twenty years, it would be impossible for me to ascertain the respective shares of the two associates. A long and intimate communication of ideas had cast our sentiments and style in the same mould: in our social labours we composed and corrected by turns; and the praise which I might honestly bestow, would fall perhaps on some article or passage most properly my own. A second Volume, (for the year 1768) was published of these Memoirs: I will presume to say that their merit was superior to their reputation: but it is not less true that they were productive of more reputation than emolument. They introduced my friend to the protection, and myself to the acquaintance, of the Earl of Chesterfield whose age and infirmities secluded him from the World; and of Mr David Hume who was under-Secretary to the office in which Deyverdun was more humbly employed. The former accepted a dedication (April 12. 1769) and reserved the author for the future education of his successor: the latter enriched the Journal with a reply to Mr

[1] *II* Lyttelton's   [2] *II added* the

Walpole's historical doubts, which he afterwards shaped into the form of a note. The materials of the third Volume were almost compleated, when I recommended Deyverdun as Governor to Sir Richard Worsley a youth, the son of my old Lieutenant Colonel, who was lately deceased. They set forwards on their travels: nor did they return to England, till some time after my father's death.

My next publication was an accidental sally of love and resentment; of my reverence for modest Genius, and my aversion for insolent pedantry. The sixth book of the Aeneid is the most pleasing and perfect composition of | Latin poetry. 76 The descent of Æneas and the Sybill to the infernal regions, to the world of spirits, expands an awful and boundless prospect, from the nocturnal gloom of the Cumæan grot

> Ibant obscuri sola sub nocte per umbram,

to the meridian brightness of the Elysian fields

> Largior hic campos æther et lumine vestit
> Purpureo —— —— —— ——

from the dreams of simple nature to the dreams, alas! of Ægyptian Theology and the Philosophy of the Greeks. But the final dismission of the Hero through the Ivory gate from[1] whence

> Falsa ad coelum mittunt insomnia manes

seems to dissolve the whole enchantment, and leaves the reader in a state of cold and anxious scepticism. This most lame and impotent conclusion has been variously imputed to the haste[2] or irreligion of Virgil: but according to the more elaborate interpretation of Bishop Warburton, the descent to Hell is not a false, but a mimic, scene; which represents the initiation of Æneas, in the character of a Law-giver, to the Eleusinian mysteries. This hypothesis, a singular chapter in the Divine legation of Moses, had been admitted by many as true, it was praised by all as ingenious; nor had it been exposed in a space of thirty years to a fair and critical discussion. The learning and[3] abilities of the author had raised him to a just eminence; but he reigned the Dictator

---

[1] *II om* from   [2] *II* taste   [3] *II added* the

and tyrant of the World of Litterature. The real merit of Warburton was degraded by the pride and presumption with which he pronounced his infallible decrees; in his polemic writings he lashed his antagonists without mercy or moderation; and his servile flatterers (see the base and malignant [1] *delicacy of friendship*) exalting the master critic far above Aristotle and Longinus, assaulted every modest dissenter who refused to consult the oracle, and to adore the Idol. In a land of liberty, such despotism must provoke a general opposition, and the zeal of opposition is seldom candid or impartial. A late Professor of Oxford (D[r] Lowth) in a pointed and polished Epistle (August 31. 1765) defended himself and attacked the Bishop: and whatsoever might be the merits of an insignificant controversy, his victory was clearly established by the silent confusion of Warburton and his slaves. *I* too without any private offence was ambitious of breaking a lance against the Giant's shield: and in the beginning of the year 1770, my Critical observations on the sixth book of the Æneid were sent without my name to the press. In this short Essay, my first English publication, I aimed my strokes against the person and the Hypothesis of Bishop Warburton. I proved, at least to my own satisfaction, *that* the ancient Lawgivers did not invent the mysteries, and *that* Æneas was never invested with the office of lawgiver. *That*, there is not any argument, any circumstance, which can melt a fable into allegory, or remove the scene from the lake Avernus to the temple of Ceres. *That* such a wild supposition is equally injurious to the poet and the man. *That* if Virgil was not initiated he could not, if he were, he would not, reveal the secrets of the initiation. *That* the anathema of Horace (*Vetabo qui Cereris sacrum, vulgârit* &c) at once attests his own ignorance and the innocence of his friend. As the Bishop of Gloucester and his party [2] maintained a discreet silence, my critical disquisition was soon lost among the pamphlets of the day, but the public coldness was over-balanced to my feelings by the weighty approbation [3] of the last and best Editor of Virgil, Professor Heyne of Gottingen, who acquiesces in my confutation, and styles the

[1] *II added* Essay on the   [2] *I* friends   [3] *I* testimony

unknown author, doctus . . . et elegantissimus Britannus.
But I | cannot resist the temptation of transcribing the [76v]
favourable judgement of Mr Hayley, himself a poet and a
scholar. 'An intricate hypothesis, twisted into a long and
'laboured chain of quotation and argument, the Dissertation
'on the sixth book of Virgil, remained some time unrefuted.
'. . . At length a superior, but anonymous critic arose; who,
'in one of the most judicious and spirited Essays, that our
'nation has produced on a point of Classical literature, com-
'pletely overturned this ill-founded edifice, and exposed the
'arrogance and futility of its assuming architect.' He even
condescends to justify an acrimony of style, which had been
gently blamed by the more unbyassed German, 'Paullo
acrius quam velis . . . perstrinxit' But I cannot forgive
myself the contemptuous treatment of a man, who, with all
his faults, was entitled to my esteem; and I can less forgive,
in a personal attack, the cowardly concealment of my name
and character.

In the fifteen years between my Essay on the study of
literature[1] and the first Volume of the decline and fall (1761-
1776), this criticism on Warburton, and some articles in
the Journal were my sole publications. It is more specially[2]
incumbent on me to mark the employment, or to confess the
waste of time from my travels to my father's death, an
interval in which I was not diverted by any professional
duties from the labours and pleasures of a studious life.
I As soon as I was released from the fruitless task of the
Swiss revolutions, [3] I more seriously undertook (1768) to
methodize the form, and to collect the substance of my
Roman decay, of whose limits and extent I had yet a very
inadequate notion. The [4] Classics as low as Tacitus, the
younger Pliny and Juvenal were my old and familiar companions: I insensibly plunged into the Ocean of the Augustan
history, and in the descending series I investigated, with

---

[1] I litterature the second t of which G deleted owing probably to his having
just transcribed Hayley's lines.   [2] II especially   [3] For the two lines
from here to decay, II substituted the corresponding passage of D (MS f 85 – M
411): I gradually advanced from the wish to the hope. from the hope to the
design, from the design to the execution, of my historical work altering,
however, the first words into I began gradually to advance   [4] I Latin

my pen almost always in my hand, the original records, both
Greek and Latin, from Dion Cassius to Ammianus Marcell-
inus, from the reign of Trajan to the last age of the western
Cæsars. The subsidiary rays of Medals and inscriptions, of
Geography and Chronology were thrown on their proper
objects: and I applied the collections of Tillemont, whose
inimitable accuracy almost assumes the character of Genius,
to fix and arrange within my reach the loose and scattered
atoms of historical information. Through the darkness of the
middle ages I explored my way in the Annals and Antiquities
of Italy of the learned Muratori; and diligently compared
them with the paralel or transverse lines of Sigonius and
Maffei, Baronius and Pagi, till I almost grasped the ruins
of Rome in the fourteenth Century, without suspecting that
this final chapter must be attained by the labour of six
quartos and twenty years. Among the books which I purchased the Theodosian Code with the commentary of James
Godefroy must be gratefully remembered. I used it (and
much I used it) as a work of history, rather than of Jurisprudence: but in every light it may be considered as a full
and capacious repository of the political state of the Empire
in the fourth and fifth Centuries. As I believed, and as I
still believe, that the propagation of the gospel and [1] triumph
of the Church are inseparably connected with the decline of
the Roman Monarchy, I weighed the causes and effects of
the Revolution; and contrasted the narratives and apologies
of the Christians themselves, with the glances of candour or
enmity which the Pagans have cast on the rising sect. The
Jewish and Heathen testimonies as they are collected and
illustrated by Dr Lardner directed, without superseding my
search of the originals; and in an ample dissertation on the
miraculous darkness of the passion I privately drew my
conclusions from the silence of an unbelieving age. I have
77 assembled the preparatory | studies directly or indirectly
relative to my history: but in strict equity they must be
spread beyond this period of my life, over the two summers
(1771 and 1772) that elapsed between my father's death,
and my settlement in London. ii In a free conversation with

[1] *II added* the

books and men, it would be endless to enumerate the names
and characters of all who are introduced to our acquaintance:
but in this general acquaintance we may select the degrees
of friendship and esteem. According to the wise maxim
'*multum* legere potius quam *multa*' I reviewed again and
again the immortal works of the French and English, the
Latin and Italian Classics. My Greek studies (though less
assiduous than I designed) maintained and extended my
knowledge of that incomparable idiom. Homer and Xenophon
were still my favourite authors; and I had almost prepared
for the press an Essay on the Cyropædia which in my own
judgement is not unhappily laboured. After a certain age
the new publications of merit are the sole food of the many:
and the most austere student will be often[1] tempted to break
the line for the sake of indulging his own curiosity and of
providing the topics of fashionable currency. A more respectable motive may be assigned for the triple[2] perusal of Blackstone's commentaries, and a copious and critical abstract of
that English work was my first serious production in my
native language iii My litterary leisure was much less
compleat and independent than it might appear to the eye
of a stranger: in the hurry of London I was destitute of
books; in the solitude of Hampshire I was not master of my
time. [3] By the habit of early rising I always secured a sacred
portion of the day, and many precious moments were stolen
and saved by my rational avarice. But the family hours of
breakfast and dinner, of tea and supper were regular and
tedious: after breakfast Mrs Gibbon expected my company
in her dressing room; after tea my father claimed my conversation and the perusal of the Newspapers. In the heat of
some interesting pursuit[4], I was called down to receive the
visits of our idle neighbours: their civilities required a
suitable return: and I dreaded the period of the full moon,
which was usually reserved for our more distant excursions.
My quiet was gradually disturbed by our domestic anxiety:
and I should be ashamed of my unfeeling philosophy, had I

---

[1] *II* often be – *III* be often   [2] *II* third   [3] *II om eleven lines from here
down to* distant excursions *which G had copied verbatim from B (see above,
p. 96) where they referred to an earlier period in his life.*   [4] *I study*

found much time or taste for study in the last fatal summer (1770) of my father's decay and dissolution.

The disembodying of the Militia at the close of the War (1762) had restored the Major, a new Cincinnatus, to a life of Agriculture. His labours were useful, his pleasures innocent, his wishes moderate: and my father *seemed* to enjoy the state of happiness which is celebrated by poets and philosophers as the most agreable to Nature, and the least accessible to Fortune.

> Beatus ille, qui, procul negotiis
> (Ut prisca gens mortalium)
> Paterna rura bubus exercet suis,
> Solutus omni fœnore.

But the last indispensable condition, the freedom from debt, was wanting to my father's felicity: and the vanities of his youth were severely punished by the solicitude and sorrow of his declining age. The first mortgage on my return from Lausanne (1758) had afforded him a partial and transient relief: the annual demand of interest and | allowance was an heavy deduction from his income: the militia was a source of expence: the farm in his hands was not a profitable adventure: he was loaded with the costs and damages of an obsolete law-suit; and each year multiplied the number, and exhausted the patience of his creditors. Under these painful circumstances, [1] my own behaviour was not only guiltless but meritorious. Without stipulating any personal advantages, I consented [2]at a mature and well-informed age to an additional mortgage, to the sale of Putney, and to every sacrifice that could alleviate his distress: but he was no longer capable of a rational effort, and his reluctant delays postponed, not the evils themselves, but the remedies of those evils, (remedia malorum potius quam mala differebat). The pangs of shame tenderness and self-reproach incessantly preyed on his vitals: his constitution was broken; he lost his strength and his sight: the rapid progress of a dropsy admonished him of his end, and he sunk into the grave on the tenth of November 1770, in the sixty fourth year of his

---

[1] *II om two lines from here to* advantages   [2] *II om* at a mature . . . age

age. A family tradition insinuates that Mr William Law has[1] drawn his pupil in the light and inconstant character of *Flatus*, who is ever confident and ever disappointed in the chace of happiness. But these constitutional failings were amply[2] compensated by the virtues of the head and heart, by the warmest sentiments of honour and humanity. His graceful person, polite address, gentle manners, and unaffected chearfulness, recommended him to the favour of every company: and in the change of times and opinions, his liberal spirit had long since delivered him from the zeal and prejudice of a Tory education. [3] The tears of a son are seldom lasting: I submitted to the order of Nature; and my grief was soothed by the conscious satisfaction, that I had discharged all the duties of filial piety: [4] Few, perhaps, are the children who, after the expiration of some months or years, would sincerely rejoyce in the resurrection of their parents; and it is a melancholy truth, that my father's death, not unhappy for himself, was the only event that could save me from an hopeless life of obscurity and indigence. ~

[1] *II* had   [2] *II* happily   [3] *II om this sentence to* lasting   [4] *II om this last sentence of the chapter.*

Chapter VII[1]

78 As soon as I had paid the last solemn duties to my father, and obtained from time and reason a tolerable composure of mind, I began to form the[2] plan of an independent life most adapted to my circumstances and inclination. Yet so intricate was the net: my efforts were so awkward and feeble, that near[3] two years (November 1770–October 1772) were suffered to elapse before I could disentangle myself from the management of the farm, and transfer my residence from Buriton to an house in London. During this interval, I continued to divide my year between town and the country: but my new freedom[4] was brightened by hope: [5]nor could I refuse the advantages of a change, which had never, (I have scrutinized my conscience), which had never been the object of my secret wishes. Without indulging the vanity and extravagance of a thoughtless heir, I assumed some additional latitude of lodging attendance and equipage: I no longer numbered with the same anxious parsimony my dinners at the club or tavern: my stay in London was prolonged into the summer; and the uniformity of the summer was occasionally broken by visits and excursions at a distance from home. [6]That home, the house and estate at Buriton were now my own: I could invite without controul the persons most agreable to my taste: the horses and servants were at my disposal: and in all their operations my rustic ministers solicited the commands, and smiled at the ignorance of their master. I will not deny that my pride was flattered by the local importance of a country gentleman: the busy scene of the farm, productive of seeming plenty, was embellished in my eyes by the partial sentiment of

---

[1] *Chapter VII gives the end of* C (*MS ff* 78-79 – *M* 288-292), *which* G *had entitled* Section iii, *and part of* E (*MS ff* 88-92 – *M* 306-307). – *The heading is the present editor's.*   [2] *II* a   [3] *II* nearly   [4] *II* situation   [5] *II om seven lines from here down to* club or tavern   [6] *II om sixty lines from here down to* enjoyment of life (*p. 153, l. 13*).

property; and still adhering to my original[1] plan, I expected the adequate offers of a tenant and postponed without much impatience the moment of my departure. My friendship for Mrs Gibbon long resisted the idea of our final separation. After my father's decease, she preserved the tenderness, without the authority | of a parent: the family and even the 78ᵛ farm were entrusted to her care; and as the habits of fifteen years had attached her to the spot, she was herself persuaded, and she tryed to persuade *me* of the pleasures and benefits of a country-life. But as I could not afford to maintain a double establishment, my favourite project of an house in London was incompatible with the farm at Buriton, and it was soon apparent that a woman and a philosopher could not direct with any prospect of advantage such a complex and costly machine. In the second summer my resolution was declared and effected: the advertisement of the farm attracted many competitors: the fairest terms were preferred: the proper leases were executed: I abandoned the mansion to the principal tenant, and Mrs G with some reluctance departed for Bath the most fashionable azylum for the *sober singleness* of widowhood. But the produce of the effects and stock was barely sufficient to clear my accounts in the country, and my first settlement in town: from the mischievous extravagance of the tenant I sustained many subsequent injuries; and a change of ministry could not be accomplished without much trouble and expence.

Besides the debts for which my honour and piety were engaged, my father had left a weighty mortgage of seventeen thousand pounds: it could only be discharged by a landed sacrifice, and my estate at Lenborough near Buckingham was the devoted victim. At first the appearances were favourable: but my hopes were too sanguine, my demands were too high: after slighting some offers by no means contemptible, I rashly signed an agreement with a worthless fellow (half knave and half madman) who, in three years of vexatious chicanery, refused either to consummate or to relinquish his bargain. After I had broken my fetters, the opportunity was lost: the public distress had reduced the

[1] *I added* original *in the margin.*

value of land: I waited the return of peace and prosperity; and my last[1] secession to Lausanne preceded the sale of my Buckinghamshire estate. The delay of fifteen years, which I may impute to myself, my friends, and the times, was accompanied with the loss of many thousand pounds. A delicious morsel, a share in the New river company, was cast, with many a sigh into the gulph of principal, interest, and annual expence; and the far greater part of the inadequate price of poor Lenborough was finally devoured by the insatiate monster. Such remembrance is bitter: but the temper of a mind exempt from avarice suggests some reasonable topics of consolation. My patrimony has been diminished in the enjoyment of life. The gratification of my desires (they were not immoderate) has been seldom disappointed by the want of money or credit: my pride was never insulted by the visit of an importunate tradesman; and any[2] transient anxiety for the past or future was soon[3] dispelled by the studious or social occupation of the present hour. My conscience does not accuse me of any act of extravagance or injustice: [4] the remant of my estate affords an ample and honourable provision for my declining age, [5] and my spontaneous bounty must be received with implicit gratitude by the heirs of my choice.—I shall not expatiate more minutely[6] on my œconomical affairs which cannot be instructive or amusing to the reader. It is a rule of prudence, as well as of politeness, to reserve such confidence for the ear of a private friend; without exposing our situation to the envy or pity of strangers: for envy is productive of hatred, and pity borders too nearly on contempt. Yet I may believe

79 and even assert | that in circumstances more indigent or more wealthy, I should never have accomplished the task, or acquired the fame, of an historian; that my spirit would have been broken by poverty and contempt; and that my industry might have been relaxed in the labour and luxury of a superfluous fortune. [7] Few works of merit and importance have been executed either in a garret or a palace. A gentle-

---

[1] *I* final   [2] *II* my   [3] *II* has been   [4] *II added* and   [5] *II om this line and the next to* choice   [6] *II om* more minutely   [7] *II om the end of the paragraph from here.*

man, possessed of leisure and independence, of books and talents, may be encouraged to write by the distant prospect of honour and reward: but wretched is the author, and wretched will be the work, where daily diligence is stimulated by daily hunger.

[1] At the time of my father's decease – 1770 November 10 –[2] 88ᵛ I was upwards of thirty three years of age the ordinary term of an human generation[3]. My grief was sincere for the loss of an affectionate parent, an agreable companion, and a worthy man. But the ample fortune which my grandfather had left was deeply impaired, and would have been gradually consumed by the easy and generous nature of his son. I revere the memory of my father, his errors I forgive, nor can I repent of | the important sacrifices which were chearfully 89 offered by filial piety. Domestic command, the free distribution of time and place, and a more liberal measure of expence were the immediate consequences of my new situation: but two years rolled away before I could disentangle myself from the web of rural oeconomy – 1772 October – and adopt a mode of life agreable to my wishes. From Buriton Mrs Gibbon withdrew to Bath; while I removed myself and my books into my new house in Bentinck street Cavendish Square, in which I continued to reside near eleven years. The clear untainted remains of my patrimony have been always sufficient to support the rank of a Gentleman, and to satisfy the desires of a philosopher.

1773 January–1783 September – I had now attained [4]the solid comforts of life, a convenient well-furnished house, a domestic table, half a dozen chosen servants[5], my own carriage, and all those decent luxuries whose value is the more sensibly felt the longer they are enjoyed. These advantages were crowned by the first of earthly blessings,

---

[1] *From here to the end of G's Memoirs the text follows E.*   [2] *G gave to E the appearance of annals, putting dates in the outer margins opposite the beginning of a paragraph, or opposite the appropriate place within a paragraph. In the present edition, these dates have been placed, for practical reasons, not in the margins, but either at the head of a paragraph, a dash separating them from the text, or at the appropriate place within a paragraph, between two dashes. These dashes are not G's. – II om these marginal dates.*   [3] *I added* the ordinary . . . generation *in the margin.*   [4] *II om five lines from here to* crowned by   [5] *I added* a domestic table . . . servants *in the margin.*

AD 1737
{ April 27 OS. }
{ May 8. NS }

AD
1737—1752.

I was

AD 1752
April 3.

AD 1753
March

I was born at his house at Putney in Surry, the eldest child of his marriage, a mar: :riage of inclination with Judith Porten. My five brothers and my sister, all died in their in infancy; and the prema: ture decease of my mother (1746) left her fond husband a disconsolate widower. Some years afterwards (1755) he was married to his second wife, Mrs Dorothea Patten whose tender friendship has often made me forget, that I had scarcely known the blessing of a mother.

From my birth to the age of fifteen, my puny constitution was afflicted with almost every species of disease and weakness; and I owe my life to the maternal tenderness of my aunt Mrs Catherine Porten, at whose name I feel a tear of gratitude trickling down my cheek. My first domestic tutor was Mr John Kirkby, the author of an English Grammar and the Philo: sophical Romance of Automathes. But my progress at Kingston and Westminster schools, were too often interrupted by my returns of illness; and the want of public discipline was imperfectly supplied by private instruction. I soon felt and indulged the love of reading, and my vague curi: osity embraced the history, chronology and geography of the ancient and modern world.

At an unripe age I was matriculated as a Gentleman Commoner at Magdalen College in the University of Oxford where I lost fourteen valuable months of my youth. The reader will ascribe this loss to my own incapacity, or to the vices of that ancient institution.

Without a master or a guide I unfortunately stumbled on some books of Popish con: :troversy; nor is it a matter of reproach, that I a boy should have believed that he believed &c. I was seduced like Chillingworth and Bayle; and like them my growing reason soon broke through the toils of sophistry and superstition.

time, temper and good
I was born &c

instruction. It is fa: :shionable for the man to envy and regret the happiness of the boy: but I never could understand the happiness of servitude; and my want of agility and strength dis: :qualified me for the joyous play of my equals. The long hours of confinement to my chamber or my couch were soothed however by an early and eager love of reading. Some books of fiction, Pope's Homer and the Arabian nights were the first food of my mind: but I soon began to devour with indiscriminate appetite the history &c

Plate V. Lower part of the first page of E, left unnumbered by G

Independence: I was the absolute master of my hours and actions: nor was I deceived in the hope, that the establishment of my library in town would allow me to divide the day between Study and Society. Each year the circle of my acquaintance, the number of my dead and living companions, was enlarged. To a lover of books the shops and sales in[1] London present irresistible temptations; and the manufacture of my history required a various and growing stock of materials. The Militia, my travels, the house of Commons, the fame of an author, contributed to multiply my connections: I was chosen a member of the fashionable clubs (27)[2]; and before I left England[3] there were few persons of any eminence in the litterary or political World to whom I was a stranger (28).[4] By my own choice I passed in town the greatest part of the year: but whenever I was desirous of breathing the air of the Country, I possessed[5] an hospitable retreat at Sheffield place in Sussex, in the family of Mr Holroyd, a valuable friend[6], whose character, under the name of Lord Sheffield, has since been more conspicuous to the public.

1773 February &c – No sooner was I settled in my house and library than I undertook the composition of the first Volume of my history. At the outset all was dark and doubtful: even the title of the work, the true æra of the decline and fall of the Empire, the limits of the Introduction, the division of the chapters, and the order of the narrative; and I was often tempted to cast away the labour of seven years. The style of an author should be the image of his mind: but the choice and command of language is the fruit of exercise: many experiments[7] were made before I could hit the middle tone between a dull Chronicle and a Rhetorical declamation; three times did I compose the first chapter, and twice the second and third, before I was tolerably satisfied with their

---

[1] *II of*   [2] *G provided E with notes which he placed all together at the end (MS ff 97-102), adding to his text the necessary references in the usual way above the line. In the present edition these references are placed on the line between round brackets. The first twenty-six notes refer to the first pages of E which are not included in the present edition. II made of G's note 27 a footnote to I was a stranger.*   [3] *II added in 1783 (see below, p. 166).*   [4] *II inserted here the text of note 28*   [5] *I found*   [6] *II family of my valuable friend, Mr. Holroyd*   [7] *I tryals*

effect. In the remainder of the way I advanced with a more
equal and easy pace: but the fifteenth and sixteenth Chapters
have been reduced by three successive revisals from a large
Volume to their present size; and they might still be compressed without any loss of facts or sentiments. An opposite
fault may be imputed to the concise and superficial narrative
of the first reigns from Commodus to Alexander, a fault of
which I have never heard except from Mr Hume in his last
journey to London. Such an oracle might have been con-
sulted and obeyed with rational devotion: | but I was soon 89ᵛ
disgusted with[1] the modest practice of reading the manuscript
to my friends. Of such friends some will praise from politeness, and some will criticise from vanity. The author himself
is the best Judge of his own performance: none[2] has so deeply
meditated on the subject, none[2] is so sincerely interested in
the event.

1774 September – By the friendship of Mr, now Lord
Eliot, who had married my first cousin (29), I was returned
at the general election for the borough of Leskeard. I took
my seat at the beginning of the memorable contest between
Great Britain and America; and supported with many a
sincere and *silent* vote the rights, though not, perhaps, the
interest of the mother country. After a fleeting illusive hope,
prudence condemned me to acquiesce in the humble station
of a mute. I was not armed by Nature or[3] education with the
intrepid energy of mind and voice

> Vincentem strepitus, et natum rebus agendis.

timidity was fortified by pride; and even the success of my
pen discouraged the tryal of my voice. But I assisted at the
debates of a free assembly, [4]which agitated the most important questions, of peace and war, of Justice and Policy:
I listened to the attack and defence of eloquence and reason;
I had a near prospect of the characters, views, and passions,
of the first men of the age. The eight sessions that I sat in
Parliament were a school of civil prudence, the first and
most essential virtue of an historian.[5]

---

[1] *I* by   [2] *II* no one   [3] *II* and   [4] *II* om *this line and a half to* Policy
[5] *II added here the text of a card, No 204 in Add. MSS 34882, which seems to
have been written at a much earlier date than the drafts of the Memoirs, at least*

1775 June – The volume of my history, which had been somewhat delayed by the novelty and tumult of a first session, was now ready for the press. After the perilous adventure had been declined by my timid[1] friend Mr Elmsley, I agreed, on very easy[2] terms, with Mr Thomas Cadell a respectable bookseller, and Mr William Strahan an eminent printer; and they undertook the care and risk of the publication, which derived more credit from the name of the shop than from that of the author. The last revisal of the proofs was submitted to my vigilance: and many blemishes of style, which had been invisible in the manuscript, were discovered and corrected in the printed sheet. So moderate were our hopes that the original impression had been stinted to five hundred, till the number was doubled by the prophetic taste of Mr Strahan. During this awful interval I was neither elated by the ambition of fame; nor depressed by the apprehension of contempt. My diligence and accuracy were attested by my own conscience.[3] History is the most popular species of writing, since it can adapt itself to the highest or the lowest capacity: I had chosen an illustrious subject; Rome is familiar to the school-boy and the statesman: and my narrative was deduced[4] from the last period of Classical reading. I had likewise flattered myself that an age of light and liberty would receive without scandal, an enquiry into the *human* causes of the progress and establishment of Christianity.

1776 February 17 – I am at a loss how to describe the success of the work, without betraying the vanity of the writer. The first impression was exhausted in a few days: a second and third Edition were scarcely adequate to the demand; and the bookseller's property was twice invaded by the pyrates of Dublin. My book was on every table, and almost on every toilette; the historian was crowned by the 90 taste or fashion of the day; | nor was the general voice disturbed by the barking of any *profane* critic. The favour of mankind is most freely bestowed on a new acquaintance of

judging from the writing. See Appendix I, 23. [1] *II om* timid [2] *II* upon – *om* very [3] *I* Of my diligence and accuracy I was myself conscious. [4] *I* narrative descended

MML N

any original merit: and the mutual surprise of the public and their favourite is productive of those warm sensibilities, which, at a second meeting, can no longer be rekindled. If I listened to the music of praise, I was more seriously satisfied with the approbation of my Judges. The candour of Dr Robertson embraced his disciple: a letter from Mr Hume (30) over paid the labour of ten years; but I have never presumed to accept a place in the triumvirate of British historians.[1]

1777 May–November – My second excursion to Paris was determined by the pressing invitation of Mr and Madame Necker, who had visited England in the preceding summer. On my arrival I found Mr Necker, Director general of the finances, in the first bloom of power and popularity: his private fortune enabled him to support a liberal establishment; and his wife, whose talents and virtues I had long admired, was admirably qualified to preside in the conversation of her table and drawing-room. As their friend I was introduced to the best company of both sexes: to the foreign ministers of all nations; and to the first names and characters of France: who distinguished me by such marks of civility and kindness, as gratitude will not suffer me to forget, and modesty will not allow me to enumerate. The fashionable suppers often broke into the morning-hours: yet I occasionally consulted the Royal library, and that of the Abbey of St Germain: and in the free use of their books at home I had always reason to praise the liberality of those institutions. The society of men of letters I neither courted nor declined: but I was happy in the acquaintance of Mr de Buffon, who united with a sublime Genius, the most amiable simplicity of mind and manners. At the table of my old friend Mr de Foncemagne[2] I was involved in a dispute (31) with the Abbé de Mably (32): and his jealous, irascible, spirit revenged itself on a work, which he was incapable of reading in the original (33).[3]

1777 December &c – Near[4] two years had elapsed between

[1] *II inserted here the full text of note 30 (see below, pp. 167-169).*   [2] *III Forcemagne*   [3] *II inserted here note 31 and, in a footnote to it, notes 32 and 33 (see below, pp. 169-170).*   [4] *II Nearly*

the publication of my first, and the commencement, of my second, Volume; and the causes must be assigned of this long delay. 1 After a short holyday, I indulged my curiosity in some studies of a very different nature; a course of Anatomy which was demonstrated by D[r] Hunter, and some lessons of Chemistry which were delivered by Mr Higgins: The principles of these sciences, and a taste for books of Natural history contributed to multiply my ideas and images; and the Anatomist or[1] Chemist may sometimes track me in their own snow. 2. I dived perhaps too deeply into the mud of the Arian controversy: and many days of reading, thinking, and writing were consumed in the pursuit of a phantom. 3. It is difficult to arrange with order and perspicuity the various transactions of the age of Constantine: and so much was I displeased with the first Essay that I committed to the flames above fifty sheets. 4. The six months of Paris and pleasure must be deducted from the account.—But when I resumed my task I felt my improvement. I was now master of my style and subject: and while the measure of my daily performance was enlarged, I discovered[2] less reason to cancel or correct. It has always been my practise to cast a long paragraph in a single mould, to try it by my ear, to | deposit it in my memory; but to suspend the action of the pen, till I had given the last polish to my work. Shall I add that I never found my mind more vigorous, or[3] my composition more happy, than in the winter hurry of society and parliament?

90[v]

1779 February 3. – [4]Had I believed that the majority of English readers were so fondly attached even to the name and shadow of Christianity; had I foreseen that the pious, the timid and the prudent would feel or affect to feel with such exquisite sensibility; I might, perhaps have softened the two invidious Chapters, which would create many enemies, and conciliate few friends. But the shaft was shot, the alarm was

---

[1] *II* and   [2] *I* found   [3] *II* nor   [4] *I began this paragraph thus:* Could I have foreseen the exquisite sensibility of Christian ears, I should probably have softened or suppressed some obnoxious passages in the fifteenth and sixteenth chapters. *These lines were cancelled and the new beginning was written in the margin.*

sounded, and I could only rejoyce, that if the voice of our [1] priests was clamorous and bitter, their hands were disarmed of[2] the powers of persecution. I adhered to the wise resolution of trusting myself and my writings to the candour of the Public, till Mr Davies of Oxford presumed to attack, not the faith, but the good faith[3], of the historian. My *Vindication* (34), expressive of less anger than contempt, amused for a moment the busy and idle metropolis: and the most rational part of the Laity and even of the Clergy, appears[4] to have been satisfied of my innocence and accuracy. [5] My antagonists[6] however were rewarded in this World: poor Chelsum was indeed neglected, and I dare not boast the making D[r] Watson a Bishop [7] (35); but I enjoyed the pleasure of giving a Royal pension to Mr Davies, and of collating D[r] Apthorpe to an Archiepiscopal living. Their success encouraged the zeal of Taylor the Arian (36), and Milner the Methodist (37), with many others whom it would [8] be difficult to remember and tedious to rehearse: the list of my adversaries [9] was graced with the more respectable names of D[r] Priestly (38), Sir David Dalrymple (39), and D[r] White (40); and every polemic of either University discharged his sermon or pamphlet against the impenetrable silence of the Roman historian (41)[10]. Let me frankly own that I was startled at the first vollies[11] of this Ecclesiastical ordnance: but as soon as I found that this empty noise was mischievous only in the intention, my fear was converted to[12] indignation; and every feeling of indignation or curiosity has long since subsided in pure and placid indifference.

1779 May – The prosecution of my history was soon afterwards checked by another controversy of a very different kind. At the request of the [13] Chancellor, and of Lord Weymouth then Secretary of State, I vindicated against the French manifesto the justice of the British arms. The whole correspondence of Lord Stormont our late Ambassador at

---

[1] *I* English   [2] *I* from   [3] *II* but the fidelity   [4] *II* appear   [5] *II in-serted here part of note 34 (see below pp. 170-171).*   [6] *II* They   [7] *II in-serted here a few words from note 35 (see below p. 171).*   [8] it would / it would *in MS (end of a line, beginning of the next).*   [9] *II* added , however,   [10] *II inserted here notes 38-41 (see below pp. 171-173).*   [11] *II* discharge   [12] *II* into   [13] *II* added Lord

Paris was submitted to my inspection; and the *Memoire Justificatif*, which I composed in French, was first approved by the Cabinet Ministers, and then[1] delivered as a state paper[2], to the Courts of Europe. The style and manner are praised by Beaumarchais himself, who, in his private quarrel, attempted a reply; but he flatters me by ascribing the *Memoire* to Lord Stormont; and the grossness of his invective betrays the loss of temper and of wit [3] (42).

1779 July 3 – Among the honourable connections which I had formed, I may justly be proud of the friendship of Mr Wedderburne, at that time Attorney General: who now illustrates the title of Lord Loughborough, and the office of Chief Justice of the Common pleas. By his strong recommendation, and the favourable disposition, of Lord North I was appointed one of the Lords Commissioners of Trade and plantations; and my private income was enlarged by a clear addition of between seven and eight hundred pounds a
91 year. The fancy of an hostile Orator | may paint in the strong colours of ridicule 'the perpetual virtual adjournment and 'the unbroken sitting vacation of the board of trade' (43) but it must be allowed that our duty was not intolerably severe, and that I enjoyed many days and weeks of repose without being called away from my library to the office. My acceptance of a place provoked some of the Leaders of opposition with whom I [4] lived in habits of intimacy; and I was most unjustly accused of deserting a party in which I had never been[5] enlisted.

The aspect of the next Session of parliament was stormy and perilous: County meetings, petitions, and committees of correspondence announced the public discontent; and instead of voting with a triumphant majority, the friends of government were often exposed to a struggle and sometimes to a defeat. The house of Commons adopted Mr Dunning's motion 'that the influence of the Crown had encreased, was increasing, and ought to be diminished' and Mr Burke's bill of reform was framed with skill, introduced with eloquence, and supported by numbers. Our late president the

---

[1] *I* after   [2] *I added* as a state paper *in the margin.*   [3] *II inserted here* note 42 (*see below p. 173*).   [4] *II added* had   [5] *II om* been

American Secretary of State very narrowly escaped the sentence of proscription: but the unfortunate board of trade was abolished in the committee by a small majority (207 to 199) of eight votes – AD 1780 March. 13.—The storm however blew over for a time. A large defection of Country Gentlemen eluded[1] the sanguine hopes of the patriots: the Lords of trade were revived: administration recovered their strength and spirit; and the flames of London – June 2. &c –, which were kindled by a mischievous madman, admonished all thinking men of the danger of an appeal to the people. In the premature dissolution which followed this Session of parliament, I lost my seat – September. 1.—Mr Eliot was now deeply engaged in the measures of opposition, and the Electors of Leskeard are commonly of the same opinion as Mr Eliot.

In this interval of my Senatorial life I published – 1781 March 1 – the second and third Volumes of the decline and fall. My Ecclesiastical history still breathed the same spirit of freedom: but Protestant zeal is more indifferent to the characters and controversies of the fourth and fifth Centuries; my obstinate silence had damped the ardour of the polemics; Dr Watson the most candid of my adversaries assured me that he had no thoughts of renewing the attack, and my impartial balance of the virtues and vices of Julian was generally praised. This truce was interrupted only by some animadversions of the Catholics of Italy [2] (44), and by some angry letters from Mr Travis (45) who made me personally responsible for condemning with the best Critics the spurious text of the three heavenly Witnesses. [3] The bigotted advocate of Popes and monks may be turned over even to the bigots of Oxford, and the wretched Travis still howls[4] under the lash of the merciless Porson (46). [5] But[6] I perceived, and without surprize, the coldness and even prejudice of the town: nor could a whisper escape my ear that, in the judgement of many readers, my continuation was much inferior to the original attempt[7]. An author who cannot ascend will

---

[1] *I* defeated   [2] *I* some Catholic animadversions in the Italian translation
of my history   [3] *II inserted here notes 44 and 45 (see below pp. 173-174).*
[4] *II* smarts   [5] *II inserted here note 46 (see below p. 174).*   [6] *II om* But
[7] *II* attempts

always appear to sink: envy was now prepared for my reception, and the zeal of my religious (47), was fortified by the malice[1] of my political, enemies. [2] I was however encouraged by some domestic and foreign testimonies of applause, and the second and third volumes insensibly rose 91ᵛ in sale and reputation to a level with the first. But | the public is seldom wrong; and I am inclined to believe, that especially in the beginning they are more prolix and less entertaining than the first: my efforts had not been relaxed by success and I had rather deviated into the opposite fault of minute and superfluous diligence. On the continent my name and writings were slowly diffused: a French translation of the first volume had disappointed the booksellers of Paris; and a passage in the third was construed as a personal reflection on the reigning Monarch (48)

AD. 1781 June. – Before I could apply for a seat at the general Election, the list was already full: but Lord North's promise was sincere, his recommendation was effectual: and I was soon chosen on a vacancy for the borough of Lymington in Hampshire. In the first Session of the new parliament administration stood their ground: their final overthrow was reserved for the second. The American War had once been the favourite of the Country: the pride of England was irritated by the resistance of her Colonies; and the executive power was driven by national clamour into the most vigorous and coercive measures. But the length of a fruitless contest, the loss of armies, the accumulation of debt and taxes, and the hostile confederacy of France, Spain and Holland indisposed the public to the American War and the persons by whom it was conducted. The representatives of the people, followed at a slow distance the changes of their opinion; and the ministers who refused to bend were broken by the tempest. As soon as Lord North had lost or was about to lose a majority in the house of Commons, he surrendered his office, and retired to a private station, with the tranquil assurance of a clear conscience, and a chearful temper: the old fabric was dissolved, and the posts of Government were occupied by the victorious and veteran troops of opposition.

---

[1] *II* motive   [2] *II inserted here note 47 (see below, pp. 174-175).*

The Lords of Trade were not immediately dismissed: but the board itself was abolished by Mr Burke's bill, which decency [1] compelled the patriots to revive: and I was stripped of a convenient salary, after I had enjoyed[2] it about three years – 1782. May 1.

So flexible is the title of my history that the final æra might be fixed at my own choice: and I long hesitated whether I should be content with the three Volumes, the fall of the Western Empire, which fulfilled my first engagement with the public. In this interval of suspense, near[3] a twelvemonth, I returned by a natural impulse to the Greek authors of antiquity. [4] In my library in Bentick street, at my summer lodgings at Brighthelmstone, at a country-house which I hired at Hampton-Court, I read, with new pleasure the Iliad and [5] Odyssey, the histories of Herodotus, Thucydides and Xenophon, a large portion of the Tragic and comic theatre of Athens, and many interesting dialogues of the Socratic school. Yet in the luxury of freedom I began to wish for the daily task, the active pursuit which gave a value to every book, and an object to every enquiry: the preface of a new edition – 1782 March 1 – announced my design, and I dropt without reluctance from the age of Plato to that of Justinian. The original texts of Procopius, and Agathias supplied the events and even the characters of his reign: but a laborious winter was devoted to the Codes, the Pandects and the modern interpreters before I presumed to form an abstract of the Civil law. My skill was improved by practise; my diligence perhaps was quickened by the loss of office, and except[6] the last chapter I had finished my[7] fourth Volume, before I sought a retreat on the banks of the Leman lake.

It is not the purpose of this narrative to expatiate on the 92 public or secret history of the times: the schism which followed the death of the Marquis of Rockingham[,] the appointment of the Earl of Shelburne, the resignation of Mr Fox, and his famous coalition with Lord North – 1783.— But I may affirm[8] with some degree of assurance, that in their

---

[1] *II added* had   [2] *II* having enjoyed   [3] *II* nearly   [4] *II om two lines from here to* Hampton-court   [5] *II added* the   [6] *II* excepting   [7] *II* the
[8] *II* assert

political conflict those great antagonists had never felt any personal animosity to each other, that their reconciliation was easy and sincere; and that their friendship has never been clouded by the shadow of suspicion or jealousy—The most violent or venal of their respective followers embraced this fair occasion of revolt, but their alliance still commanded a majority in the house of Commons: the peace was censured, Lord Shelburne resigned; and the two friends knelt on the same cushion to take the oath of Secretary of State. From a principle of gratitude I adhered to the coalition: my vote was counted in the day of battle; but I was overlooked in the division of the spoil. There were many claimants more deserving, and importunate than myself: the board of trade could not be restored; and while the list of places was curtailed, the number of candidates was doubled. An easy dismission [1] to a secure seat at the board of customs or excise was promised on the first vacancy: but the chance was distant and doubtful: nor could I solicit with much ardour, an ignoble servitude which would have robbed me of the most valuable of my studious hours. At the same time the tumult of London, and the attendance on Parlia[ment] were grown more irksome; and without some additional income I could not long or prudently maintain the style of expence to which I was accustomed.

[1] *I* from Parliament

Gibbon's Notes to Chapter VII[1]

27. [2] From the mixed, though polite company of Boodle's, White's and Brooks's I must honourably distinguish a weekly society which was instituted in the year 1764, and which still continues to flourish under the title of the literary club. (Hawkins's life of Johnson p 415. Boswell's Tour to the Hebrides p. 97.) The names of D[r] Johnson, Mr Burke, [3] Mr Garrick, D[r] Goldsmith, Sir Joshua Reynolds, Mr Colman, Sir William Jones, D[r] Percy, Mr Fox, Mr Sheridan, D[r][4] Adam Smith, Mr Steevens, Mr Dunning, Sir Joseph Banks, D[r] Warton and his brother Mr Thomas Warton, D[r] Burney &c. form a large and luminous constellation of British stars.

28. [5] It would most assuredly be in my power to amuse the reader with a gallery of portraits, and a collection of anecdotes. But I have always condemned the practise of transforming a private memorial into a vehicle of satire or praise.

29. [6] Catherine Elliston; whose mother Catherine Gibbon was my grandfather's second daughter. The education of Lady Eliot, a rich heiress, had been entrusted to the Mallets; and she is thus invited to their Hymenæal feast.

> Last comes a Virgin—Pray admire her!
> Cupid himself attends to squire her:
> A welcome guest! we much had mist her
> For 'tis our Kitty, or his sister.
> But Cupid, let no knave or fool
> Snap up this lamb to shear her wool;

---

[1] *This heading is the present editor's. − The division into two chapters − VII and VIII − of the text of E, a division for which the present editor is alone responsible, made it advisable to divide G's notes also into two groups.* [2] *II turned note 27 into a footnote to the sentence about G's election to fashionable clubs (see p. 155, n 2).* [3] *II added here* Mr. Topham Beauclerk and [4] *II* Mr. [5] *II inserted note 28 in the text (see p. 155, n 4).* [6] *II om note 29.*

No Teague of that unblushing band,
Just landed or about to land;
Thieves from the womb, and train'd at nurse
To steal an heiress, or a purse.
No scraping, saving, saucy cit,
Sworn foe of breeding, worth and wit;
No half-form'd insect of a peer,
With neither land, nor conscience, clear;
Who, if he can, 'tis all he can do,
Just spell the motto on his Landau,
From all, from each of these defend her;
But thou and Hymen both befriend her,
With truth, taste, honour in a mate
And much good sense and some estate.

The poet's wishes were soon accomplished by her marriage
with Mr Eliot of Port Eliot in Cornwall. In the year 1784
he was raised to the honour of an English peerage; and their
three sons are all members of the house of Commons.

30. [1] That curious and original letter will amuse the reader;
and his gratitude should shield my free communication
from the reproach of vanity.

'Edinburgh 18 of March. 1776
Dear Sir,
As I ran through your Volume of History with great
avidity and impatience, I cannot forbear discovering somewhat of the same impatience, in returning you thanks for
your agreable present, and expressing the satisfaction which
the performance has given me. Whether I consider the
dignity of your style, the depth of your matter, or the
extensiveness of your learning, I must regard the work as
equally the object of esteem, and I own that if I had not
99 previously had the happiness of your personal | acquaintance,
such a performance from an Englishman in our age would
have given me some surprize. You may smile at this sentiment; but as it seems to me, that your countrymen, for
almost a whole generation have given themselves up to
barbarous and absurd faction, and have totally neglected all

[1] *II inserted note 30 in the text (see p. 158, n 1).*

polite letters, I no longer expected any valuable production ever to come from them. I know it will give you pleasure (as it did me) to find that all the men of letters in this place concur in their admiration of your work, and in their anxious desire of your continuing it.

When I heard of your undertaking (which was some time ago) I own, that[1] I was a little curious to see how you would extricate yourself from the subject of your two last chapters. I think you have observed a very prudent temperament: but it was impossible to treat the subject so as not to give grounds of suspicion against you, and you may expect that a clamour will arise. This, if any thing, will retard your success with the public; for in every other respect your work is calculated to be popular. But, among many other marks of decline, the prevalence of superstition in England prognosticates the fall of Philosophy, and decay of taste; and, though no body be [more][2] capable than you to revive them, you will probably find a struggle in your first advances.

I see you entertain a great doubt with regard to the authenticity of the poems of Ossian. You are certainly right in so doing. It is indeed strange that any men of sense could have imagined it possible that above twenty thousand verses, along with numberless historical facts, could have been preserved by oral tradition during fifty generations by the rudest perhaps of all the European nations, the most necessitous, the most turbulent, and the most unsettled. Where a supposition is so contrary to common sense, any positive evidence for[3] it ought never to be regarded. Men run with great avidity to give their evidence in favour of what flatters their passions and their national prejudices. You are therefore over and above indulgent to us, in speaking of the matter with hesitation.

I must inform you that we are all very anxious to hear that you have fully collected the materials for your second volume, and that you are even considerably advanced in the composition of it. I speak this more in the name of my friends than in my own; as I cannot expect to live so long as to see the publication of it. Your ensuing Volume will

[1] *II om* that   [2] *II added* more   [3] *II of*

be still[1] more delicate than the preceding; but I trust in your prudence for extricating you from the difficulties; and in all events you have courage to despise the clamour of Bigots.

I am with great regard, Dear Sir
Your most obedient and most humble Servant
David Hume.

Some weeks afterwards I had the melancholy pleasure of seeing Mr Hume in his passage through London; his body feeble, his mind firm. On the 25th of August of the same year (1776) he died at Edinburgh the death of a Philosopher.

31. [2] As I might be partial in my own cause, I shall transcribe the words of an unknown Critic [3] (Supplément à[4] la maniere d'ecrire l'histoire p 125 &c): observing only that this dispute had been preceded by another on the English constitution at the house of the Countess de Froulay an old Jansenist 99ᵛ Lady. 'Vous étiez chez M. de Foncemagne, mon cher Theodon, le jour que M. l'Abbé de Mably et M. Gibbon y dinerent en grande compagnie. La conversation roula presque entierement sur l'histoire. L'Abbé etant un profond politique la tourna sur l'administration, quand on fut au dessert: et comme, par caractère, par humeur, par l'habitude d'admirer Tite-Live, il ne prise que le systême Républicain il se mit à vanter l'excellence des Républiques; bien persuadé que le savant Anglois l'approuveroit en tout et admireroit la profondeur de génie, qui avoit fait deviner tous ces avantages à un François. Mais M. Gibbon instruit par experience[5] des inconvéniens d'un gouvernement populaire, ne fut point du tout de son avis, et il prit généreusement la defense du gouvernement monarchique. L'Abbé voulut le convaincre par Tite-Live, et par quelques argumens tirés de Plutarque en faveur des Spartiates. M. Gibbon doué de la memoire la plus heureuse et ayant tous les faits présens à la pensée, domina bien-tôt la conversation; l'Abbé se fâcha, il s'emporta,

---

[1] *II om* still   [2] *II inserted note 31 in the text (see p. 158, n 3).*   [3] *II shifted this parenthesis to the end of the quotation.*   [4] *II de*   [5] *II l'expérience*

il dit des choses dures. L'Anglois, conservant le flegme de son pays, prenoit ses avantages, et pressoit l'Abbé avec d'autant plus de succès que la colère le troubloit de plus en plus. La conversation s'echauffoit, et M. de Foncemagne la rompit en se levant de table, et en passant dans le sallon, où personne ne fut tenté de la renouer.[']

32. [1] Of the voluminous writings of the Abbé de Mably (see his *Eloge* by the Abbé Brizard), the *Principes du Droit public de l'Europe*, and the first part of the *Observations sur l'histoire de France* may be deservedly praised; and even the *Maniere d'ecrire l'histoire* contains several useful precepts and judicious remarks. Mably was a lover of virtue and freedom; but his virtue was austere, and his freedom was impatient of an equal. Kings, Magistrates, Nobles and successful writers were the objects of his contempt, or hatred or envy; but his illiberal abuse of Voltaire, Hume, Buffon, the Abbé Raynal, Dr Robertson, and *tutti quanti* can be injurious only to himself.

33. Est-il rien de plus fastidieux (says the polite Censor) qu'un M. *Guibbon*, qui, dans son eternelle histoire des Empereurs Romains, suspend à chaque instant son insipide et lente narration, pour vous expliquer la cause des[2] faits que vous allez lire? (Maniere d'ecrire l'histoire p 184 see another passage p 280). Yet I am indebted to the Abbé de Mably, for two such advocates, as the Anonymous French Critic (Supplément p 125-134) and my friend Mr Hayley (Vol. ii p 261-263).

34. *A Vindication of some passages in the fifteenth and sixteenth Chapters of the history of the decline and fall of the Roman Empire, by the Author: London 1779 in octavo*, for [3] I would not print it in quarto lest it should be bound and preserved with the history itself. At the distance of twelve years I calmy affirm my judgement of Davies, Chelsum &c. A victory over such antagonists was a sufficient humiliation.

---

[1] *II turned notes 32 and 33 into footnotes to note 31 (see p. 158, n 3).*   [2] *II de – III des*   [3] *II inserted the latter part of note 34, from* I would not, *in the text (see p. 160, n 5), but replaced* print it *by* print this Vindication

35. Dr Watson now Bishop of Landaff [1]is a prelate of a large mind and liberal spirit. I should be happy to think that his Apology for Christianity had contributed, though at my expence to clear his Theological character. He has amply repaid the obligation by the amusement and instruction which I have received from the five Volumes of his Chemical Essays. It is a great pity that an agreable and useful science should not yet be reduced to a state of *fixity*.

100   36. [2]The stupendous title, *Thoughts on the causes of the Grand Apostacy* at first agitated my nerves; till I discovered that it was the apostacy of the whole Church, since the Council of Nice from Mr Taylor's private Religion. His book is a strange mixture of *high* enthusiasm, and *low* buffoonery, and the *Millennium* is a fundamental article of his creed.

37. From his Grammar-school at Kingston upon Hull, Mr Joseph Milner pronounces an anathema against all rational Religion. *His* faith is a divine taste[3], a spiritual inspiration; *his* Church is a mystic and invisible body: the *natural* Christians, such as Mr Locke, who believe and interpret the Scriptures, are in his judgement, no better than profane infidels.

38. [4]In his History of the Corruptions of Christianity (Vol ii.), Dr Priestly throws[5] down his two gauntlets to Bishop Hurd and Mr Gibbon. I declined the challenge in a polite[6] letter, exhorting my opponent to enlighten the World by his philosophical discoveries, and to remember that the merit of his predecessor Servetus is now reduced to a single passage, which indicates the smaller circulation of the blood through the lungs, from, and to, the heart. [7](Astruc de la structure du Coeur. Tom i. p 77-79) Instead of listening to this friendly advice, the dauntless Philosopher of Birmingham

---

[1] *From note 35 II took the words* is a prelate of a large mind and liberal spirit *and, putting* he *in front, inserted them in the text* (*see p. 160, n 7*).
[2] *II kept notes 36 and 37 as footnotes to the names of* Taylor *and* Milner (*see p. 160*)   [3] *I* sense   [4] *II inserted notes 38-41 in the text* (*see p. 160, n 10*).   [5] *II* threw   [6] *II om* polite   [7] *II turned this parenthesis into a footnote.*

continues[1] to fire away his double battery against those who believe[2] too little, and those who believe[2] too much. From *my* replies he has nothing to hope or fear: but his Socinian shield has repeatedly been pierced by the spear of the mighty[3] Horsley; [4] and his trumpet of sedition may at length awaken the magistrates of a free country.

39. The profession and rank of Sir David Dalrymple (now a Lord of Session) have[5] given a more decent colour to his style. But he scrutinizes[6] each separate passage of the two Chapters with the dry minuteness of a special pleader, and as he is[7] always solicitous to make, he may sometimes succeed[8] in finding, a flaw. In his Annals of Scotland, he has shewn himself a diligent Collector, and an accurate Critic.

40. I have praised, and I still praise the eloquent sermons which were preached in St Mary's pulpit at Oxford by Dr White. If he assaults[9] me with some degree of illiberal acrimony[10], in such a place, and before such an audience he was obliged to speak the language of the country. I smiled at a passage in one of his private letters to Mr Badcock. 'The 'part where we encounter Gibbon must be brillant and 'striking'

41. In a sermon lately[11] preached before the University of Cambridge, Dr Edwards compliments[12] a work, 'which can 'only perish with the language itself', and esteems the author as[13] a formidable enemy. He is indeed astonished that more learning and ingenuity has not been shewn in the defence of Israel, that the prelates and dignitaries of the Church[14] (alas! good man) did not vie with each other, whose stone should sink the deepest in the forehead of this Goliah. 'But the force of truth will oblige us to confess that 'in the attacks which have been levelled against our Sceptical

---

[1] *II* continued   [2] *II* believed   [3] *II om* the mighty – *III* by the mighty spear of   [4] *I* and it would perhaps be more consistent if he renounced the character of a Christian and a subject.   [5] *II* has   [6] *II* scrutinized   [7] *II* was   [8] *II* have succeeded sometimes   [9] *II* assaulted   [10] *I* language   [11] *II om* lately   [12] *II* complimented   [13] *II om* as   [14] *I added* of the Church *in the margin*.

'historian we can discover but slender traces of profound
'and exquisite erudition—of solid criticism and accurate
'investigation; but are too frequently disgusted by vague
'and inconclusive reasoning; by unseasonable banter and
'senseless witticisms; by unlettered[1] bigotry, and enthusiastic
100v 'jargon; by futile cavils and illiberal invectives. Proud | and
'elated by the weakness of his antagonists, he condescends
'not to handle the sword of controversy &c (Monthly Review
for October 1790. Vol. iii p 287)[2].

42. [3]See Oeuvres de Beaumarchais. Tom iii p 299-355. 'Le
style ne serait pas sans graces[4] ni la logique sans justesse,[']
&c if the facts were true [,] which he undertakes to disprove.
For these facts my credit is not pledged; I spoke as a lawyer
from my brief: but the veracity of Beaumarchais may be
estimated from the assertion that France, by the treaty of
Paris (1763) was limited to a certain number of ships of
War. On the application of the Duke of Choiseul he was
obliged to retract this daring falsehood.

43. [5]See Mr Burke's speech on the bill of reform, p. 72-80.
I can never forget the delight with which that diffusive and
ingenious Orator [6] was heard by all sides of the house, and
even by those whose existence he proscribed. The Lords of
Trade blushed at their own insignificancy, and Mr Eden's
appeal to the two thousand five hundred volumes of our
reports served only to excite a general laugh. I take this
opportunity of certifying the correctness of Mr Burke's
printed speeches which I have heard and read.

44. [7]The piety or prudence of my Italian translator has provided an antidote against the poison of his original. The vth
and viith Volumes are armed with five letters from an anony-

---

[1] *II* embittered   [2] *II turned this parenthesis into a footnote, curtailing it to*
Monthly Review, Oct 1790.   [3] *II inserted note 42 in the text (see p. 161,
n 3), linking text and note by the addition of* he acknowledged that *and
making a footnote of the first sentence.*   [4] *II* grace   [5] *II kept note 43
as a footnote to the Burke quotation (see p. 161), but inverted the order of the
first two sentences.*   [6] *II added here* , Mr. Burke,   [7] *II inserted notes
44 and 45 in the text (see p. 162, n 3).*

mous Divine to his [1] friends, Foothead and Kirk, two English students at Rome, and this meritorious service is [2] commended by *Monsignore* Stonor, a prelate of the same nation who discovers much venom in the *fluid* and nervous style of Gibbon. The critical Essay at the end of the iii[d] Volume was furnished by the Abbate Nicola Spedalieri, whose zeal has gradually swelled to a more solid confutation in two quarto Volumes. Shall I be excused for not having read them?

45. The brutal insolence of his[3] challenge can only be excused by the absence of learning, judgement and humanity; and to that excuse he has the fairest or foulest title[4]. Compared with Archdeacon Travis, Chelsum and Davis assume the character[5] of respectable enemies.

46. [6] I consider Mr Porson's answer to Archdeacon Travis, as the most acute and accurate piece of Criticism which has appeared since the days of Bentley. His strictures are founded in argument, enriched with learning, and enlivened with wit; and his adversary neither deserves nor finds any quarter at his hands. The evidence of the three heavenly witnesses would now be rejected in any court of Justice: but prejudice is blind, authority is deaf, and our vulgar Bibles will ever be polluted by this spurious text *'sedet æternumque sedebit.'* The more learned Ecclesiastics will indeed have the secret satisfaction, of reprobating in the Closet what they read in the Church.

47. [7] Bishop Newton [8] (see his life in Posthumous works. Vol. I p 173. 174. octavo Edition) was at full liberty to declare how much he himself and two eminent brethren were disgusted by Mr G's [9] prolixity, tediousness and affectation. But the old man should not have indulged his zeal in a false and feeble charge against the historian who had faith-

---

[1] *I* English   [2] *I* much   [3] *II* Mr. Travis's   [4] *II* pretension   [5] *II* title   [6] *II inserted note 46 in the text (see p. 162, n 5).*   [7] *II inserted note 47 in the text (see p. 163, n 2).*   [8] *II replaced the parenthesis by the words* writing his own life   [9] *II* Gibbon's

fully and even cautiously rendered Dr Burnet's meaning by
the alternative 'of sleep *or repose*' That philosophic Divine
supposes that in the period between death and the resurec-
tion human souls exist without a body, endowed with in-
101 ternal | consciousness, but destitute of all active or passive
connection with the external World. 'Secundum communem
dictionem Sacræ Scripturæ, Mors dicitur *somnus* et
morientes dicuntur *obdormire*: quod innuere mihi videtur
statum mortis esse statum quietis silentii et αεργασιας' (*de
statû Mortuorum* C v. p 98).

48. [1] It may not be generally known that Louis xvi is a
great reader, and a reader of English books. On the perusal
of a passage of my history (Vol iii p 636) which seems to
compare him with Arcadius or Honorius, he expressed his
resentment to the Prince of B— from whom the intelligence
was conveyed to me. I shall neither disclaim the allusion, nor
examine the likeness: but the situation of the *late* King of
France excludes all suspicion of flattery; and I am ready to
declare that the concluding observations of my third Volume
were written before his accession to the throne.

[1] *II turned note 48 into a footnote to the sentence alluding to Louis XVI (see
p. 163).*

Chapter VIII[1]

1783 May 20 – From my early acquaintance with Lausanne, ₉₂ I had always cherished a secret wish, that the school of my youth might become the retreat of my declining age. A moderate fortune would secure the blessings of ease, leisure and independence: the country, the people, the manners the language were congenial to my taste; and I might indulge the hope of passing some years in the domestic society of a friend. After travelling with several English, Mr Deyverdun was now settled at home in a pleasant habitation, the gift of his deceased aunt: we had long been separated, we had long been silent; yet in my first letter I exposed with the most perfect confidence, my situation, my sentiments and my designs. His immediate answer was a warm and joyful acceptance: the picture of our future life provoked my impatience; and the terms of arrangement were short and simple, as he possessed the property, and I undertook the expence, of our common house. Before I could break my English chain, it was incumbent on me to struggle with the feelings of my heart, the indolence of my temper, and the opinion of the World, which unanimously condemned this voluntary banishment. In the disposal of my effects, the library, a sacred deposit, was alone excepted: as my post-chaise moved over Westminster bridge, I bid a long farewell to the 'fumum, et opes, strepitumque Romae'; my journey – September. 15-27 – by the direct road through France was not attended with any accident, and I arrived at Lausanne, near[2] twenty years after my second departure. Within less than three months the Coalition struck on some hidden rocks: had I remained aboard[3] I should have perished in the general shipwreck.

AD 1783. September 27–1787. July 29. – Since my _{92v} establishment at Lausanne, more than seven years have

---

[1] *Chapter VIII gives the end of E (MS ff 92-96 – M 327-349). The heading is the present editor's.*   [2] *II* nearly   [3] *II* on board

176

elapsed: and if every day has not been equally soft and serene, not a day, not a moment has occurred in which I have repented of my choice. During my absence, a long portion of human life, many changes had happened: my elder acquaintance had left the stage: virgins were ripened into matrons, and children were grown to the age of manhood. But the same manners were transmitted from one generation to another: my friend alone was an inestimable treasure: my name was not totally forgotten, and all were ambitious to welcome the arrival of a stranger, and the return of a fellow-citizen. The first winter was given to a general embrace without any nice discrimination of persons and characters: after a more regular settlement, a more accurate survey I discovered three solid and permanent benefits of my new situation. 1. My personal freedom had been somewhat impaired by the house of commons and the board of trade; but I was now delivered from the chain of duty and dependence, from the hopes and fears of political adventure: my sober mind was no longer intoxicated by the fumes of party, and I rejoyced in my escape, as often as I read of the midnight debates which preceded the dissolution of Parliament. 2. My English œconomy had been that of a solitary batchelor who might afford some occasional dinners. In Switzerland I enjoyed at every meal, at every hour, the free and pleasant conversation of the friend of my youth; and my daily table was always provided for the reception of one or two extraordinary guests. Our importance in society is less a positive than a relative weight: in London I was lost in the crowd; I ranked with the first families of Lausanne, and my style of prudent expence enabled me to maintain a fair balance of reciprocal civilities. 3. Instead of a small house between a street and a stable-yard, I began to occupy a spacious and convenient mansion, connected on the north side with the City, and open on the south to a beautiful and boundless horizon. A garden of four acres had been laid out by the taste of Mr Deyverdun: from the garden a rich scenery of meadows and vineyards descends to the Leman lake, and the prospect far beyond the lake is crowned by the stupendous mountains of Savoy. My books and my acquaintance had been first united in London; but this happy position of my library in town *and* country was finally reserved for Lausanne. Possessed of every comfort in this triple alliance I could not be tempted to change my habitation with the changes of the seasons.

My friends had been kindly apprehensive, that I should not be able to exist in a Swiss town at the foot of the Alps, after so long conversing[1] with the first men of the first cities of the World. Such lofty connections may attract the curious and gratify the vain; but I am too modest or too proud to rate my own value by that of my associates; and whatsoever may be the fame of learning or genius, experience has shewn me that the cheaper qualifications of politeness and good sense are of more useful currency in the commerce of life. By many, conversation is esteemed as a theatre or a school: but after the morning has been occupied by the labours of the library, I wish to unbend rather than to exercise my mind; and in the interval between tea and supper I am far from disdaining the innocent amusement of a game at cards. Lausanne is peopled by a numerous gentry whose companionable idleness is seldom disturbed by | the 93 pursuits of avarice or ambition: the women, though confined to a domestic education, are endowed for the most part with more taste and knowledge than their husbands or[2] brothers; but the decent freedom of both sexes is equally remote from the extremes of simplicity and refinement. I shall add as a misfortune rather than a merit that the situation and beauty of the Pays de Vaud, the long habits of the English, the medical reputation of Dr Tissot, and the fashion of viewing the mountains and *glaciers* have opened us on all sides to the incursions of foreigners. The visits or Mr and Madame Necker (49), of Prince Henry of Prussia (50), and of Mr Fox (51) may form some pleasing exceptions: but in general Lausanne has appeared most agreable in my eyes, when we have been abandoned to our own society.[3]

AD. 1784. July &c – My transmigration from London to Lausanne could not be effected without interrupting the

---

[1] *II* having so long conversed   [2] *II* and   [3] *II* inserted here notes 49-51 (*see below, p. 190*).

Plate VI. View of La Grotte (arrowed) from the west, painted in 1815 by J. H. Bleuler, Jr. (*By permission of the Lausanne Musée cantonal des Beaux-Arts*)

Plate VII.   View of La Grotte, north side, painted in 1893 by Ch. Vulliermet.
(*By permission of the Musées du Vieux-Lausanne*)

course of my historical labours. The hurry of my departure, the joy of my arrival, the delay of my tools suspended their progress; and a full twelvemonth was lost before I could resume the thread of regular and daily industry. A number of books, most requisite and least common had been previously selected: the Academical library of Lausanne which I could use as my own, contains[1] at least the fathers and councils, and I have derived some occasional succour from the public collections of Bern, and Geneva. The fourth volume was soon terminated by an abstract of the controversies of the Incarnation (52), which the learned Dr Prideaux was apprehensive of exposing to profane eyes[2] (53). In the fifth and sixth Volumes, the revolutions of the Empire and the World are most rapid various and instructive[3]: and the Greek or Roman historians are checked by the hostile narratives of the Barbarians of the East and [4] West. It was not till after many designs and many tryals, that I preferred, as I still prefer, the method of groupping my picture by nations (54); and the seeming neglect of Chronological order[5] is surely compensated by the superior merits of interest and perspicuity. The style of the first Volume is in my opinion somewhat crude and elaborate: in the second and third it is ripened into ease correctness and numbers: but in the three last, I may have been seduced by the facility of my pen; and the constant habit of speaking one language and writing another may have infused some mixture of Gallic idioms. Happily for my eyes, I have always closed my studies with the day, and commonly with the morning: and a long but temperate labour has been accomplished without fatiguing either the mind or body. But when I computed the remainder of my time, and my task, it was apparent, that, according to the season of publication, the delay of a month would be productive of that of a year. I was now straining for the goal; and in the last winter many evenings were borrowed from the social pleasures of Lausanne. I could now wish that a pause, an interval had been allowed for a serious revisal.

[1] *II* contained   [2] *II inserted here note 53 (see below, p. 191).*   [3] *I* interesting   [4] *II added* the   [5] *I* of Chronology

1787 June 27. – I have presumed to mark the moment of conception: I shall now commemorate the hour of my final deliverance. It was on the day or rather the[1] night of the 27th of June 1787, between the hours of eleven and twelve that I wrote the last lines of the last | page in a summer- 93ᵛ house in my garden. After laying down my pen, I took several turns in a *berceau* or covered walk of Acacias which commands a prospect of the country the lake and the mountains. The air was temperate, the sky was serene; the silver orb of the moon was reflected from the waters, and all Nature was silent. I will not dissemble the first emotions of joy on the[2] recovery of my freedom and perhaps the establishment of my fame. But my pride was soon humbled, and a sober melancholy was spread over my mind by the idea that I had taken my[3] everlasting leave of an old and agreable companion, and that, whatsoever might be the future date of my history, the life of the historian must be[4] short and precarious.—I will add two facts which have seldom occurred in the composition of six or at least of five quartos. 1 My first rough manuscript, without any intermediate copy has been sent to the press (55). 2. Not a sheet has been seen by any human eyes except[5] those of the Author and the printer: the faults and the merits are exclusively my own.[6]

AD 1787. July 29 – After a quiet residence of four years, during which I had never moved ten miles from Lausanne it was not without some reluctance and terror that I undertook in a journey of two hundred leagues to cross the mountains and the sea. Yet this formidable adventure was atchieved without danger or fatigue, and at the end of a fortnight I found myself in Lord Sheffield's house and library, safe happy and at home. The character[7] of my friend (Mr Holroyd) had recommended him to a seat in Parliament for Coventry, the command of a regiment of light Dragoons, and an Irish peerage. The sense and spirit of his political writings have decided the public opinion on the great questions of our commercial intercourse[8] with America (56)

---

[1] *II om* the   [2] *II om* the   [3] *II an*   [4] *I* that of the historian himself was   [5] *II excepting*   [6] *II inserted here note 55 (see below, p. 191) as a distinct paragraph.*   [7] *I* spirit   [8] *II interest*

and Ireland (57).[1] He fell (in 1784) with the unpopular coalition, but his merit has been acknowledged at the last general election (1790) by the honourable invitation and free choice of the city of Bristol. During the whole time of my residence in England I was entertained at Sheffield place and in Downing Street by his hospitable kindness, and the most pleasant period was that which I passed in the domestic society of the family. In the larger circle of the Metropolis, I observed the country and the inhabitants with the knowledge, and without the prejudices, of an Englishman: but I rejoyced in the apparent encrease of wealth and prosperity which might be fairly[2] divided between the spirit of the nation and the wisdom of the minister. All party resentment was now lost in oblivion; since I was no man's rival, no man was my enemy: I felt the dignity of independence, and as I asked no more I was satisfied with the general civilities of the World. The house in London which I frequented with the[3] most pleasure and assiduity was that of Lord North: after the loss of power and of sight he was still happy in himself and his friends, and my[4] public tribute of gratitude and esteem could no longer be suspected of any interested motive. Before my departure from England, I assisted[5] at the august spectacle of Mr Hastings's tryal in Westminster hall. – 1788 June –: I shall not[6] absolve or condemn the Governor of India: but Mr Sheridan's eloquence demanded[7] my applause; nor could I hear without emotion the personal compliment which he paid me in the presence of the British nation (58) [8]

94   As the publication of my three last volumes was the principal object so it was the first care of my English journey – 1787. August – 1788. April –. The prævious arrangements with the bookseller and the printer were settled in my passage through London, and the proofs, which I returned more correct, were transmitted every post from the press to Sheffield place. The length of the operation, and the

---

[1] *II inserted here notes 56 and 57 (see below pp. 191-192) as a single distinct paragraph.*   [2] *I added* fairly *in the margin.*   [3] *II om the*   [4] *I a*   [5] *II was present*   [6] *II It is not my province to*   [7] *II commanded*   [8] *II added here note 58 (see below, p. 192) as a distinct paragraph.*

leisure of the Country allowed some time to review my manuscript: several rare and useful books, the Assises de Jerusalem, Ramusius de bello C. Pano[1], the Greek acts of the Synod of Florence, the Statuta Urbis Romæ &c were procured, and I introduced in their proper places the supplements which they afforded. The impression of the fourth volume had consumed three months: our common interest required that we should move with a quicker pace: and Mr Strahan fullfilled his engagement, which few printers could sustain of delivering every week three thousand copies of nine sheets. The day of publication was however delayed that it might coincide with the fifty first anniversary of my own birth-day – 1788. May 8. –: the double festival was celebrated by a chearful litterary dinner at Cadell's house; and I seemed to blush while they read an elegant compliment from Mr Hayley (59) whose poetical talent had more than once been employed in the praise of his friend. [2] As most of the former purchasers were[3] naturally desirous of compleating their sets, the sale of the quarto edition was quick and easy: and an octavo size was printed to satisfy at a cheaper rate, the public demand. The conclusion of my work appears to have diffused a strong sensation: it was generally read and variously judged. The style has been exposed to much Academical criticism; a religious clamour was revived; and the reproach of indecency has been loudly echoed by the rigid censors of morals (60). [4] Yet upon the whole the history of the decline and fall seems to have struck a root both at home (61) and abroad (62), and may, perhaps, an hundred years hence, still continue to be abused. [5] The French, Italian, and German translations (63) have been executed with various success; but instead of patronizing, I should willingly suppress such imperfect copies which injure the character while they propagate the name of the author. [6] The Irish pyrates are at once my friend and my enemies: but I cannot be displeased with the two numerous and correct impressions of the English original, which have

[1] *II* Paro   [2] *II inserted here note 59 (see below, p. 192).*   [3] *I* would be
[4] *II inserted here note 60 (see below, p. 193).*   [5] *II inserted here notes 61 and 62 (see below, pp. 193-194).*   [6] *II inserted here note 63 (see below, p. 194).*

been published for the use of the continent at Basil in Switzerland (64). The conquests of our language and litterature are not confined to Europe alone; and the writer who succeeds in London is speedily read on the banks of the Delaware and the Ganges.

In the preface of the fourth Volume, while I gloried in the name of an Englishman, I announced my approaching return to the neighbourhood of the lake of Lausanne. This last tryal confirmed my assurance that I had wisely chosen for my own happiness: nor did I once, in a years visit, entertain a wish of settling in my native country. Britain is the free and fortunate island: but where is the spot, in which I could unite the comforts and beauties of my establishment at Lausanne? The tumult of London astonished my eyes and ears: the amusements of public places were no longer adequate to the trouble: the clubs and assemblies were filled with new faces and young men; and our best society our 94v long and late dinners would | soon have been prejudicial to my health. Without any share in the political wheel[1] I must be idle and insignificant: yet the most splendid temptations would not have enlisted[2] me [3] a second time in the servitude of parliament or office. At Tunbridge some weeks after the publication of my history, I [4]tore myself from the embraces of Lord and Lady Sheffield, and with a young Swiss friend whom I had introduced to the English world, I pursued the road of Dover and Lausanne – AD 1788. July 21-30 –. My habitation was embellished in my absence, and the last division of books which followed my steps, encreased my chosen library to the number of six or[5] seven thousand volumes. My Seraglio was ample, my choice was free, my appetite was keen. After a full repast on Homer and Aristophanes, I involved myself in the philosophic maze of the writings of Plato, of which the dramatic is perhaps more interesting than the argumentative part: but I stept aside into every path of enquiry which reading or reflection accidentally opened.

Alas! the joy of my return and my studious ardour were

---

[1] lottery   [2] *II* enticed   [3] *II added here* to engage   [4] *II replaced six words from here by* reluctantly quitted   [5] *II* of between six and

soon damped by the melancholy state of my friend Mr
Deyverdun. His health and spirits had long suffered a
gradual decline; a succession of Apoplectic fits announced
his dissolution, and before he expired – 1789 July 5. – those
who loved him could not wish for the continuance of his life.
The voice of reason might congratulate his deliverance, but
the feelings of Nature and friendship could be subdued only
by time: his amiable character was still alive in my remembrance; each room, each walk was imprinted with our
common footsteps, and I should blush at my own philosophy
if a long interval of study had not preceded and followed the
death of my friend. By his last will he left [1] me the option of
purchasing his house and garden or of possessing them during
my life: on the payment either of a stipulated price, or of an
easy retribution, to his kinsman and heir. I should probably
have been tempted by the Dæmon of property (65): if
some legal difficulties had not been started against my title:
a contest would have been vexatious, doubtful and invidious:
and the heir most gratefully subscribed an agreement which
rendered my life-possession more perfect, and his future
condition more advantageous. [2] The certainty of my tenure
has allowed me to lay out a considerable sum in improvements[3] and alterations: they have been executed with skill
and taste; and few men of letters, perhaps, in Europe, are
so[4] desirably lodged as myself. But I feel, and with the decline
of years, I shall more painfully feel, that I am alone in
paradise. Among the circle of my acquaintance at Lausanne,
I have gradually acquired the solid and tender friendship of
a respectable family: the four persons of whom it is composed are all endowed with the virtues best adapted to their
age and situation; and I am encouraged to love the parents
as a brother, and the children as a father. Every day we seek
and find the opportunities of meeting: yet even this valuable
connection cannot supply the loss of domestic society.

Within the last two or three years our tranquillity has
been clouded by the disorders of France: many families of[5]
Lausanne were alarmed and affected by the terrors of an

[1] *II added* to   [2] *II inserted here note 65 (see below, pp. 194-195).*   [3] *I*
repairs   [4] *I more*   [5] *II at*

impending bankruptcy; but the revolution or rather the dissolution, of the Kingdom (66) has been heard and felt in the adjacent lands[1]. [2] A swarm of emigrants of both sexes, who escaped from the public ruin[3], has been attracted by
95 the | vicinity, the manners, and the language of Lausanne: and our narrow habitations in town and country are now occupied by the first names and titles of the departed Monarchy. These noble fugitives are entitled to our pity; they may claim our esteem; but they cannot, in the present state of their mind[4] and fortune, much contribute to our amusement. Instead of looking down, as calm and idle spectators, on the theatre of Europe, our domestic harmony is somewhat embittered by the infusion of party spirit: our ladies and gentlemen assume the character of self-taught[5] politicians; and the sober dictates of wisdom and experience are silenced by the clamours[6] of the triumphant *Democrates*. The fanatic missionaries of sedition have scattered the seeds of discontent in our cities and villages, which had[7] flourished above two hundred and fifty years without fearing the approach of war, or feeling the weight of government. Many individuals, and some communities appear to be infected with the French disease[8], the wild theories of equal and boundless freedom: but I trust that the body of the people will be faithful to their sovereign and [9] themselves; and I am satisfied that the failure or success of a revolt would equally terminate in the ruin of the country. While the Aristocracy of Bern protects the happiness, it is superfluous to enquire whether it be founded in the rights, of man: the œconomy of the state is liberally supplied without the aid of taxes (67); and the magistrates *must* reign with prudence and equity, since they are unarmed in the midst of an armed nation. [10] For myself (may the omen be averted) I can only declare that the first stroke of a rebel drum would be the signal of my immediate departure.

[1] *I* countries   [2] *II inserted here note 66 (see below, p. 195) as a distinct paragraph.*   [3] *I* from the ruin of their country   [4] *II* in their present state of mind   [5] *I* untaught   [6] *II* clamour   [7] *III* have   [8] *II* with the Gallic phrenzy   [9] *II added* to   [10] *II inserted here note 67 (see below, p. 195), making of it and of the last sentence of G's paragraph a single distinct paragraph.*

When I contemplate the common lot of mortality, I must acknowledge that I have drawn a high prize in the lottery of life. The far greater part of the globe is overspread with barbarism or slavery: in the civilized world the most numerous class is condemned to ignorance and poverty; and the double fortune of my birth in a free and enlightened country in an honourable and wealthy family is the lucky chance of an unit against millions. The general probability is about three to one that a new-born infant will not live to compleat his fiftieth year (68). I have now passed that age, and may fairly estimate the present value of my existence in the three-fold division of mind body and estate.

I The first [1] indispensable requisite of happiness is a clear conscience unsullied by the reproach or remembrance of an unworthy action

> —— —— —— Hic murus aheneus esto,
> Nil conscire sibi, nullâ pallescere culpâ.

I am endowed with a chearful temper, a moderate sensibility and a natural disposition to repose rather than to action[2]: some mischievous appetites and habits have perhaps been corrected by philosophy or time. The love of study, a passion which derives fresh vigour from enjoyment, supplies each day, each hour, with a perpetual source of independent and rational pleasure; and I am not sensible of any decay of the mental faculties. The original soil has been highly improved by labour and manure[3]: but it may be questioned whether some flowers of fancy, some grateful errors, have not been eradicated with the weeds of prejudice. ii Since I have escaped from the long perils of my childhood, the serious advice of a physician has seldom been requisite. 'The madness of superfluous health', I have never known; but my tender constitution has been fortified by time: [4] the play | 95ᵛ of the animal machine still continues to be easy and regular; and the inestimable gift of the sound and peaceful slumbers of infancy may be imputed both to the mind, and body. [5] About the age of forty I was first afflicted with the gout

---

[1] *II added* and *to* regular   [2] *II* activity   [3] *II* by cultivation   [4] *II om this line*   [5] *II om ten lines from here to* agreable sensations.

which in the space of fourteen years has made seven or eight different attacks: their duration though not their intensity appears to encrease; and after each fit I rise and walk with less strength and agility than before. But the gout has hitherto been confined to my feet and knees: the pain is never intolerable; I am surrounded by all the comforts that art and attendance can bestow: my sedentary life is amused with books and company; and in each step of my convalescence I pass through a progress of agreable sensations. iii. I have already described the merits of my society and situation: but these enjoyments would be tasteless and[1] bitter; if their possession were not assured by an annual and adequate supply. [2]By the painful method of amputation, my father's debts have been compleatly discharged: the labour of my pen, the sale of lands, the inheritance of a maiden aunt (Mrs Hester Gibbon (69)) have improved my property, and it will be exonerated on some melancholy day from the payment of Mrs Gibbon's jointure. According to the scale of Switzerland I am a rich man; and I am indeed rich, since my income is superior to my expence, and my expence is equal to my wishes. My friends more especially Lord Sheffield kindly relieve[3] me from the cares to which my taste and temper are most adverse: [4]the oeconomy of my house is settled without avarice or profusion: at stated periods all my bills are regularly paid, and in the course of my life, I have never been reduced to appear, either as plaintiff, or defendant, in a court of Justice. [5]Shall I add, that, since the failure of my first wishes, I have never entertained any serious thoughts of a matrimonial connection?

I am disgusted with the affectation of men of letters, who complain that they have renounced a substance for a shadow; and that their fame (which sometimes is no insupportable weight) affords a poor compensation for envy, censure and persecution (70). My own experience at least has taught me a very different lesson: twenty happy years have been animated by the labour of my history; and it's success has given

---

[1] *II* or   [2] *II om five lines from here to* jointure   [3] *II* My friend Lord Sheffield has kindly relieved   [4] *II om four lines from here to* court of Justice.   [5] *I added this last sentence of the paragraph in the margin.*

me a name a rank, a character in the World to which I should not otherwise have been entitled. The freedom of my writings has indeed provoked an implacable tribe: but as I was safe from the stings, I was soon accustomed to the buzzing of the hornets: my nerves are not tremblingly alive: and my litterary temper is so happily framed, that I am less sensible of pain than of pleasure. The rational pride of an author may be offended rather than flattered by vague indiscriminate praise: but he cannot, he should not be indifferent to the fair testimonies of private and public esteem. Even his social[1] sympathy may be gratified by the idea, that, now in the present hour, he is imparting some degree of amusement or knowledge to [2]his friends in a distant land: that, one day his mind will be familiar to the grandchildren of those who are yet unborn (71). I cannot boast of the friendship or favour of princes: the patronage of English litterature has long since been devolved on our booksellers, and the measure of their liberality is the least ambiguous test of our common success. Perhaps the golden mediocrity of my fortune has contributed to fortify my application: [3]few books of merit and importance have been composed either in a garret or a palace. A Gentleman, possessed of leisure and competency may | be encouraged by the assurance of an 96 honourable reward: but wretched is the writer, and wretched will be the work, where daily diligence is stimulated by daily hunger.

The present is a fleeting moment: the past is no more; and our prospect of futurity is dark and doubtful. This day may *possibly* be my last: but the laws of probability, so true in general, so fallacious in particular, still allow me about fifteen years (72); and I shall soon enter into the period, which, as the most agreable of his long life, was selected by the judgement and experience of the sage Fontenelle. His choice is approved by the eloquent historian of Nature, who fixes our moral happiness to the mature season, in which

---

[1] *II* moral   [2] *I* many distant readers, and his personal existence may be extended to countries and perhaps to ages, which he will never see but to which he shall be familiarly known. I cannot boast . . .   [3] *II om from here the end of the paragraph which G had taken over from C (see pp. 153-154).*

our passions are supposed to be calmed, our duties fullfilled, our ambition satisfied, our fame and fortune established on a solid basis (73). [1] I am far more inclined to embrace than to dispute this comfortable doctrine: I will not suppose any præmature decay of the mind or body; but I must reluctantly observe, that two causes, the abbreviation of time and the failure of hope, will always tinge [2] with a browner [3] shade the evening of life. [4] 1. The proportion of a part to the whole is the only standard by which we can measure the length of our existence. At the age of twenty, one year is a tenth perhaps of the time which has elapsed within our consciousness and memory: at the age of fifty it is no more than a fortieth, and this relative value continues to decrease till the last sands are shaken by the hand of death. This reasoning may seem metaphysical; but on a tryal it will be found satisfactory and just. 2. The warm desires, the long expectations of youth are founded on the ignorance of themselves and of the World: they are gradually damped by time and experience, by disappointment or [5] possession; and after the middle season the crowd must be content to remain at the foot of the mountain; while the few who have climbed the summit, aspire to descend or expect to fall. In old age, the consolation of hope is reserved for the tenderness of parents who commence as new life in their children; the faith of enthusiasts who sing Hallelujahs above the clouds (74); and the vanity of authors who presume the immortality of their name and writings.

Lausanne. March 2: 1791

[1] *II inserted here note 73 from* In private . . . (*see p. 196*)   [2] *I colour*
[3] *I dark*   [4] *from here II om the end of E – III restored it, but as a footnote.*
[5] *III and*

49. [1] I saw them frequently in the summer of 1784 at a [101] country house near Lausanne, where Mr Necker composed his treatise of the administration of the Finances. I have since (in October 1790) visited them in their present residence the castle and barony of Copet near Geneva. Of the merits and measures of that Statesman various opinions may be entertained; but all impartial men must agree in their esteem of his integrity and patriotism.

50. In the month of August 1784, Prince Henry of Prussia in his way to Paris, passed three days at Lausanne. His military conduct is [2] praised by professional men; his character has been vilified by the wit and malice of a Demon [3] (Memoires secrets de la cour de Berlin) [4] but I was flattered by his affability, and entertained by his conversation.

51. In his tour of [5] Switzerland (September, 1788) Mr Fox gave me two days of free and private society. He seemed to feel and even to envy the happiness of my situation; while I admired the powers of a superior man, as they are blended in his attractive character, with the softness and simplicity of a child. Perhaps no human being was ever more perfectly exempt from the taint of malevolence, vanity or falsehood.

52. [6] In one of the Dialogues of the dead (xvi) Lucian turns into ridicule the Pagan Theology concerning the double Nature of Hercules, God and Man. (Opp. Tom i p 402-405 Edit Reitz) As truth and falsehood have sometimes an apparent similitude, I am afraid that even the Synods of

---

[1] *II inserted notes 49-51 in the text (see p. 178, n 3); he added note 49 to the paragraph on the Lausanne society, altering it so that it might refer to Mr. Necker only:* I had frequently seen Mr. Necker . . . where he . . . visited him . . . *while of notes 50 and 51 he made two distinct paragraphs.* [2] *II has been* [3] *I* malice of Mirabeau [4] *II turned this parenthesis into a footnote, to which III added* par Mirabeau. [5] *II to* [6] *II om note 52.*

Ephesus and Chalcedon would not have been safe from the arrows of his profane wit.

53. [1]It had been the original design of the learned Dean Prideaux to write the history of the ruin of the Eastern Church. In this work it would have been necessary not only to unravel all those controversies which the Christians made about the Hypostatical Union, but also to unfold all the niceties and subtil notions, which each sect did hold[2] concerning it. The pious historian was apprehensive of exposing that incomprehensible Mystery to the cavils and objections of unbelievers, and he durst not, considering[3] the nature of this book, venture it abroad in so wanton and lewd an age (see preface to the life of Mahomet. p x.xi)

54. [4]I have followed the judicious precept of the Abbé de Mably (Manière d'ecrire l'histoire p 110) who advises the historian not to dwell too minutely on the decay of the Eastern Empire; but to consider the Barbarian Conquerors as a more worthy subject of his narrative. 'Fas est et ab hoste doceri.'

101[v] 55. [5]I cannot help recollecting a much more extraordinary fact which is affirmed of himself by Rètif de la Bretonne, a voluminous and original writer of French novels. He laboured, and may still labour, in the humble office of Corrector to a printinghouse. But this office enabled him to transport an entire Volume from his mind to the press; and his work was given to the public without ever having been written with[6] a pen.

56. [7]*Observations on the commerce of the American states by John Lord Sheffield: the sixth edition London 1784 in octavo.*

---

[1] *II inserted note 53 in the text (see p. 179, n 2), turning, however, the parenthesis at the end into a footnote.* [2] *II entertained* [3] *II seeing* [4] *II kept note 54 as a footnote to the paragraph on the fifth and sixth volumes.* [5] *II inserted note 55 in the text as a distinct paragraph (see p. 180, n 6).* [6] *II by* [7] *II inserted notes 56 and 57 in the text as a single distinct paragraph (see p. 181, n 1), turning, however, the first two lines of note 56 into a footnote to the sentence on Holroyd's political writings.*

Their sale[1] was diffusive, their effect beneficial: the Navigation act, the Palladium of Britain, was defended and perhaps saved by his pen; and he proves, by the weight of fact and argument, that the mother-country may survive and flourish after the loss of America. My friend has never cultivated the arts of composition, but his materials are copious and correct, and he leaves on his paper the clear impression of an active and vigorous mind.

57. [2]*Observations on the trade, manufactures and present state of Ireland by John Lord Sheffield:* [3]*the third Edition London 1784 in octavo.* Their useful aim was to guide the industry, to correct the prejudices and to asswage the passions of a country which seemed to forget that she could only be free and prosperous[4] by a friendly connection with Great Britain. The concluding observations are expressed[5] with so much ease and spirit that they may be read by those who are the least interested in the subject.

58. [6]From this display of Genius, which blazed four successive days, I shall stoop to a very mechanical circumstance. As I was waiting in the Managers' box, I had the curiosity to enquire of the short-hand writer, how many words a ready and rapid Orator might pronounce in an hour. From 7000 to 7500 was his answer. The medium of 7200 will afford one hundred and twenty words in a minute, and two words in each second. But this computation will only apply to the English language.

59. [7]Before Mr Hayley inscribed with my name his Epistles on History, I was not personally[8] acquainted with that amiable man and elegant poet. He afterwards thanked me in verse for my second and third Volumes, and in the summer of 1781, the Roman Eagle (a proud title) accepted

---

[1] *II* The sale of his Observations on the American States   [2] *II added* His
[3] *For this line* the third . . . aim was *II substituted the two words* were intended   [4] *II* could be free and prosperous only   [5] *II* written   [6] *II inserted note 58 in the text as a distinct paragraph (see p. 181, n 8).*   [7] *II inserted note 59 in the text (see p. 182, n 2).*   [8] *II om* personally.

the invitation of the English sparrow, who chirped in the groves of Eartham near Chichester.

60. [1] I never could understand the clamour which[2] has been raised against the indecency of my three last Volumes 1. An equal degree of freedom, in the former part, especially in the first Volume had passed without reproach. 2. I am justified in painting the manners of the times; the vices of Theodora form an essential feature in the reign and character of Justinian, [3] and the most naked tale in my history is told by the Reverend Mr Joseph Warton, an instructor of Youth. (Essay on the Genius and writings of Pope p 322-324) 3. My English text is chaste and all licentious passages are left in the obscurity of a learned language.
        Le Latin dans ses mots brave l'honnêteté
says the correct Boileau in a country and idiom more scrupulous than our own.

61. [4] I am less flattered by Mr Porson's high encomium on the style and spirit of my history than I am satisfied with his honourable testimony to my attention, diligence and 102 accuracy; | those humble virtues which Religious Zeal has[5] most audaciously denied. The sweetness of his praise is tempered by a reasonable mixture of acid. (see his preface p xxviii-xxxii)[6]

62. As the book may not be common in England I shall transcribe my own character from the Bibliotheca historica of Meuselius a learned and laborious German (Vol. iv P. i p 342-344[)]. 'Summis aevi nostri historicis Gibbonus sine dubio adnumerandus est. Inter Capitolii ruinas stans primum hujus operis scribendi consilium cepit. Florentissimos vitæ annos colligendo et laborando eidem impendit. Enatum inde monimentum ære perennius, licet passim appareant sinistre dicta, minus perfecta, veritati non satis consentanea. Videmus

---

[1] II inserted note 60 in the text (see p. 182, n 4). [2] II that [3] II om three lines from here to the end of the parenthesis, but III restored them. [4] II inserted notes 61 and 62 in the text (see p. 182, n 5). [5] II had [6] II turned this reference into a footnote.

quidem ubique fere studium scrutandi veritatemque scribendi maximum: tamen sine Tillemontio duce, ubi scilicet hujus historia finitur, saepius noster titubat atque hallucinatur. Quod vel maxime fit, ubi de rebus Ecclesiasticis vel de Jurisprudentiâ Romanâ (Tom iv) tradit, et in aliis locis. Attamen nævi hujus generis haud impediunt quo minus operis summam et οικονομιαν præclare dispositam, delectum rerum sapientissimum, argutum quoque interdum, dictionemque seu stilum historico æque ac philosopho dignissimum et vix a quoque alio Anglo, Humio ac Robertsono haud exceptis, prærepto[1] (*præreptum?*), vehementer laudemus, atque sæculo nostro de hujusmodi historiâ gratulemur ... Gibbonus adversarios cum in tum extra patriam nactus est, quia propagationem Religionis Christianae, non, ut vulgo fieri solet, aut more Theologorum, sed ut historicum et philosophum decet exposuerat.[']

63. [2]The first Volume had been feebly though faithfully translated into French by Mr Le Clerc de Septchênes a young Gentleman of a studious character and liberal fortune. After his decease the work was continued by two manufacturers of Paris M.M. Desmeuniers and Cantwell: but the former is now an active member in[3] the national assembly, and the undertaking languishes in the hands of his associate. The superior merit of the Interpreter or his language inclines me to prefer the Italian, version: but I wish [4] it were in my power to read the German which is praised by the best Judges.

64. [5]Of their fourteen octavo Volumes, the two last include the whole body of the notes. The public importunity had forced *me* to remove them from the end of the Volume to the bottom of the page: but I have often repented of my complyance

65. [6]Yet I had often revolved the judicious lines in which Pope answers the objection[7] of his long-sighted friend

---

[1] *II om* praerepto   [2] *II inserted note 63 in the text (see p. 182, n 6).*
[3] *II of*   [4] *II added* that   [5] *II kept note 64 as a footnote.*   [6] *II inserted note 65 in the text (see p. 184, n 2).*   [7] *II objections*

'Pity to build without a child or wife!
'Why you'll enjoy it *only* all your life
Well, if the use be mine does it concern one
Whether the name belong to Pope or Vernon.

66. [1] I beg leave to subscribe my assent to Mr Burke's creed on the Revolution of France. I admire his eloquence, I approve his politics, I adore his Chivalry, and I can almost excuse his reverence for Church establishments. I have sometimes thought of writing a dialogue of the dead, in which Lucian, Erasmus, and Voltaire should mutually acknowledge the danger of exposing an *old* superstition to the contempt of the blind and fanatic multitude.

67. [2] The revenue of Bern, (I except[3] some small duties) is derived from Church-lands, tythes, feudal rights, and interest of money. The Republic has near[4] 500,000 pounds sterling in the English funds, and the amount of their treasure is unknown to the Citizens themselves.

102ᵛ 68. [5] See Buffon. Supplement à l'histoire naturelle. Tom vii p 158-164. Of a given number of new born infants, one half, by the fault of Nature or Man, is extinguished before the age of puberty and reason. A melancholy calculation!

69. [6] My pious aunt and her profane sister are described under the names of Miranda and Flavia in Law's Serious Call, a popular and powerful book of Devotion. Mr William Law, a Nonjuror, a Saint and a wit, had been my father's domestic Tutor. He afterwards retired with his spiritual daughter Miranda to live and dye in a Hermitage at Cliffe in Northamptonshire.

70. [7] Mr d'Alembert relates, that as he was walking in the gardens of Sans-souci with the King of Prussia, Frederic said

---

[1] *II inserted note 66 in the text as a distinct paragraph (see p. 185, n 2).*
[2] *II inserted note 67 in the text, beginning a new paragraph with it (see p. 185, n 10).*   [3] *II* excepting   [4] *II* nearly   [5] *II kept note 68 as a footnote.*
[6] *II om note 69*   [7] *II kept notes 70, 71, 72 and the first two words of note 73 as footnotes.*

to him 'Do you see that old woman, a poor weeder, asleep on that Sunny bank? She is probably a more happy Being than either of us.' The King and the Philosopher may speak for themselves: for my part I do not envy the old woman.

71. In the first of ancient or modern Romances (Tom Jones L xiii C 1[1]) this proud sentiment, this feast of fancy is enjoyed by the Genius of Fielding 'Foretell me that some future[2] maid whose grandmother is yet unborn &c.' [3] But the whole of this beautiful passage deserves to be read.

72. See Buffon. p 224. From[4] our disregard of the possibility of death within the four and twenty hours he concludes (p 56-58)[5] that a chance which falls below or rises above ten thousand to one, will never affect the hopes or fears of a reasonable man. The fact is true, but our courage is the effect of thoughtlessness rather than of reflection[6]. If a public lottery was[7] drawn for the choice of an immediate victim, and if our name were inscribed on one of the ten thousand[8] tickets, should we be perfectly easy?

73. See Buffon p 413[9]. [10] In private conversation, that great and amiable man added the weight of his own experience: and this autumnal felicity might be exemplified in the lives of Voltaire, Hume, and many other men of letters.

74. [11] This celestial hope is confined to a small number of the Elect, and we must deduct, 1 All the *mere* philosophers who can only speculate about the immortality of the soul. 2. All the *earthly* Christians, who repeat, without thought or feeling, the words of their Catechism. 3. All the *gloomy* fanatics who are more strongly affected by the fear of Hell, than by the hopes of Heaven. 'Strait is the way, and narrow is the gate, and *few* there be, who find it!'

---

[1] *II* Book xiii, chap. 1 (*this reference being shifted to the end of the note*).
[2] *II* tender   [3] *II replaced the last two lines of note 71 by the end of Fielding's paragraph.*   [4] *II* Mr. Buffon, from   [5] *II om this reference.*   [6] *I* reason   [7] *II* were   [8] *I* added ten thousand *in the margin.*   [9] *II om* p 413   [10] *II inserted note 73 in the text (see p. 189, n 1).*   [11] *II om* note 74.

Appendices

Appendix I

Extracts from Sketches A and D, and from those
parts of Sketches B and C which have not been
included in the above edition of *The Memoirs*

1

I had long and modestly acquiesced in the knowledge of my two immediate predecessors, a country-gentleman and a wealthy merchant.
Beyond these, I found neither tradition nor memorial: and as our
Genealogy was never a topic of family conversation, it might seem
probable that my grand-father, the Director of the South-Sea-Company,
was himself a son of the Earth, who by his industry, his honest industry
perhaps, had raised himself from the work-house or the Cottage. It is
not two years since I acquired in a foreign land some domestic intelligence
of my own family: and this intelligence was conveyed to Switzerland
from the heart of Germany. I had formed an acquaintance with Mr
Langer a lively and ingenious Scholar, while he resided at Lausanne as
preceptor to the Hereditary prince of *Brunswick*. On his return to his
proper station of librarian to the Ducal library of *Wolfenbuttel*, he accidentally found among some litterary rubbish a small old English volume
of Heraldry, inscribed with the name of *John Gibbon*. From the title
only Mr *Langer* judged that it might be an acceptable present to his
friend: and he judged rightly: for I soon convinced myself that the
author was not only my namesake, but my kinsman. To his book I am
indebted for the best and most curious information: but in my last visit
to England I was tempted to indulge a curiosity which had been excited
by this odd discovery. Some Wills, parish-registers, and monumental
inscriptions were consulted at my request, and my enquiries were assisted
by Mr *Brooke* the Somerset-Herald, whose knowledge deserves my
applause, and whose friendly industry is entitled to my thanks.

(A, Gibbon's pp. 5-6 – MS f 7)

2

But alas these honours are obliterated and my scutcheon is irretrievably
stained if we adopt the lofty prejudices of French and German nobility.
I cannot deny, that the younger branch of the Gibbons of Kent migrated
in the reign of James I from the Country to the City, and that they
persevered during three generations in the profession of trade (. . . .)
These facts I can relate without a blush: the good-sense of the English

has embraced a system more conducive to national prosperity; the character of a merchant is not esteemed incompatible with that of a Gentleman; and the first names of the peerage are enrolled in the books of our trading Corporations. The descent of landed property to the eldest son is secured by the common law: and though Kent, under the name of *Gavelkind*, retains a more equal partition, this provincial custom is defeated by the practise of settlements and entails. The pride and indolence of younger brothers might frequently acquiesce in the life of a William Wimble so incomparably described by the Spectator: but a more rational pride must often prevail over their indolence and urge them to seek in the World the comforts of independence. Since the auspicious reign of Elizabeth the commerce of England had opened a thousand channels of industry and wealth, and the more splendid resources which now divert a Gentleman's younger sons from the mercantile profession were much less frequent and beneficial. After the reformation the Church assumed a graver and less attractive form, and though many might be content to sleep in the possession of a patrimonial living, the bench of bishops was long filled by indigent scholars; before the gentry, or at least the nobility became fully sensible of the value of a calling which bestows riches and honours without requiring either genius or application. In every age the youth of England has been distinguished by a martial spirit; and the subjects of Elizabeth and her successors sought every occasion of danger and glory by sea and land. But these occasions were rare and voluntary: nor could they afford such an ample and permanent provision as is now supplied by an hundred regiments, and an hundred ships of the line. Our civil establishment has gradually swelled to its present magnitude; nor did India unfold her capacious bosom to the merit or fortune of every needy adventurer. The common alternative was the bar and the counter; but the success of a lawyer unless he be endowed with superior talents is difficult and doubtful: the various occupations of commerce are adapted to the meanest capacity, and a modest competency is the sure reward of frugality and labour, since those humble virtues have so often sufficed for the acquisition of riches.

(A, pp. 12-13 – MS ff 10ᵛ-11)

3

Of the life and character of Matthew Gibbon (. . . .) I am totally ignorant, and must be content to repeat that he was a Linnen-Draper in Leadenhall Street. After his decease, Hester his relick remarried with Richard Acton third son of Sir Walter Acton Baronet, who exercised the same trade in the same street and in due time their union was confirmed by the marriage of the son of Hester and the daughter of Richard by their former marriages. This Lady who survived both her husbands

and lived to a great age was of an active and notable spirit. While her
son my Grandfather Edward Gibbon was in Flanders where he had a
contract for supplying King William's arms, his mother managed all
his mercantile affairs at home; and I have seen some of her letters in a
character no longer legible and on business no longer interesting.
Besides my grand-father she had another son Thomas Gibbon who
became Dean of Carlisle: in my childhood I have known *his* son William
Gibbon, a drunken Jacobite parson who obtained by party-interest the
Rectory of Bridewell.

(A, p. 14 – MS ff 11ᵛ-12)

4

By Hester, the wife and widow of (. . .) Matthew, three links were
formed between the Gibbons and the Actons: by her second nuptials
with Richard Acton; by the marriage of their children of the first adventure, and by the union of her daughter with Sir Whitmore Acton.
This triple alliance and especially the second gives me a deep and
domestic interest in the name and honours of a worthy family, which
has flourished in Shropshire since the thirteenth and fourteenth Centuries,
which has been propagated by a series of adequate connections, and of
which the younger branches have been supported without being dis-
graced by the profession of trade. In the eyes of the Tories the Actons
may claim the merit of firm and untainted loyalty, not only in their
distant province far from the vortex of new opinions, but even in the
occupations and offices of the Capital. Sir Richard Acton, of a branch
now extinct was created a Baronet in 1629: in the year 1643 he was
chosen Lord Mayor of London; and was removed by the House of
Commons for his attachment to the King, and his opposition to their
proceedings. His cousin Edward Acton of Aldenham the Chief of the
elder was created a Baronet by Charles i in 1643, a few months after he
had erected his standard at Nottingham. Sir Edward was succeeded by
Sir Walter his eldest son, and the father of seven sons who all exceeded
the ordinary proportion of the human stature. One of these, Francis
who died a batchelor in my grandfather's, his nephew's house at Putney,
confessed or boasted that he was a pygmey of six feet two inches, the
least of the seven; and he added in the true spirit of party, that such
men had not been born since the Revolution. Of the other brothers, I
shall mention three who left a numerous posterity: Sir Edward the
father of Sir Whitmore who married my grandfather's sister, by whom
he had Sir Richard the present Baronet, now almost fourscore years of
age; Richard the father of my grandmother; and Walter whose descendants by strange accidents have migrated to foreign Countries. Walter
himself and his son Edward passed their lives, a Mercer, and a Goldsmith, in the City of London: but of the two sons of Edward, the one,

who accompanied my father on his travels, was tempted to marry and
settle at Besançon in France, while the other a Captain in the East-India
Company's service was invited to command at Leghorn the fleet of the
Emperor Great Duke of Tuscany. The Commodore died a batchelor:
the two younger sons of the Physician are still, if they are alive in the
French service, but the fortune of the elder has been much more singular
and splendid; after a visit to England in the year 1762, with the design
perhaps of obtaining the daughter and heiress of his kinsman Sir Richard
Acton, he devoted himself with spirit and success to the naval service
of Tuscany and Naples. In the expedition against Algiers, the Chevalier
Acton who commanded a Frigate was distinguished by his courage and
conduct; and his abilities have since raised him to the first honours of
the State. The Courts of Versailles and Madrid have laboured in vain
to drive him from his station; and he still enjoys with the title or at
least the power of prime Minister, the entire confidence of the King, I
should rather say of the Queen, of the two Sicilies.

(A, pp. 19-21 – MS ff 14-15)

5

The act of Parliament which stripped the Directors of the greatest part
of their property has been condemned by the more impartial judgement
of posterity, and without suspicion of personal resentment, I may be
allowed to prove that the proceedings against those unfortunate men
were *unjust*, *illegal*, and arbitrary. In the year 1711 the South-sea
Company had been incorporated by Lord Oxford: their original stock
was composed of near ten millions of the unfunded debt; and the creditors
now transformed into merchants were invested with an executive
charter of trade and establishment in the South-seas. But their ambition
was soon checked by the conclusion of the peace: the treaty of Utrecht
did not afford an adequate compensation; their commercial privileges
were eluded or infringed by the jealousy of Spain; nor could these new
adventurers pretend to rival the firm credit of the Bank, or the rising
greatness of the East-India Company. Yet they were encouraged by the
favour of the crown and the people, and a project was adopted in the
year 1720, for consolidating in their hands the greatest part of the
national debt. They were authorised by parliament to encrease their
stock, and to acquire by subscription or purchase the redeemable and
irredeemable debts on such terms as they should be able to stipulate with
the public creditors. Their first operations were seconded by the enthusiasm of the times: the rapid rise in the price of their stock enabled
them to conclude an advantageous bargain: all parties were united by
the lust of gold; and all men rushed forwards to grasp those ideal
treasures, which were realized only for those, who had prudence to
withdraw before the impending ruin. In these wonderful transactions,

I am at a loss to discern the precise and specific crime of the Directors: nor could it be very obvious to the majority of Country-Gentlemen who sat as their Judges in the house of commons: The least justifiable of their measures, the vague letter of Attorney which was inserted in their books, and unknowingly signed by the thoughtless subscribers was afterwards ratified at *their* expence by the authority of parliament. If the directors promised an enormous dividend, if they opened a subscription at one thousand per cent they were countenanced and almost compelled by the popular frenzy; nor are they accused, at least they are not convicted of inflaming that frenzy for their private emolument. They acted under the legal controul of the Lords of the Treasury, and whatever might be the guilt, the largest share must be assigned to the Earl of Sunderland the first Lord, and above all to Mr Aislabie Chancellor of the Exchequer. Yet these Ministers were peaceably dismissed or imperfectly punished. Their resignation attoned for their offences; and the friendless directors were the victims to appease the blind vehemence of popular resentment.

(A, pp. 21-23 – MS ff 15-16)

6

Such were once the proceedings of a British parliament: but it was the same house of Commons which had forfeited the trust of their constituents; and voted their own continuance four years beyond their legal term of existence: it was the same parliament which passed the Riot-Act and introduced Martial law in time of peace; which stripped the Irish peerage of their right of judicature and had almost stripped the Scotch peerage of their right of election. It must be lamented that the Whigs have too often sullied the principles of freedom by the practise of violence and tyranny.

(A, p. 24 – MS f 16ᵛ)

7

After he could persuade himself to try not the pleasures but the consolations of friendship and society, the two houses at Putney, which he most familiarly frequented were those of the Gilberts and the Mallets. The former were three maidens of middle age and small fortunes, the sisters of the *leaden* Gilbert stigmatized by Pope, and who without either talents or virtue could ascend the Ecclesiastical ladder as high as the station of Archbishop of York. The younger sister Emily Gilbert was a Lady of some spirit and accomplishments who had been the intimate friend of my mother; and she secretly aspired to supply as well as to alleviate the widower's loss. But he was exasperated at the first suspicion of her design, and as his indignation was artfully fomented, he threw himself without reserve into the arms of the Mallets. The Poet's conversation, (we may trust Dr Johnson an unforgiving enemy) was easy and elegant; and his wife, though far different from my mother in character and person, was not deficient either in wit or cunning. Their society soothed and occupied his grief: and as they both thought with freedom on the subjects of Religion and Government they successfully laboured to correct the prejudices of his education.

(A, p. 31 – MS f 17)

8

Such was truly the most interesting and respectable cause of my father's retirement: but I may not dissemble that it was precipitated by a motive of baser alloy, the encreasing disorder of his circumstances. By a wise dispensation, which preserves the balance of riches, idleness is the heir of industry; and the thirst of gain is succeeded by the desire of enjoyment. OEconomy is seldom the virtue of a gay and sanguine temper; my father's youth had been penuriously stinted; he was dazzled by a sudden influx of gold: but his possessions proved inadequate to his hopes, and his expences soon exceeded the measure of his income. To this illusion my grandfather had in some degree been accessory by leaving to his daughters the clearest and most solid parts of his personal fortune, while he bequeathed to his son such unsettled accounts such complicated plans as might have been productive in his own hands but which tended rather to deceive than to enrich a less careful manager. Among these was a lucrative contract for supplying the Court of Spain with naval stores, of which large quantities were already deposited in his warehouses at Cadiz. In spite of the most solemn engagements, these effects were sequestered on the rupture between the two nations, and in the vote which my father gave against the Spanish convention, I must admire either his patriotism or his credulity. He anticipated the payment of his debt with a large arrear of interest and damages, which he confidently expected from the justice of the Catholic King: but alas! on the return of peace our agents and memorials were referred by the Ministers to the Judges, and by the judges to the ministers till the obsolete demand has finally evaporated in delay, disappointment and fruitless cost. Of dress and diversions, of house and equipage the expences may be foreseen and must be limited: but the gaming-table is a dark and slippery precipice. My father did not enjoy with impunity the honour of being a member of the old club at White's: his contemporaries seemed to think less highly than himself of his skill at Whist; some large and nameless charges in his books must be placed to the Debtor side of play; and the tryals to which I have alluded were the anxious hours and sleepless nights of his wife, while she felt that too much of her children's fortune was depending on a card or a die. By these means his ready-money was speedily exhausted, his landed estate was entailed, and as soon as the first debts were contracted, the rapid accumulation of principal and interest encreased the want, and diminished the facility of new supplies. His temper was soured by pecuniary embarrassements, and had my mother lived he must have withdrawn with more comfort, but with less grace from a public life, in which he could not support or retrench his customary figure. But if we search still deeper, we shall discover a third motive of retirement in the natural inconstancy of his disposition, which, perhaps, has been painted by his tutor Mr William Law under the name of *Flatus* 'Flatus (says the devout satirist) is rich and in health: yet always uneasy and always searching after happiness Every time you visit him you find some new project in his head; he is eager upon it as something that is more worth his while and will do more for him than any thing that is already past. Every new thing so seizes him that if you were to take him from it, he would think himself quite undone. His sanguine temper and strong passions promise him so much happiness in every thing that he is always cheated and satisfied with nothing.' Mr Law's wit then pursues him through the various pursuits of dress [,] gaming, diversions, drinking, hunting, building, riding and travelling, with each of which Flatus is by turns delighted and disgusted. All these features cannot indeed be applied to the same person, and as the *second* Edition of The serious call to a devout and holy life was published in the year 1732, the prophetic eye of the tutor must have discerned the butterfly in the caterpillar. But our family-tradition attests his laudable or malicious design; and from my own observation, I can acknowledge the skill of the painter and the likeness of the portrait.

(A, pp. 33-34 – MS ff 18-18ᵛ)

9

Christianity has not shed it's mildest influence on her temper naturally proud and morose: she hates all the enemies of God, and how can *her* enemies be *his* friends? After their separation she seldom saw and never forgave my father: his connection with the Mallets marked him as a reprobate, and when I notified his death the sister did not drop a tear of sorrow or sympathy. That event however renewed our correspondence which had been interrupted from my childhood, and I have been admitted to her presence in her two short and necessary visits to London. I found her external appearance such as has been described; her health confirmed by temperance; her natural understanding clear and manly; and her attention to the interest of this World, as keen and intelligent, as if she had never thought of another. My aunt Hester has now lived above eighty five years on this earth, an improper habitation, and if she survives to the conclusion of these Memoirs, I shall mention my hopes and fears which may depend on her final dispositions.

(A, pp. 37-38 – MS f 20)

10

By my grandfather's [1]last Will, his two daughters were enriched at the
expense of his son to whose marriage he was not perfectly reconciled.
Of my two Aunts, Catherine became the wife of Mr Edward Elliston
[2]an East-India Captain; their daughter and heiress Catherine was married
in the year 1756 to Edward Eliot Esq[re] (now Lord Eliot) of Port-Eliot
in the County of Cornwall, and their three sons are my nearest [3] relations
on the father's side. A life of devotion and celibacy was the choice of my
aunt Mrs Hester Gibbon, who at the age of eighty five still resides in a
hermitage at Cliffe in Northamptonshire, having survived many years [4]
her spiritual guide and faithful companion Mr William Law.

(B, p. 5 – MS f 24)

11

It is on the tender and vacant mind that the first characters of science
and language are most deeply engraved: and I am often conscious that
the defects of my first education have not been perfectly supplied
by the voluntary labour of my riper years. Yet in my progress from
infancy to the age of puberty, the faculties of memory and reason were
insensibly fortified, my stock of ideas was encreased and I soon discovered the spirit of enquiry and the love of books to which I owe the
happiness of my life. My Aunt Mrs Porten, whom I must always mention
with respectfull gratitude possessed a clear and manly understanding
and her natural taste was improved by the perusal of the best authors
in the English language. In sickness or in health I was often resigned
to her care, and my long vacations from school were chiefly passed in
her father's house near the bridge and church-yard at Putney. She was
truly my mother, she became my friend: all distance and reserve were
banished between us; we freely conversed on the most familiar or abstruse
subjects, and it was her delight and reward to observe the first shoots of
my childish fancy. During many hours, as she sat anxious and watchful
by my bed-side have I listened to the books which she read, and the
stories which she related: and a favourite tale from the English translation of Hippolitus Earl of Douglas is still present to my memory: the
cavern of the winds, the palace of felicity, and the fatal moment, at the
end of three months, or three Centuries, in which Prince Adolphus is
overtaken by old time who had worn out so many pairs of wings in the
fruitless chase. I soon tasted the Arabian nights entertainments, a book
of all ages, since in my present maturity I can revolve without con-

---

[1] *II altered these first two lines or so down to* Catherine *into*   ; and by his last will,
at the expense of Edward, his only son (with whose marriage he was not perfectly
reconciled,) enriched his two daughters Catherine and Hester. The former   [2] *II*
om an East India Captain   [3] *II added* male   [4] *II having long survived*

tempt, that pleasing medley of Oriental manners, and supernatural fictions. But it is in rude ages and to youthful minds that the marvellous is most attractive: the decoration of the imaginary world is more splendid, its events more interesting, its laws more – more consonant to justice, and virtue, and our ignorance is easily reconciled to the violation of probability and truth. From these tales I rose to the father of poetry, but I could only embrace the phantom of Homer; nor was I then capable of discerning that Pope's translation is a portrait endowed with every merit, except likeness to the original. His elegant and sonorous verse I repeated with emphasis, and retained without labour, I was delighted with the exploits of the Iliad and the adventures of the Odyssey, the Heroes of the Trojan war soon became my intimate acquaintance and I often disputed with my aunt on the characters of Hector and Achilles. From Pope's Homer to Dryden's Virgil was an easy transition: but I know not how, by the fault of the author or the translator or the reader the pious Æneas less forcibly seized on my imagination; and I could read with more pleasure some parts of the Metamorphoses, the fall of Phaethon, and the speeches of Ajax and Ulysses in the old version of Sandys's Ovid. Our English writers of poetry[,] Romances, history and travels were my daily and indiscriminate food: my aunt's partiality encouraged me to open the works of philosophy and divinity least adapted to the capacity of a child, but I was either too young or too old to partake of her enthusiasm for the Characteristics of Shaftsbury. During the nine months (from March to December 1747) between my grandfather's absconding and the sale of his effects, I rioted without controul in his library which had been hitherto locked, and I should distinguish this period, the eleventh year of my age, by the plentiful nourishment and rapid growth of my mind.

(B, pp. 10-12 – MS ff 26ᵛ-27ᵛ)

12

To complete this account of my puerile studies, I shall here observe that I soon attempted and soon abandoned two litterary projects far above my strength; a critical enquiry into the age of Sesostris, and the paralel lives of the Emperor Aurelian and Selim the Turkish Sultan, who in their cruelty, valour, and Syrian victories may indeed support some kind of resemblance.

(B, p. 14 – MS f 28ᵛ)

13

The defects of private tuition might have been supplied by public discipline and example: but the example of the old monks (I mean the fellows)[1] was not likely to incite the emulation and diligence of the

[1] *I* example of the senior members of the society

novices and undergraduates. The forty principal members of our opulent
foundation who had been amply endowed with the means of study and
subsistence, were content to slumber in the supine enjoyment of these
benefits; they had absolved themselves from the labour of reading, or
thinking or writing; and the first shoots of learning or genius rotted on
the ground without producing any fruits either for the owners or the
public.

(B, p. 17 – MS f 30)

14

In the exercises of the body which have been reduced to a polite art, I
was less successful than in those of the mind. A skillful fencing master
could never communicate to my arm the dextrous management of a foil
or sword; and once in a boyish quarrel, my awkwardness was punished
by the loss of some drops of blood. My total want of an ear and taste
for music disqualified me for the profession of a dancer: I attempted,
with indifferent grace to walk a minuet: but I have never been able to
unravel the mazes of a country dance. The Manage or Riding-house then
flourished under the care of Mr de Mesery, a Gentleman[1] of Lausanne:
but he could not be proud of such a disciple as myself; and after the
fruitless expence and labour of five months, I gladly withdrew from his
Equestrian school without an hope of being ever promoted to the use of
stirrups or spurs. This unfitness for bodily exercise reconciled me however to a sedentary life: and many precious hours were employed in my
closet, which, at the same age are wasted on horseback by the strenuous
idleness of my countrymen.

(C, pp. 14-15 – MS ff 64^v-65)

15

I should be ashamed if the warm season of youth had passed away
without any sense of friendship or love: and in the choice of their objects,
I may applaud the discernment of my head or heart – Mr George
Deyverdun of Lausanne was a young Gentleman of high honour, and
quick feelings, of an elegant taste and a liberal understanding: he became the companion of my studies and pleasures; every idea, every
sentiment was poured into each other's bosom: and our schemes of
ambition or retirement always terminated in the prospect of our final
and inseparable union – The beauty of Mademoiselle Curchod, the
daughter of a country clergyman, was adorned with science and virtue:
she listened to the tenderness which she had inspired; but the romantic
hopes of youth and passion were crushed, on my return, by the prejudice
or prudence of an English parent. I sighed as a lover: I obeyed as a son:
my wound was insensibly healed by time, absence, and the habits of a

[1] *I* in every sense of the word

new life: and[1] my cure was accelerated by a faithful report of the tranquillity and chearfulness of the Lady herself. Her equal behaviour under
the tryals of indigence and prosperity has displayed the firmness of her
character. A citizen of Geneva, a rich banker of Paris made himself
happy by rewarding her merit; the genius of her husband has raised him
to a perilous eminence; and Madame Necker now divides and alleviates
the cares of the first minister of the finances of France.

(C, p. 16 – MS f 65[v])

16

Whatsoever have been the fruits of my education they must be ascribed
to the fortunate shipwreck which cast me on the shores of the Leman
lake. I have sometimes applied to my own fate the verses of Pindar
which remind an Olympic champion that his victory was the consequence
of his exile, and that at home, like a domestic fowl his days might have
rolled away inactive or inglorious

$$\text{ἤτοι καὶ τεά κεν,}$$
$$\text{Ἐνδομάχας ἀτ' ἀλέκτωρ,}$$
$$\text{Συγγόνω παρ' ἐστία}$$
$$\text{Ἄκλεης τιμὰ κατεφυλλοροησε —}$$
$$\text{Εἰ μὴ στάσις ἀντιάνειρα}$$
$$\text{— — αμερσε πατρας.}$$

(*Olymp.* xii)

If my childish revolt against the Religion of my country had not stripped
me in time of my Academic gown, the five important years, so liberally
improved in the studies and conversation of Lausanne would have been
steeped in port and prejudice among the monks of Oxford. Had the
fatigue of idleness compelled me to read, the path of learning would not
have been enlightened by a ray of philosophic freedom: I should have
grown to manhood ignorant of the life and language of Europe, and
my knowledge of the World would have been confined to an English
Cloyster. Had I obtained a more early deliverance from the region of
sloth and pedantry; had I been sent abroad with the indulgence which
the favour and fortune of my father might have allowed I should probably
have herded with the young travellers of my own nation, and my attain-
ments in language, and manners and science would have been such as
they usually import from the continent. But my religious error fixed me
at Lausanne in a state of banishment and disgrace: the rigid course of
discipline and abstinence to which I was condemned invigorated the
constitution of my mind and body: poverty and pride estranged me
from my countrymen: I was reduced to seek my amusement in myself

---

[1] *I ended this sentence* against the dangers of a serious attachment, my heart has
been steeled by the image of that amiable woman.

and my books, and in the society of the natives who considered me as
their fellow-citizen, I insensibly lost the prejudices of an Englishman.
My friends may indeed complain that this foreign education had eradi-
cated the love and preference of my native country: my mother-tongue
was grown less familiar; and I had few objects to remember and fewer
to regret in the British islands. If I was impatient of my situation, it
was rather as a prisoner than as an exile, and I should gladly have
accepted a small independent estate on the easy terms of passing my life
in Switzerland with the two persons who possessed the different affec-
tions of my heart.

(C, pp. 16-17 – MS ff 65^v-66)

17

During the seven years (1758-1760 [,] 1765-1770) which I divided
between London and Buriton my ordinary expences were reduced to this
moderate stipend: the extraordinaries of the Militia and my travels
(1760-1765) were defrayed, the former by my pay of Captain; the
latter by a stipulated supply of twelve hundred pounds, and I may claim
the singular merit of never having borrowed a shilling during the whole
term of my filial dependence. From the fashionable follies of English
youth, the vanity of dress, the mischief of play, and the impulse of perpetual motion, I was saved by temper as well as by oeconomy: and with
the private establishment of a lodging, a servant and a chair, my amusements were simple, and my appetites moderate. As soon as my purse
was emptied by the unavoidable charges of a town life, I retired without
a murmur to the shelter of domestic hospitality; and all circulation was
suspended for some months: like those animals who repose in a torpid
state without any occasion to exhaust or renovate their vital juices.

(C, p. 19 – MS f 67)

18

The better habits which I had formed at Lausanne induced to seek a
more rational and elegant society: but my search was not easy or successful, and the first tryal of a capital did not correspond with the gay
pictures of my fancy. I had promised myself the pleasure of conversing
with every man of litterary fame: but our most eminent authors were
remote in Scotland, or scattered in the country, or buried in the Universities, or busy in their callings, or unsocial in their tempers, or in a
station too high or too low to meet the approaches of a solitary youth.

(C, pp. 19-20 – MS f 67)

19

After my library, I must not forget an occasional place of weekly study;
the parish Church which I frequented, commonly twice, every Sunday

in conformity with the pious or decent custom of the family. I deposited in our pew the octavo Volumes of Grabe's Septuagint, and a Greek testament of a convenient edition: and in the lessons, Gospels and Epistles of the morning and evening service, I accompanied the reader in the original text, or the most ancient version of the Bible. Nor was the use of this study confined to words alone: during the psalms, at least, and the sermon I revolved the sense of the chapters which I had read and heard; and the doubts, alas or objections that invincibly rushed on my mind, were almost always multiplied by the learned expositors whom I consulted on my return home. Of these Ecclesiastical meditations, few were transcribed, and still fewer have been preserved: but I find among my papers a polite and elaborate reply from Dr Hurd (now Bishop of Worcester) to whom I had addressed, without my name, a critical disquisition on the sixth Chapter of the book of Daniel. Since my escape from Popery I had humbly acquiesced in the common creed of the Protestant Churches; but in the latter end of the year 1759, the famous treatise of Grotius (de veritate Religionis Christianae) first engaged me in a regular tryal of the evidence of Christianity. By every possible light that reason and history can afford I have repeatedly viewed the important subject: nor was it my fault if I said with Montesquieu 'Je lis pour m'edifier, mais cette lecture produit souvent en moi un effet tout contraire' since I am conscious to myself, that the love of truth and the spirit of freedom directed my search. The most accurate philosophers, and the most orthodox Divines will perhaps agree that the belief of miracles and mysteries cannot be supported on the brittle basis, the distant report, of human testimony: and that the faith, as well as the virtue, of a Christian must be formed and fortified by the inspiration of Grace.

(C, additional paragraph, p. 21 – MS f 68ᵛ)

20

My first work the *Essai sur l'etude* de la Literature was published in the year 1761 during the service of the Militia. If I had yielded to the impulse of youthful vanity, if I had given my Manuscript to the World, because I was tired of keeping it in my closet the venial sin might be honestly confessed and would be easily pardoned. But I can affirm, in truth and conscience, that it was forced from my reluctant hands by the advice and authority of my father. He was himself impatient to enjoy the glory of his son; and he fondly conceived that the success of a Classical performance in the French language might recommend the author to some honourable employment in the approaching congress of Augsburgh which indeed was refused to the pacific wishes of Europe.

(C, pp. 23-24 – MS f 70)

21

A youth of liberal education may be allowed to make a tryal of his strength in a foreign language; and some applause will attend the successful adventure: but his riper judgement will teach him that it is in his own country, and in his mother-tongue that he must build the solid fabric of his fame. After my second return I gradually adopted the style and sentiments of an Englishman: it was in my power to act as a magistrate; it might be my fortune to sit in Parliament: I investigated with some care the principles and history of the British constitution; and a copious, rational abstract of Blackstone's Commentaries was the first and indeed the sole fruit of my legal studies The generality of readers feed only on the popular publications of the winter; and the most austere student will often break the line to indulge his curiosity, and provide the fashionable topics of conversation. But I was ever mindful of the adage 'old wine, old friends, *old books*' the classics of Greece and Rome were my perpetual feast, and, 'the *Critical observations on the sixth book of the Æneid* arose, perhaps, from the thirtieth perusal of Virgil.

(D, pp. 10-11 – MS ff 84ᵛ-85)

22

the neighbourhood enjoyed the presence of an active magistrate and charitable landlord: his polite address and chearful conversation recommended him to his equals: he was not dissatisfied with his son, and he had been fortunate or rather judicious in the choice of his two wives. . . . There can be no merit in the discharge of a duty: but, alone, in my library, at such a distance of time and place, without a witness or a judge, I should be pursued with the bitterness of remembrance; had I not obeyed the dictates of filial piety, had I not consented to every sacrifice that might promise some relief to the distress of a parent.

(D, p. 12 – MS f 85ᵛ)

23

The cause of government was ably vindicated by *Lord North*, a statesman of spotless integrity, a consummate master of debate, who could wield with equal dexterity the arms of reason and ridicule. He was seated on the Treasury bench between his Attorney and Solicitor General, the two pillars of the law and state, *magis pares quam similes*: and the minister might indulge in a short slumber whilst he was upheld on either hand by the majestic sense of *Thurlow*, and the skillful eloquence of *Wedderburne*. From the adverse side of the house an ardent and powerful opposition was supported by the lively declamation of *Barré*, the legal acuteness of Dunning, the profuse and philosophic fancy of *Burke* and the argumentative vehemence of *Fox*, who in the conduct of a party approved himself equal to the conduct of an Empire. By such men every operation of peace and war, every principle of justice or policy, every question of authority and freedom was attacked and defended; and the subject of the momentous contest was the union or separation of Great Britain and America

(Add. MSS 34882, No 204)

Appendix II

Surviving letters of D. Pavillard
to Gibbon's father
(1753-1758)
in the British Museum Add. MSS 34887

1

Monsieur

Quoique je vous aie promis de vous donner tous les q[uin]ze jours des nouvelles de Monsieur votre Fils, j'ai laissé pa[sser] un Courier, plus que je n'aurois du le faire; mais dans l[a] suite je serai plus exact.

Monsieur De Gibbon se porte très bien par la grace de Dieu, et il me paroit qu'il ne se trouve pas mal de notre maison; j'ai même lieu de penser qu'il prend de l'attachement pour moi, ce dont je suis charmé & que je travaillerai a augmenter, parce qu'il aura plus de confiance e[n] moi, dans ce que je me propose de lui dire.

Je n'ai point encor entrepris de lui parler sur les matieres de Religion, parce que je n'entens pas assez la langue Angloise pour soutenir une longue conversation en cette Langue, quoique je lise les Auteurs Anglois avec assez de facilité; et Monsr De Gibbon n'entend pas assez de François, mais il y fait beaucoup de progrès.

J'espère que vous ne désaprouverez pas, Monsieur, que je lui aïe fait faire un petit habit d'été, qu'il m'a demandé, de même que quelques chemises, dont il m'a paru qu'il avoit besoin. J'aurai l'honneur de vous envoier le compte du tout. Je vous prie aussi de me marquer si vous trouvez à propos que je lui donne quelque argent de poche, et combien je puis lui en donner par mois. Au reste il s'applique beaucoup à la lecture. Il me paroit jusqu'ici que les Domestiques de la maison peuvent lui rendre tous les services dont il a besoin, ainsi, a moins que vous ne l'ordonniez autrement, je ne lui en donnerai point, d'autant plus qu'il n'en a point demandé.

Il voit quelquefois Mylord Blesinton & Monsieur son Fils qui est venu passer trois semaines auprès de son cher Pere, pendant que les Professeurs de Geneve suspendent et interrompent leurs leçons â cause des moissons. Il a amené avec lui Monsieur Arran, qui est de la connoissance de Monsr De Gibbon, ces Messieurs m'ont paru se revoir avec plaisir.

Je suis fort content de la politesse & de la douceur du caractere de Monsr votre Fils, & je me flatte que je pourrai toujours vous parler de lui avec éloge. Je fais des voeux très sincères pour votre conservation & pour votre prosperité & j'ai l'honneur d'être avec les sentimens de la consideration la plus distinguée

Monsieur

à Lausanne ce   Votre très humble et très obeissant
25e Juillet 1753   serviteur Pavillard Pasteur

2

Monsieur

J'ai eu l'honneur de vous écrire dans ma précédente lettre que je travaillois avec Monsieur De Gibbon sur la Langue Françoise, afin qu'il soit bientot en état de pouvoir expliquer avec moi quelques Auteurs Classiques & les autres choses qu'il doit étudier; parce que n'aiant pas l'accent Anglois, & ne connoissant pas à fond le genie de cette Langue, je ne pourrois pas, assez utilement pour lui, le faire traduire un Auteur Latin en Anglois.

Mais nous ne tarderons pas à y venir, parce qu'il s'applique au François et qu'il y fait beaucoup de progrès.

Monsieur De Gibbon se porte bien, par la grace de Dieu; je l'aime et je me suis extrémement attaché à lui, parce qu'il est doux et tranquille. Pour ce qui regarde ses sentimens, quoique je ne lui aie encor rien dit là dessus, j'ai lieu d'esperer qu'il ouvrira les yeux à la verité. Je le pense ainsi, parce qu'etant dans mon Cabinet il a choisi deux livres de controverse qu'il a pris dans sa chambre et qu'il les lit.

J'ai eu l'honneur de vous marquer ci devant les noms des Seigneurs et des Gentilshommes Anglois que nous avons ici; mais il est plus particulierement attaché à Mylord Huntinghtower, qu'il a connu au College, et qui paroit l'aimer beaucoup.

Il ne m'a point temoigné avoir aucune envie d'aller dans quelque Ville Catholique, et comme il ne m'a pas paru souhaitter d'aller dans nos Eglises, je ne le lui ai pas proposé: quand son esprit s'éclairera il prendra du gout pour le culte raisonnable que nous professons.

Comme Monsieur De Gibbon a besoin de quelque argent de poche, je vous prie, Monsieur, de me marquer si vous voulez lui assigner quelque chose de fixe par mois, ou si vous trouvez bon de le laisser le maitre là dessus, à la charge de vous rendre compte de sa depense: Ou enfin si vous trouvez à propos que je lui donne plus ou moins suivant que je verrai qu'il aura eu quelque occasion legitime de faire quelque depense.

Je ne vous envoierai aucun compte qu'à la fin des trois mois, afin de ne pas multiplier les comptes.

J'ai dit à Monsieur votre Fils que je me proposois de vous écrire aujourd'hui, et il m'a chargé de vous offrir ses très humbles respects, et de vous demander la permission de le laisser monter au manege: cet exercice pourroit contribuer a donner de la force à son corps, c'est l'idée qu'il en a: mais je n'ai rien voulu decider là dessus, jusqu'à ce que vous m'aiez appris votre sentiment.

Agréez, Monsieur, les vœux que je fais pour votre prosperité, de même que la consideration distinguée avec laquelle j'ai l'honneur d'être.

Monsieur

a Lausanne ce   Votre très humble et très obeissant
15e Aout 1753   Serviteur Pavillard Pasteur

3

Monsieur

Depuis ma lettre du 15<u>e</u> Aout, je receus le 18<u>e</u> du même mois la lettre que vouz m'avez fait l'honneur de m'écrire en datte du 24<u>e</u> Juillet. Je l'ai lue avec attention: Permettez moi de vous marquer les reflexions que j'y ai fait.

Vous souhaittez que je tienne Monsieur votre Fils à la maison attaché à ses études, et qu'il sorte peu. Vous êtes Pere, et par là même, Monsieur, vous avez droit de prescrire la maniere dont vous voulez qu on le conduise. Sans doute vous ne prenez ce parti, que parce que vous croiez qu'on reussira mieux par cette voie à le ramener des préjugés auxquels il s'est livré. Mais, je vous prie de considerer que Monsieur votre Fils est d'un caractère sérieux, qu'il se plait a réfléchir, qu'étant dans sa chambre occupé à lire, il suivra ses idées, et il s'y attachera toujours plus, parce que personne ne le contredira; D ailleurs regardant comme une peine l'obligation qu'on lui impose, il sera toujours moins porté à écouter favorablement ce que je lui dirai; il envisagera tous mes discours, comme venant d'un homme qui est dans les idées qu'il desaprouve, et qui veut cependant les lui faire recevoir parce qu'il est paié pour cela.

Je crois, Monsieur, qu'il seroit plus à propos de le distraire un peu, de l'egaier un peu pour lui faire passer ce qu'il a de trop sombre dans le caractere: en voiant bonne compagnie il apercevroit qu'on pense juste sur bien des sujets, il s'accoutumeroit à être contredit quelquefois, et à ceder aussi dans l'occasion, il examineroit avec plus de soin, et avec moins de preoccupation les principes qu'il adopte, et les voiant souvent condamnés par des personnes qu'il voit qui ont du gout pour la verité, il ne les regarderoit pas comme infaillibles, et convaincu qu'on ne le hait pas à cause de ses sentimens, il ecouteroit ce qu'on lui diroit avec plus de confiance. Tout ce que je viens de dire est une suite des re-marques que j'ai fait sur son caractere, & sur ce que vous m'avez fait l'honneur de m'en dire dans votre lettre. Mais, Monsieur, vous avez droit de décider, & je suivrai vos idées plutot que les miennes. Je me suis aperçu qu'il était attaché au parti du Pretendant; il s'en est declaré assez ouvertement dans la suite. J'ai combattu ses idées sans faire semblant que c'étoit les siennes, & sans marquer aucune intention de lui faire de la peine; il a repliqué plusieurs fois, mais à la fin j'ai tellement renversé tous ses raisonnemens qu'il n'en parle plus, & qu'il s'exprime sur le sujet du Roi d'une maniere bien différente, de ce qu'il faisoit autrefois. Je n'assurerai pas cependant qu'il ait entierement changé d'idées, parce qu'il parle peu, & que je n'ai pas voulu faire connoitre que j'avois dessein de l'emporter sur lui. Au reste il se porte très bien, par la grace de Dieu, et il me paroit qu'il a de l'affection pour moi.

J'ai pris la liberté d'envoier une lettre de change de la somme de vingt livres sterlings a M.ᵉ Boissier, comme vous me l'avez marqué dans votre lettre. Ces 20 livres font, argent de notre Païs, la somme de 290 livres, à raison de 14 ll. 10ss la livre. Je vous demanderai 60 livres par mois, pour la pension, pour le dejeuner, pour la chambre et la chandelle. Pour le bois je lui en acheterai une provision: comme il aime le feu, il a pris une chambre à cheminée; s'il aime à faire bon feu, il en consumera une plus grande quantité, ce que je ne saurois determiner, mais j'aurai soin de le lui acheter au meilleur prix & comme pour moi-même. Quelques jours après son arrivée il me demanda de l'argent, ne sachant point ce que vous lui destiniez par mois, je le priai de me dire combien il en souhaittoit, il me demanda deux Louis neufs. Est-ce là, lui dis-je, ce que Monsieur votre Pere a accoutumé de vous donner, il me repondit qu'ouï, et même que vous lui en donniez davantage. Alors je les lui donnai, et je lui en ai donné autant le mois suivant, mais aiant recu votre lettre, je ne lui ai donné qu'un Louis pour le mois de 7bre. et un pour le mois d'Octobre.

Comme il faisoit fort chaud quand il arriva, Mons.ᵉ Frey me dit qu'il lui paraissoit qu'il avoit besoin d'un habit d'été, je lui en fis faire un de Camelot de Bruxelles qui n'est pas cher. Je vous rends compte de ce que j'ai fait, et des raisons qui me l'ont fait faire. Aiez la bonté, Monsieur, de decider ce que je dois lui donner d'argent de poche, à moins que vous ne m'en laissiez la disposition pour lui en donner plus ou moins, suivant que je verrai qu'il pourra en avoir besoin; cela pourra encor l'attacher à moi, & je ne pousserai pas trop loin, la permission que vous me donnerez là dessus. Pour l'habit j'ai été faché de l'avoir fait, quand j'ai vu que vous ne le trouviez pas à propos, mais il était fait, quand votre lettre est arrivée. Je lui ai fait faire aussi quelques chemises dont il avoit besoin. Je vous envoierai les comptes detaillés de tout cela, si vous le trouvez à propos, ou j'attendrai à vous les faire tenir par le moien de quelque Anglois qui partira pour s'en retourner.

Voila, Monsieur, une longue lettre, que je vous prie d'excuser; je vous rendrai compte exactement de tout ce qui arrivera dans la suite. Daignez encor m'apprendre si vous trouvez bon qu'il monte au manege.

Je fais des voeux de tout mon coeur pour votre prosperi[té] & j'ai l'honneur d'être avec une parfaite consideration & mon entier devouement

Monsieur

à Lausanne ce   Votre très humble et très obeissant

31e 8bre 1753   Serviteur   Pavillard Pasteur

Monsieur De Gibbon me
charge de vous offrir
ses très humbles respects

4

Monsieur

J'espere que vous me pardonnerez mon long silence en faveur des nouvelles que j'ai à vous apprendre. Si j'ai tant tardé, ce n'a été ni par oubli, ni par negligence, mais je croiois de semaine en semaine pouvoir vous annoncer que Monsieur votre fils avoit entierement renoncé aux fausses idées qu'il avoit embrassées; mais il a fallu disputer le terrein pié à pié, et je n'ai pas trouvé en lui un homme leger, et qui passe rapidement d'un sentiment à un autre. Souvent apres avoir détruit toutes ses idées sur un article, de maniére qu'il n'avoit rien a repliquer, ce qu'il m'avouoit sans detour, il me disoit qu'il ne croioit pas qu'il n'y eut rien à me repondre. Là dessus je n'ai pas jugé qu'il fallût le pousser à bout, et extorquer de lui un aveu que son cœur desavoueroit; je lui donnois alors du tems pour réfléchir; tous mes Livres étoient à sa disposition; je revenois à la charge quand il m'avouoit qu'il avoit étudié la matiere aussi bien qu'il l'avoit pu, et enfin j'etablissois une verité.

Je me persuadois que quand j'aurois détruit les principales erreurs de l'Eglise Romaine, je n'aurois qu'à faire voir que les autres sont des consequences des prémiéres, et qu'elles ne peuvent subsister, quand les fondamentales sont renversées; mais, comme je l'ai dit, je me suis trompé, il a fallu traitter chaque article dans son entier. Par la grace de Dieu, je n'ai pas perdu mon tems, et aujourdhui, si même il conserve quelques restes de ses pernicieuses erreurs, j'ose dire qu'il n'est plus membre de l'Eglise Romaine. Voici donc ou nous en sommes.

J'ai renversé l'infaillibilité de l'Eglise; j'ai prouvé que jamais St Pierre n'a été Chef des Apôtres: que quand il l'auroit été le Pape n'est point son successeur; qu'il est douteux que St Pierre ait jamais été à Rome, mais supposé qu'il y ait été, il n'a pas été Evêque de cette Ville. Que la transubstantation est une invention humaine, et peu ancienne dans l'Eglise, que l'adoration de l'Eucharistie et le retranchement de la Coupe sont contraires à la Parole de Dieu: Qu'il y a des Saints, mais que nous ne savons pas qui ils sont, et par consequent qu'on ne peut pas les prier: que le respect et le culte qu'on rend aux reliques est condamnable; qu'il n'y a point de Purgatoire, et que la Doctrine des Indulgences est fausse: Que le Carème et les jeunes du Vendredi et du Samedi sont ridicules aujourdhui, et de la maniere que l'Eglise Romaine les prescrit: Que les imputations que l'Eglise de Rome nous fait de varier dans notre Doctrine, et d'avoir pour Reformateurs des personnes dont la conduite et les moeurs ont été en scandale, sont entierement fausses.

Vous comprenez bien, Monsieur, que ces articles sont d'une longue discussion, qu'il a fallu du tems à Monsr votre Fils pour mediter mes raisons & pour y chercher des reponses. Je lui ai demandé plusieurs fois si mes preuves et mes raisons lui paroissoient convaincantes, il m'a toujours assuré qu'ouï, de façon que j'ose assurer aussi, comme je le lui ai dit à lui même, il y a peu de tems, qu'il n'etoit plus Catholique Romain. Je me flatte qu'après avoir obtenu la victoire sur ces articles, je l'aurai sur le reste avec le secours de Dieu. Tellement que je compte de vous marquer dans peu que cet ouvrage est fini. Je dois vous dire encor, que quoique j'aie trouvé Mr votre Fils très ferme dans ses idées, je l'ai trouvé raisonnable, qu'il s'est rendu à la lumiére, et qu'il n'est pas, ce qu'on appelle, chicaneur. Par raport à l'article du jeune les Vendredi et Samedi, long tems après que je vous eus écrit, qu'il n'avoit jamais marqué qu'il voulut l'observer, environ le commencement du mois de Mars, je m'aperçus un Vendredi qu'il ne mangeoit point de viande; je lui parlai en particulier pour en savoir la raison craignant que ce ne fut par indisposition; il me répondit qu'il l'avoit fait à dessein, et qu'il avoit cru être obligé de se conformer à la pratique d'une Eglise dont il étoit membre: nous parlames quelque tems sur ce sujet, il m'assura qu'il n'envisageoit cela que comme une pratique bonne, à la verité, et qu'il devoit suivre, quoiqu'il ne la crut pas sainte, en elle même, ni d'instittution divine. Je ne crus pas devoir ins[is]ter pour lors, ni le forcer à agir contre ses lumiéres: j'ai traitté cet article, qui est certainement un des moins importans, des moins fondés, et cependant il m'a fallu un tems considerable pour le detromper & lui faire comprendre qu'il avoit tort de s'assujettir à la pratique d'une Eglise qu'il ne reconnoissoit plus pour infaillible. Que si même cette pratique avoit eu quelque utilité dans son institution, cependant elle n'en avoit aucune en elle même, puisqu'el[le] ne contribuoit en rien à la pureté des moeurs; qu'ainsi il n'y avoit aucune raison, ni dans l'institution de cette pratique, ni dans la pratique en elle même qui l'autorisât à s'y soumettre: qu'aujourdhui ce n'étoit qu'une affaire d'intérêt, puisqu'avec de l'argent on obtenoit des dispenses pour manger gras &c., de maniére que je l'ai ramené à la liberté Chrétienne, avec beaucoup de peine et seulement depuis quelques semaines.

Au reste je puis vous assurer, Monsieur, que Mr votre Fils joui[t] d'une santé parfaite, qu'il n'a eu que quelques maux de tête, mais très rarement, pour lesquels je l'ai fait purger et saigner, ce qui a parfaitement reussi. Je l'ai engagé à vous écrire, pour vous manifester les sentimens ou il est et l'état de sa santé, et je crois qu'il l'a fait. Je continue à faire des voeux ardens pour votre conservation & pour l'heureux succès de vos entreprises, et j'ai l'honneur d'être avec une parfaite consideration et un entier devouement.

Monsieur

Lausanne ce   Votre très humble & très obeissant
26e Juin 1754   serviteur   Pavillard Pasteur

5

This letter is not in Pavillard's hand, nor is the signature his. As Mr Low says (Edward Gibbon, *p. 55, n. 1*) '*It is probably in Gibbon's hand – a boyish best-behaviour fist.*' *It is most probably the translation to which Gibbon refers in his February letter to his aunt* (*see* Letters, *i, p. 4*); *It may be conjectured that Pavillard, hearing from Gibbon that Catherine Porten did not know French, had asked him for a translation to be sent along with his letter.*

Madam

As I have a piece of news extremely interesting to acquaint you with I cannot any longer defer answering to the letter you honoured me with. God has at length blessed my cares & heard your prayers; I have had the satisfaction of bringing back Mr. Gibbon to the bosom of our Reformed Church he has communicated with us Christmas day last with devotion he appears satisfied with what he has done, & I am persuaded is at present as little inclined to the sentiments of the Church of Rome as I am myself. I have made use with him neither of vigour nor artifice. I have never hurried him in his decisions but have always left him the time to reflect on every article. he has been persuaded of the integrity of my intentions, he has heard me as a friend & I have served him as guide to enter into the road of the truth. God Almighty be blessed for it. I pray that God to strengthen him more & more in the right way & to make him a faithful member of his church. I ought to render him the justice to say I never found him obstinate. He has been fixed in his Ideas, but when he has seen the light he has rendered himself.[1] His behaviour has been very regular & [he] has made no slips, except that of Gaming twice & losing much more than I desired. I hope Madam you will acquaint Mr. Gibbon with your satisfaction & restore him your affection which tho his errors may have weakened they have not I am sure destroyed. As his father has allowed him the bare necessaries but nothing more, I dare beg you to grant him some tokens of your satisfaction. I am convinced he will employ them well & I even flatter myself he will give me the direction of them, for he has promised me never to play any

[1] *Translated from the French* il s'est rendu = *he has yielded.*

more any games of Chance. I wish you Madam all kinds of prosperity.
Lausanne, Jan:ʳʸ 28.1755

>I am with respect
>   Madam
>your most obedient
>& most humble servant
>Daniel Pavillard Pastor
>and Professor

addressed to
Mademoiselle Porten in College Street Westminster a Londres

6

Monsieur
Je me fais un devoir de repondre dabord à la lettre que vous m'avez
fait l'honneur de m'écrire le 14ᵉ du mois passé, pour vous assurer des
vœux que je fais de tout mon coeur pour votre prosperité et pour celle
de Madame votre Epouse, a qui je vous prie, Monsieur, de faire agréer
mes très humbles respects. Dieu veuille repandre sur votre mariage ses
precieuses benedictions, et vous faire gouter l'un avec l'autre le contente-
ment le plus parfait.

Je n'ai point changé de sentimens pour Monsieur votre Fils; je
m'interresse de tout mon coeur à sa santé, a ses études et à ses intérets
autant qu'il m'est possible. Il se porte très bien, par la grace de Dieu, à
présent, mais il a eu beaucoup de maux de dents, qui lui ont occasionné
quelques fluxions, ce qui m'a engagé a apeller un Medecin.

Il vous rend compte de ses études, et je puis vous assurer qu'il ne vous
dit rien qui ne soit très vrai. Il emploie très bien son tems, et il s'applique
extremement, aussi a-t-il fait beaucoup de progrès. Il entend très bien
le Latin, et il a lu les meilleurs Auteurs que nous aions, et cela plus
d'une fois: il a lu la Logique de Mʳ De Crousaz et l'Essai sur l'entende-
ment humain de Mʳ Locke dont il a fait des extraits; il a commencé le
Grec, et il s'y attache; il va commencer l'Algebre comme vous le lui
ordonnez. Vous jugerez par ses lettres s'il entend le François; car je
vous assure que je n'y ai fait aucune correction.

Par rapport à la Religion, il n'a pas laissé echaper un seul mot, qui ait
pu me faire soupçonner, qu'il eût encor quelque attachement pour la
Religion Romaine, et quoique nous parlions souvent sur ces matiéres,
je le trouve toujours penser très juste sur toutes les questions qu'on
traitte. Le petit voiage que nous avons fait lui a beaucoup valu à cet
egard; il a été temoin des superstitions epouvantables qui y regnent; il
en a été d'autant plus frappé qu'il ne les connoissoit pas, et qu'il ne
pouvoit s'imaginer qu'elles fussent aussi grandes. Quand il n'auroit
pas deja renoncé à cette Communion, il l'auroit fait indubitablement
tant elles lui ont paru excessives et deraisonnables. Je suis persuadé

MML R

qu'il a embrassé le parti Protestant par raison, et qu'il y a peu de personnes qui aient plus examiné et mieux senti la force de nos preuves que lui. Je lui dois ce temoignage et je le lui rends avec plaisir, de meme que sur sa bonne conduite.

Je lui ai fait faire un habit de drap pour l'hiver; il en avoit besoin, je crois que vous ne le desaprouverez pas, non plus que de lui fournir, comme je l'ai fait, tout ce qui lui sera necessaire, mais je ne donnerai rien pour le superflu. Je lui ai retranché les deux Louis que vous lui avez alloué par mois pendant que nous avons été en voiage.

J'aurai soin que les lettres de change que je tirerai sur vous, Monsieur, ne soient paiables qu'à dix jours de vue. Je vous envoie le compte de la demi année, et je ne remettrai mon Billet à un Banquier que la semaine prochaine.

A la Blanchisseuse	18 lb	6 ss	
Pr un habit de drap, façon et fournitures	119	10	9d
Au perruquier	34		
Au cordonnier	19	4	
Pr louage de livres, et gazette	15	7	
Pr six mouchoirs	13	10	
Pr Medecin, Chirurgien, Apoti-	8	10	
Pr 2 paires bas de laine	4	12	
Pr la blanchisseuse de bas	24		
Pr un manchon	16	15	
Pr Cartes de Geographie, port de lettres	8	8	
Pr argent de poche	160		
Pr le bois	36		
Pr la pension	360		
Pr une paire culottes de soie et façon	24		
Pr 2 paires bas de soie	16		
Pr le maître a danser 4 mois	48		
Pr le maitre de dessein 2 mois	16		
Pr 2 paires caleçons	3	10	6
Pr un Chauffepied	3		
	948 lb	13 ss	3d

J'ai l'honneur d'être avec une consideration distinguée et un entier devouement

Monsieur   Votre très humble et très obeissant
            Serviteur   Pavillard Pasteur

P.S. La lettre que vous avez ecrit à Monsieur votre Fils l a extremement touché, parce qu'elle lui a fait voir que vous etiez mecontent de lui. Rien ne peut le mortifier davantage que cette idée. Rendez lui, je vous supplie, votre affection, il la merite, par l'attachement qu'il a pour vous.

This letter is undated, but can be dated January 1766 – lb = livres (Berne money); ss = sous; d = deniers; see Editor's Notes to p. 70.

7

Monsieur

Vous avez souhaitté que Monsieur votre Fils s'appliquât a l'Algebre; le gout qu'il a pour les Belles Lettres lui faisoit apprehender que l'Algebre ne nuisit à ses études favorites; je lui ai persuadé qu'il ne se faisoit pas une juste idée de cette partie des Mathematiques; l'obeissance qu'il vous doit jointe à mes raisons l'ont determiné a en faire un cours. Je ne croiois pas qu'avec cette repugnance il y fit de grands progrès: je me suis trompé: il fait bien tout ce qu'il fait; il est exact à ses leçons, il s'applique à lire avant sa leçon, et il repasse avec soin, de maniére qu'il avance beaucoup, et plus que je ne m'y serois attendu: il est charmé d'avoir commencé, et je pense qu'il fera un petit Cours de Géometrie, ce qui en tout ne lui prendra que sept à huit mois. Pendant qu'il fait ces leçons il ne s'est point relaché sur ses autres études, il avance beaucoup dans le Grec, et il a presque lu la moitié de l'Iliade d'Homere, je lui fais regulierement des leçons sur cet Auteur: il a aussi fini les Historiens Latins, il en est à present aux Poetes; et il a lu entierement Plaute et Terence et bientot il aura fini Lucrece. Au reste il ne lit pas ces auteurs à la legere, il veut s'eclaircir sur tout: de façon qu'avec le genie qu'il a, l'excellente memoire et l'application il ira loin dans les sciences.

J'ai eu l'honneur de vous dire ci devant, que malgré ses etudes il voioit compagnie, je puis vous le dire encor aujourdhui.

J'ai pris la liberté, Monsieur, de tirer une lettre de change pour les depenses des derniers six mois, qui se monte a 73 livres sterlings. Vous y trouverez 2 articles qui ont grossi le compte: cinq mois de leçons de manege. Monsieur Gibbon vous en a demandé la permission plusieurs fois, et comme vous ne vous êtes point expliqué là dessus, il a cru que vous lui permettiez cet exercice: j'ai aussi fait accommoder son linge, dont je prens soin comme du mien propre; vous verrez qu'il a fallu remettre des manchettes &c: mais malgré mes attentions il a fallu lui faire six chemises, six mouchoirs & huit tours de col: ses chemises et tours de col etoient usés; pour les mouchoirs il en a perdu quelques uns.

Agreez, Monsieur, les voeux que je fais pour votre prosperité, et pour celle de Madame votre Epouse. Dieu veuille vous conserver à Monsieur votre fils, & vous donner la consolation de le voir en etat de faire honneur à sa Patrie par ses lumieres, comme j'espere que cela arrivera. J'ai l'honneur d'être avec la consideration la plus parfaite et un entier devouement

Monsieur

A Lausanne ce   Votre très humble et très obeissant
12e Janv: 1757.   Serviteur   Pavillard Pasteur

Monsieur Gibbon me charge de vous dire qu'il se porte bien et qu'il vous prie d'agréer ses tres humbles respects, de même que Madame votre Epouse.

Compte pour Monsieur Gibbon le fils

Pour toile batiste pour racommoder ses chemises et p^r façon	23 lb	7 ss
Pour garnir, racommoder et marquer des bas	3	
P^r louage de chevaux	9	
P^r un voiage de 2 jours en Savoie	6	15
P^r 2 saignées & quelques remedes	5	3
P^r un ceinturon	3	
P^r se faire inscrire dans le livre de l'Academie	4	
P^r racommoder les fenetres de son cabinet		15
P^r façon d'une paire culottes noires et racomodage d'habits	6	4
P^r le Perruquier, suivant son compte	44	26
P^r la blanchisseuse de linge	27	
P^r la blanchisseuse de bas	13	5
P^r le Cordonnier suivant son compte	23	4
P^r le Chapelier suivant son compte	26	10
P^r le bois	22	
P^r 5 mois leçons de manege suivant le compte	165	16
P^r ½ douzaine tasses a caffé et une jatte	4	10
P^r la pension de 6 mois	360	
P^r trois mois leçons de Mathematiques	48	
P^r argent de poche	192	
P^r rubans a son manchon	1	10
P^r papier, encre, plumes &c.	2	10
P^r 20 aunes toile de Hollande p^r 6 chemises a 2 lb 15 ss	55	
P^r 4 au. ½ et 1/3 meme toile p^r 6 mouchoirs	13	6
P^r 3 au. 1/4 toile de batiste a 5 lb 10 ss pour garnir les chemises et p^r 8 tours de col	17	18
P^r façon des chemises, mouchoirs & tours de col	12	
P^r restat du precedent compte	4	11
	1'095 lb	8 ss[1]

Pour laquelle Somme j'ai tiré une lettre de change sur Messieurs Surman

[1] *The third column of this account (for deniers) is hidden by the guard, which accounts for the apparent error of this addition, the total should be 1095 lb 8 ss 120 dd.*

et Comp. de 73 liv. sterl. La livre sterling a 15 lb faisant la somme de 1'095 lb.

8

Monsieur

J'ai eu l'honneur de vous ecrire le 27ᵉ Juillet & le 26ᵉ 8ᵇʳᵉ passés, et je vous ai rendu compte de la santé, des études & de la conduite de Monsieur votre Fils. Je n'ai rien à ajouter à tout ce que je vous en ai dit: il se porte parfaitement bien, par la grace de Dieu; il continue à étudier avec application, et je puis vous assurer qu'il fait des progrès considérables dans les études, et il se fait extrémement estimer par tous ceux qui le connoissent, et j'espére que quand il vous montrera en détail ce qu'il sait, vous en serez très content. Les Belles Lettres, qui sont son étude favorite, ne l'occupent pas entierement; il continue les Mathematiques, et son Professeur m'assure qu'il n'a jamais vu personne avancer autant que lui, ni avoir plus d'ardeur et d'application qu'il en a. Son génie heureux et pénétrant est secondé par une memoire des plus heureuses, tellement qu'il n'oublie presque rien de ce qu'il apprend. Je n'ai pas moins lieu d'être content de sa conduite; quoiqu'il étudie beaucoup, il voit cependant compagnie, mais il ne voit que des personnes dont le commerce peut lui être utile.

J'ai eu l'honneur de vous marquer qu'il souhaittoit d'avoir un valet; comme vous ne lui avez point écrit, non plus qu'à moi que vous désaprouviez son dessein, je n'ai pas osé m'y opposer plus longtems. Je vous ai aussi écrit qu'il a fait un voiage à Geneve pour y faire connoissance avec quelques Savans et pour voir la Comedie; ces deux articles ont fait une augmentation au compte, mais vous ne la desaprouverez pas, puisqu'il fait un bon usage de son argent et de son tems, et qu'il est dans un âge dans lequel on accorde un peu plus de liberté aux jeunes gens.

Ma femme vous offre ses très humbles obeissances, nous nous joignons tous deux pour les présenter à Madame votre Epouse, pour la prospérité de laquelle nous faisons bien des voeux de même que pour la vôtre, Monsieur. Monsieur Gibbon me charge aussi de vous assurer de ses très humbles respects, et de les offrir de sa part à Madame Gibbon. J'ai l'honneur d'être avec une très parfaite consideration et un entier devouement.

Monsieur

a Lausanne ce   Votre très humble et très obeissant
14ᵉ Janv. 1758   Serviteur   Pavillard Pasteur

Compte de la depense de Monsieur Gibbon pour les six derniers mois depuis le 1er Juillet jusqu'au 31 Xbre

	lb	ss
Pour argent de poche	192 lb	
Pr le valet depuis le 1er Aout 5 mois	160	
Pr quelques louages de chevaux	7	
Pr la voiture et le sejour a Geneve avec son domestique	225	
Pr 4 paires bas de soie	39	
Pr garnir, acommoder et blanchir les bas de soie pendant six mois	25	17 ss
Pr 12 paires bas de fil, de dessous	18	
Pr raccommoder ses chemises	3	15
Pr faire la charité à un Anglois	3	
Pr louage de livres	4	10
Pr 3 paires bas de laine	5	12
Pr bois pour Monsieur Gibbon, pour la chambre et le bois du valet	42	
Pr un ecran de chandelle	3	
Pr une cloche pr apeller son valet	3	8
Pr parties de billard	21	18
Pr affranchir 2 lettres, papier, encre, cire &c.	2	7
Au Marchand Drapier suivant son compte	172	
Au Tailleur suivant son compte	35	10
Au Chapelier suivant son compte	26	8
Au Perruquier suivant son compte	38	
A la Blanchisseuse de linge	22	10
Au Fabriquant pour une culotte de soie	20	
Pr une epée d'acier damasquinée, couteau de chasse et 3 ceinturons &c.	92	
Au Cordonnier	28	12
Pr la pension	360	
Pr le montant total	1'551 lb	7 ss
Je redevais du dernier compte	1	14
Reste	1'549	13

Ce qui revient a 104 livres sterlings, la Livre comptée a 14 livres de notre monnoie et 16 sols. Ainsi il me sera redu à compte nouveau 10 livres 9 sols.[1]

---

[1] £104 at the rate of 14 livres 16 sols (or 296 sols) = 1539 livres 4 sols. After remitting £104 to Pavillard (see next page), Mr Gibbon was still owing 10 livres 9 sols.

Et comme le 26.ᵉ 8ᵇʳᵉ 1757, j'ai tiré une lettre de change de 14 livres sterlings, qui est sans doute deja paiée, je ne tirerai celle-ci que de quatre vingt dix livres, a dix jours de vue, que je prie Monsieur Gibbon de donner ordre à Monsʳ Surman et Comp d'acquitter.

9

Pavillard's Draft of his Account for January to June 1757

Magdalen College Library MS 359 Part I, No. 13 Gibbon Accounts 1753-1794 (the writing is Pavillard's).

Compte de Monsieur Gibbon depuis le 1ᵉʳ Janvier 1757 jusqu'au 1ᵉʳ Juillet 1757

Janv. 1	étrennes aux domestiques, au porteur de lettres	11 lb.	4 ss
22	Pʳ un falot	5	
11	Pʳ la gazette d'Utrecht	4	
Fév. 6	Donné a un Irlandois par charité	4	
	au Tailleur	29	16
	au Cordonnier	38	8
	au Perruquier pʳ la demi année	43	10
	au Libraire Vaney pour louage de livres	5	16
	Pʳ la Gazette de Berne	4	
	Pʳ le Bois	32	
	Pʳ la pension	360	
	Pʳ sept paires bas de soie et blanchissage de bas	81	6
	Pʳ un habit de drap gris &c et pr. un habit de Camelot de Bruxelles bleu, &c	199	26
	Pʳ argent de poche	192	
	Pʳ 2 mois leçons de Mathematiques	32	
	Pʳ les Elemens de Mathematiques	6	
	Pʳ les Sections coniques	8	
	Pʳ quelques parties de Billard	29	16
	(plus racommodage & blanchissage)	29	68
	Total	1112	40 [1]

[1] *Total is inaccurate, but this account is a mere draft.*

Editor's Notes

There are three more or less fully annotated editions of Gibbon's Memoirs:

1 *The Autobiographies of Edward Gibbon, edited by John Murray*, London, Murray, 1896 (2nd ed. 1897).
2 *The Memoirs of the Life and Writings of Edward Gibbon, edited by O. F. Emerson*, Boston, Ginn & Co., 1898.
3 *The Memoirs of the Life of Edward Gibbon, edited by George Birkbeck Hill*, London, Methuen, 1900.

The present editor is deeply indebted to these editors, in whose notes students will find much additional information. In his own notes, he has tried to limit himself to whatever may be thought useful to a full understanding of Gibbon's text.

List of Abbreviations

used in the Editor's Notes

A B C D E F   refer to the six fragments (sketches, drafts) of Gibbon's Memoirs in Add. MSS 34874.

Bibliography   *A Bibliography of the Works of Edward Gibbon by J. E. Norton*, Oxford, 1940.

B.M.   British Museum Library.

Bn   Bentinck Street, London.

B.U.   *Biographie universelle (Michaud) ancienne et moderne, nouvelle édition*, Paris and Leipzig, 1854, 45 vols.

D.F.   *The History of the Decline and Fall of the Roman Empire.*

D.N.B.   *Dictionary of National Biography*, Oxford, 1908-1909 (re-issue).

ed. edns   edition(s).

f. ff.   following page(s) or line(s).

f ff   folio(s).

G   Edward Gibbon, the historian.

Ev. Lib. ed.   *Gibbon's Decline and Fall ... in six vols*, London, Dent (Everyman's Library).

Hill   G. B. Hill's ed. of *The Memoirs*, London, 1900.

Journal A   *Gibbon's Journal to January 28th, 1763 ... with Introductory Essays*, London, 1929.

Journal B   *Le Journal de Gibbon à Lausanne*, Lausanne, 1945.

Journey   *Gibbon's Journey from Geneva to Rome*, London, 1961.

L.   Lausanne.

Low, *Gibbon*   D. M. Low, *Edward Gibbon 1737-1794*, London, 1937.

Letters   *The Letters of Edward Gibbon*, edited by J. E. Norton, 3 vols, London, 1956.

M   *The Autobiographies ...* , *edited by John Murray*, London 1896.

Misc. Gibb.   *Miscellanea Gibboniana*, Lausanne, 1952.

Misc. Wks   *The Miscellaneous Works of Edward Gibbon*, 5 vols, London, 1814.

n.   note (this abbreviation is not used for Gibbon's own notes).

N.E.D.   *New English Dictionary.*

P. p. pp.   Page(s).

All references to Gibbon's Library are based on *Edward Gibbon's Library / A Catalogue, Edited and Introduced by Geoffrey Keynes*, London, 1940.

Editor's Notes

The numbers in the left-hand margins refer to the line(s) of the text to which the corresponding note is relevant

Page 2

9 *Biographia Britannica*: This is the title of the 18th-century dictionary of British biography, 6 vols, f⁰, 1747-1766; 2nd ed., 5 vols, f⁰, 1778-1793. Both edns were in G's library at L.

12 Thuanus: Jacques Auguste de Thou (1553-1617). His *Commentariorum de vita sua libri sex* are in vol. vii of the London 1733 ed. of his *Historariarum sui temporis libri cxxxviii*, 7 vols, f⁰; this was in G's library at L.

13 Hume: The *Life of David Hume, written by himself*, was published by Adam Smith after the philosopher's death in vol. i of the 1778 ed. of *The History of England*, 8 vols, 8⁰, which ed. of Hume's *History* was in G's library at L.

20 ff. In his library at L., G had two edns of the younger Pliny's *Epistolae*, as well as W. Melmoth's translation (1770); Petrarch's *Epistolarum familiarium libri XIV*; two edns and one selection of Erasmus' *Epistolae*, besides the Leyden ed. of his *Opera*; two edns of Montaigne's *Essais*; two of Sir W. Temple's *Works*; Benvenuto Cellini's *Vita de lui medesimo scritta; An Apology of the life of C. Cibber*; Rousseau's *Confessions*; Huet's *Commentarius de rebus ad eum pertinentibus*; Goldoni's *Mémoires* (Paris, 1707) as well as his *Commedie* in 17 vols; Whiston's *Memoirs* in their 1st and their 2nd edns. For Pierre-Daniel Huet (1630-1721) and Michel de Marolles (1600-1680), see *B.U.* Huet's *Demonstratio evangelica* (1679) was his most widely known work. Being in great demand from theologians everywhere, it was reprinted in Germany, Holland and Italy. De Marolles published a first instalment of his *Memoirs* in 1656 and stopped there. For William Whiston, Anthony Wood and Bishop Newton, see *D.N.B.* Whiston's *Memoirs of the Life and Writings of Mr. William Whiston . . . written by Himself* were published three years before his death in 1752, and a 2nd ed. followed in 1753. Among the papers which Anthony Wood committed to the care of his executor were an autobiography and diaries for the years 1657-1695; the *Autobiography* was published in 1730; it was reprinted, with the addition of notes from the diaries, by William Huddesford in *The Lives of John*

Leland, Thomas Hearne, and Anthony à Wood, 2 vols, 8⁰, Oxford, 1772. This book was in G's library at L.

Page 4

28-34 I exhort them—This admonition to the Spencers occurs in the independent draft of G's introduction to the history of his family (MS *ff* 128-129 – M 417-419). Though the exact date of this fragment cannot be ascertained, it must have been written some time in the years 1787-1793. The Spencer family was then represented by several descendants of Charles Spencer (1674-1722), 3rd Earl of Sunderland, who had married in 1700 Anne Churchill, the younger daughter of the Duke of Marlborough. These were, on the one hand: the three sons of Charles Spencer (1706-1758), second son of Sunderland, who, on the death of his elder brother Robert (1701-1729), 4th Earl of Sunderland, had become the 5th Earl, and had succeeded his aunt, the Dowager Duchess of Marlborough, as 3rd Duke of Marlborough; they were George Spencer (1739-1817), 4th Duke of Marlborough, Lord Charles Spencer, M.P., (1740-1820), and Lord Robert Spencer (?-1831)—whom G knew particularly well as they had sat together on the Board of Trade—and, on the other hand, the descendants of John Spencer, youngest son of Sunderland, to whom the Sunderland estates were conferred when his brother inherited the Marlborough dukedom. His son John (1734-1783) was created Earl Spencer in 1765. G knew him (see *Letters*, ii, p. 162). His widow was at L. in the summer 1792 (*Ibid.*, iii, p. 266). Their son George John (1758-1834), 2nd Earl Spencer, was G's friend.

The family relation of Edmund Spenser to the noble family of Sir John Spencer of Althorpe, Sunderland's ancestor, has never been elucidated and is doubtful; but neither Sir John, nor his three daughters, the Phyllis, Charillis and Amaryllis of *Colin Clout* (ll. 530 ff.) ever denied the poet's right to claim their kinship.

Page 5

1-14 Fielding descended from the younger son of Sir William Feilding (*d.* 1643), who had been created Earl of Denbigh by James I in 1622. The Feildings did not pretend 'to draw their origin from the Counts of Habsburgh' until 1664 when Basil Feilding, 2nd Earl of Denbigh, was duly authorized to assume the title of Count of Hapsburg, Lauffenburg and Rheinfelden. He appears to have commissioned an unscrupulous antiquary to work up into a history of his family various deeds and documents, all of them forgeries, according to which the head of the younger branch of the Hapsburg family, reduced to poverty by his cousin, the future emperor, sent his son Geoffrey to England. There Geoffrey took the name of Feilding (from Rheinfelden) and married. His right to the title of Count was later acknowledged by the Hapsburgs.

This fake history was accepted by Dugdale himself and henceforth no one, not even the Austrian emperor, disputed the claim of the earls of Denbigh to draw their origin from the Hapsburgs, until J. H. Round, in an article of *The Genealogist*, N.S., X (1894), p. 193 ff. (reprinted in his *Studies in Peerage*, 1901, p. 210 ff.) conclusively showed it to be entirely unfounded. It disappeared from Burke's *Peerage* in 1900. For Fielding's real ancestry, see W. L. Cross, *The History of Henry Fielding*, Yale University Press, 1910, i, p. 1 ff.

Page 7

8 ff. Nearly all the information given here about the early history of the Gibbon family is drawn from various Latin and English passages of John Gibbon's *Introductio ad Latinam Blasoniam | Essay to a more correct Blazon in Latin than formerly hath been used . . . Authore Johanne Gibbono Armorum Servulo, quem à Mantelio dicunt Caeruleo . . .* London, 1682: 'Natus sum Ego Johannes Gibbon, patre Roberto Cive & Pannario Londinensi, qui obiit An.1643, & fuit filius junior Roberti Gibbon de Rolvenden (Militiae Cantianae Capitanei) obeuntis An.1618. . . . Nedum mentionem sum facturus, Gibbonos Terras tenuisse & possedisse in Rolvenden Anno 1326, vicesimo Ed. 2. . . . mention is made of a Grant of Edw 3 (13⁰ Regni) to *John Gibbon* of the profits of the Passage between *Sandwich* and *Stonat* in the Isle of Thanet, wherein the said *John* is stiled *Marmarius Regis—Marmarius* is no other than Marmorarius (the King's chief Marbler, Master Mason, or Surveyor of his Stone-works) no contemptible Office: For . . . such a one was Armiger . . . It's more than supposed, the Granté was the chief Architect in building *Quinborough Castle . . .*'.

30-32 Pope, *Epistle III to Allen Lord Bathurst (Moral Essays)*, ll. 287-8. In a note to l. 287, the poet explains that he is referring to 'The Parish-register'. In the preface to his *Introductio*, J. Gibbon, the Herald, gives 1548 as the date of the institution of parish registers. But in his *note 5*, G dates it 1538, referring to A. Anderson's *An Historical and Chronological Deduction of the Origin of Commerce*, 2 vols, f⁰, London, 1764, i, p. 367—a work which he had owned when in Bn. It probably was still in his library at L.

Page 8

11-26 armorial ensigns—'A Lyon rampant between three Ogresses . . . was granted to *Edmond Gibbon* (his Father always sealed with a Lyon rampant gardant between three Schallops). But himself assumed a new Coat out of dislike against three Ladies his kinswomen, Daughters of *Gervase Gibbon* . . . The falling out was about the Will of *Edmund Gibbon*, Founder of the Free-School in *Benenden*, the next Parish to *Rolvenden*. . . . As for *Edmund* aforesaid, he lyes buried in the Temple Church

London' (J. Gibbon's *Introductio*, p. 161). From what J. Gibbon says here, it seems probable that Edmund substituted black roundles (called 'pellets' or 'ogresses' in heraldry) for scallop-shells merely to show that he did not belong to the same family as his three cousins. Not knowing what 'ogresses' were, G imagined that *Edmund* had altered his arms to convey the idea that his cousins were 'female cannibals'.

33 ff. checking his pen—'Omitto Bercleos de *Beauston*, Hextallos, Ellenbriggos, Calverleos, & Whetenallos Cestrenses (Equestri dignitate olim nobiles) ne videas vanitati Genealogicae nimis-nimium indulgero. Et genus & proavos &c' (*Introductio*, p. 160).

Page 9

1 'Nam genus et proavos et quae non fecimus ipsi, Vix ea nostra voco,' says Ulysses in Ovid's *Metam.*, xiii, 140-141.

8-13 Peckham—'madame Wetenhall . . . étoit ce qu'on appelle proprement une beauté tout angloise: pétrie de lis et de roses, de neige et de lait quant aux couleurs, faite de cire, à l'égard des bras et des mains, de la gorge et des pieds; mais tout cela sans âme et sans air. Son visage étoit des plus mignons; mais c'étoit toujours le même visage: on eût dit qu'elle le tiroit le matin d'un étui pour l'y remettre en se couchant, sans s'en être servie durant la journée. . . . La nature en avoit fait une poupée des son enfance, et poupée jusqu'à la mort resta la blanche Wetenhall.' Her husband spent his days in his library and neglected her and 'ce n'étoit pas sans raison qu'elle s'ennuyoit de la vie qu'on lui faisoit mener à Peckham. L'oisiveté d'un lieu si triste lui parut insupportable . . . Elle y séchoit sur pied, et ce fut de peur d'y mourir de solitude . . . qu'elle eut recours à la pitié de mademoiselle Hamilton' who took her to London and Tunbridge where she met Hamilton, who fell in love with her. But, not obtaining her favours, Hamilton turned his attentions elsewhere, and tried to obtain those of the king's mistress. The pursuit was fraught with danger and Grammont persuaded his friend to give it up and, instead, pay a visit to Peckham, but he does not say that the visit ever took place, and G's suspicions are wholly unwarranted. (A. Hamilton, *Mémoires du Chevalier de Grammont*, ch. xii.)

13-19 In his *Introductio*, p. 159, J. Gibbon traces his descent from *James Fiens, Baron Say and Seal* (Summus Angliae Thesaurus) and from William Cromer, twice Lord Mayor of London (ejusdem civitatis Praetor Anno 1413, 1424) as follows: Cromer's son William, twice Sheriff of Kent (Vicecomes Cantii 23 & 28 Henry VI) married Elizabeth Fiens, daughter of the Baron. The granddaughter of William and Elizabeth Cromer married William Whetnal of Peckham, whose daughter Rose married Edward Phillips de la Weld. Margaret Phillips, Edward's granddaughter, married Robert Gibbon (militiae Cantianae Capitaneus) who died in 1618 and whom G wrongly assumed to be his ancestor.

Page 10

5-13 'Natus sum Ego Johannes Gibbon, patre Roberto Cive & Pannario Londinensi, qui obiit An. 1643, & fuit filius junior Roberti Gibbon . . . obeuntis An. 1618' (*Introductio*, p. 159). Matthew Gibbon, G's great-grandfather, is not mentioned by John Gibbon; G vainly tried to make sure that Matthew was a younger son of the second Robert, but when he wrote this passage he had persuaded himself that it must be so.

15 ff. G found all, or nearly all, he says about J. Gibbon the Herald in the *Introductio*. He secured some additional information from his visits to the College of Arms in May-June 1787, as is shown by his *note 9*: 'Mr Brooks Lancaster Herald', which is a reference to J. C. Brooke, the Herald to whom he wrote twice in June (*Letters*, iii, pp. 110, 114).

20-23 Allesborough—'my very good Lord Coventry of Allesborough in Worcestershire, whose servant I was, and whilst so, was blessed with retired content, which makes me call to mind that of Mr. Hobbes, acknowledged in the like case' (*Introductio*, p. 19). For Hobbes's acknowledgment, see his *Vita carmine expressa*, published in 1679 and again in 1681, which is just about the time J. Gibbon was writing his treatise.

31-34 'while I lived in Virginia, I saw once a War-dance acted by the Natives. The Dancers were painted . . . and carried little ill-made Shields of Bark . . . They were not ignorant of Countermarches and Wheelings, and sometimes would come up towards the Spectators, holding forth their Tamahawks . . . ' (*Introductio*, p. 156).

Page 11

7 G's statement that his grandfather inherited from the Herald a house near the Tower reads like a figment of his imagination, intent on finding some proof of his connection with the author of the *Introductio*. There is no mention of a house in J. Gibbon's will (*Journal A*, p. xxix). Perhaps he was told at the College of Arms that J. Gibbon had lived near the Tower, and as he knew that his grandfather had a house in the same vicinity, he assumed it to have been an heirloom from the son of Robert.

14 Of Nehemiah Grew (see *D.N.B.*) J. Gibbon says that 'semper erga me omnimodo usus est benevolentia'. He calls Dr John Betts, Physician-in-ordinary to His Majesty (see *D.N.B.*) 'my exceeding good friend' (*Introductio*, pp. 18 and 164).

24 J. Gibbon ends his *Introductio* with a Latin prayer: May King Charles, his brother James, and all the royal family be safe from 'turba Fanatica Antimonarchica: Quibus Symbolum & Insigne est: Bellua multorum Capitū, coloris Diabolici (viz. nigri) in Campo sanguineo.' This 'most Diabolical scutcheon' is of course dedicated to Shaftesbury's republican faction.

33 Lord Sheffield corrected 'the Roman idiom' into 'a Roman idiom', which
may be what G meant to write since Camden used Latin in his Patents,
but French in his descriptions of the Arms themselves. (Preface to the
Introductio.)

Page 12

11-16 The only editor of G's *Autobiography* to give a translation of these lines
is O. Smeaton (Everyman's Library ed., p. 11 f.). As apparently he had
not inspected the *Introductio*, J. Gibbon's meaning in his first line
escaped him. The little book is made up of a series of Latin descriptions
of the coats of arms of well-known families, in which a large number of
the terms of heraldry have been latinized, but not all, far from it, as the
author is the first to know. Hence his 'Usque huc corrigitur Romana
Blasonia per me' (so far have I corrected Roman heraldry). The last
two lines, coming close to his prayer for the safety of the King and the
royal family, probably allude to his counting on their protection against
the wrath of the 'turba fanatica Antimonarchica' which he had just insulted in his 'most diabolical scutcheon'. His hopes were defeated by the
Revolution.

19 To the end of his paragraph on J. Gibbon, G added his *note 33*: 'Oblivion
—From Wolfenbuttel to Lausanne.' He apparently meant to add, when
revising his text, a long note or another paragraph on how he became
acquainted with the *Introductio*. This might have been what he had
written in his first attempt (A). See Appendix I, 1, p. 201.

37 notable woman—'Notable: Of women: Capable, managing, bustling,
clever and industrious in household management or occupations' (*N.E.D.*,
4 b).

Page 13

1-11 Acton—See the A passage on the Actons in Appendix I, 3.

14 Prior was appointed to the Commission of Customs in 1711 and took his
seat at the Board in January 1712. (See Swift's letters to Mrs. Johnson
of 15 Oct. 1711, 18 and 31 Jan., and 13 March 1711/12.)

31 ff. In his *note 13* (G's own notes to F are *ff* 124-127 of the MS. M used
their numbers but turned them into footnotes, see Preface, p. xxxii),
which no doubt G would have placed here, (but the reference to which
is lacking in the margin of F, MS *f* 105), he gives his authorities for his
account of the proceedings in Parliament against the Directors of the
South-Sea Company: 'Tindal and Anderson—a private narrative.'
   Nicholas Tindal (1687-1774) translated Paul de Rapin, Sieur de
Thoyras's *Histoire d'Angleterre* in 15 vols published 1726-1731, and
added to the twenty-four Books of Rapin (Origins to 1688) three more
on the reigns of William, Anne and George I, in 13 vols published 1745-

1747. In Book XXVII, he gave a very full account of the South-Sea Bubble, its consequences, and in particular of the debates in Parliament. Though Tindal's continuation of Rapin does not seem to have been in G's library at L., his account appears to be based chiefly on it. He may, of course, have used the French translation.

Anderson's history of commerce (see above, p. 233), which was in G's library, gives a rather technical account of the finances of the South-Sea Company, but hardly any of the parliamentary proceedings.

As to the 'private narrative' mentioned by G, it might be supposed to be his grandfather's, had he not written in A (MS *f* 15 – M 374) that 'the books and papers' of his grandfather were not in his possession. There were, however, three works in his library at L. which he may have used in working up his story of his grandfather's ruin: 1. *Journals of the House of Commons* (1547-1774), 1 vol. f°. 2. *History and proceedings of the House of Commons from the Restoration to the present time*, 14 vols, 1742-1744. 3. *Reports from committees of the House of Commons* (1715-1773), 4 vols, 1773.

Whatever his sources or authorities were, G's account is accurate in all respects, as can be ascertained by comparing it with Cobbett's *Parliamentary History*, vii, p. 678 ff. (passim).

36 G's *note 14* (M 12): 'Molesworth in B.B., his Denmark, erroneous, partial, and arising from personal pique.' Molesworth was in the front rank of those who attacked the Directors of the South-Sea Company. Years before he had been Envoy Extraordinary to the Court of Denmark where, according to *Biographia Britannica*, he had made himself obnoxious by using the King's private road to Elsinore, and hunting in the King's private hunting-ground. He had to be recalled and spent his enforced leisure in writing his *Account of the State of Denmark as it was in the Year 1692*, which he published in 1694.

Page 15

18 In his *note 15* (M 14) on *il serrar di Consiglio*, G refers to Abraham Nicolas Amelot de la Houssaie's *Histoire du Gouvernement de Venise*, 2 vols, Paris, 1677, i, pp. 4-11: 'Après la mort de Vital Michieli . . . le peuple lassé de la longue domination de ses Ducs reprit le Gouvernement, et continua pourtant d'élire un Prince pour donner plus de crédit aux affaires; mais il resserra son pouvoir à un point, qu'il ne lui laissa presque plus rien que le titre et la préséance. Et tout se faisoit alors par le Grand Conseil, qui étoit composé de 470 Citoiens, nommés par 12 Electeurs, tirés des six Quartiers de la Ville . . . et ces 470 se changeoient tous les ans . . . afin de contenter tout le monde à son tour. Ce qui dura jusques au tems du Duc Pierre Gradenigue second qui réforma le Grand Conseil l'an 1298, en faisant passer . . . une nouvelle Ordonnance, dont la teneur étoit: Que tous ceux qui dans cette année-là composoient le

Corps du Grand Conseil ou en avoient été dans les quatre années pré-
cédentes en fussent eux et leurs descendans à perpétuité & que tous les
autres, quels qu'ils fussent, Nobles ou Populaires . . . fussent exclus à
jamais de l'administration civile. Si bien que . . . la Puissance fut trans-
férée du Peuple aux Nobles. Ce changement produisit . . . la fameuse
conjuration des Quirins des Tiepoles & de quelques autres familles
anciennes qui furent excluses totalement ou en partie; car il y en eut
beaucoup qui se trouverent partagées entre la Servitude & la Liberté.
Témoin les Minii, les Bons, les Nani . . . qui virent par le succez de
cette Ordonnance, leurs Maisons melées de Nobles & de Populaires; de
Maîtres & de Sujets; sur quoi les Quirins fondoient leurs plaintes, disant,
que cette reformation coupoit le noeud de la concorde de toutes les
Familles Venitiennes. Mais ce fut en vain que l'on en murmura . . .'.
Amelot cite encore la 'Harangue de Marc Quirin: "Questo dose", dit-il
en parlant du Duc Gradenigue, 'Spento da sperito Diabolico, ha vogiù
serrar el Mazor Consiglio, e privar qualunque bon Citadin de poter
pervenir alla prerogativa de Nobile Veneto . . .'.

   G's *note 15* reads like a hastily written summary of Amelot's account:
'In 1298, 470 annually chosen at Michaelmas: voted perpetual and
hereditary for all the actual, and of the last years, if they had 12 votes
in the Quarantia—Families broken, new ones added—Stability of
Venice.' G appears to have confused the '12 Electors' with the *Quarantia*
ou Conseil des Quarante who supported the Duke's initiative.

31 suspicious secret—Both M and Hill believe this to refer to the £574,000
   of South-Sea stock which had been distributed by the Directors to
   facilitate the passing of the South-Sea Act. This, however, does not seem
   to explain the 'suspicious secret' in which the name of G's grandfather
   was 'reported'.

Page 16

11 Francis Acton was an uncle of G's grandfather. See Appendix 1, 4, p. 201.
12-17 the use of fraud—The corresponding passage in A, if there was one,
   would have been on G's p. 25, which was destroyed (see Preface, p. xvi).
   G wrote in B: 'it is suspected that he had found means to elude the impending stroke by previous settlements and secret conveyances' (MS
   f 24 – M 109). This became in C: 'Some part of my grandfather's fortune
   was legally and perhaps honestly secured by prævious settlements and
   conveyances' (MS *f* 59 – M 215). In D he wrote: 'Yet something had
   been secreted by his foresight' (MS *f* 80 – M 391). In E he is content to
   say: 'he was stripped of his apparent fortune' (MS *f* 87 – M 294).

Page 18

1-12 younger brother of a younger brother—Richard Acton, a younger son
   of Sir Walter Acton, of Aldenham in Shropshire, had a daughter,

Katherine, from his first wife. A widower, he married in 1698 the widow of Matthew Gibbon, G's great-grandfather. Katherine Acton married her step-mother's son Edward, G's grandfather, who by his marriage became the nephew of Richard Acton's brothers and a first cousin of their children. He was thus the nephew of Francis Acton and the cousin of Sir Whitmore Acton who married one of the two daughters of Matthew Gibbon and so became his brother-in-law. He was also the first cousin of another Acton, Edward, goldsmith in London, son of his uncle Walter. This Edward Acton had two sons, second cousins of G's father. One of them, Edward, was studying medicine in Paris when G's father, travelling in France, fell ill at Besançon and called him to his assistance. Edward Acton married and settled at Besançon. His brother Richard became chief officer (Commodore) of the small navy of the Grand-Duchy of Tuscany (see *Journey*, pp. 227, n. 2; 230; 233), and remained a bachelor. Edward's eldest son, John Francis Edmond, followed the same career as his uncle the Commodore, entered the naval service of the Emperor, distinguished himself and eventually became a minister of the King of the Two Sicilies (see *Journal A*, pp. 121-122 and Hill's n., p. 276). His two brothers were officers in the French army.

14 A burgage tenure is 'a tenure whereby lands or tenements in cities and towns are held of the King or other lord for a certain yearly rent' (*N.E.D.*).

34 Robert Darrell, of Richmond, married a younger sister of G's mother, who gave him two sons, both merchants in the City: Edward (1728-1814), who became Director of the Bank of England in 1770, and Robert (1734-1801), a Director of the South-Sea Company.

Page 19

11-14 Quotation from the tale of Pyramus and Thisbe as told by Ovid, *Metam.*, iv, 59-62.

32 G's parents were married on 3 June 1736.

Page 20

6-7 Hester Gibbon (1706-1790)—Katherine Gibbon (?-*c.* 1737).

9 styles his nephew—G seems to have been unaware that Edward Elliston (?-*c.* 1737) was really his grandfather's nephew; he was the son of a younger sister of Edward Gibbon, G's grandfather.

13 ff. William Law's *Serious Call*, in chapters vii, viii, and xii of which the portraits of Flavia, Miranda and Flatus appear, was first published in 1728 when Hester was twenty-two, Edward twenty, and Katherine, whose date of birth has not been found, less than twenty. These portraits do not really fit the circumstances of the Gibbon family, so they can hardly be portraits of G's aunts and father. But Law may have drawn

on his shrewd observation of their youthful characters, and on his premonitions of what they might well turn out to be.

G's sketch of Flavia is only a very general summing-up of Law's pp. 95-101 in the 2nd ed. of *A Serious Call*, which was in his library at L., while his portrait of Miranda is practically made up of quotations from pp. 108-119.

Page 21

32 Law was a native of King's Cliffe (Northamptonshire). The house to which he retired in 1740, where he was joined by Mrs. Hutchinson and Hester Gibbon and where he died on 9 April 1761, had been left to him by his father.

34 Nonjuror—In 1689 all holders of civil and ecclesiastical offices were required to take the oaths of supremacy and allegiance to the new sovereign. About four hundred of the clergy refused to swear and were deprived of their offices. They formed a sort of sect and were known by the name of 'nonjurors'. See G. N. Clark, *The Later Stuarts* (*Oxford History of England*, vol. x), 1934, p. 150.

Page 22

5 Jacob Behmen—All 17th- and 18th-century English translations of Boehm's Works were published under the name of Behme or Behmen, with the single exception of Law's translation of *The Way to Divine Knowledge*, published in 1752.

6 The passage of *The Absolute Unlawfulness of the Stage Entertainments Fully Demonstrated*, 1726, which G seems to be quoting, actually reads: 'When . . . you are tempted to go to a Play . . . fancy that you was asked in plain Terms to go to *the Place of the Devil's Abode, where he holds his filthy Court of evil Spirits* . . . Fancy that you are going to a Place that as certainly belongs to the Devil, as the *heathen Temples* of old, where Brutes were worshipped, where wanton Hymns were sung to *Venus*, and drunken Songs to the *God of Wine*. Fancy that you was as certainly going to *the Devil's Triumph* . . . Now whilst you consider the Play-House in this View, I suppose you can no more go to a Play, than you can renounce your Christianity' (p. 13). So G must have quoted it from memory, though he had Law's *Works* (1762) in his library at L.

20 the Bangorian controversy—so called from the Bishop of Bangor, Benjamin Hoadly (1676-1761) who started it in 1717 by a sermon preached before the King, and a pamphlet. In these he denied that the Established Church had any justification for claiming doctrinal or disciplinary authority. A committee of Convocation, appointed to examine Hoadly's opinions, 'reported strongly against them. The report drew from him a dexterous reply' (M, n. p. 25) to which Law answered in *A*

Reply to the Bishop of Bangor's Answer to the representation of the committee of Convocation, 1719. Several members of the clergy had also endeavoured to refute the Bishop who defended his position in an open *Letter* to one of them, Dr Snape. So Law returned to the fray with *The Bishop of Bangor's late Sermon, and his letter to Dr. Snape in defence of it*, 1721. Both pamphlets were in G's library at L. On the Bangorian Controversy see B. Williams, *The Whig Supremacy (Oxford History of England*, vol. xi), 1939, p. 83.

22 the plain account—In 1735 Hoadly, who was then Bishop of Winchester, published *A Plain Account of the Nature and End of the Sacrament*, which Parson Adams, as G points out in his *note 22*, 'By the pen of an angel, says Adams (J. A. Book i, chap. 17)', describes as 'that excellent Book . . . written with the pen of an Angel, and calculated to restore the true Use of Christianity, and of that sacred Institution; for what could tend more to the noble Purposes of Religion than frequent chearful Meetings among the Members of a society, in which they should, in the Presence of one another, and in the Service of the Supreme Being, make promises of being good, friendly, and benevolent to each other?' And Adams adds that 'this excellent book was attacked by a party, but unsuccessfully'. Law was one of that party. He published in 1737 *A Demonstration of the Gross and Fundamental errors of a late book, called A Plain Account . . .* This was also in G's library at L.

28 the fable of the Bees—Bernard (de) Mandeville published in 1705 his *The Grumbling Hive*, a verse squib which jokingly propounded the theory that the love of money was really the source of all progress. He republished it in 1714 under the title of *The Fable of the Bees: or Private Vices, Publick Benefits*, adding in prose *An Enquiry into the Origin of Moral Virtue* and some *Remarks* in which he seriously explained his meaning. A 2nd ed., with the *Remarks* much enlarged, came out in 1723. It was then, and only then, that the indignation of a large part of the public found expression in attacks by Dennis and Law in 1724, Hutcheson in 1725, Watts in 1728. A copy of the 1738 ed. of Law's *Remarks upon a late Book entitled the Fable of the Bees* was in G's library at L.

Page 24

1-2 For G's dating of his birth, see the *Note on Dates* in B. Williams, *op. cit.*, p. xx.

6 My five brothers—*Journal A*, p. xxix, n., gives, from the Registers of Putney Parish Church, the names and dates of baptism of G's brothers and sister: James, 20 October 1738; Edward James, 15 August 1740; William, 1 September 1741; Judith, 16 November 1743; Stanier, 15 May 1745; James, 20 December 1746.

Page 25

4 About four months—G's grandfather died 'about Christmas 1736' (D, MS f 80 – M 391), and was buried at Putney on 31 December.

12 hostilities between the two nations—In October 1739, Great Britain declared war on Spain, which had long been endeavouring to restrict all English trade with her American colonies. What began as a colonial war developed into a general European war owing to England siding with the enemies of France and Spain in the struggle over the Austrian succession to which the congress of Aix-la-Chapelle put an end in 1748, restoring peace between Spain and Great Britain. In 1761 war between them broke out again as France had persuaded Spain to become her ally in the Seven Years' War. Peace was restored by the Treaty of Paris, signed in February 1763.

16-20 According to G's *note 1* to Chapter ii (M 29) (G used a separate numbering for the notes to each of his chapters in F) 'Ferdinand VI held a consult of Lawyers and Divines—not obliged to pay former debts'; G found this piece of information in 'Nouv. Voy. en Esp. tom ii, pp. 30, 31'. This was identified by M as the *Nouveau voyage en Espagne, ou Tableau de l'état actuel de cette monarchie*, 3 vols, Paris, 1789, by the Baron J. F. de Bourgoing. Here is the passage to which G refers:

'Philippe V laissa des dettes pour plus de 168 millions de livres Tournois. A sa mort, Ferdinand VI, son fils et son successeur, Prince équitable & pieux, effrayé d'un fardeau si énorme, flottant entre la crainte de le faire supporter à l'Etat & le scrupule de frustrer ses créanciers de leurs droits, assembla une Junte composée d'Evêques, de Ministres & de gens de loi, & lui proposa cette question singulière: si un Roi est tenu d'acquitter les dettes de son prédécesseur? Croira-t'on qu'elle fut décidée à la négative par la pluralité, sous prétexte que l'Etat étoit un patrimoine dont le Souverain n'étoit que l'usufruitier, & ne répondoit que de ses propres engagemens? Cette décision, contre laquelle réclamoient à l'envi l'équité, la raison & la politique, tranquillisa la conscience du monarque, & légitima à ses yeux ce qui étoit une véritable banqueroute. Le payement des dettes de l'Espagne fut donc entièrement suspendu . . . Charles III, en montant sur le trône, trouva dans ses coffres plus de 165 millions de livres Tournois. Ce nouveau Souverain, plus conséquent dans ses scrupules que son prédécesseur, crut devoir réparer la fatale omission de Ferdinand VI. Dès l'année 1761, il fit payer 6% des capitaux dûs par Philippe V; mais commençant par les créanciers nationaux, il renvoya les étrangers à l'époque où toutes les créances des Espagnols seroient acquittées. . . . En 1767 les 6% furent réduits à 4 . . . enfin en 1769 les charges de l'Etat qui s'étoient accrues obligèrent de suspendre entièrement le payement de ces à-comptes.'

25-27 For Sir Robert Henley, earl of Northington (1708-1772) see *D.N.B.*, where neither Mr Delmé nor Mr Dummer are recorded.

37 Strange coalitions—In his *note 2* (M 30), G wrote: 'Of P. of W. and Jac.—Allowance in 37'. In 1737, Frederick, Prince of Wales, who had married the year before, unsuccessfully appealed to Parliament for a substantial increase of his yearly allowance. He then openly joined the opposition (to Walpole's government) which had so far been divided and powerless. His alliance with it, in spite of its including a remnant of die-hard Jacobites, made it clear that it was not directed against the Hanover dynasty, and strengthened it considerably. See B. Williams, *op. cit.*, p. 194.

Page 28

9-14 G's memory was at fault here: only one of his brothers was called Edward. He quoted *Æneid*, vi, 143 from memory. Virgil has *primo avulso* . . .

Page 29

10-11 For Sir Hans Sloane (1660-1753), Richard Mead (1673-1754), Joshua Ward (1685-1761) and John Taylor (1703-1772), see *D.N.B.*

19 In his *note 7* (M 37) G refers to the 2nd vol. of *Commentarii de rebus pertinentibus ad . . . cardinalem Quirinum*, 5 vols, Brescia, 1749-1761, which were in his library at L. For Girolamo (Angelo Maria in religion) Quirini, 1680-1759, bishop of Brescia, promoted cardinal in 1727, librarian of the Biblioteca Vaticana, see *Grande Encyclopédie*.

21 In his *Discours préliminaire*—which, in his *note 8* (M 37), G calls 'a very good preface'—the first editor of the *Journal du voyage de Michel de Montaigne en Italie, par la Suisse & l'Allemagne en 1580 & 1581* gives the explanation of Montaigne's 'naked frankness'. He was taking advantage of his travels to try the effect on his health of the waters of all the spas he came across; he was suffering from lithiasis (gravel) and had little trust in doctors. On his return journey from Rome he stopped at the Bagno della Villa near Lucca: 'C'est là que Montaigne, de sa seule ordonnance, s'imposa la résidence & l'usage de ces eaux de la façon la plus stricte. Il ne parle plus que de son régime, des effets successifs que les eaux font sur lui, de la manière dont il les prenoit chaque jour; en un mot, il n'omet aucune des plus petites circonstances concernant son habitude physique, & l'opération journalière de ses boissons, de ses douches, &c. Ce n'est plus le Journal d'un Voyageur . . . c'est le Mémoire d'un malade attentif à tous les procédés du remède dont il use à discrétion, aux plus petits incidens de son action sur son être . . .: c'est un compte bien circonstancié qu'il semble rendre à son Médecin, pour l'instruire, & pour avoir ses avis sur les suites de ses infirmités. Il est vrai que Montaigne, en se livrant à tous ces fastidieux détails,

prévient que comme il s'est autrefois repenti de n'avoir pas écrit plus particulièrement sur les autres Bains . . . il veut cette fois s'étendre et se mettre au large sur cette matière; mais la meilleure raison pour nous c'est qu'il n'écrivoit que pour lui.' Montaigne wrote all this part of his *Journal* in Italian.

Page 30

62 To this passage G added his *note 10* (M 39): 'English better than foreigners, present age than last—Compare reformers, etc., in Jortin's *Erasmus* with our round Robin in Boswell.' In J. Jortin's *Life of Erasmus*, 2 vols, 1758-1759, which was in G's library at L., there are two plates of specimens of 16th-century handwriting. Dr Johnson had composed a Latin epitaph on Goldsmith, and submitted it to the judgment of Sir Joshua Reynolds, asking him to 'shew it to the Club'. Reynolds had it discussed one day at a dinner to which he had invited twelve of his friends, most of whom were members of the Club (Gibbon, Burke, Sheridan, etc.). After the discussion Burke drew up a short letter to Johnson begging him to revise his epitaph and write it in English. This letter was given a round shape, and all present signed it, their signatures forming a circle round it, so that nobody could know who had signed it first. The 'Round Robin' was reproduced in facsimile by Boswell in his *Life of Johnson*, 1791 (see Hill-Powell ed., iii, p. 82 ff.).

Page 31

8 For John Kirkby see *D.N.B.*

9 His own words—G's quotation is the opening of Kirkby's *Automathes*, the real title of which is *The Capacity and extent of the human understanding exemplified in the extraordinary case of Automathes, a young nobleman, left in his infancy upon a desolate island*, London 1745. It is followed by these words: 'I had not long continued in this pensive Mood, ere I was diverted from it by the Sight, as I imagined, of a small cylindrical Trunk, about a Foot long, rolling along with the Tide, just below where I sat, with a Key tied to the Handle. I stepped into the Water, to seize the supposed Prize, which upon opening, I found to contain nothing but a kind of written Journal, rolled up, belonging (as I then conjectured) to some shipwrecked Mariner.' Read in this context, G's quotation, which he appears to have taken as a fragment of autobiography, is clearly as much of a fiction as the rest of the story.

34 forgot—in C Kirkby's dismissal is ascribed to 'his public refusal to name King George'.

Page 32

23 E. Pocock (see *D.N.B.*) published in 1671 a Latin translation, entitled *Philosophus Autodidactus*, of the Arabic romance *Hai Ebn Yokdhan*, the

1700 ed. of which was in G's library at L. On 23 August 1762, G had read in Le Clerc's *Bibliothèque Universelle & Historique de l'Année 1686*, iii, pp. 77-98, 'un "extrait un peu circonstancié" de *The history of Hai Ebn Yokdhan, Or the Self-taught Philosopher*, écrite en Arabe par Jaaphar Ebn Tophail, traduite en Anglois sur la version latine d'Edouard Pocock, M.A.' (see *Journal A*, p. 100).

28 discovery of fire—'One Evening, as I was cutting down the Reliques of an old rotten Tree . . . I struck the Hatchet against a Stone, which occasioned Sparks to fly forth in abundance. I beheld some of the Chips, lying close by the remaining Stump, to send up a Vapour, something like what I had seen arise in the Morning from the dewy Savannahs, but far more gross and dense. And, on approaching nigher, I perceived the Flame, which immediately brought to mind the . . . Glow-worms; but when I came to handle this, as I had done the Worms, the Pain . . . made me draw in my Fingers . . .; by and by the Flame, catching hold of the stump of the Tree, began to burn with some vehemence. I stood wondering how this strange Thing came here, which I took at first to be a living Animal . . .' Understanding that the sparks emitted by the hatchet were the cause of the curious phenomenon, he amused himself with repeating the experiment until the fire he had kindled caught hold of a coppice, so that the forest was soon ablaze. 'I was in the utmost Consternation to see the Devastation I had caused, my Ears being quite stunned with the incessant roaring of the Flames . . . mixed with the loud Yells of the Beasts and Fowls, all endeavouring to escape. . . . But when I came to think of the Injuries this indifferent Piece of Curiosity must bring upon my Fellow-creatures, and imagined I heard the Cries of several helpless Animals perishing in the Flames; O Heavens! with what Horror was I seized . . . This Accident raised a Tumult in my Bosom, as much beyond my own Power to appease, as it was beyond my Power to quench the Flames which occasioned it. For it gave me the first sad Experience of the severe Lashes of a *Self-condemning Conscience*: a Trouble, to which all my other Griefs were comparatively as Nothing' (pp. 187-192).

Page 33

2 Woodson—For Richard Wooddesdon (1704-1774) see *D.N.B.* and M's n., p. 43.

23 A Phaedrus, *Fabulae*, The Hague, 1718, and a Cornelius Nepos, *Vitae excellentium imperatorum*, Amsterdam, 1707, were in G's library when the L. catalogue on playing-cards was made in 1789 (see Keynes, p. 23).

33 Rousseau—In his *note 13*, G refers to *L'Emile*, Book ii.

Page 34

5 Thracian slave—In his Prologue to Book iii, Phaedrus calls himself a

Macedonian: 'Ego quem Pierio mater enixa est jugo' (The district called Pieria, east of the Strymon, was part of Macedonia). According to the heading of the best MS he had been a slave: 'Augusti libertus.'

8-12 Pierre Pithou (Pithaeus) published his ed. of *Phaedrus* in 1596. Pieter Burman edited *Phaedrus* in 1718 and again in 1727, Bentley in 1726. As to the number of edns of *Phaedrus*, G refers (in his *note 14*) to vol ii, pp. 24-35 of J. A. Ernest's 1773-1774 ed. of J. Fabricius' *Bibliotheca Latina*, 2 vols, which he had in his library at L.

17 The last child of G's mother was born on 20 December 1746. She was buried in January 1747. See Low, *Gibbon*, p. 28, n. 2.

29 G's *note 16* (M 45) 'Prevot's Marquis—Selima—English translation read and compared at the time' does not refer to anything in F, in the margin of which (MS *ff* 112-113) there is no reference 16 between 15 and 17. But it refers to a few lines of A which G left out when copying into F the description of his father's grief: 'That interesting romance of the Abbé Prevot d'Exiles, the Memoires d'un homme de qualité had lately been translated into English, and as soon as I read them the grief of the Marquis on the death of his beloved Selima most forcibly brought to my mind the situation and behaviour of my poor father' (MS *f* 17 – M 378-9). An English translation of Prévost's romance was published in 1738. A 1775 reprint of the French original was in G's library at L. Why did he buy it so late in life? Was it perhaps because he wanted to reread the passage he remembered and turn it to his own use? The marquis himself relates how he behaved after the death of his wife, fourteen years earlier: 'Je louai une maison . . . entourée de tous côtez d'un bois fort épais qui en fait une profonde solitude . . . Mon premier soin fut de faire couvrir les murs & le pavé de la chambre que j'avois choisie pour ma demeure, d'un drap noir. Les fenêtres furent bouchées, n'aiant plus envie de revoir la lumière du Soleil, mais de me servir seulement de celle de quelques flambeaux . . . Si les pleurs & les soupirs ne peuvent porter le nom de plaisirs, il est vrai néanmoins qu'ils ont une douceur infinie pour une personne mortellement affligée.'

Page 35

10 A paraphrase of ll. 3-7 of G's quotation from Mallet's *Wedding-day* may not be superfluous: The god of Love (Cupid, Hymen's brother) first sent off one of his underlings (a pensive Love) who for three years had borne his torch reversed (i.e. put out, in token of grief) and had bound with cypress the place where it had once brightly burned, to call . . .

37 a secret inconstancy—In his *note 18* 'Flatus in Law . . . mum' (mum = memorandum), G refers to the portrait of Flatus in ch. xii of *A Serious Call* which he had quoted from in A (see Appendix I, 8, p. 205). Perhaps

he meant to use the quotation either here in his text or in a note when revising F.

29 a favourite tale—In his *note 19* G refers to the *Histoire d'Hipolite, Comte de Duglas* par Mme Catherine La Mothe, 1699, an English translation of which appeared in 1708. The episode to which G refers is p. 176 ff. of the translation: 'King Adolph, losing his way in hunting, arrived at the Cave of the Winds. Zephyrus bore him away to the Isle of Felicity, where he was entertained by the Princess. One day she asked him how long he thought he had been there. "I think it cannot be much less than three months," he replied. She burst out laughing. "Dear Adolph," said she with a very serious air, "you must know it is no less than three hundred years." He was struck with shame at having done no glorious action in all that time, and insisted on leaving her to render himself more worthy of her favours. She gave him a horse which would bear him safely home so long as he did not touch the ground before he reached his own country. In the way lay a cart overthrown, laden with wings of divers shapes and sizes, and by it the carter, a very old man, who called for help. The King alighted, when up sprang the old man, calling out: "At last I have met you. My name is Time. I have been in search of you these three ages. I have worn out all these wings to find you out." '

34 *Arabian Nights Entertainment. Translated into French from the Arabian MSS by M. Galland . . . and now done into English* was published in 1713 and again in 1718, 1725, 1728, etc. The French translation remained a favourite with G who added it twice to his own books: he had the 1745 ed. in 6 vols at Bentinck street, and the 1773 ed. in 8 vols at La Grotte.

36 Specious miracles is Horace's 'speciosa miracula' (*Ars Poetica*, 144).

10 fall of Phaeton: *Metam.* ii, 153 ff., speeches of Ajax and Ulysses: xiii, 1-381.

32 G entered Westminster school in January 1748 (see *Journal A*, p. xlii, n. 1, and *Letters*, iii, p. 345, n. 4).

34 John Nicoll, 1683-1765, was appointed second master of Westminster school in 1714, headmaster in 1733.

15 mimic scene of a rebellion—G may be thinking here of a passage in Johnson's *Life of Addison*: 'The practice of *barring-out* was a savage licence . . . by which the boys, when the periodical vacation drew near, growing petulant at the approach of liberty, some days before the time

of regular recess, took possession of the school, of which they barred the doors, and bade their master defiance from the windows. It is not easy to suppose that on such occasions the master would do more than laugh, yet . . . he often struggled hard to force or surprise the garrison.' (*Lives of the English Poets*, ed. G. B. Hill, ii, p. 80.)

18 Spartan king—In his *note 22* (M 51) G quotes Agesilaus' precept in its Greek form, and in Estienne's Latin translation, from Henri Estienne's *Apophthegmata Graeca Regum et Ducum*, 1568, pp. 306-7.

23 G is here quoting Adam Smith (to whom he refers in his *note 23*) who had said that 'in the schools the youth are taught, or at least may be taught, Greek and Latin, that is, everything that the masters pretend to teach'.

33 In his *note 24* (M 52) 'Burke's Vectigal', G refers to Burke as one 'who possessed the sense and spirit of the Classics', though, not having the benefit of a public school education and being merely 'a private and voluntary student', he could be guilty of a false quantity as when he mispronounced vectigal in the House of Commons. Here is the anecdote as told by Sir James Prior in his *Life of Edmund Burke*, 1824: 'On the 15th December 1780, Burke opened a brief but lucid exposition of his plan . . . While enforcing the necessity of frugality, and recommending to the Minister the old and valuable Roman apophthegm *magnum vectigal est parsimonia*, he made a false quantity, pronouncing the second word vectĭgal. Lord North, in a low tone corrected the error, when the orator with his usual presence of mind, turned the mistake to advantage. "The noble Lord, said he, hints that I have erred in the quantity of a principal word in my quotation; I rejoice at it; because it gives me an opportunity of repeating the inestimable adage",—and with increased energy he thundered forth—"magnum vectīgal est parsimonia".' (Bohn's Standard Library ed., 1908, p. 184.)

G was a witness of the scene (see his *note 43* to E, *above*, p. 173) and probably intended to describe it in a full note. Another witness was William Wilberforce who had just been elected to the House of Commons and was only twenty-one; he was so impressed that, in old age, he would recount it to his young friend J. S. Herford. And so the anecdote found a place in the *Recollections of William Wilberforce* which Herford dictated to his wife in 1862-1863 and published in 1864.

Page 39

16 Lord H. is Lionel Tollemache, 3rd viscount Huntingtower (1734-1799), whom G mentions as being at L. in July 1753 (*Letters*, i, p. 2), but so briefly that his intimate friend of Westminster schooldays seems to have already begun to repel him by his coldness, though Pavillard in his 2nd letter says that he 'paroit l'aimer beaucoup' (see *above*, p. 215).

Page 40

21 For Rev. Philip Francis (1708-1773), see *D.N.B.*

Page 41

32 G's reference is to the 'Ancient Part' of the *Universal History from the earliest accounts of Time to the present* which, first printed in folio, was reprinted in 21 vols 8⁰ from 1747 to 1754. The 'Modern Part', in 43 vols, was published from 1759 to 1766. It was a joint undertaking both of publishers and authors. According to a manuscript list in the British Museum, drawn up by an Oxford don at the request of Dr Johnson and Sir Robert Chambers, the authors were Mr Sale, Mr Shelvock, Mr Belmanazar, Dr Campbell, Mr Bower. See Johnson's *Letters*, ed. Chapman, iii, p. 252.

34 The First Book of Thomas Hearne's *Doctor Historicus: or a short System of Universal History, and an Introduction to the study of it*, 1704 (4th ed. 1723) deals with chronology, the Second is *An Introduction . . . wherein an Account is given of the Writings of the ancient Historians, Greek and Roman, with the Judgment of the best Criticks upon them.*

37 *The Ægyptian and Grecian History of Herodotus. Translated from the Greek* by Isaac Littlebury, 2 vols, 1709.

38 *The Expedition of Cyrus into Persia. Translated, with notes,* by Edward Spelman, 2 vols, 1742. G had a copy of the 1749 ed. at Bn and L.

Page 42

1 *The Works of Tacitus:* Vol. I *The Annals* 1728 (dedicated by T. Gordon to Sir Robert Walpole); Vol. II *History, Germania, Agricola* 1731 (dedicated . . . to Frederick, prince of Wales). G had them at Bn; he probably sold these two folios, as ponderous as they are 'pompous' (an epithet they fully deserve), before moving his library to L. where he no longer had them.

a ragged Procopius—This was probably *Historiarum Procopii libri VIII nunc primum editi . . . opera D. Hoeschelii*, Augusta Vindelicorum, 1607, which G still had in his library at L.

11-12 John Speed (?1552-1629) published his *History of Great Britain from the Roman Conquest to King James* in 1611. The 1627 f⁰ ed. was in G's library at Bn and L.

For Rapin, see *above*, n. to p. 13, l. 31.

François Eudes de Mézeray (1610-1683) published his *Histoire de France depuis Faramond jusqu'à Louis le Juste* in 3 vols from 1643 to 1683. An English translation, by I. Bulteel, in 3 vols, appeared in 1683: *A general chronological history of France, beginning before the reign of King Pharamond, and ending with the reign of King Henry the Fourth.*

Enrico Caterino Davila (1576-1631). His *Istoria delle guerre civili di Francia*, translated into English by Sir Charles Cotterell and William Aylesbury, was published in 1647-1648 in 2 vols.

Machiavelli (1469-1527). His *Istorie fiorentine*, published posthumously in 1532, was twice translated into English before G's youth: 1. *The Florentine Historie . . .* by Thomas Bedingfeld, 1595 and 2. *The Florentine History in VIII Books . . . now exactly translated by M.K.*, 1674.

Father Paul: Paolo Sarpi (1552-1623). His *Istoria del Concilio de Trente* was published in London under an anagrammatic pseudonym (Pietro Soave Polano) in 1619, and was translated into English in 1676 by Sir N. Brent.

Archibald Bower (1686-1766) published his *History of the Popes from the Foundation of the See of Rome to the present Time* in 7 vols from 1748 to 1766.

27 Laurence Echard (?1670-1730). His *Roman History*, published in 5 vols in the last years of the 17th and the early years of the 18th centuries, was very popular, each of its volumes being often reprinted. Echard is responsible for the first two only (down to 'Constantine the Great'); the last three ('from Constantine to . . . the Taking of Constantinople by the Turks') were the work of a continuator and merely revised by Echard.

31 The passage of the Goths over the Danube is related towards the end of the 1st chapter of Vol. iii of the *Roman History*: 'The Huns were in the mean time grown so terrible to . . . the Goths, that they thought of removing from a Storm which they saw rolling irresistibly upon 'em, and resolved upon *Thrace*, both for that it was a fertile Country, and was separated by the *Ister* from these Tracts which lay expos'd to the Fury of the Huns. Having therefore seized on the Banks of the *Danube . . .* they sent their orators to *Valens*, by whom, in a most submissive manner, they begg'd leave to be admitted into *Thrace*, where they promised to live peacably in Subjection to the Empire, to whom they would be ready to send Aid upon all Occasions.

. . . there were not wanting some Sycophants about the person of the Emperor, who had the impudence to flatter him, and extol his good Fortune upon the Occasion, which had unexpectedly brought him a perpetual supply of soldiers. . . . The imaginary Prospect of this Advantage made him . . . give Order for their immediate Transportation which was done with so much Care and Diligence, as if it had been a Sin to leave any Person, who was to be concerned in the Subvertion of the *Roman* Empire, behind: For several Nights and Days together, without any intermission, did they come over in such Multitudes, that they, who were appointed to see the Business effected, were in no manner able to compute their Numbers, exceeding, saith Ammianus, the Sands upon the Libyan shore.'

36 William Howell (?1638-1683). His *An Institution of general history from the beginning of the World till the Monarchy of Constantine the Great*, published in 1661, was afterwards brought down to the fall of Augustulus and, in its complete form, published in 1685.

Page 43

3 Simon Ockley (1678-1720). His *History of the Saracens* was published in 2 vols, 1708, 1718. It was in G's library at Bn and L.

9 So also was the *Bibliothèque orientale ou dictionnaire universel contenant tout ce qui regarde la connaissance des peuples de l'Orient* of B. d'Herbelot de Moulainville (1625-1695) which was completed by A. Galland and published in 1697.

10 Edward Pocock (1604-1691) published in 1650, in a Latin translation, part of the Syriac *Chronicle* of Bar-Hebraeus (Abu 'l Faraj, latinized Abulfaragius, 1226-1286) under the title of *Specimen Historiae Arabum, sive . . . de origine et moribus Arabum succincta narratio*, and in 1663 an edition with a Latin translation of the same Syriac historian's *Compendious History of the Dynasties*. Both books were in G's library at Bn and L.

14-18 Christophorus Cellarius (1638-1707). His *Notitia orbis antiqui* was published, the 1st vol. at Cambridge in 1703, the 2nd at Amsterdam in 1706.

Edward Wells (1667-1727). His *Treatise of antient and present Geography, together with a sett of maps*, Oxford 1701, reached a 5th ed. in 1738.

Aegidius Strauch (1632-1682). His *Breviarium chronologicum* was 'done into English by R. Sault' as, according to its subtitle, '*a treatise describing the terms used in Chronology*' and published in 1722. It was in G's Library at Bn and L.

Christophorus Helvicus (1581-1617): *Theatrum chronologicum, sive chronologiae systema novum*, 1609.

James Anderson (?1680-1739): his *Royal Genealogies: or the Genealogical Tables of Emperors, Kings, and Princes, from Adam to these Times*, was published in 1732. The 1736 ed. was in G's library at Bn and L.

James Usher (1581-1656) published his *Annales veteris et novi Testamenti* in 1650-1654. The Geneva 1733 ed. was in G's library at Bn and L.

Humphrey Prideaux (1648-1724) published in 1716 *The Old and New Testament connected in the history of the Jews*. The 1718 ed. was in G's library at Bn. At L. he only had the 1749 8⁰ ed. in 4 vols.

23 J. J. Scaliger's *Opus de emendatione temporum* (1583), was carried on by Denys Petau (1583-1652) in his *Opus de doctrina temporum* (1627). Sir John Marsham (1602-1685) published his *Chronicus Canon aegyptiacus, ebraicus, graecus, et disquisitiones* in 1672, and Isaac Newton's *The Chronology of Ancient Kingdoms amended* came out after his death, in 1728.

24 study in the originals—Though the chronological works of Scaliger, Marsham and Newton were all in G's library at Bn, what he says here probably means that previously he had to borrow them. When, in January 1758, he wrote at L. his *Remarques critiques sur le nouveau système de chronologie du Chevalier Newton*, he was using Castillon's French translation.

Page 44

6 the sprightly race—In his *note 26* (M 59), G explains that, instead of quoting Gray's lines in the *Ode on a Distant Prospect of Eton College*, he merely gives 'images extricated from metre'; and then adds, smilingly mocking himself for coupling Westminster with Eton: 'Father Thames at Westminster, instead of margent green, has trading barges and carpenters yards.'

24 parva leves . . . Ovid, *Ars Amatoria*, i, 159.

32 under the scourge—G's *note 27* (M 60): 'Ὑπο μαστιγος, familiar to the readers of Herodotus.' The allusion is to the soldiers of Xerxes who were compelled to dig a channel through the isthmus of Mount Athos peninsula under *the scourge* (Herodotus, vii.22). Here again, G was quoting from memory: the Greek historian has ὑπὸ μαστίγων.

Page 46

1 A traveller—That G had in mind a particular traveller is shown by his *note 1* to chapter III (M 62): 'Le nombre des Etudians d'Oxford va à 2000. Ils ne portent ni bâton ni epée. Tous portent la robe et le bonnet quarré, l'habillement differe suivant le degré et la qualité . . . Tout est bien reglé dans cette Université: les desordres n'y regnent pas comme dans celles d'Allemagne (*Voyage Litteraire en* 1733, par M. Jordan [the correspondent of Frederic], pp. 174, 175)' (MS *f* 127 – M 62). The *Histoire d'un voyage littéraire fait en MDCCXXXIII en France, en Angleterre, et en Espagne*, by Charles Etienne Jordan (1700-1745), La Haye, 1735, was in G's library at L. On the author see *B.U.* For his correspondence with Frederic, see vol. x of F's posthumous *Works*.

8 quarrels of youth and wine—In his *note 2* (M 62), G refers to G. Burnet's *Some Letters Containing an Account of what seemed most remarkable in travelling thro' Switzerland, Italy &c in the Years 1685 and 1686*, Rotterdam, 1686 (a copy of the 1737 ed. was in G's library at L.); 'The University here,' says Burnet of Padua, 'tho' so much supported

by the *Venetians*, that they pay fifty Professors, yet sinks extremely:
there are no men of any great Fame now in it; and the Quarrels among
the Students have driven away most of the Strangers that used to come
and study here; for it is not safe to stir abroad here after Sun-set.'
(London 1724 ed., p. 133.)

20 The eyes of the traveller—Jordan, *op. cit.*, p. 174: 'Je logeai à Oxford
au *Blow Board* [?Blue Boar], où on est fort bien. La Ville est petite, &
il y a peu de belles Maisons. Les Colleges y sont magnifiques . . . .'

Page 47

8 banks of the Ilissus—To this passage on Magdalen College, G appended
his *note 3* (M 64): 'Praised by Hurd. (Dialogues, iii. pp. 165-169)
—Spartan halls, Attic symposia are or *may be* united.' In his *Dialogue
viii On the uses of Foreign Travel*, Hurd represents Locke as a champion
of the English Universities 'where the discipline of Spartan HALLS and
the civility of Athenian BANQUETS are, or may be, united'.

14 (says Bishop Lowth)—On Robert Lowth (1710-1787), see *D.N.B.* G's
quotation is from Lowth's *Letter to the Rt. Rev. Author of the Divine
Legation of Moses Demonstrated* (1765). In the course of his long controversy with Lowth, Warburton had attacked him and his University in
an Appendix added to the fifth vol., published in 1765, of the 4th ed.
of the *Divine Legation*. Lowth answered it at once. His famous *Letter*
was in G's library at L.

32 And do you reproach me—In his *note 4* (M 65) G first refers to 'p. 62-
65' of Lowth's *Letter* and then adds 'by an happy quot. from Clarendon
charges W, with having been an attorney's Clerk'. Warburton had
ascribed what he pretended to regard as Lowth's advocacy of intolerance
to the influence of Oxford University, as though its former student and
professor must still feel it. Lowth ironically retorted that Warburton
himself had overcome the deplorable influence of his education, since he
had been an attorney's clerk, an employment which, according to
Clarendon, 'inclines young men to more pride than any other kind of
breeding and disposes them to be pragmatical and insolent', whilst, in
spite of it, he 'had always distinguished himself by humility, lenity,
meekness, forbearance, &c' . . . qualities which no one would have
attributed to Lowth's adversary.

37 Locke—While saying that he would refrain from examining whether
Locke derived any benefits or rewards from his Oxford education, G
took care to attach a note to the name of the philosopher (*note 5*, wrongly
numbered 6 and misplaced in M 66): 'Locke owed no thanks—Student
of Christ-Church—expelled, never restored after Revol. (Biograph.
Brit., vol. v)—Heads of houses—no public censure—He [Locke]
laughed a good jest, a recommendation, yet was anxious to know

MML T

(His Works, 4° Edit., Vol. iv, p. 618, 19, in his letters).' The first
part of this note is explained by these lines in *Biographia Britannica*:
(returning from Holland in 1688) Locke 'put in a claim to his student's
place at Christ Church, but that society rejected his pretensions, as the
proceedings in his deprivation were conformable to their statutes.' To
this B.B. added a note to the effect that 'The bare fact alone of going
out of the kingdom without leave from the college . . . was in strictness,
a forfeiture of his studentship, by the statutes of that as well as other
colleges'. As to the second part, G's reference is to pp. 618-9 of vol. iv
of the 7th ed. of Locke's *Works* (G's '4° Edit.' is the 7th, the first to be
in 4 vols; G had the 8th 1777 ed., also in 4 vols, in his library at L.).
This vol. iv contains Locke's *Letters*; on pp. 618-619 are found two
letters addressed to Anthony Collins in February 1703/4 and introduced by the editor thus: 'It was proposed at a meeting of the heads of
the houses of the University of Oxford, to censure and discourage the
reading of Mr Locke's *Essay concerning Human Understanding*; and,
after various debates among themselves, it was concluded, that each
head of a house should endeavour to prevent its being read in his college,
without coming to any public censure.' Collins had informed his friend
of this meeting. On February 21, Locke wrote to him: 'It will be a
kindness to get a particular account of these proceedings; but therein
must be contained the day, the names of those present, and the very
words of the order or resolution; and to learn, if you can, from whence it
had its rise. When these particulars are obtained, it will be fit to consider what use to make of them. In the meantime, I take what has been
done as a recommendation of that book to the world, as you do; and I
conclude when you and I meet next we shall be merry upon the subject.
For this is certain, that because some men wink, or turn away their heads,
and will not see, others will not consent to have their eyes put out.'
Three days later, he wrote again repeating his request, begging Collins
to let his informer 'get the precise time, the persons present, and the
minutes of the Register taken of their proceedings; and this without
noise, or seeming concern to have them, as much as may be, and I
would beg you not to talk of this matter, till we have got the whole
matter of fact, which will be a pleasant story, and of good use . . . .'

39 This angry controversy—For the subject and the course of the controversy between Warburton and Lowth, see Mark Pattison's essay on the
Life of Bishop Warburton (Nettleship's collected ed. of Pattison's *Essays*,
ii, p. 140 ff.) and A. W. Evans, *Warburton*, Oxford, 1932, p. 247 ff.

Page 48

1 intolerant zeal—G saw traces of intolerance in the earlier part of the
Letter where Lowth excludes from toleration 'all those who make
practices shocking to humanity, and destructive of the human race itself,

parts of their religious worship', and in his *note 6* (wrongly numbered 5 in M 65) laughed at the notion of setting up the Inquisition in Bengal and punishing the worshippers of the Lingham and the rite of Suttee: 'Idolatry excluded from toleration—and Bengal—the Lingham, Suicide? Inquisition at Calcutta? Ha!'

11 'G was admitted as a member of the College on 2 April 1752, and matriculated in the Easter vacation. His name disappears from the Buttery Book on July 1753.' (Hill, p. 283.)

31 this 'separate annotation' was never written.

Page 49

17-21 In his *note 7* (M 68) G refers to two plans of reform of the Universities, drawn up at the request of Viscount Townshend when he was secretary of state under George I, one for Oxford by H. Prideaux (1648-1724), the other for Cambridge, by W. Whiston (1667-1752). (See M 101.)

Page 50

4 our *budge* Doctors—In his *note 8* (M 69) G refers to Milton's *Comus*, 707-710, and to Warton's note on the passage. A. W. Verity's comment is more to the point: 'It looks as if Milton, perhaps with a recollection of budge-trimmed hoods seen at Cambridge, used *budge* to suggest a learned professor, very much as we use *ermine* in special association with the judges.' (Cambridge University Press ed. of *Comus & Lycidas*, 1912, p. 102.) In the same *note 8* G ironically added: 'I do not apply lean and sallow abstinence (*Comus* 710) to our learned professors.'

18 general contempt—To these words G appended his *note 9*: 'Here Vicesimus Knox must be used.' In his *Liberal Education* (1781), a treatise in forty sections on the education of boys, V. Knox devoted a whole section to the Universities, the opening words of which are: 'It is easy to perceive, that the English Universities are in less repute than they formerly were. The rich and great . . . now frequently place their sons under some private tutor to finish them, as it is called, and then immediately send them on their travels. There seems . . . to prevail a discontent on the relaxation of discipline, and the useless and frivolous exercises required for the attainment of academical honours.' (p. 320 f.) And further: 'I consider the sending of a son thither [*i.e.* to our Universities] at present, . . . as a most dangerous measure . . . which may probably make shipwreck of his learning, his health, his character, and his fortune.' (p. 324.)

19-24 Universities of Europe—In his *note 10* G says he got his information from Göttingen. No letter from G asking for information has been found at Göttingen. But he may have applied to his friend Langer, just as he applied to him for help when he was engaged in his researches on the history of the House of Brunswick (see *Letters*, iii, p. 202). Göttingen is the nearest University to Wolfenbüttel where Langer resided.

32, p. 50-6, p. 51

The passage of *The Wealth of Nations* to which G refers is near the beginning of Article ii (not iii as G has it in his *note 11*) of Part iii of the 1st chapter of Book v (vol. ii). Adam Smith's *Inquiry into the nature and causes of the wealth of nations*, 2 vols, 1776, was in G's library at L.

Page 51

4-6 Professors are secure—In his *note 12*, G gave Thomas Gray as a typical example: 'Gray Prof. of modern history at Cambridge, £400 a year (Mem., p. 333), in three years never once read—his remorse—Mason's excuses, p. 395-399—Never admonished by any superiors.' G's reference is to W. Mason's ed. of Gray's *Poems. To which are prefixed memoirs of his life and writings*, 1775, which was in his library at L. The passages of Mason's *Memoirs* to which G refers are quoted by M, pp. 71-72.

6-11 It has been observed—G is most probably thinking here of what Johnson had said to Boswell in February 1766: 'People have now a-days got a strange opinion that every thing should be taught by lectures. Now, I cannot see that lectures can do so much good as reading the books from which the lectures are taken. I know nothing that can be best taught by lectures, except where experiments are to be shewn.' (Boswell's *Life of Johnson*, ed. Hill-Powell, ii, p. 7.)

12-14 To this passage M appended G's *note 13* (M 72): 'Dodwell. Prael. Camden—read on the August. hist. 25 lectures only for the authors and private life of Hadrian (Life, vol. [G's slip for pp.] 190-217 by Brokesby); must be now worth (since 1722) at least £400 per annum (*B.B.*, p. 168, new Edit. *Camden*, Ayliff, vol. ii, p. 186).' Though there is no reference 13 between 12 and 14 in MS *ff* 118-118ᵛ, the place given to *note 13* by M is right, as it adduces a good example of an office and salary which, having become useless, should be abolished. In 1622 Camden instituted a readership in history which, early in the 18th century was worth £140 and may have been worth £400 at the end of it. Now this readership had produced one book only, Henry Dodwell's *Praelectiones*, a series of 25 lectures on the *Augustan History* (collection of biographies of the Roman emperors by different authors, the Scriptores Historiae Augustae) which F. Brokesby summarizes in his *Life of Mr Henry Dodwell*, 2 vols, London, 1715. For the founding of the Camden readership G refers to John Ayliffe's *Ancient and present state of the University of Oxford*, 2 vols, London, 1714 and to the article on Camden in the 2nd ed. of *Biographia Britannica*. All these works were in G's library at L.

32 In his *note 14* (M 73), G refers to the 3rd ed. of Lowth's *De sacra poesi Hebraeorum praelectiones*, which was in his library at L., but notes that the 1st ed. had appeared in 1753, and adds 'Interesting without Hebrew or faith—good abstract in Blair (Lectures on Rh., Vol. ii. p. 385-406)'. Hugh Blair's *Lectures on rhetoric and belles lettres*, 2 vols, London, 1783 were also in his library at L.

34 In his *note 15* (M 73), G gives the name of the founder and the date of the foundation of Magdalen College, referring to Ayliffe's history of Oxford University, and adds: 'Merit under James II., zeal, privileges.' Perhaps he intended to make some amends for what he had said of his college by praising the courageous attitude of its fellows in 1687.

Page 52

2 loosely—'vaguely' (*N.E.D.*, which quotes Paley's 'loose traditions and reports').

4 quit-rents—'A rent, usually of small amount, paid by a freeholder or copy-holder in lieu of services which might be required of him' (*N.E.D.*).

5 fines—'sum of money paid by the tenant in order that his rent may be small or nominal' (*N.E.D.*). Hill quotes Adam Smith: 'Some landlords instead of raising the rent, take a fine for the renewal of the lease.'

16 In his *note 16* (M 74), G refers to a passage of the *Eloge de M. le Cardinal Quirini* in the *Histoire de l'Académie royale des Inscriptions et Belles Lettres* (tom. 27, p. 215 ff.) by the perpetual secretary of the Academy, Ch. Le Beau who, in the course of his sketch of the Cardinal's life, speaks of his stay in Paris: 'Il arriva à Paris au mois de mai 1711; & pour choisir un séjour favorable à la fois à sa piété & à sa curiosité, il logea à St Germain-des-Prés . . . Ce que sent Enée dans Virgile (Artificumque &c Æneid, i.455) lorsqu'il considère avec transport tant de bras en mouvement, tant de beaux édifices qui s'élèvent, le P. Quirini le sentit en entrant dans cette illustre Abbaye: on y travailloit alors aux annales des Bénédictins . . . à la collection des Décrétales, au glossaire de Du Cange . . . (etc.).' In this account, Le Beau followed Quirini's own narration in his autobiography to which G also refers. His *note 16* ends: 'burnt till extinction more or less', which cannot refer to the fire that destroyed part of the library on 19 August 1794, and is puzzling.

33 a young fellow—George Horne (1730-1792), elected a fellow in 1750, became Bishop of Norwich forty years later. When G arrived at Magdalen, Horne was 'deeply immersed' in the composition of *A Fair, Candid, and Impartial Statement of the Case between Sir Isaac Newton and Mr Hutchinson*, which was published anonymously in 1753. Horne's position as Newton's adversary is clear from the outset: 'The Newtonian system has now been in possession of the chair for some years. But there

have appeared, since it's first publication, some treatises on philosophical subjects, by a very curious and inquisitive person ... Mr Hutchinson, who thought that by the light revelation afforded him, compared with his own observations, he saw further into the constitution of the universe, and the operations carried on in it, than Sir Isaac had done.' (p. 4 f.) Though one might have expected these treatises to be eagerly read at a time when 'Sir Isaac had set the learned on a warm pursuit after physical knowledge', their claim remained 'slighted and neglected', which is the reason why Horne undertook to support their author who, on the cause of attraction was 'very sensible': considering that 'such knowledge is too excellent for man's wisdom, Mr Hutchinson thought there was but one way in the world by which we could possibly arrive at the knowledge of it, viz. by examining, with humility and diligence, what account was given of it in the bible where it's creation and formation were described at large by him who created and formed it.' (p. 66 f.)

For John Hutchinson (1674-1737) see *D.N.B.* He had attacked Newton's system in a series of pamphlets from 1726 to 1733. 'He seems to have started from the opinion that Newton's doctrines were of dangerous consequence. He denied ... gravitation, ... found a number of symbolical meanings in the Bible and in nature, and thought, for example, that the union of fire, light, and air was analogous to the Trinity.' (*D.N.B.*)

Page 53

1　George Ballard (1706-1755), who was not a chaplain, but a choral clerk of Magdalen College ... 'published, by subscription, his *Memoirs of Several Ladies of Great Britain who have been celebrated for their Writings, or Skill in the Learned Languages, Arts, and Sciences* in 1752' (J. R. Bloxam, *Register of the Members of Magdalen College*, quoted by M p. 75).

6-11　To illustrate this passage, G referred in his *note 17* (M 76) to the *Journal of a Senior Fellow*, published as No. 33 in *The Idler* by an anonymous contributor jeered at by G: 'his awe, nonsense, air!' The four-days *Journal* itself, which gives a fairly vivid picture of a Fellow who idles away his time, is not necessarily fictitious.

15　Neither Lord Wenman nor Sir James Dashwood are recorded in *D.N.B.* Both gentlemen represented the 'old interest' and both were defeated when the election was fought in 1754. See Emerson's note on the contest. Hill's quotation from an Oxford letter of May 1754 to *The Gentleman's Magazine* describes 'all the malevolence of party zeal' that characterized the election. See also No. XI of *The Connoisseur*.

22　This quotation is from Horace, *Odes*, III.3, 35-6.

36　Hill regards 'Burman an unfortunate instance' (p. 59, n. 4), owing to the variety of the chairs he held; but G only thought of the single devotion with which Burman edited the Latin classics.

Page 54

8 For Thomas Waldegrave (1721-1784), unrecorded in *D.N.B.*, see M's n., p. 77. His two manuscript volumes of *Annotationes in Platonis Opera* (on which see Hill's note, p. 288) are preserved as MS. 231 in the Library of Magdalen College. They are based on a 1578 edition in three vols of Plato's Works, including the spurious Dialogue and Letters, by de Serre (Serranus) and refer throughout to the page numbers and subdivisions of this edition, but stop at p. 304 of the third vol. What Waldegrave says at the end of his second vol. refers to the spurious works added by de Serre to his vol. iii (pp. 309-416). These Waldegrave did not think worth annotating. (For this information the editor's thanks are due to the Librarian of Magdalen College, Mr Neil Ker.)

31 avocation at home or abroad—the slightest distraction that detained me in or out of College. *N.E.D.* defines 'avocation' as 'that which has the effect of calling away or withdrawing one from an occupation'.

Page 55

1 without advice or account—without any advice from my tutor or any account given him of how I spent my time.

6 For Thomas Hyde (1636-1703) and Edward Pocock (1604-1691), orientalists, see *D.N.B.*

14 lost sight of my first tutor—Late in 1758 G wrote to Waldegrave informing him of his return to the Protestant faith, and apparently adding that he intended paying him a visit at Washington (about thirty miles from Buriton on the road from Worthing to London). This letter is lost (see *Letters*, iii, p. 453). Waldegrave answered on 7 December (*Misc. Wks*, ii, p. 37): 'it will give me great pleasure to see you at Washington.' From what G says here, it appears that his intended visit was never paid.

21 alteration of the style—'By Lord Chesterfield's Act of 24 George II . . . (1751), the Julian calendar was superseded by the Gregorian . . . and, in order to correct the error of eleven days in the Julian calendar, the eleven days between 2 and 14 September were omitted from the calendar for that year, the day after 2 September 1752 being called 14 September (the succession of days of the week thus not being interfered with).' B. Williams, *The Whig Supremacy*, 1939, p. xx (*Oxford History of England*, xi).

29 Voltaire's *Siècle de Louis XIV* was published in 1751; the first English translation was published in 1752.

31 the Conqueror of Asia—This phrase can hardly have been suggested by Herodotus' chapters on the reign of Sesostris (*Euterpe,* 102-10), but may well be due to what G had read about Sesostris in Sir John Marsham's *Chronicus Canon Ægyptiacus, Ebraicus, Graecus, et Disquisitiones* f⁰ London, 1672. (This, which G calls the 'best edition' in his *note 18* (M 79), was in his library at Bn and L. A later, 4⁰ ed., published at Frankfurt in 1696, was also in his possession at Bn. He may have bought it when at Oxford.) 'Sesostris Aegyptiaci in Asia imperii auctor fuit . . . Rex hic bellicâ civilique gloria inclytus erat, & parto Asiae imperio splendidissimus' (p. 353). Marsham himself seems to have based his pages 352-368 on the reign of Sesostris, in part at least, on Flavius Josephus' quotation from the Egyptian chronicler Manetho in his *Contra Apionem,* to which G refers in his *note 19* (M 80): 'Fragments in Joseph. contra Apion. in . . . Tom. ii, p. 447. Edit. Havercamp . . . .' Here is, in Havercamp's Latin translation, what Manetho, according to Josephus, had written on Sesostris' conquests: 'Hic (Sethosis) fratrem Armain procuratorem Aegypti constituit . . . Ille vero in Cyprum et Phoenicen, rursusque in Assyrios et Medeos expeditione suscepta, universos . . . magnae suae potestatis terrore sibi subiugavit atque, prospero rerum successu valde elatus, aliquanto audacius progrediebatur, orientales urbes et provincias subvertendo.'

36, p. 55-2, p. 56
As to the dating of Sesostris's reign, this is what Marsham has to say: 'Sesostris Ægyptiaci in Asia imperii auctor fuit. Hunc Regem Graeci ad Danai tempora perperam retulerunt. Ex deducta Thebanorum regum serie illius aetas incidit in posteriora XIV hujus seculi tempora: Ex collata modo Ebraeorum Chronologia illi contemporaneus fuit Roboboam Rex, Solomonis filius; cujus anno regni quinto, Sesostris cum exercitu in Asiam profectus est.' So Marsham rejects the Greek in favour of the Hebrew dating of Sesostris.

38 Newton's shorter chronology—In his paper on *Les principales époques de l'histoire de la Grèce et de l'Egypte,* dated 'Lausanne, Janvier 13, 1758' (*Misc. Wks,* iii, p. 150 f.), G showed that Newton dated most of the earlier events of Greek and Egyptian history several centuries later than Marsham, beginning with 1440 B.C. as against Marsham's 1643 or even 2184. Newton, like Marsham, dated Sesostris' expedition into Asia as 974. But for him the Flight of Danaus from Egypt to Greece took place ten years later whilst Marsham dated it 1511 B.C. Had Newton's dating been accepted by G, there would have been no 'formidable objection' to remove.

Page 56

1-5 This 'formidable objection' was the partial agreement of the Parian Chronicle and Manetho's story, the former giving the date of Danaus' arrival at Argos and the latter identifying Sesostris' brother with Danaus. For Manetho's story as related by Josephus, see M's appendix, p. 103 (where *vini* should be *vim*). G appears to have thought the Parian Chronicle reliable, whilst Manetho, because he was a priest, could well be suspected of deliberate falsehood. G may have studied the Chronicle in his youth, its first ed. being Selden's (1628); at any rate he was sufficiently interested in it late in life to buy *The Parian Chronicle, or the Chronicle of the Arundelian marbles. With a dissertation by Joseph Robertson, London 1788*, which was in his library.

To his *note 19*, partly quoted above (p. 55, l. 31), G added 'real loss, see Fabricius and Gerard Voscius'. These words refer to Manetho, and to Fabricius' *Bibliotheca graeca*, III, xx, 'De Manethone Ægyptico', as well as to what G. A. Voss says of the Egyptian chronicler: 'Quanquam vero optandum esset, ut scriptor hic integer ad nos pervenisset, tamen bene saltem est, quod luculenta quaedam fragmenta conservavit nobis Fl. Josephus lib. I contra Apionem.' (*De Historicis Graecis*, 1701, p. 91.) Both Fabricius' *Bibliotheca graeca* and Voss's *De Historicis Graecis* were in G's library at L.

11 fabulous or illegitimate pedigree—G's *note 20* (M 80): 'Quidam Philippo genitum esse credebant, certum pellice ejus ortum constabat Q.C., L.ix.C.8'. In chapter viii of his Book IX, Quintus Curtius relates how, in the attack of an Indian fortress, many soldiers were wounded by poisoned arrows, to Alexander's great concern: 'Praecipue Ptolemaeus ... regis sollicitudinem in se converterat: Sanguine conjunctus erat et quidam . . . .'

33 For Dr Winchester, see Bloxam's *Register*, vi, pp. 220-5. Though Bloxam quoted what G says here of his second tutor, there is nothing in the long notice to support his allegation.

Page 57

10 my frequent absence—According to the note in his own hand (Add. MSS 37.772) published by Low (*Journal A*, p. xlvi f.), G spent three weeks in London from 16 December to 8 January, a full week in February (16-24), and almost a fortnight in April (18-30). Besides this, he was away at the end of March on visits to Buckinghamshire and was at Bath for a week in May (10-18).

17 manly Oxonian in town—G's *note 21* (M 82): 'See Conoisseur No. XI. worked up in Colman's farce—Pallas quas condidit arces/ipsa colat, good.' In his library at L. G had a late ed. of *The Connoisseur* (4 vols, 12⁰, 1777), a periodical published in 1754-1756 by two Oxford students, George Colman and Bonnel Thornton. For it, see E. R. Page's Columbia dissertation 1935, on *George Colman the Elder*, chapter ii. The title of No. XI is given by M, p. 82, who also quotes the epigraph with its

translation (a specific feature of *The Connoisseur*) and adds a few extracts from the opening paragraphs. Here is another: 'The love of pleasure and a few supernumerary guineas draws the student from his literary employment, and entices him to this theatre of noise and hurry, this grand mart of pleasure, where, as long as his purse can supply him, he may be as idle as he pleases. I could not help smiling at a dialogue between two of these gentlemen which I overheard . . . at the Bedford coffeehouse. "Ha! Jack (says one accosting the other) is it you? How long have you been in town?"—"Two hours"—"How long do you stay?"— "Two guineas." . . .'. G also possessed Colman's *Dramatick Works*, 4 vols, 1777. The farce he refers to is *The Oxonian in Town* (vol. iv, p. 157 ff.): 'This short play describes the adventures of two young Oxonians, Knowell and Careless, during a visit to London. Three scoundrels attempt to trick Careless out of all his money, but Knowell saves him by winning their confidence and so discovering their methods' (Page, *op. cit.*, p. 167). It can hardly be said to be a 'working up' of the essay. G's exclamation 'good' after his quotation of the epigraph from Virgil is simply the expression of his approval of Colman's and Thornton's implicit blame of their University.

Page 58

14 incredible neglect—G's *note 22* (M 83): 'Ignorance, religious, of under graduates, who are soon ordained—complaint of Dr Prideaux—Dr Busby offered to endow two Cathechists—rejected by both Univers.— Confessional, p. 435-440.' G possibly meant to adduce in proof of the incredible neglect from which he suffered the following passage from an anonymous treatise (the work really of an archdeacon, Rev. Francis Blackburne), *The Confessional* (full title in M, p. 83) which had been in his library at Bn and was probably still in it at L.: 'Many of them [candidates for orders], in the northern dioceses especially, come immediately from a grammar-school, where they have thought of nothing but learning Latin and Greek. At the universities, the point for the first four years, is to qualify themselves for their first degree, which they may take with the utmost honour and credit, without ever having seen the inside of a Bible. And it should seem, by an anecdote in the Life of Dr *Humphrey Prideaux*, as if it were determined, that, during that interval, it is better they should not. Dr Busby offered to endow two catechetical lectures . . . provided the undergraduates should be obliged to attend, and none of them be admitted to the degree of Bachelor of Arts till after having been examined by the Catechist as to their knowledge in the doctrine and precepts of the Christian religion. But this condition being rejected by *both* universities, the benefaction was rejected therewith . . .'. To this passage there is added this footnote: 'Young men, said Dr Prideaux, frequently come to the University, without any

knowledge or tincture of religion at all; and have little opportunity of improving themselves therein . . . they are usually admitted to their first degree of Bachelors of Arts, with the same ignorance, as to all sacred learning, as when first admitted into the university; and many of them, as soon as they have taken that degree, offering themselves for orders, are too often admitted to be teachers in the church, when they are only fit to be catechumens.'

25 In his *Introductory Discourse* to *A Free Inquiry* (1749) Conyers Middleton wrote: 'It is an opinion commonly received among Christians, and above all, among those of the Romish communion, that after the days of the Apostles, there resided still in the Primitive Church, through several successive ages, a divine and extraordinary power of working miracles, which was frequently and openly exerted, in confirmation of the truth of the Gospel, and for the conviction of unbelievers. This is generally alledged by the Divines of all Churches, in their disputes with the Sceptics, as a subsidiary proof of the Divinity of the Christian Doctrine . . . This being universally adopted by the Papists, as an indisputable fact, or an article rather of the Christian Faith, and espoused likewise in part by the Protestants, I thought it my duty to inquire into the grounds of it.' In the opening pages of the *Inquiry* itself, Middleton gives the plan of his work thus: 'I. To draw out, in their proper order, all the principal testimonies, which relate to the miraculous gifts of the Church . . . found in the writings of the Fathers. II. To throw together all, which those Fathers also have delivered, concerning the condition of the persons who are said . . . to have wrought the miracles. III. To illustrate the particular characters and opinions of the Fathers, who attest those miracles. IV. To review all the several kinds of miracles . . . and to observe . . . how far the credibility of them may be reasonably suspected.' Middleton's conclusion is clearly given in his title: 'By which it is shewn That we have no sufficient Reason to believe, upon the Authority of the Primitive Fathers, that any such Powers were continued to the Church, after the Days of the Apostles.' Middleton's *Miscellaneous Works*, 4 vols, 4⁰, were in G's library at Bn and L.

28-30 the two dullest of their champions—On William Dodwell (1709-1785) 'the university of Oxford conferred the degree of D.D. by diploma, in recognition of his services to religion by his answer to Dr Middleton's *Free Inquiry*' (*D.N.B.*). 'For his *Vindication of the Miraculous Powers which subsisted in the three first centuries of the Christian Church*, the university of Oxford conferred upon Thomas Church (1707-1756) the degree of D.D.' (*Ibid.*).

37-8 As Aeneas was told by the Sibyl (*Æneid*, vi, 96-97) that his salvation would come from a town of the Greeks, his worst enemies, so a Roman

Catholic Gibbon might have ascribed his salvation from heresy to heretic Middleton.

Page 59

25 Molesworth—Such a name has not been found in the Books of Magdalen College (Hill, p. 69, n. 5).

29 *An Exposition of the Doctrine of the Catholique Church . . . translated into English by W.M.* (William Montague) was published in Paris in 1672. Another translation, by Joseph Johnston, was published in London in 1683 and several times reprinted, in 1686, 1729, 1735 and 1753. *The History of the Variations of the Protestant Churches, Translated from the 6th ed.* was published at Antwerp in 1742.

37 ten-horned Monster—The monster of *Revelation*, ch. xii, in which Protestants used to see the Roman Church.

Page 60

1 This echoes the opening lines of Dryden's *The Hind and the Panther*.

7 This line may also be an echo of Dryden's 'One is the Church, and must be to be true' (*Ibid.*, ii, 526).

9 When writing 'transsubstantiation', G often, but not always, failed to write the fourth syllable.

11 As Hill observes (p. 71, n. 2), Bossuet does not use the Latin form of 'the sacramental words'. Nor do his translators. But G may have thought it more in keeping with his 'oppressed me'.

16 ff. *The Hind and the Panther*, i, 141 ff.

Page 61

5 at present ignorant—In the 1814 ed. of the *Misc. Works*, (i, p. 64), Lord Sheffield added this footnote: 'His name was Baker, a Jesuit, and one of the chaplains of the Sardinian Ambassador. Mr. Gibbon's conversion made some noise; and Mr. Lewis, the Roman Catholic bookseller of Russel-street, Covent Garden, was summoned before the Privy Council, and interrogated on the subject. This was communicated by Mr. Lewis's son. 1814'. Lord Sheffield would probably not have published the information he had received from Lewis's son, at some time between 1796 and 1813, unless he had felt sure it was correct. But there does not seem to be any letter from the bookseller's son, or to him, among the Gibbon papers at the B.M., nor is any listed in the typewritten *Catalogue of the Sheffield Papers used for the editions of Gibbon's Miscellaneous Works* (B.M., *Add. MSS 11907*, dd, 25/1), which are at Yale. And no trace has been found of Lewis's interrogation in the records of the Privy Council at the Public Records Office. (These records have been searched at the present editor's request by another Gibbonian, M. Michel Baridon, of Dijon

University.) This absence of any record of the interrogation need not mean that it did not actually take place: Mr D. Foxon has also failed to find in the records any confirmation of John Nichols's account of the citation before the Privy Council of John Cleland, the author of *Memoirs of a Woman of Pleasure* (see *Times Literary Supplement*, 4 January 1964, p. 35). But since as many as fifty years or more elapsed between G's conversion and the information received by Lord Sheffield from the bookseller's son, whose father died in 1802, the fact of Lewis's interrogation by the Privy Council should perhaps be questioned.

15 Blackstone's *Commentaries on the Laws of England*, 4 vols, 4⁰, was in G's library at L. His quotation is from vol. iv, p. 56.

20 Epistle—'He described the letter to his father, announcing his conversion, as written with all the pomp, the dignity, and self-satisfaction of a martyr.' (Lord Sheffield's footnote to *Misc. Works*, i, p. 63.)

31 'turned Papist'—G may be alluding here, as Hill suggested, to a passage in Boswell's account of his conversation with Johnson on 20 March 1776 (ed. Hill-Powell, ii, p. 447 f.): 'The authour had been an Oxonian, and was remembered there for having turned Papist.'

Page 62

8 The quotation is from Milton's *Lycidas*, 128-9.

10 What G says of Chillingworth is apparently based on the *Life* by P. Desmaizeaux rather than on that by T. Birch prefixed to the 1742 ed. of Chillingworth's *Works*, which is itself based on Desmaizeaux's.

13-18 '. . . a famous Jesuit, who went under the name of John Fisher . . . was very busy in making Converts, particularly at Oxford, and attacking Mr *Chillingworth* upon the Necessity of an infallible Judge in Matters of Faith . . . the latter forsook the Communion of the Church of England and soon after wrote . . . to his friend Sheldon [Gilbert Sheldon, the future archbishop] asking him to consider most seriously of these two Quæries: I Whether it be not evident from Scripture, and Fathers and Reason, from the Goodness of God, and the Necessity of Mankind, that there must be some one Church infallible in Matters of Faith? II Whether there be any Society of Men in the World, besides the Church of Rome, that can . . . challenge to itself the Privilege of Infallibility in Matters of Faith' (Birch's *Life*, p. ii).

25 In his reply to G's letter (see above n. to l. 14, p. 55) Dr Waldegrave had written: 'Had I in the least suspected your design of leaving us, I should immediately have put you upon reading Mr Chillingworth's Religion of Protestants; any one page of which is worth a library of Swiss divinity.'

31 In a private letter—another letter to Sheldon on the subject of his refusal of the preferment offered him: 'If I can have no Preferment without Subscription, I neither can, not will have any . . . as long as I keep that modest and humble Assurance of God's Love and Favour which I now enjoy, so long I may, and shall, and will be happy. But if I once lose this . . . I shall and must be extremely miserable. Now this inestimable Jewel, if I subscribe . . . I shall wittingly, and willingly, and deliberately, throw away . . . if I subscribe, I subscribe my own Damnation . . . whenever I make such a preposterous choice [preferment rather than happiness], I will give you leave to think I am out of my wits' (*op. cit.*, pp. v-vi).

Page 63

1 without a date—Desmaizeaux does not date it, but it is dated by Birch 21 September 1635.

12 This sentence is from an undated letter which Chillingworth wrote to one of his friends who wanted to know what he thought of arianism. Birch thinks it contemporary with *The Religion of Protestants a safe way to Salvation.*

Page 64

4 falling sect—The suppression of the Edict of Nantes had been prepared by fifteen years of increasing persecution of the Protestants.

10 favour—Hill (p. 77, n. 2) proposes to correct 'favour' into 'fervour'. But 'favour' refers to the physical appearance and completes 'genius'. *N.E.D.* defines it as 'that which wins goodwill, attractiveness'.

34 paradox of Plutarch—G is referring here to Plutarch's moral essay 'Περί Δεισιδαιμονία'.

38 the *false* Religions—In B, his second attempt at writing his *Memoirs*, G said: 'Bayle balanced the Religions of the Earth in the scales of his sceptical philosophy'; for G, all religions were equally *false*, but by using this adjective he may have calculated that his readers would instinctively think he made an exception for the Christian religion and spare him their criticism.

Page 65

4-9 See Voltaire's *Lettre . . . sur Rabelais & d'autres auteurs accusés d'avoir mal parlé de la religion chrétienne* (1767), Lettre VII *Sur les Français*, 'De Bayle': 'il est rapporté dans un de ces dictionnaires historiques, où la vérité est si souvent mêlée avec le mensonge que le cardinal de Polignac, en passant à Rotterdam, demanda à Bayle s'il était anglican, ou luthérien, ou calviniste, et qu'il répondit: "Je suis protestant; car je proteste contre toutes les religions."' Voltaire then gives several good reasons for doubting the authenticity of the story, but adds: 'Il est vrai que Bayle avait dit quelquefois ce qu'on lui fait dire: il ajoutait qu'il était comme Jupiter assemble-nuages d'Homère.' (Voltaire, *Oeuvres*, ed. Beuchot, xliii, p. 518.)

21-31 For Edward Bentham (1707-1776) and John Burton (1696-1771) see *D.N.B.* Bentham published in 1771 his *Epistola De Vita et Moribus Johannis Burtoni*. The portrait he draws of his friend forms a complete contrast with what G says of tutors in general (see p. *53 above*): 'Mathesin non attigit, Hebraica nescivit . . . Pupillis auctor erat ut utriusque Eruditionis elementa in quadriennale suo cursu, condiscerent. Quae ipse non intellexit adeo non damnavit ut Suis adjumenta aliunde conquireret, prece, aliquando etiam pretio, conducta, ut ex omni parte officio suo, quanquam alienâ operâ, satisfaceret . . . Quo melius Pupillos suos in *Dialectices* et *Metaphysices* elementis institueret, Sandersoni Logica, subjectis iis observationibus quas ex *Lockio* decerpserat *J. Clericus*, plerumque utebatur. Inde via ad *Lockium* ipsum explicandum complanatior. . . .'

24 Francis Burgerdyk (1590-1629), professor of logic and moral philosophy at Leiden University. Of his popular *Institutionum logicarum libri duo*, Lugduni Batavorum, 1632, B.M. possesses the second ed. of 1634 and other edns of 1637, 1647, 1651, 1666, and 1680, mostly published at Cambridge.

34 Sir William Scott was King's Advocate-General when G was writing this sentence. He had been Camden Professor of Ancient history from 1774 to 1785. See Hill's appendix 18, p. 292.

Page 66

10 What G calls 'the second part of Lord Clarendon's history' is *The Life of Edward Earl of Clarendon*, published at Oxford in 1759. In the preface, the printers explain that 'The reason, why this History has lain so long concealed, will appear from the Title of it, which shews that his Lordship intended it only for the Information of his Children. But the late Lord Hyde . . . left by his Will this, and the other Remains of his Great Granfather, in the Hands of Trustees, to be printed at our Press, and directed that the Profits arising from the Sale should be employed towards the establishing a Riding-School in the University.' It was soon found that the aforesaid profits were so small that years would elapse before there was enough money to build a riding-school. So a fund was instituted into which the profits were paid. See Powell's long note in Boswell's *Life of Johnson*, ed. Hill-Powell, ii, p. 527 f.

13-22 In the preface to the first volume, published in 1765, of his *Commentaries*, Blackstone wrote: 'The following sheets contain the substance of a course of lectures on the laws of England which was read by the author in the university of Oxford. His original plan took it's rise in the year

1753 ... he had the satisfaction to find ... that his efforts were encouraged and patronised by those ... whose ... esteem he was desirous
to obtain. The death of Mr Viner in 1756, and his ample benefaction
to the University for promoting the study of the law, produced about
two years afterwards a regular and public establishment of what the
author had privately undertaken. The knowledge of our laws and constitution was adopted as a liberal science of general academic authority;
competent endowments were decreed for the support of a lecturer and
the perpetual encouragement of students; and the compiler of the ensuing commentaries had the honour to be elected the first Vinerian
professor.'

Page 67

2 The allusion is probably to the foreign education of the sons of George III.
In 1780 Frederick Augustus was sent to Hanover to study French,
German, and military tactics, and in 1786 Ernest Augustus and his
younger brothers were sent to the University of Göttingen (Emerson).

Page 68

1 Ch. IV gives the text of B from where it may be said to continue F, *i.e.*
from MS *f* 31 (M 104). The earlier pages of B (MS *ff* 22-30 – M 104-
129) correspond to the whole of F, but the narrative is much less
detailed. For some extracts from the pages of B not included in the text,
see Appendix I, 10-13.

15 Mr Mallet—'The author ... of some forgotten poems and plays ...
—His tenets were deistical; perhaps a stronger term might have been
used.' (Lord Sheffield's footnote, *Misc. Wks*, i, 79.) Though Mallet's
poetry mostly justifies this contempt, the literary historian cannot pass
it over entirely. See, *e.g.*, B. Dobree's *English Literature in the Early
Eighteenth Century*, 1959 (*Oxford History of English Literature*, vii),
passim. Mallet's less despicable poetry shows him to have been a deist.
To suggest that he was an atheist was gratuitous.

23 advice of Mr Eliot—Lord Chesterfield sent Philip Stanhope to L. on
the advice of his secretary, Salomon Dayrolles, who was a native of the
Pays de Vaud. Philip's friend Eliot went with him (Sir G. de Beer in
Revue Historique Vaudoise, 1953, p. 212). Eliot, who married Catherine
Elliston, G's first cousin, in 1756 (*Letters*, i, p. 57), had probably met
her at the Mallets' to whose care Mr Gibbon, a widower himself, had
entrusted his orphan niece and ward. Falling in love, Eliot, a young man
in his early twenties, but already an M.P., had ingratiated himself with
the uncle and won his confidence.

26 travelled post—From Henry Frei's *Account of travelling expenses made
for Mr Gibbon from London to Lausanne* (Magdalen College Library,

MS. 359, I, 1), a single sheet listing, on one side, Frei's expenses in sterling and, on the other, his expenses in French livres, a clear idea of the journey can be formed:

[June 19] *1. Paid for 2 places in ye stage-coach from London to Dover*   £1 17

       2. Paid for ye Luggage   1 7

[June 20] *3. Expenses for ye Inn from London to Dover* [i.e. between London and Dover, probably at Sitting-bourne]   19

[June 21] *4. at ye Inn at Dover*   1 2

       5. Custom house fees & porters   12

       6. For the passage from Dover to Calais   1 6

                            £7 3

France

[June 22] *1. Paid for several little expenses at Calais*   Livres   36

       2. for the hiring of a Post-chaise   144

       3. Paid from Calais to Besançon, Post 67 at L.4 10 [i.e. 301 livres 10 sous] *each post 15 sous ye Guide makes*   351 15

       [From Calais to Besançon there were 67 posts: fresh horses were put in at each post at a cost of 4 livres 10 sous for the horses and 15 sous for the man in charge of them, the 'guide'.]

       4. Expenses upon ye Road from Calais to Besançon   90

       5. bought a knife for Mr Gibbon   12

       6. From Besançon to Lausanne   126

               french money 759 15

   at Livres 24 for a Guinea makes Sterling £33 4

      transferred from ye other side   7 3

             Total   £40 7

   Received from Madame Morel at Calais June 22.1753 for Mr Gibbon's account   £42

           Deducted   40 7

      Due to Mr Gibbon   £1 13

            Henry Frei

Thirty years later, in 1783, G followed the same route and in a note in the B.M. (*Add MSS 34882, f 259*) gave a full list of the places where he stopped for the night. See *below*, p. 329.

Page 69

2 Daniel Pavillard (1704–1776) was not only, from 1748 to 1765, one of the four 'pasteurs' of Lausanne, he was also teaching Latin and ancient history at the 'collège' (grammar-school), and was professor of history at the 'Académie' (now the University). By calling him 'a calvinist minister', G meant no more than 'a protestant' one; calvinism had long ceased to be the doctrine of the Canton of Berne (see below, p. 73, what G says of J.-P. de Crousaz's influence).

Page 70

The money then current in the Canton de Berne, and therefore in the Pays de Vaud, as well as in France, was the 'livre' of 20 sols (sous), the sol being subdivided into 12 deniers. According to Pavillard (see p. 226 *above*, end of his letter of 14 January 1758) £1 was equivalent to 14 'livres' 16 sols of Berne money. At this rate 1 'livre' was equivalent to $1/4\frac{1}{4}$d, and 1/- was worth 14 sols 8d. This should be remembered when reading the following notes. The Berne 'livre' was therefore worth more than the French one which, according to Frey (see his *Account*, n. to p. 68, l. 26), was equivalent to 1/-.

6 Payments 'pour le bois' entered in what has survived of M. and Mme Pavillard's respective accounts:

For the winter 1755–1756	36 livres	(see p. 222, *above*)	
1756–1757	22 ,,	(see p. 224, *above*)	
	25 ,,	(Mme P.'s account for July–December 1756—*Magdalen College Library*: MS. 359, *f* 42)	
	32 ,,	(see p. 227, *above*)	
1757–1758	42 ,,	(see p. 226, *above*)	

Even if we regard Mme P.'s entry for 22*l* as distinct from her husband's for 25*l*, which is questionable, the expense for G's wood in the 5 to 6 months of the winter 1756–1757 was only 79*l*, *i.e.* 13 to 16*l* per month. Low, *Gibbon*, p. 49, n. 1, does not give his reasons for saying that heating cost 60*l* a month.

9 Small monthly allowance—It is impossible, on the basis of the surviving documents, to calculate with any degree of assurance, how much pocket-money G received from M. and Mme P. The surviving documents are (a) P.'s 3 accounts for the last six months of 1755, 56 and 57 sent to Mr Gibbon (see pp. 222–226, *above*); (b) what seems to be the draft of a similar account for the first six months of 1757 (see p. 227, *above*); (c) P.'s four-page memorandum or list of his expenses for G, dated month by month, for the two years 1755 and 1756, ending with a general entry of G's pocket-money for 1757 (see *Magdalen College*

Library MS. 359, *ff* 6-9); (d) lastly, Mme P.'s *compte pour M. Gibbon* from July 1756 to December 1757 (*Ibid*, *ff* 42, 17, 18).

There are serious difficulties in trying to use these documents. P.'s accounts sent to Mr Gibbon may be supposed to give the best information, but they only cover three half-years. His draft of an account for January-June 1757 is only a draft: the fair copy may have been different. Further it is difficult to reconcile the memorandum or list of his expenses with the accounts sent to Buriton. And, lastly, the relation of Mme P.'s accounts to those of her husband is far from clear: it may be argued that they are complementary and should be added to find out the true amount of their expenses for G, and in particular that of the pocket-money he was given; it may also be argued that, in part at least, they refer to the same expenses noted twice, by husband and wife independently, and should therefore not be added.

However that may be, here is what these documents tell about G's pocket-money:

Writing to Mr Gibbon on 25 July 1753, P. asked him whether he should give his son some pocket-money, and how much (see p. 214, *above*). In fact he had already given him two 'Louis d'or'. And he had again given him the same sum for August when a letter, written on 24 July, arrived on 18 August with instructions as to pocket-money. To his annoyance he saw he had given his boarder more than the father intended. So G had to be content with one 'Louis d'or' only for September and again for October, (see p. 217, *above*). No record has survived for the end of 1753 and 1754.

In his Memorandum, P. noted in the first six months of 1755 the following remittances 'pour l'argent de poche': Jan. 4: 12*l* 5*s*—Feb. 2: 12*l*—25: 12*l*—March 12: 12*l*—30: 12*l*—April 20: 12*l*—May 18: 12*l*—June 9: 12*l*—26: 12*l* (altogether 9 remittances totalling 108*l* 6*s*). In the last six months of the same year, he noted: July 3: 6*l*—Aug. 3: 12*l*—21: 12*l*—Sept. 16: 13*l* (during the Swiss tour, Sept. 21 to Oct. 20, P. paid all expenses himself and had them refunded by Mr. Gibbon separately (see Low, *Gibbon*, p. 60).—Oct. 30: 2*l*—Nov. 5: 6*l*—18: 6*l*—30: 4*l*—Dec. 16: 12*l*—28: 4*l* (altogether 11 remittances totalling 77*l*. But in the account sent to Mr Gibbon for July-Dec. 1755, P. charged 'pour argent de poche' 160*l* (see p. 222, *above*). Is it then that Mme P. gave 83*l* in addition to what P. himself had given?

In the first six months of 1756, P. noted in his Memorandum: Jan. 4: 8*l*—25: 12*l*—Feb. 15: 12*l*—March 10: 12*l*—21: 4*l*—April 3: 8*l*—22: 12*l*—May 3: 4*l*—9: 8*l*—30: 12*l*—June 20: 12*l* (*i.e.* 11 remittances and 104*l*)—and in the last six months: July 19: 12*l*—Aug. 5: 12*l*—22: 12*l*—Sept. 11: 8*l*—19: 4*l*—25: 4*l*—Oct. 3: 8*l*—19: 4*l*—26: 8*l*—Nov. 13: 12*l*—17: 4*l*—28: 8*l*—Dec. 20: 12*l* (*i.e.* 13 remittances and 108*l*); now in her own account for the same period, Mme P. noted 'for argent de poche': July 19: 12*l*—Aug. 5: 12*l*—22: 12*l*—Sept. 11: 8*l*—19: 4*l*—25: 4*l*—Oct. 3: 8*l* 10*s*—19: 4*l*—26: 8*l*—Nov. 13: 12*l*—19: 4*l*—25: 8*l*—Dec. 20: 12*l* (*i.e.* 13 remittances and 108*l* 10*s*, the same number of remittances and each time the same amount as her husband). Together the Ps. gave G 217*l*, but in the account P. sent to Mr Gibbon. he charged 192*l* for pocket-money (see p. 224, *above*), that is 25*l* less than he and his wife had noted, but 83*l* 10*s* more than either of them had noted. This seems to show that, whenever he was in need of some pocket-money, G had to go to each of them for half the sum he could be given. Rather curious!

At the end of his Memorandum, P. noted: '1757 Janvier à Décembre compte de l'argent de poche, au total 296*l* 4*s*.' Now this does not agree with the total of his charges 'pour argent de poche' in his two half-yearly accounts for 1757 (see pp. 226, 227, *above*), which is 384*l*. Nor does it agree with Mme P.'s 14 remittances from January to June, totalling 128*l*, and 8 remittances from July to December amounting to 96*l*, altogether 224*l* for the whole year. And the total of the remittances of both P. and his wife, which is 520*l* 4*s*, does not agree either with the 384*l* he charged Mr Gibbon for 1757.

At any rate one can understand the bitter memory G, who was a proud young man, kept of his dependency on the Ps. for his pocket-money. Not only had he to ask whenever he was short of money, but it was often given him in absurdly small amounts and each time he had apparently to apply successively to his tutor and to his tutor's wife.

18 they never attempted—For the sake of peace between the two confessions, more or less equally represented in Switzerland, there was a tacit understanding that the Protestants would abstain from any propaganda in the Catholic Cantons, and the Catholics in the Protestant ones.

Page 71

6 One evening early in January 1755, G went to see a Mr Gee, found him playing at 'Pharaon' (faro) with some other gentlemen, was persuaded to take a hand, and lost 40 guineas. He demanded his revenge, and, at a second meeting lost 110 guineas. For what happened as a consequence, see G's letters to his aunt Catherine (*Letters*, i, pp. 3-4 and 6-8) and Low, *Gibbon*, p. 54 ff.

33 Jean Le Sueur (?-1681), 'pasteur' of the protestant congregation of La Ferté-sous-Jouarre, published an elaborate *Histoire de L'Église et de l'Empire* from the birth of Christ to the year 1000, 6 vols, 4⁰, Geneva 1672-1679. Written in the form of annals, this unpretentious History enjoyed a certain popularity and was re-edited at Amsterdam in 1730 with a continuation to the year 1100.

Page 72

6 In his *Compte pour Monsieur Gibbon* (*Magd. Coll. Lib.*, MS. 359, I, *ff* 6-9), Pavillard entered several payments for dancing lessons from March 1755 to March 1756.

7 expensive—In his letter of 15 August 1753 (see p. 216, *above*) Pavillard asked Mr Gibbon to allow his son to take riding-lessons (monter au manège). This request seems to have been disregarded. But P. had already given his boarder the permission to 'monter au manège': G had begun riding on the 13th and went on for five months at a total cost of 196 livres 16 sols. As, in spite of repeated demands, the permission never came, P. dared not forward the riding-master's heavy bill to Mr Gibbon until three years later when, on 12 January 1757, he sent him his half-yearly account (see p. 224, *above*) with a slightly reduced bill 'pour leçons de manège', amounting to 165 livres 16 sous (*Ibid.*, MS. 359, I. *f* 3). Apparently, Mr Gibbon refused to honour his son's debt, and the riding-master, Henri Crousaz de Mésery, did not get his money until, in Dec. 1757, he had his original bill for 196 liv. 16s. accepted in payment of a sum he happened to be owing to a certain 'Monsieur Pradez'. This man got Pavillard's promise to pay by Jan. 13 1758 (*Ibid.*, *f* 4). Whether P. kept his promise and was subsequently refunded by Mr Gibbon is not known, though the presence of the two bills among the papers bought by Magdalen College makes it probable. However that may be, G's trouble over the payment of his riding-lessons explains why he found them 'expensive'.

Page 73

5 For professor de Crousaz (1663-1750), see J. E. de la Harpe, *Jean-Pierre de Crousaz et le conflit des idées au siècle des lumières*, Genève & Lille, 1955; Pope, *An Essay on Man*, ed. M. Mack, p. xix ff. (Twickenham ed., vol. iii, 1, 1950).

10 Philip van Limborch (1633-1712) and Jean Le Clerc (1657-1736) were both professors at the Remonstrant (Arminian) Seminary of Amsterdam, the former from 1668 and the latter from 1684, Limborch of theology and Le Clerc of philosophy and later of Church history. G had devoted some of his leisure hours in the summer of 1762 to Le Clerc's *Bibliothèque Universelle* and, in vol. ii, read a long extract from Limborch's *Theologia Christiana* which he described in his Journal as 'moderate and judicious, the general character of the Arminian Divines' (*Journal A*, pp. 79 and 87). Limborch's *De veritate religionis christianae* was in G's library at L., and so were the 26 vols of the *Bibliothèque Universelle*.

15 J.-P. de Crousaz's *Logique ou Système de réflexions*, first published in 1712 in 3 vols, had grown to 6 vols in its 4th ed. (1741).

26 some of his letters—See Appendix II.

28 a firm . . . defence—In a n. to this passage, *Misc. Wks*, i, p. 82, Lord Sheffield wrote: 'M. Pavillard has described to me the astonishment with which he gazed on Mr Gibbon standing before him: a thin little figure, with a large head, disputing and urging, with the greatest ability, all the best arguments that had ever been used in favour of popery. . . .' Written in 1795, this n. can only refer to 1763 when Holroyd met Pavillard in G's company.

Page 74

5 I received the sacrament—See Pavillard's letter to G's aunt, Catherine Porten, p. 220, *above*, and J. E. Norton's n. 3 in *Letters*, i, p. 3.

13 But in the life—This sentence is clearly incorrect. The MS shows what happened: after writing *there is an æra from*, G saw that the image he had in mind (*he soars*) demanded another word than 'æra', replaced it by *a level from whence* but crossed out *from* only and not *æra* as well, as he should have done. When, some time later, he rewrote B into C, he was dissatisfied with his sentence and wrote the passage over again in two sentences, dissociating *level* and *æra*, and giving up the image.

Page 75

1 Vertot—For René Aubert, abbé de Vertot (1655-1735) see *B.U.*; his *Histoire des révolutions de la république romaine* was published in 1719.

18 Dr Middleton's history—Conyers Middleton's *Life of Cicero*, largely told in the orator's own words, appeared in 1741.

21 Olivet—For Joseph Thoulier d'Olivet (1682-1768) see *B.U.*; his ed. of Cicero—*Ciceronis opera omnia cum selectu commentariorum*, 9 vols, 4⁰, Paris 1740-1742—is said to be unrivalled 'pour la beauté typographique, la correction du texte, la netteté, la précision, le savoir et le goût qui brillent dans les remarques'. (Michaud).

22 Ernesti—For Johann Augustus Ernesti (1707-1781) see *B.U.*; his epoch-making ed. of Cicero's *Opera omnia* was published in 1734.

23 John Ross (1719-1792), bishop of Exeter, published in 1749 'a competent edition of Cicero's letters *Ad familiares* with numerous notes' (*D.N.B.*).

24 Verbruggius—Lord Sheffield rightly corrected Verbruggius into Verburgius. Verburgius (1684-?) was professor at Leyden; his *Ciceronis Opera quæ supersunt omnia, cum Asconio et scholiaste veteri, ac notis . . . Isaacus Verburgius . . . recensuit*, Amsterdam, 1724, filled two big f⁰ vols.

29 observation of Quintilian—'. . . ab hominibus aetatis suae regnare in judiciis dictus est; apud posteros vero id consecutus ut Cicero jam non

hominis nomen, sed eloquentiae habeatur; hunc igitur spectemus; hoc propositum nobis sit exemplum; ille se profecisse sciat, cui Cicero valde placebit.' (*Institutio*, X.1.)

Page 76

17 studied—in the sense of 'endeavoured' (*N.E.D.* s.v. *study*, 4).

22-24 Torrentius—Latin name of Lievin Vander Beken (1525-1595) whose ed. of Horace was published after his death at Antwerp, in 1602. (*B.U.*).

Dacier—For André Dacier (1659-1757) see *B.U.*; his *Oeuvres d'Horace, en latin et en français, avec des remarques historiques et critiques*, 10 vols, was published in Paris, 1681-1686.

Catrou—For François Catrou (1659-1757) see *B.U.*; his translation of Virgil was poor and soon superseded, but G may have found his notes of some use.

Meziriac—For Claude-Gaspar Bachet, sieur de Meziriac (1581-1638) see *B.U.*; his *Epitres d'Ovide, traduites en vers français avec des commentaires fort curieux* is said to be 'une mine où n'ont pas manqué de puiser tous les auteurs qui ont écrit depuis sur la mythologie' (Michaud). It was published in 1626. 'Meziriae', said G, 'as usual compiles without a thought of reasoning' (*Journal A*, p. 95).

28 a dissertation—This, which is dated 'At Lausanne, 13 Mai 1757' was published by Lord Sheffield in *Misc. Wks*, iv, pp. 446-466.

Page 77

5 Horace, *Ars Poetica*, 268.

11 etymology—is used in the now obsolete sense of 'accidence'.

23 darkly and through a glass—*I Cor.*, xiii, 12 (A.V.).

24 in an English dress—Pope's. See pp. 36-37, *above*.

35 my father—See Pavillard's letter of 12 January 1757, p. 223, *above*.

Page 78

2 Théodore-Louis de Treytorrens (1726-1794) was giving private lectures in 1756-1757; he was appointed professor of mathematics and physics at the Académie of L. in 1758. See *Journal B*, pp. 21 and 23.

4 For Guillaume Lhopital (1661-1704), known as 'marquis de Lhopital, though really 'marquis de Ste-Mesme', see *B.U.*; his *Traité analytique des sections coniques*, by which he is best remembered, was only published in 1707.

9 relinquished for ever—In 1762 G was still hoping one day to resume his study of mathematics. See *Journal A*, pp. 64 and 70.

17 Béat-Philippe Vicat (1715-1770), professor of law at the Académie of L. since 1741. His *Cours abrégé de droit naturel* is still extant in MS, but his *Traité de droit naturel et de son application au droit civil et au droit des gens* was published in 1777 at L.

26 For Jean Barbeyrac (1674-1744), professor of law first at L. (1711-1717), then at Groningen, see Philippe Meylan, *Jean Barbeyrac... Contribution à l'histoire du droit naturel*, Lausanne 1937. In his study of Grotius and Pufendorf, G had probably recourse to the following publications of Barbeyrac: *Le Droit de la Nature et des Gens* (1706) and *Les Devoirs de l'Homme et du Citoyen* (1707), both translated from Pufendorf's Latin; *Hugo Grotii de jure belli et pacis, cum notis* (1720).

33 de Crousaz attacked Bayle in the latter part of his *Examen du Pyrrhonisme ancien et moderne* (1733): see de la Harpe, *op. cit.*, p. 223 ff.

Page 79

1 G rightly considers Locke's works as a school of argument and Bayle's as a school of objection.

3 Philosophic dictionary—The context makes it clear that the reference is here to Bayle's *Dictionnaire historique et critique* and not, as Emerson suggests, to Voltaire's *Dictionnaire philosophique* which came out in 1764 only.

15 For Jean-Philippe René de la Bletterie (1696-1772) see *B.U.*; his *Vie de l'empereur Julien* was published in 1735 and re-issued with additions and corrections in 1746.

19 Pietro Giannone (1676-1748): his *Istoria civile del Regno di Napoli* (1723) was translated into French by P. Desmaiseaux and published at Geneva in 1742.

21 Revolutions—G uses the word in the then normal sense of 'changes' (*N.E.D.*, III 6).

30 '... Others I have found unalterably persuaded, that nothing is certainly remembered but what is transcribed; and they have therefore passed weeks and months in transferring large quotations to a common-place book. Yet, why any part of a book, which can be consulted at pleasure, should be copied, I was never able to discover. The hand has no closer correspondence with the memory than the eye. The act of writing itself distracts the thoughts, and what is read twice is commonly better remembered than what is transcribed. This method therefore consumes time without assisting memory.' (*Idler*, No. 74.)

Page 80

14 French journal—G's *Journal de mon voyage dans quelques endroits de la Suisse* has been published in *Miscellanea Gibboniana*, Lausanne 1952.

17 printed accounts—such as Thomas Coryat's (1611), Gilbert Burnet's (1686), Joseph Addison's (1705), William Coxe's (1779, 1789) and others. See Sir Gavin de Beer, *Travellers in Switzerland*, London, 1949.

21 Einsidlen—see *Misc. Gibb.*, pp. 28-32.

32 Geneva—G stayed at Geneva from 15 September to 15 October 1757 (*Journal A*, p. 6; *Letters*, i, p. 74). It cost his father 225 livres (see p. 226, *above*).

30 Zwingli—For Zwingli at Einsiedlen, see Abraham Ruchat, *Histoire de la Réformation en Suisse*, Geneva 1727, Livre premier. Ruchat's History was in G's library at L.

36 For 'the languid state of science at L.' in mid 18th century see Philippe Meylan, *Grands projects à l'Académie de Lausanne il y a deux cents ans* in *Revue de théologie et de philosophie* (Lausanne), N.S. xxviii (1940), pp. 17 ff.

Page 81

3 Livy (XXX.44)—the sentence which G proposed to correct occurs in Hannibal's speech to the senate of Carthage and used to read in all edns, including Crevier's (1748): *Nec esse in vos odio vestro consultum ab Romanis credatis.* G's was 'an obviously sound correction for which he deserves all the more credit seeing that no one before him had felt its necessity. It has since been supported by MS authority.' (D. M. Low in *Letters*, i, p. 390.)

11 For Crevier, Jean-Baptiste-Louis (1693-1765) and Charles Rollin (1661-1741) see *B.U.* Neither was professor at the University. Though Crevier was professor of rhetoric at the Collège de Beauvais in Paris (merged in Louis-le-Grand in 1764 when the Paris secondary school system was re-organized), and Rollin had been 'coadjuteur', *i.e.* principal, of the same collège, Crevier can hardly be said to have been Rollin's successor. But Rollin, at his death, had only published the first five vols of his *Histoire romaine* which Crevier completed by writing eight more vols: Crevier was Rollin's continuator. This is what G probably meant. G's letter to Crevier is missing, but Crevier's letter, now in B.M. (*Add. MSS* 34886), was published by Lord Sheffield in *Misc. Wks*, i, 433.

15 Latin correspondence—G's five letters to Breitinger are in the Zentral-bibliothek at Zürich; they have been published, with translations by D. M. Low, in *Letters*, i, pp. 14-68. Three of Breitinger's Latin replies are in B.M. (*Add. MSS*, 34886, *ff* 10-15); they were published, with translations, in *Misc. Wks*, i, pp. 436-486. The whole correspondence is the subject of an essay by D. M. Low given in *Appendix I* of *Letters*, i, pp. 387-390.

25 G's letters to Gesner are missing, but elaborate drafts, in French, of

two of them are in B.M. (*Letters*, i, Nos 19 and 22); they were published in *Misc. Wks*, i, pp. 486-530 together with Gesner's two Latin replies.

31 foolish enumeration—See *Misc. Wks*, i, p. 514.

34 For François-Louis Allamand (1709-1784) see Henri Vuilleumier, *Histoire de l'Eglise réformée du Pays de Vaud*, Lausanne 1933, iv, pp. 288-300.

Page 82

4 an anonymous letter—See *Journal B*, p. 197, n. 3 and Vuilleumier, *op. cit.*, iv, pp. 449 ff.

15 Est sacrificulus . . .—According to Vuilleumier, *op. cit.*, iv, p. 290, G borrowed this saying from a German scholar of the 17th century.

19 G's letters to Allamand are missing, but two of Allamand's replies were kept by G; Lord Sheffield published them in *Misc. Wks*, i, pp. 436-455; they are now in B.M. Both deal exclusively with Locke's doctrine of innate ideas. Soon after his arrival at L. in May 1763 G went with a party of young Englishmen on an excursion to Bex (see *Revue Historique Vaudoise*, 1961, p. 181), where Allamand was still the local 'pasteur'. There is no evidence that he took this opportunity of renewing his acquaintance with his 'personal friend' of 1756, though he could write in his Journal on 1 January 1764, 'Allamand m'intéresse beaucoup'. (*Journal B.*, p. 197). Nor is there any evidence that G ever met him after he had settled at L. in September 1783 when Allamand was, and had been for ten years, professor of Greek at the Académie.

23 *Paradise Lost*, ii, 561.

28 his secret scepticism—Had G ever seen Allamand's major work, *L'Anti-Bernier* (1770), on which see Vuilleumier, *op. cit.*, iv, pp. 294-300, he would hardly have suspected him of scepticism. But the interest which he still professed in 1764 had apparently vanished long before he returned to L. in 1783.

35 Voltaire broke with Frederick and left Berlin in March 1753; he reached Geneva, where he bought Les Délices, in December 1754.

37 two winters—Voltaire stayed at Lausanne for some of the winter months in 1755-1756, 1756-1757 and 1757-1758. He lived at Montriond, a large house about half-way between the town on the heights and the lake, 'in the neighbourhood' of L., from December 1755 to March 1756, and again from January to April 1757. He left it to occupy 'in town' Nº 6, rue du Grand-Chêne. Both houses have disappeared.

Page 83

3 he received me—D. M. Low, in his *Gibbon*, p. 71, n. 2, dates G's visit as 'probably in December 1755, when Voltaire first resided at Monrion'.

This seems rather too early: G then was only seventeen; after two and a half years at Lausanne, he would not yet have spoken French fluently; he does not appear to have begun seeing 'some company', as Pavillard put it, before the latter part of 1756 (see *above*, p. 223); besides, G himself gives for Voltaire's residence at Lausanne the two winters 1756-1757 and 1757-1758 when Voltaire had some of his plays performed at Monrepos, as though he did not know that the poet had already been there in the winter 1755-1756. Sir Gavin de Beer is no doubt nearer the truth when he prefers to date G's introduction to Voltaire as taking place in 1757. See his article on *Voltaire's British visitors* in *Studies on Voltaire*, ed. Th. Besterman, iv (1957), pp. 14-18. It may be conjectured that the pretext of the visit was to solicit an invitation to the performances in February-March 1757 of some of Voltaire's plays.

4 Virgilium vidi tantum—Ovid, *Tristia*, IV.10, 51.

5 The Ode is, in fact, Epistle XCI with its sub-title '*L'auteur arrivant dans sa terre, près du lac de Genève*' (Beuchot's ed. of Voltaire's *Works*, xxiii, p. 210).

8 imparted as a secret—Meredith Read, in his *Historic Studies in Vaud . . .* i, p. 90, claimed to have discovered in a collection of de Brenles' papers a manuscript copy of Voltaire's Epistle which he felt was 'unquestionably' the very 'copy which Voltaire enclosed in his letter' to de Brenles of 18 June 1755. But there is no reason to believe that the words 'Je vous envoie des vers. Ils ne sont pas trop bons, mais c'est l'éloge de votre pays' refer to a manuscript rather than to a printed copy, sent separately and not enclosed within the letter, in which there is not a word that could justify G's 'imparted as a secret' (see Besterman's ed. of *Voltaire's Correspondence*, xxvii, p. 43). The Epistle was published about the middle of June (*Ibid.*, p. 53), but anonymously, Voltaire, as so often, wishing to be able to disavow it in case it was attacked by his adversaries for its praise of liberty. As de Brenles was the first of his friends to receive a copy directly from him, he may have told G, while allowing him to read it, that the author's name was for the moment a secret not to be divulged. Even if Read's reason for identifying the Gentleman who introduced G to Voltaire cannot be retained, the identification may well be right: we know that, during his first stay at Lausanne, G was often the guest of the de Brenles (see *Journal B*, p. 246) and, of all the gentlemen whom Voltaire knew at Lausanne, none is more likely to have introduced a young Englishman to him than Jacques-Abram Clavel, a jurist with a charge in the local administration, who was to end his career as professor of law at the Académie, and who, for all he was 'seigneur de Brenles', was not exactly a member of the local aristocracy.

11 When he wrote this line, many years after the event, G probably remem-

bered only Clavel's advice not to risk displeasing Voltaire by revealing his authorship of the Epistle, and he took it for granted that his circulating among his acquaintances the copy he had written from memory must have annoyed the author. In fact, the poem was almost at once known to be Voltaire's and the poet does not appear to have been displeased.

20 Monrepos—a house at a little distance from what was then the eastern suburb of L.; its owner had turned a large room on the second floor into an auditorium and opened a wall separating it from an adjoining hay-loft used as a stage. The house was pulled down early in the 19th century and a new house built on the site.

24-25 *Zaïre* was performed at Monrepos on 18 or 19 February (*Voltaire's Correspondence*, ed. cit., xxi, pp. 44 and 60); *L'Enfant prodigue* on 10 and 13 March (*Ibid.*, pp. 88 and 99), 1757; *Zulime* (as *Fanime*) on 19 March (*Ibid.*, pp. 104, 108 and 109); *Alzyre* early in March 1758 (*Ibid*, xxxii, p. 163 and n. 2).

31 Hannah Pritchard (1711-1768) was the leading actress of Garrick's company at Drury Lane, and much admired by G (see *Journal A*, p. 186).

32 her age—Voltaire's niece was born in 1711.

33 Lusignan in *Zaïre*, Alvarez in *Alzire*, Benassar in *Zulime*, Euphemon in *L'Enfant prodigue*.

Page 84

15 early love—For an account of G's early love, see *Journal B*, Appendix II: 'Edward Gibbon et Suzanne Curchod jusqu'en septembre 1763' and *Letters*, i, 391-400: 'The Letters of Edward Gibbon and Suzanne Curchod.'

21 Amor omnibus idem—Virgil, *Georgics*, iii, 244.

Page 85

4 Crassy (the Swiss-French frontier runs through the village; the Swiss part is now called *Crassier*, while the French one has retained the old form) is not in, but at the foot of, the Jura range.

17 two or three visits—G paid four visits at Crassy: at the beginning of August 1757, on 2 October, in November from the 17th to the 23rd, and at the end of February or early in March 1758.

Page 86

5 Dutchess of Grafton—The 3rd Duke of Grafton divorced in 1769 and his wife married in the same year John Fitzpatrick Ossory; G does not appear to have known her before her second marriage. See *Letters*, *passim* (Index, iii, p. 438).

14 prosperity and disgrace—The Genevese Jacques Necker (1732-1804), banker in Paris, had become finance minister of France in 1776, but Louis XVI, acting under the influence of the Queen, dismissed him in 1781. Seven years later, yielding to the pressure of public opinion, the King recalled him and, in September 1788, Necker was once again at the head of the country's finances. In the following months, he was more and more regarded as the only man who could save France from financial ruin by bringing about the necessary reforms if he was given the power. Writing in the spring of 1789 G, by calling him 'perhaps the Legislator', was reflecting the trend and the hopes of public opinion.

Page 87

7-8 midst of a war—the Seven Years' War. 'War was not actually declared by England till news had come of the French landing in Minorca in May 1756.' In April of the previous year 'Boscaswen had been sent out with a squadron to intercept the French fleet with reinforcements for Canada, but without clear instructions as to how he should act if he met the French before war had been declared. Unfortunately he only captured two French frigates without doing any damage to the rest of their fleet, so that this dubious act of war, while putting us in the wrong, gave us no material advantage'. (Basil Williams, op. cit., pp. 328 and 330, n. 3.)

13 In the early pages of his first Journal, begun at the end of August 1761, G set down 'some few events of my past life'. He there gave a slightly more detailed account of his journey back to England and says he 'determined to pass through France under the name of my friend D'Eyverdun and set out in a hired coach with M.M. le Maire Crousaz (sic)'. These are the names of the two Swiss officers in whose company he was travelling, Daniel Lemaire and Jean-Louis Crousaz, both captains in the service of Holland; their names occur in Journal B.

26 Austrian dutchy—Luxemburg had been a possession of the dukes of Burgundy for more than a century when, in 1477, as a consequence of the marriage of Charles the Bold's daughter with Maximilian I, it became an Austrian duchy.

31 Stanislaus Leszczynski, whom Charles XII had placed on the throne of Poland and maintained there for a few years, was driven from it on the defeat of the King of Sweden at Poltava; he was succeeded by his predecessor, the legitimately elected Augustus. Stanislaus retired to Lorraine and his daughter married Louis XV. When Augustus died in 1733 Stanislaus was duly elected King of Poland but, owing to Russia's opposition, could not ascend his throne. In compensation his son-in-law obtained for him the duchy of Lorraine.

33 For Louis de Beaufort (?-1795) see B.U. G discussed the *Dissertation sur l'incertitude des cinq premiers siècles de l'histoire romaine* (1738) in ch. xxvii ff. of his *Essai sur l'étude de la littérature*.

36 stepped aside—On 26 April, G passed in sight of Rotterdam and went on to The Hague, but on 2 May he turned back to spend the night at Rotterdam whence, on the following day, he went to Brielle. (*Journal A*, p. 8.)

Page 89

2 prayers of the Church—'. . . we commend to thy fatherly goodness all those, who are any ways afflicted, or distressed, in mind, body, or estate, that it may please thee to comfort and relieve them . . .' (*Book of Common prayer . . . of the Church of England*, A Collect or Prayer for all Conditions of men).

20 hinted—this alludes to a passage in the early pages of B. (See *Appendix I*, p. 206, *above*.)

Page 90

10 levied a fine and suffered a recovery—'The person to whom the land was to be conveyed sued the holder for wrongfully keeping him out of possession; the defendant acknowledged the right of the plaintiff; the compromise was entered on the records of the court; and the particulars of it were set forth in a document called the *foot of the fine*. This method of conveyance was resorted to as a means of barring an entail. The defendant was said to *acknowledge* or *levy* a fine'. (*N.E.D.*, *s.v.* fine.)

Page 91

21 During my absence—Mr Gibbon married Dorothea Patton on 8 May 1755 but did not inform his son of it until December in a letter published in Low, *Gibbon*, p. 60. Three months earlier G had heard of it when the news was brought him by a Buriton acquaintance three days after he had received a letter from his father in which there was 'not a syllable' about it. See *Letters*, i, p. 8.

28 Euripides, *Alcestis*, 309. Before dying Alcestis beseeches her husband not to marry again, 'for a step-mother hates the children of a first bed, being as cruel to them as an adder'.

Page 92

3 *Eclogues*, iii, 33.

14 In 1758 G's step-mother was 43. He had been anxiously wondering whether his father was perhaps intending to disinherit him in favour of a child from his second wife. See *Letters*, *loc. cit.*

31 Horace, *Ars Poetica*, 82.

Page 93

36 Lord Chesterfield's word—'Monsieur and Madame Fogliani will, I am sure, show you all the politeness of Courts, for I know no better bred people than they are. Domesticate yourself there while you stay at

Naples, and lay aside the English coldness and formality.' (*Letters written by the Earl of Chesterfield to His son*, 4 vols, London 1775, iii, p. 2, Letter dated 29 March 1750.) Chesterfield's *Letters to his Son* was in G's library at L.

Page 94

2 unforgiving enemy—There is no evidence of Johnson being Mallet's enemy, but much evidence of his contempt for the Scottish poet. After writing, at the end of his penultimate paragraph of his *Life of Mallet*, 'His conversation was elegant and easy', he added 'The rest of his character may without injury to his memory sink into silence', and in Boswell's *Life of Johnson*, which G had not yet read, of course, when writing this passage, Johnson is reported by his friend as calling Mallet a 'beggarly Scotchman . . . ready for any dirty job . . . the prettiest drest puppet about town'.

3 defects of his wife.—'I found her exactly the same talkative, positive, passionate conceited creature as we knew her twenty years ago' (G's account to his step-mother of his visit to Mrs Mallet at Paris in 1777: *Letters*, ii, p. 155).

5 For Lady Mary Hervey (1706-1768) see *D.N.B.*

6 the present Earl of Bristol—Frederick Augustus Hervey, 4th Earl of Bristol (1730-1803) was the third son of Lady Hervey.

18 Bond Street—For the winter 1758-1759, G had lodgings at a linen-draper's in Bond Street.

Page 95

7-9 This sentence is curious and possibly incorrect, though G copied it out *verbatim* in C (MS *f* 67ᵛ – M 246) and Lord Sheffield did not think it necessary to change it. G had first written *His attendants were multiplied by the intermixture of domestic and rural servants*. He then stopped to change or sharpen his pen and added in the margin ⟨*The produces maintained a number of men and horses*, repeating the sign for insertion ⟨ in front of *His attendants*; he then deleted heavily (angrily?) the *s* of *produces* and completed the marginal addition by adding *, which* and lightly crossed out *His attendants*. The result was the curious sentence in B, C and Sheffield's two editions. Might it not be surmised that the change or sharpening of his pen induced an instant of inattention, produced the wrong deletion of *His attendants* and the mistaken addition of *, which*? And the correct text should no doubt be *The produce maintained a number of men and horses. His attendants were multiplied by the intermixture of domestic and rural servant;*

26 For Charles Lennox, 3rd Duke of Richmond (1735-1806) see *D.N.B.*

Page 96

1 never less alone than when by myself—According to Cicero (*De officiis,*
iii, 1) Publius Scipio Africanus used to say 'nunquam se minus otiosum
esse quam cum otiosus, nec minus solum quam cum solus esset'.

21 Militia business—The militia bill had been passed by the Commons in
1756, but rejected by the Lords in 1757. Soon after his return to power
in June, Pitt got it passed. The organisation of the militia, however,
took a fairly long time and it was not until the summer of 1759 that
captain Edward Gibbon (he received his commission on 12 June, see
Journal A, p. 10) had to give much of his time to 'Militia business'.
'This summer,' he wrote in his Journal, 'was unfavourable to Letters,
being taken up with continual journeys to Winchester and Alton upon
Militia business' (*Ibid.,* p. 9).

24-27 According to *D.N.B.,* Henry Bilson Legge, who was then chancellor of
the exchequer, 'was returned for Hampshire early in December 1759.
This gave great offence to Bute who had supported the candidature of
Mr (afterwards Sir Simeon) Stuart.'

Page 97

15 thus expressed—in ch. v of the *Essai sur l'étude de la littérature.*

29 The elder Pliny's maxim is known from what his nephew, the younger
Pliny, says of his uncle's studious habits in a letter to Marcus (Pliny's
Letters, iii, 5).

32 See *Appendix I,* 19, p. 211, *above.*

Page 98

2 solution of a passage of Livy—'Argenti probi duodecim millia Attica
talenta dato intra duodecim annos pensionibus æquis (talentum ne
minus pondo octoginta Romanis ponderibus pendat)' (Livy, xxxviii, 38).
On this passage G wrote in his *Principes des poids, des monnoies . . . des
Anciens* (*Misc. Wks,* v, p. 73): 'Les historiens nous ont conservé ce
traité orgueilleux que les Romains firent signer à Antiochus. On lui
impose un grand tribut qu'il doit payer en talens attiques. On stipule
que le talent pèsera 80 livres Romaines . . . Il a donc dû exister un
talent Attique du poids de quatre-vingt livres Romaines.'

3-5 dry and dark treatises—For John Greaves (1602-1652), author of *A
Discourse on the Roman Foot and Denarius* (1649)—John Arbuthnot
(1667-1735) who published his *Table of Ancient Coins, Weights and
Measures* in 1727—John Hooper (1640-1727), bishop of Bath and Wells,
whose *Inquiry into the State of the Ancient Measures, the Attick, the Roman
and the Jewish* was published in 1721—and Edward Bernard (1638-
1696), author of *De mensuribus et ponderibus antiquis Libri tres* (1688),

see *D.N.B.* For Jean-Gaspard Eisenschmid (1656-1712) mathematician, Johann-Friedrich Gronovius (1611-1671) and Nicolas Fréret (1688-1749), see *B.U.* Eisenschmid: *De ponderibus et mensuris veterum Romanorum, Graecorum, Hebraeorum nec non de valore pecuniae veterus* (1708, 2nd ed. 1737); Gronovius: *De sesterciis* (1643, further edns 1656, 1691); Fréret: *Dissertations sur les mesures itinéraires des anciens*, 1736. De La Barre is not recorded in *B.U.*; for him, see *Misc. Wks*, v, pp. 67-68, where G lists and briefly describes 'les principaux auteurs chez qui j'ai puisé' (Greaves, Eisensch[m]idt, de la Barre, Arbuthnot, Hooper).

6 ridiculously—In a note to ch. xx of the *Essai* G calculates what Sulla would have had to pay his soldiers had he paid them on the scale later adopted by Augustus, and reaches an enormous sum; he adds that, on the basis of Arbuthnot's *Table*, it would be somewhat less, but 'quelques recherches que j'ai faites' confirm his own and not Arbuthnot's results. To which he appended a footnote: 'V. mes Rem. MSS; sur les poids, &c des anciens. . . .'

37 The old reproach—In his Appendix No. 21, Hill quotes passages from Addison, Voltaire, Bolingbroke and Johnson in illustration of 'the old reproach'.

Page 99

1 recently—Robertson's *History of Scotland* was published in 1759 and Hume's *History of the Stuarts* from 1754 to 1757.

19 three Royal societies—Académie française, Académie des sciences, Académie des inscriptions et belles-lettres.

22-25 . . . la mémoire, la raison proprement dite et l'imagination, sont les, trois manières différentes dont notre âme opère sur les objets de ses pensées . . . Ces trois facultés forment d'abord les trois divisions générales de notre système, et les trois objets généraux des connaissances humaines: l'Histoire, qui se rapporte à la mémoire; la Philosophie, qui est le fruit de la raison; et les Beaux-Arts, que l'imagination fait naître. . . . La division générale de nos connaissances suivant nos trois facultés pourrait fournir aussi les trois divisions du monde littéraire, en Erudits, Philosophes et Beaux-Esprits: en sorte qu'après avoir formé l'arbre des sciences, on pourrait former sur le même plan celui des gens de lettres. La mémoire est le talent des premiers; la sagacité appartient aux seconds, et les derniers ont l'agrément en partage . . . Les trois espèces de républiques dans lesquelles nous venons de distribuer les gens de lettres, n'ont pour l'ordinaire rien de commun, que de faire assez peu de cas les unes des autres . . . La société doit sans doute aux beaux esprits ses principaux agréments, et ses lumières aux philosophes; mais ni les uns ni les autres ne sentent combien ils sont redevables à la mémoire; elle renferme la matière première de toutes nos connaissances, et les travaux de l'érudit ont souvent fourni au philosophe et au poète les sujets sur lesquels ils s'exercent. . .' (D'Alembert, *Discours préliminaire de l'Encyclopédie*, ed. F. Picavet, pp. 63-71). These pages form the conclusion of the first part of the *Discours*, in which D'Alembert explains his system of classification of all human notions; G does not seem to have read them very carefully: had he done so he would not have written the end of his sentence. The *Discourse*, which was published in 1763, was not among his books.

31 before my departure—See *Journal A* (8 March 1758), p. 7.

32 'hurry' means here 'excitement'.

34 no more than ten days—*Ibid.* (11 July 1758), p. 9.

38 'M. Burdet, a french prisoner at Petersfield began to copy my Essai which he finished in a few days.' *Ibid.*, 24 August 1759. See *Letters*, i, 117.

Page 100

6-18 For Matthew Maty (1718-1776), see *D.N.B.* He was appointed underlibrarian at the foundation of the B.M. in 1753 and principal librarian in 1772. The *Journal Britannique*, written in French and published in Holland, was in G's library at one time (24 vols), but he must have left it behind when he removed to L. The 'eighteen Volumes' is probably due to imperfect recollection.

18 his angry son—For Paul-Henry Maty (1745-1787) see *D.N.B.*; in January 1782 he launched a review meant to draw the reading public's attention to new foreign publications; it came to an end in 1785.

32 short preface—this is entitled *Avis au lecteur*.

37 *Ars Poetica*. i, 388.

38 For Jacques Sirmond (1559-1654) see *B.U.*

Page 101

3 d'Olivet (P. J. Thoulier, abbé d', 1682-1768) published in 1729 *Histoire de l'Académie françoise*, in one 4⁰ vol. made up of two vols bound together, the first being an ed. 'avec des Remarques & des Additions' of P. Pellison's (1624-1693) *Histoire de l'Académie françoise Depuis son établissement jusqu'à 1652*, published in 1653, and the second being his own continuation entitled *Histoire de l'Académie françoise, Depuis 1652 jusqu'à 1700*. A new ed. in 2 vols 8⁰ was issued in 1730. G's reference is to this 1730 ed., which was in his library at L. (see Keynes, p. 216, under Pellison-Fontanier; Pellison usually added to his own name, that of his mother). The advice given by J. Sirmond to 'a young friend' occurs in d'Olivet's

notice of La Motte le Vayer as something he had heard from P.-D. Huet, the future bishop of Avranches: 'La première fois qu'il vit le P. Sirmond, qui étoit alors plus que nonagénaire: *Ne vous pressez pas,* lui dit ce sage & docte vieillard, *de rien donner au Public; il n'y a rien dans les sciences, qui n'ait ses coins & ses recoins, où la vue d'un jeune homme ne perce pas; attendez que vous ayez cinquante ans sur la tête, pour vous faire auteur.* Il ne s'agit pas ici des Orateurs; encore moins des poëtes; leur objet demande qu'ils profitent du temps où l'imagination a toute sa force.'

9 This 'great Edition' of Sirmond's *Opera varia* was in G's library. In the *Vita* prefixed to vol. i, the anonymous biographer, referring to Sirmond's youth, writes: 'Hoc ipso tempore complura, ut videtur, Patrum Graecorum opera Latine vertit, & Apollinarem Sidonium doctissimis illustravit Notis; qui primus excellentis viri partus, antequam publicam in lucem exiret, eruditorum, quibus ejus copiam [*i.e.* copy] fecit, plausis, admiratione, praeconiis exceptus, viam illi ad summam qua postmodum floruit ingenii & doctrinae existimationem aperuit. Extant virorum ea tempestate in re literaria principum [here follows a list of such well-known names as Lipsius, Pithoeus, etc.] literae quibus Sirmondum rogant, hortantur, urgent, ut eximium opus ne diutius premat. Quod tamen nonnisi longo post tempore in lucem emittere potuit . . .' The biographer does not give the date of the publication of this 'eximium opus', but his *Vita* is followed by a *Syllabus operum Jacobi Sirmondi* which begins with a catalogue of his numerous editions—'ab ipso Sirmondo edita sunt'—with their dates; there *Apollinaris Sidonius* is dated 1614.

11 in the spring of 1761—See *Journal A,* p. 24 (23 April), and *Misc. Wks,* iv, pp. 1-2.

15 overtures of peace—For a full account of these negotiations, see R. Waddington, *La Guerre de Sept Ans,* iv (1909), ch. ix and x.

17 which never met—In 1761, after five years of war, a general desire for peace was making itself increasingly felt in nearly all the countries and governments involved. France, Austria, and their allies on the continent, proposed that a general congress should meet at Augsburg, but only after France and England had reached a separate agreement as to the conditions they would accept for the restoration of peace between them. These proposals were duly accepted in April, and delegates to the future congress named at once, while envoys extraordinary were exchanged between the courts of St James's and Versailles. Choiseul sent M. de Bussy to London with a memorandum of the conditions the French were ready to subscribe to, and Pitt sent Hans Sloane Stanley to Paris with a similar document. From June to August negotiations were pursued through the envoys who, at every step, had to refer to their respective minister. No agreement could be reached, partly owing to Pitt's resentment at the French support of the claims of Spain against

Great Britain, her ally. In August the negotiations were broken off and in mid-September Pitt and Choiseul recalled their envoys. The plan of a general congress was tacitly given up.

21 G completed his 'last revisal' on 23 April (see *Journal A*, pp. 24-25). I consulted with . . .—see *Ibid.*, p. 28.

30 without my knowledge—In the early pages of his first Journal, written from memory between 14 August and 10 September 1761, G wrote under 10 June 1761: 'Finding the printing of my book went on slowly, I went up to town where I found the whole was finished except an introductory letter from Dr Maty, who showed me what he had wrote of it' (*Journal A*, p. 27). As Maty's *Epitre* is dated 16 June (the day no doubt when it was finished), G's 'without my knowledge' is questionable: was it perhaps due to the unconscious desire to conceal the fact that he had allowed the insertion in his book of an 'Epitre' which, on reflection, he found ungracious, at least in part?

34 Did G underline these three words because he somewhat resented Maty's insistence on his youth, nationality and social condition in the opening paragraph of the 'Epitre à l'auteur' (see *Misc. Wks*, iv, pp. 7-8)?

38 pious—written with filial piety.

Page 102

3 I marched—The sentence should probably be completed: 'into Winchester camp.' See *Journal A*, p. 28.

5 Duke of York—Edward Augustus, King George III's younger brother (1739-1767).

11-17 G probably copied this list of presentation copies from his journal, where, instead of an &c, there are the names of Mallet, Maty and M. de Bussy. Did he suppress them simply to shorten a rather long list, or because he felt they added no lustre to it?—'Great part of these were only my father's or Mallet's acquaintance.' (*Journal A*, p. 27), which was probably the case with Caernavon (Henry Brydges, 2nd duke of Chandos and marquis of—), Litchfield (George Henry Lee, 2nd earl—, 1737-1805), Waldegrave (James, 2nd earl—, 1715-1763), Shelburne (William Petty, earl of—, 1737-1805), the duchesse d'Aiguillon and the comte de Caylus. But it may have been with a view to supporting G's eventual application for a post of Secretary of the Augsburg congress that copies were sent to two of the British delegates named in April, Charles Wyndham, 2nd earl of Egremont (1710-1763), and Sir Joseph Yorke, baron Dover (1724-1792) as well as to Bute and to other influential members of the government, Hardwicke (Philip Yorke, 1st earl of—, 1690-1764) and Granville (John Carteret, earl —, 1690-

1763). G's father may have wished copies to be sent in homage to the old statesmen, now living in retirement, who had been Sir Robert Walpole's chief opponents: William Pulteney, earl of Bath, and the earl of Chesterfield. Mallet was probably responsible for adding to the list Horace Walpole, George Lewis Scott (1708-1780), the mathematician, who was a friend of his and trustee for his divorced daughter. Presentation copies to G's school-fellow Charles Lennox, 3rd duke of Richmond (1735-1806), to Daniel Wray (1701-1783), the antiquary, who had quite recently married Mary Darrel, G's first cousin, to Sir Matthew Fetherston, on whom see *Journal A, passim*, and to M. de Bussy, Choiseul's envoy to London, to whom his father may have introduced him (see *Journal A*, p. 26), were sent perhaps at the author's own request.

23 See G. A. Bonnard, *Gibbon's Essai sur l'Etude de la Littérature as judged by contemporary reviewers and by Gibbon himself* in *English Studies* (Amsterdam), xxxii (1951), pp. 145-153.

26 a new Edition—See *Bibliography*, p. 8 (No. 4).

32 The English translation was advertised early in June 1761 (*Ibid.*, p. 4) as preparing 'under the inspection of the author'. But the translation, apparently in manuscript, only reached G in April 1762, sent him by his publisher Becket (see *Journal A*, p. 54). He kept it many months. On 11 January 1763 he wrote in his journal: '. . . I went to Becket, paid him his bill (fifty-four pounds) and gave him back his translation. It must be printed, tho' very indifferent' (*Ibid.*, p. 200). How was it that G allowed the translation to be printed such as it was? The only explanation seems to be that he would not, or could not, take the trouble of correcting it, correcting really implying doing it all over again. But why did he not give up the idea of having his *Essai* appear also in an English translation? A possible conjecture is that Becket had accepted to publish the little book on the terms proposed by Mallet, on condition that the author *paid* for the translation which he, the publisher, would provide and publish, and which G would control. This would account for G's payment of £54 on returning it to Becket, and for his accepting the publication as something he could not oppose. Other explanations have been offered. R. B. Mowat's (see *Bibliography*, p. 5, n. 2) is ruled out by what G says here of Mallet's 'easy agreement'. J. E. Norton's suggestion that the bill G paid to Becket was one for books, and had nothing to do with the publication of the *Essai* or its translation, is more acceptable. But G's mention in the same sentence of the bill and the translation seems to establish a connection between them.

Page 103

3 pyrated copy—See *Ibid.*, p. 8 (No 5).

17 For the comte de Caylus, see *B.U.* and *Misc. Gibb.*, pp. 97 and 104. He appears to have received his presentation copy of the *Essai* through Lady Hervey to whom he wrote his thanks and admiring appreciation of the unknown author. Lady Hervey sent the letter to Mallet who hastened to pass it on to G who kept it. Lord Sheffield found it among his friend's papers and published it in the *Miscellaneous Works* (see *Misc. Wks*, ii, pp. 43-44). Caylus had praised G's 'impartialité qui le rend juste et modeste, malgré l'impression qu'il a dû recevoir des auteurs sans nombre qu'il a lus et très bien lus'.

21 naming the Greek masters—In the *Essai* are named: Aeschylus in ch. iii, Euripides in ix, Homer in xi, Aristotle in xxii, etc.

32 brevis esse . . .—Horace, *Ars Poetica*, 25-26.

Page 104

7 defence of the early history of Rome—*Essai*, ch. xxvii-xxxiii (*Misc. Wks*, iv, p. 40-44).

8 defence of the new Chronology—Note [a] to ch. xxxviii (*Ibid.*, pp. 49-51).

9 specious—was commonly used until the end of the 18th century without any derogatory connotation, meaning merely 'brilliant'. See *N.E.D.*

design of the Georgics—*Essai*, ch. xix-xxi (*Misc. Wks*, iv, pp. 32-36).

14 remarks on the study of history and man—ch. xlviii-lv (*Ibid.*, pp. 63-69).

15 Gods of Polytheism—ch. lvi-lxxiii (*Ibid.*, pp. 70-84).

17 curious question—'Quelle fut la nature & l'origine de ces Dieux? Furent-ils des Princes, des Fondateurs de Sociétés, des grands Hommes, inventeurs des Arts? . . . Ou bien faut-il reconnoître dans ces Divinités autant de parties de l'Univers, auxquelles l'ignorance des premiers hommes avoit accordé la vie & la pensée? Cette question est digne de notre attention: elle est curieuse, mais elle est difficile—*Ibid.*, ch. lvii (*Misc. Wks*, iv, p. 70).

25 progeny—as, *e.g.*, Achilles, son of the sea-goddess Thetis and Peleus; Æneas, son of Anchises and Aphrodite; Heracles, son of Zeus and Alcmene.

27 similar Apotheosis—had almost attained the status of Gods, become quasi-divinities.

36 Osiris . . . Bacchus—See Pauly-Wissowa, Supplement Band ix (1962), *s.v. Osiris*, section XII 'Verbindung mit Dionysos'.

37 Bishen—The editor is indebted to his colleague, Professor C. Regamey, for identifying Bishen with Vishnou, Kishen with Krishna, and directing him to the most likely source of G's information, *viz.* Alexander Dow's

translation of the Persian historian Ferishta's *History of Hindostan*. This, in its 2nd ed., was the only one of the books in G's library which gives the forms Bishen and Kishen, neither Sir William Jones nor Charles Wilkins using these dialectal forms in those of their translations which G also possessed. As a kind of preamble to vol. i of his translation, Dow added a long *Dissertation concerning the Religion and Philosophy of the Brahmins* of which he was apparently the author (*History of Hindostan*, i, pp. xxi-lxix of the 1st (1768) ed.).

The idea of Bishen is a metaphysical abstraction—This assertion may rest on passages of the dialogue between Brimha and Narud quoted at length by Dow from what he calls the Bedang Shaster (Vedanga Shastra), such as these *e.g.*: 'Affection (or Passion) dwelt with God from all eternity. It was of three kinds, the creative, the preserving, and the destructive. The first is represented by Brimha, the second by Bishen, and the third by Shibah. You, O Narud! are taught to worship all the three, in various shapes and likenesses, as the creator, the preserver, and the destroyer.'—'Brimha perceived the idea of things, as if floating before his eyes. He said, LET THEM BE, and all that he saw became real before him. Then fear struck Brimha, lest those things should be annihilated. He cried, who shall preserve those things which I behold. In the instant a spirit issued from Brimha's mouth, and said aloud, I WILL, Then shall thy name be Bishen, because thou hast undertaken to preserve all things.' (*History of Hindostan*, i, pp. xl-xli, xlvii.) G may also have remembered Dow's general conclusion on the nature of the divinities of Hinduism: '. . . the Brahmins . . . believe in the unity, eternity, omniscience and omnipotence of God: the polytheism of which they have been accused, is no more than a symbolical worship of the divine attributes . . . Under the name of Brimha, they worship the wisdom and creative power of God; under the appellation of Bishen, his providential and preserving quality; and under that of Shibah, that attribute which tends to destroy.' (*Ibid.*, p. lxvii.)

Page 105

1 the adventures of Kishen . . . are those of a man—From the Persian translation of the *Mahābhārata*, Ferishta tells the story of the adventures of Kishen, 'the son of Basdeo . . . esteemed a great prophet among the Hindoos' as those of a man, though 'the superstitious pay him divine honours, believing him to be still alive'. (*Ibid.*, pp. 6-7.)

2-3 'The first credible account we have of the Bedas, is, that about the commencement of the Cal Jug [Kaliyuga], of which æra the present year 1768, is the 4886th year, they were written, or rather collected by a great philosopher, and reputed prophet . . . called Krishen Basdeo [Krishna Vasudava] . . . near the present city of Delhi.' (*Ibid.*, pp.

xxvii-xxviii.) A few lines further, Dow calls Krishen the 'first monarch of Hindostan', rightly making no distinction between the divinity and the monarch though Ferishta mistakenly distinguishes them: '. . . the first who placed his foot on the manud of empire, in the region of Hindostan, was Krishen, but not the Krishen whom the Hindoos worship, but a man of wisdom, policy, and courage.' (*Ibid.*, p. 10.)

12 At Lausanne—between 8 March and mid-April 1758, according to *Journal A*, p. 7.

17 Bentley—G probably remembered Addison's remark in Nº 165 of *The Spectator*: 'The histories of all our former wars are transmitted to us in our vernacular idiom, to use the phrase of a great modern critic.' Richard Bentley had used 'vernacular' in his *Dissertation upon the Epistles of Phalaris* (1697). Taken to task for coining a new word, he defended himself in the preface of his *Works* by asserting that the word had been used before, in which *N.E.D.* shows him to have been right.

18 Anti-gallican clamour—G borrowed the phrase from Maty's *Epitre* prefixed to the *Essai*. See *Misc. Wks*, iv, p. 9. The fact that the book was written in French had irritated some of the reviewers.

21 Dedication—For his 2nd ed. of the *Essai*, dated 1762 (*Bibliography*, p. 7, Norton's No. 3), the publisher had the Dedication translated into English, probably by the man whom Becket had committed to the translation of the *Essai* itself. G does not appear to have been aware of this 2nd ed., at least to judge from what he says *above*, pp. 101 and 102.

37 *Ciceronianus*—G read the famous dialogue in September-October 1762 and wrote a critical analysis of it in his journal. See *Journal A*, pp. 151-154.

Page 106

5-10 G here refers to two passages of the *Epistolae ad Atticum*: 'Commentarium consulatus mei Graece compositum misi ad te, in quo si quid erit, quod homini Attico minus Graecum eruditumque videatur, non dicam, quod tibi, ut opinor, Panormi Lucullus de suis historiis dixerat, se, quo facilius illas probaret Romani hominis esse, idcirco barbara quaedam et σόλοικα dispersisse: apud me si quod erit ejus modi, me imprudente erit et invito.' (Liber I, 19)—'Meus autem liber totum Isocrati μυροθήκιον, atque omnis ejus discipulorum arculas, ac nonnihil etiam Aristotelia pigmenta consumpsit . . . Tu, si liber placuerit, curabis, ut et Athenis sit et in ceteris oppidis Graeciae.' (Liber II, 1.)

30 their printed letters—For Sir William Temple, see the 1770 ed. of his *Works*, which was in G's library at L. For Chesterfield, see his *Miscellaneous Works* (1777).

31 may have published in French—This publication has not been traced but G had possibly heard of it from Mallet who was the editor of several works of Bolingbroke published after his death in 1752, as well as of his *Collected Works* in 5 vols, published in 1754.

32 the address of Voltaire—Voltaire dedicated his *Discours sur la tragédie* which prefaces his tragedy of *Brutus* to Lord Bolingbroke in these words: 'Souffrez . . . que je vous présente *Brutus*, quoique écrit dans une autre langue, *docte sermonis utriusque linguae*, à vous qui me donneriez des leçons de français aussi bien que d'anglais . . . .' Horace, in the ode *ad Maecenatem*, has 'sermones' which Donat corrected into 'sermonis'. G preferred to follow the text of Bentley (which is that of all modern edns) in preference to Voltaire's.

33 English dedication—in 1727, Voltaire, then staying in England, advertised a subscription for a 4^0 ed. of *La Henriade*, which ed. came out in 1728 with a dedication to Queen Caroline, written in English. In most subsequent edns of the poem, the original dedication was replaced by a French translation. For the English text, see Voltaire, *Œuvres*, ed. Beuchot, x, pp. 4-5.

Page 107

3 omission of his English verses—In his library at L. G had two edns of Hamilton's *Œuvres*, one in 6 vols published in Paris in 1772 and another published in London in 1776, in 7 vols. Neither of them includes Hamilton's English verses. One can almost see G laying down his pen and going up to his shelves to ascertain whether Hamilton was as good a poet in English as he was in French, and disappointed that he could not make the comparison.

5 primus ego . . .—I might therefore assume to be the first Englishman to publish a book written in French just as Virgil hoped he would be the first to bring the Muses from the summit of Helicon to the land of his fathers. (*Georgics*, iii, 10-11.)

9 For the quotation from Maty's epistle '*A l'Auteur*', see *Misc. Wks*, iv, p. 13.

24 the war before the last—the Seven Years' War (1756-1763), the last being the American War (1775-1783).

Page 108

9-19 Dryden, *Cymon and Iphigenia*, 399-408.

Page 109

26 Virgil, *Æneid*, vi, 814: Anchises sees among the shades that of Tullus and describes him to Æneas as he who will put an end to the sloth of his country and send its idle sons to the army.

30 The Militia bill laid by Pitt before Parliament in 1756, and again in
1757, was 'for the better ordering of the Militia forces in several counties
of England'.

Page 110

10 It is reported—In his 'Brief account of the military force of England'
at the time of the Armada (Appendix III), Hume quotes various contemporary estimates which can hardly be reconciled ('such uncertainty
and contradictions are there in' them all). G has retained one of them
only: 'Harrison [*i.e.* W. Harrison's *Description of England*, 1577] says
that in the musters taken in the years 1574 and 1575 the men fit for
service amounted to 1.172.674, yet it was believed that a full third was
omitted.' The 'last 8⁰ ed.' of Hume's *History* was in G's library at L.

14 the difference—in the number of men in the militia between the days
of Elizabeth I and the days of George II, due to the many who in 1756-
1763 served in the navy and the regular army, was compensated by . . .

16 G possibly remembered his 1759 summer 'taken up with continual
journeys upon Militia business'. (*Journal A*, p. 9.)

17 reduced the national defence—The Hanoverian and Hessian regiments
brought over in 1756 had provided some protection against the threatened
French invasion in the absence of the regular regiments in service
abroad. But when Pitt sent the Germans back to their country, England
was left practically without defence except for the militia, which it took
a long time to re-organize and train.

34 the danger—The French fleet which Hawke destroyed in Quiberon bay
was meant as an escort to the troops assembled in South Brittany for the
proposed invasion.

36 embodied—On 10 May 1760, G wrote in his journal: 'The King's sign
manual passed for embodying the South Battalion of the Hampshire
militia from which time we entered into pay.' (*Journal A*, p. 11.)

Page 111

3 the principals—those soldiers who had 'a Family not of Ability to
support themselves during [their] Absence', as was enacted in the December 1757 'Act to explain and enforce' the Militia Act passed in the
previous June. (*Public General Acts*, 31 George II 1757-1758, p. 844.)
The word 'principal' used by Gibbon does not appear in the Act, but
N.E.D. records it as obsolete in the sense of 'master of a household'
without, however, giving any example of its use in that sense. (The
editor's thanks are due to M. M. Baridon, of Dijon University, who
kindly copied for him the Act quoted above.)

12 specious name—G seems to have regarded a militia as, in principle,

superior to an army of mercenaries, and the name itself as highly honourable, and 'specious' may be taken to mean here 'illustrious'.

16 George III who succeeded his grandfather in October 1760 was born in
England.

19 Brunswick—'An English subject may be prompted . . . to investigate
the origin and story of the House of Brunswick, which, after an alliance
with the daughters of our kings, has been called by the voice of a free
people to the legal inheritance of the crown.' *Antiquities of the House of
Brunswick* in G's *Misc. Wks*, iii, p. 359. The 'daughters of our kings'
are Elizabeth, daughter of James I and wife of Frederic V, Elector
Palatine, and their daughter Sophia, mother of George I.

24 general meeting—of the Hampshire country gentlemen.

33 our Colonel—Alexander Thistlewayte, colonel-commandant of the
county militia since 1741, resigned his commission after the Militia Acts
had assigned the command to the Lord Lieutenant. (*Journal A*, p. cx.)

Page 112

6 passionate dispute—See *Journal A*, pp. cix-cxv.

23 foreign education—training at a distance from the home district.

28 'Major Sturgeon is the *miles gloriosus* of Foote's rather thin farce, *The
Mayor of Garratt* (1763)' (*Journal A*, pp. c-ci). See also *Journal B*,
p. 21, n. 3.

Page 113

31 persecutions—from the duke of Bolton; the dispute between Sir Thomas
Worsley, the lieutenant-colonel, and the Lord-lieutenant, had been
settled by a decision of the government: see *Journal. A*, p. 31.

Page 114

18 Virgil, *Æneid*, v. 196—Mnestheus' rowers, ashamed of being the last
in the boat-race, ended it in second place.

Page 116

2-6 G altered Cicero's order of his sentences in his letter *ad Atticum*, V,
xv, 1-3: '. . . est incredibile, quam me negotii taedeat . . . denique haec
non desidero; lucem, forum, urbem, domum, vos desidero. Sed feram, ut
potero, sit modo annuum: si prorogatur, actum est . . . clitellae bovi sunt
impositae, plane non est nostrum onus; sed feremus, modo sit
annuum . . .'

5 *libros*—G's substitution for Cicero's 'forum'.

20 Adjutant—'. . . a thoroughly objectionable man, McCombe, was trans-
erred to the South [Battalion] as adjutant, and proved a constant
annoyance to the battalion'. (*Journal A*, pp. cx-cxi, 15-20.)

Page 117

14 For Guichard, Karl Gottlieb (1724-1775) see the article in the 11th ed. of *Encyclopaedia Britannica*. His *Mémoires militaires sur les Grecs et les Romains*, published in 1757, were frequently reprinted. G bought them in May 1762 and read them at once. They gave him, he wrote in his journal, 'a much clearer notion of ancient tactics than I ever had before. Indeed, my own military knowledge was of some service to me, as I am well acquainted with the modern discipline and exercise of a battalion. So that . . . I am a much better judge than Salmasius, Casaubon, or Lipsius; mere scholars, who perhaps had never seen a battalion under arms.' (*Journal A*, pp. 71-75.)

24 Blandford—from 18 June to 22 August 1760. See *Ibid.*, p. 12.

25 Portsmouth—in September-November 1760. See *Ibid.*, pp. 15-20.

29 Dover—in May 1761. See *Ibid.*, pp. 25-26.

31 a volume of Tully—namely the *De deorum natura*.

35 For Isaac de Beausobre (1659-1738) see *B.U.* His *Histoire critique de Manichée et du Manichéisme* was published at Amsterdam in two vols, the 2nd being edited by a friend from the notes he had left.

38 the holy circle of the Author—'the holy circle' which de Beausobre traced round his work, beyond which he declined to pass, was presumably his persuasion that the Christian revelation was absolutely true and that any researches that might lead to doubt should be renounced. This idea runs through the first part, pp. vi-xxiii, of his *History*: 'Le Devoir d'un Historien exigeoit de moi, que je rapportasse les raisons de l'Hérétique. Mais le Devoir d'un Chrétien n'en exigeoit pas moins, que je prévinsse le scandale, qui en pourroit résulter' (p. xi). And again 'Il faut . . . justifier la méthode, que j'ai suivie, & prévenir, autant qu'il est possible, les jugemens de certains Lecteurs, qui ont de l'amour et du zèle pour la Religion & dont on trouvera peut-être que je ne ménage pas assez la délicatesse ou l'humeur. J'aurai pour eux toute la complaisance possible, mais ils ne doivent pas exiger de moi que je leur sacrifie la justice & la sincérité. Ecrivant en Historien la Vie, les Actions, les Dogmes & la Morale d'un fameux Hérésiarque, je dois le faire avec une exacte Impartialité. Ainsi, je ne dissimule point ses raisons. Seulement, quand elles sont assez spécieuses pour causer du scandale, je tâche d'y remédier. Je le disculpe, lui & sa Secte, des accusations qui me paroissent mal fondées . . . mais je ne le fais jamais aux dépens, ni au préjudice de la Vérité Catholique . . . Il est vrai que j'ai un grand penchant à excuser les Erreurs humaines, mais c'est lorsqu'elles ne sont ni volontaires ni malicieuses, lorsqu'elles ne touchent point les Fondemens de la Foi: lorsqu'elles ne sont point en contradiction avec les Décisions claires &

formelles de l'Ecriture: Et enfin lorsqu'elles ne détruisent en aucune sorte le culte, l'obéissance, & la profonde vénération qui appartiennent à la Divinité' (pp. xx-xxi). With de Beausobre's principles as a critical historian, G felt in agreement, but of course disregarded the Christian's scruples.

Page 118

4 Winchester camp—July-October 1761. See *Journal A*, pp. 28-41.

6 Devizes—November-December 1761. See *Ibid.*, pp. 41-44.
Blandford—March-May 1762. See *Ibid.*, pp. 48-79.
Southampton—August-October 1762. See *Ibid.*, pp. 121-161.

9 Buriton—June-August 1762. See *Ibid.*, 81-117.

12 I consulted—G's letter to G. L. Scott is missing. Scott's reply was kept by G, and found among his papers by Lord Sheffield who published it: *Misc. Wks*, ii, pp. 44-59. For Abraham de Moivre (1667-1754) see *B.U.*

21 equal number of weeks—G started reading *The Iliad* in October 1761 (*Journal A*, p. 42) and got to the end in August 1762 (*Ibid.*, p. 115).

25 Ulysses' ship, which had brought Calchas' daughter back to her father, sets sail on the return to the Greek camp:
The breeze fills the sail. On either side of the rushing prow the waves swirl and sizzle. Swift over the flood, the vessel pursues her way. *Iliad*, A, 481-483.

31 Gale—*Opuscula mythologica et ethica (ex recensione T. Gale)*, Amsterdam, 1688.

Page 119

5 Richard Hurd, who had become bishop of Lichfield in 1774, was translated in 1781 to the see of Worcester, and died in 1808. He had published his edition of Horace's *Epistolae ad Pisones et Augustum* in 2 vols (1749-1751). G owned the 1757 Cambridge ed.

7 fifty—G's observations on Hurd's Notes to Horace's *Epistolae* together with his dissertations on the 'Provinces of the Drama' and on 'Poetical Imitation' were published by Lord Sheffield in the *Miscellaneous Works* (*Misc. Wks*, iv, pp. 113-152). They end on these words: 'I have at last finished Mr Hurd's performance. I reckoned upon six or seven pages; I am now writing the thirtieth.' They are now in B.M. (*Add. MSS* 34880) and belong to two separate note-books, pp. 33-44 of the first and 1-18 of the second, that is, 30 pp. in all. Lord Sheffield's correction is therefore justified.

11 Johnson—wrote 'The true genius is a mind of large general powers, accidentally determined to some particular direction' (*Life of Cowley,*

§3, B. Hill's ed. of the *Lives*, i, p. 2). G cannot have read either Reynolds's *Discourses* or Northcote's *Reynolds*, but he probably discussed the question of what is 'true genius' with Reynolds on more than one occasion when the painter alleged Johnson's opinion.

26 two Memoirs—'*Eclaircissemens historiques sur quelques circonstances du voyage de Charles VIII en Italie; & particulièrement sur la cession que lui fit André Paléologue, du droit qu'il avait à l'empire de Constantinople.*'; '*Observations sur deux Ouvrages historiques, concernant le règne de Charles VIII* (*le Vergier d'honneur* d'André de la Vigne, et le *Journal* de Burchard . . . les seuls ouvrages qui puissent nous instruire des détails de la conquête du royaume de Naples').

28 dissertation—*Critical Researches concerning the title of Charles VIII to the Crown of Naples* in *Misc. Wks*, iii, pp. 206-222.

Page 120

1 Major Gibbon and his son left the Camp on 4 August and rejoined it on 10 September (see *Journal A*, p. 30).

21 Birch—For Thomas Birch (1705-1766) see *D.N.B.*—The *General Dictionary, Historical and Critical* was published in 10 vols, London, 1734-1741.

24 G stayed at Buriton from December 25 to February 2 (see *Ibid.*, pp. 43-44).

28 Bacon papers—*Memoirs of the Reign of Queen Elizabeth from the year 1581 till her death . . . From the original papers of . . . Anthony Bacon,* 2 vols, 1754.

30 For Sir Robert Naunton (1563-1635) see *D.N.B.* His *Fragmenta Regalia* (*or, observations on the late Queen Elizabeth, her times and favorites*) were published in 1641 in a thin 4to.

33 For Sir William Monson (*c.* 1569-1643) see *D.N.B.* His *Naval Tracts* were first published by the Brothers 'A. and J. Churchill, booksellers' in their *Collection of Voyages and Travels, some now first printed from original MSS,* 4 vols, f⁰, 1704.

34 Sir Walter Raleigh, *History of the World, the 11th ed. To which is prefixed the Life of the Author, by Mr. Oldys,* London, 1736.

Page 121

15 Arthur Collins, the genealogist, published in 1746, under the title of *Letters and Memorials of State written and collected by sir Henry Sidney* (and others), two vols of documents relating to the history of England from the reign of Mary Tudor to that of Charles II, which he had transcribed from the originals at Penshurst Place.

32 Walpole—G must be thinking here of Horace Walpole's *Catalogue of Royal and Noble Authors of England* (1758): *curious* here means *inquisitive*, proceeding from curiosity (*N.E.D.*).

Hurd—G is probably thinking here of Richard Hurd's two dialogues on the age of Queen Elizabeth, Nos II and III of the *Moral and Political Dialogues* (1759): Robert Digby, Arbuthnot and Addison, on a visit to Warwick and Kenilworth, discuss the age and politics of the Queen.

Page 122

12-14 rescued from ... Austria—at the battles of Morgarten (1315) and Sempach (1386).

defended against—the future Louis XI, at the battle of St Jakob on the Birs (1444).

Charles of Burgundy—Charles the Bold was defeated at Grandson and Morat (1476) and killed at Nancy (1477).

Page 123

4 After resigning his chair at Leyden in June 1591, Justus Lipsius was uncertain where to go. From Augusta (Trèves), he wrote to a friend on 15 November: 'In hac urbe nunc sumus, non ut domo tamen, sed hospitio & nisi fallor, hic vere migrabo. Quo? nondum constitui, & patriam vellem, sed ea sic turbat, ut vix prudenter de ea cogitemus. Vocamur tamen ad veterem sedem nostram & Musarum, Louanium: etiam in Italiam, à magna Etruriae Dynastâ. Neque nollem, vel Mediceae stirpis causa, fataliter poenè dixerim natae ad haec studia instauranda vel fovenda quod Cosimus, Laurentius, Leo dicent: sed imbecillitas me tenet, neque per eam decîdo.' (Letter to Marco Velsero in *J. Lipsi Epistolarum selectarum centuria singularis Ad Germanos & Gallos*, Antwerp, Plantin, 1613. pp. 5-6, Epistola vii.)

10 Virgil, *Æneid*, vi, 266. Entering Hades, Æneas addresses the gods who reign over the dead—Di quibus imperium est animarum—asking for their permission to reveal those things—res alta terra et caligine mersas —which he is now likely to see.

Page 124

8 three or four weeks—from 19 December 1762, when G took leave of his company and returned to Buriton (*Journal A*, p. 192) to 23 January 1763, when he 'set out from London' on his way to Paris (*Ibid.*, p. 204).

11 Mallet's *Elvira*—see *Ibid.*, pp. 202-204.

13 the packet—In his journal (*Ibid.*, p. 204), G noted that he crossed with two gentlemen 'who had taken a yacht ... and agreed to his going with them. This is confirmed by the short letter he wrote to his father on

arriving at Boulogne (*Letters*, i, p. 132). He appears to have forgotten this detail though the two Gentlemen were a duke and a marquis.

14 twenty-six days—Major Gibbon's battalion was disembodied on 23 December 1762 (*Journal A*, p. 202).

19 first visit—During 'this first visit', G managed to keep his journal for a few days in February, from the 21st to the 26th, and later on, attempting to write an 'Idée générale de mon séjour à Paris', filled eight pages but was interrupted, and gave it up as an 'Enterprise vaine'. These fragments have been published in *Misc. Gibb.*

Page 125

15 Inverary is the seat of the dukes of Argyll, Wilton house near Salisbury that of the earls of Pembroke.

21-23 See *Misc. Gibb.*, p. 96.

36 Words taken from Cato's panegyric of Pompey in Lucan, *De bello civili*, ix (202).

Page 126

9 dress and equipage—See *Letters*, i, p. 135.

13 For Louis Charles, duc de Nivernais (1716-1798) see *B.U.* Ambassador at Rome and Berlin successively, Choiseul sent him in the autumn of 1762 to London, there to resume the peace neogtiations with Great Britain.

14 letters of recommendation—In his journal (*Journal A*, p. 202) G recorded two 'credentials' from Lady Hervey (for the comte de Caylus and Mme Geoffrin) and seven from the duke of Nivernais (for Caylus, la Bletterie, Ste-Palaye, Capperonnier, Duclos, Foncemagne and D'Alembert), but none from Walpole. None are mentioned either in G's Paris journal where, to the 'credentials' listed in *Journal A*, G added two from Maty (for La Condamine and Raynal), two from Mrs Mallet (for Mme Bontems and La Motte), one from the Duke of Richmond for the English ambassador at the court of Versailles, the Duke of Bedford (*Misc. Gibb.*, pp. 102-103).

16 their reception and success—See *Ibid.*, pp. 103-104.

24-27 Montesquieu had died in 1755, Fontenelle in 1757; Voltaire had bought Ferney in 1758 and resided there until his departure for Paris, and his death, in 1778; Rousseau had been driven from Montmorency—not from l'Ermitage which Mme d'Épinay had fitted up for him in 1756, but which he left early in 1758 when he became the guest at the château of the duke and duchess of Luxembourg—by the condemnation of *L'Emile* and had taken refuge in Switzerland.

30 associates—D'Alembert had been Diderot's chief collaborator for the first volume of the *Encyclopédie*, but their association had come to an

end long before 1763. The condemnation in 1757 of their joint undertaking by the Paris 'parlement' had frightened him and he ceased to
contribute to it. Whether G met either of them is not clear from his
ambiguous sentence; he may merely refer to the reputation they had
among the men of letters he saw, all rather minor figures; none the less,
his comparison of D'Alembert to the element of water, of Diderot to
fire and a volcanic eruption is far from inapt.

35 The comte de Caylus (1692-1765), the abbés de la Bletterie (1696-
1772) and Barthélemy (1716-1795) were prominent members of the
'Académie des Inscriptions' to which they had been elected in 1742,
1742 and 1747 respectively. The abbé Raynal was not. For them, see
B.U., the notes in *Autobiographies*, p. 201 and *Hill*, pp. 305-306. Caylus,
G saw 'trois ou quatre fois et je vis un homme simple, uni bon, et
qui me témoignait une bonté extrême' (*Misc. Gibb.*, p. 104). Barthélemy, who was keeper of the Royal collection of Medals, showed it
himself to G who found him 'fort aimable' (*Ibid.*, pp. 98-99).

Page 127

1-2 The Abbé François Arnaud (1721-1784), MM. Duclos (1704-1772), de
Ste Palaye (1697-1774), de Bougainville (1722-22 June 1763), Capperonnier (1716-1775) and de Guignes (1721-1800) were also members
of the 'Académie des Inscriptions' since 1742, 1739, 1746, 1749 and
1753 respectively. Charles-Marie de la Condamine, the explorer, had
been elected to the 'Académie française' in 1760. Jean-Baptiste Suard
(1734-1817), a young man when G met him, entered the 'Académie
française' in 1772. For all these 'académiciens' see Hill's and Murray's
notes and *B.U.* G's visits to de Bougainville and Ste Palaye were recorded by him (see *Misc. Gibb.*, p. 100).

15 fragment from *The Golden Race* (χρυσοῦν γένος), a comedy of Eupolis,
Aristophanes' contemporary and rival; see J. M. Edmonds, *The Frag-
ments of Attic Comedy*, Leiden 1957, where (p. 415) this line is translated:
'The brave go uninvited to the banquets of the craven.'

26 the Italians—The 'Comédie Italienne' was already in 1763 the home of
light opera, which it has remained under the appellation of 'Opéra
comique'. For the history of the Paris 'Comédie Italienne', see the
article in *La Grande Encyclopédie*.

29 famous actresses—Claire Leris, 'La Clairon' (1723-1803) and Marie-
Françoise Marchand, 'La Dumesnil' (1713-1803) were both at the
'Comédie Française'.

Page 128

3 For Marie-Jeanne Bontems (1718-1768) and G's visits to her, see *Misc.
Gibb.*, pp. 96-97 and 106-107. G had met her son who was private secret-

ary to the Duke of Nivernais, at the Mallets' (*Journal A*, pp. 184 and 199).

18 Mirabeau—Victor Riqueti, marquis de Mirabeau (1715-1789), disciple of the economist Quesnay, was, like him and all the future 'Physiocrats', an adversary of the 'Encyclopédists' and their materialistic philosophy. Mme Bontems was a friend of his; he claimed in 1762 to have urged her to translate Thomson's *The Seasons*, in order apparently to strengthen his circle's opposition to the atheistic outlook of Diderot and the 'philosophes'. (See Y. Châlon, *Les Saisons de J. Thomson* in *Revue de littérature comparée*, xxxii (1958), pp. 34-46.)

33 ff. For G's stay at L. from May 1763 to April 1764, see *Journal B*.

Page 129

6 Prince Louis-Eugen von Wirtemberg (1731-1795) had been educated at Lausanne where he lived from 1763 to 1767. He succeeded his brother in 1793.

7 frequently—G was invited to dinner at the Prince's three times only in the early months of his stay at L., on 23 August for the last time (*Ibid.*, pp. 5-6, 8). He then let more than three months elapse before calling on his noble host, which was hardly polite; the Prince naturally resented it and refused to receive him. Henceforth their relations were rather strained (*Ibid.*, pp. 174, 217).

21 quarrel—A bitter quarrel actually broke out between Voltaire and one of the first 'pasteurs' of L., but in 1759, months after the poet had retired to Ferney. G was misinformed. See H. Vuilleumier, *op. cit.*, iv, pp. 280-286.

Page 130

27 Madame Henri Crousaz de Mézery, née Suzanne Bergier, was born in June 1716. Her husband, also born in 1716, died in 1782. She survived him many years and died, aged 94, in 1810 (Archives cantonales vaudoises, Lausanne registers). The dates given in *Letters*, iii, p. 406, are wrong.

Page 131

9 riotous acts—For the only riotous act of intemperance recorded by G during his months at L., see *Journal B*, pp. 31-32.

15 our Italian journey—Holroyd left L. for Italy in the middle of June 1763, about one month after G; he arrived at Florence in September when he and G had a few days together; they met again in Rome, but from what Holroyd's letters home (B.M. *Add. MSS 34887*) tell of his life in Italy, they were hardly together again in the subsequent stages of their separate journeys. In his letters, Holroyd never mentioned G.

See G. Bonnard, *John Holroyd in Italy* in *Etudes de Lettres* (Lausanne) S^te II, 2 (1959), pp. 122-135.

27 Jean Mabillon (1622-1707) and Bernard de Montfaucon (1655-1741) were both Benedictine monks of the Congregation of St. Maur, attached to the abbey of St Germain. The *De Re diplomatica* (1681) and the *Palaeographica graeca* (1708), two works which may be said to have created the science of palaeography, were when G tried to study them, and have long remained, the standard works on their subjects.

Page 132

For authors and works listed in this page, refer to the Index, text and notes of *Journal B*.

22 G's 'collections and remarks on the Geography of Italy' were published by Lord Sheffield (*Misc. Wks*, iv, pp. 157-328) under the title of *Nomina Gentesque Antiquae Italiae*.

23 For his 'long and learned notes' on: the Insulae, see *Journal B*, pp. 47-50; the Social War, pp. 122-130; Hannibal's passage of the Alps, pp. 105-113.

37 For William Guise (1737-1783) see *Journey*, pp. vii-ix, notes and 'Appendix'; G. A. Bonnard, *Un Anglais à Lausanne en 1762-1764* in *Revue Historique Vaudoise*, LXIX (1961), pp. 177-184.

Page 133

1 my Italian tour—*Gibbon's Journey from Geneva to Rome. His Journal from 20 April to 2 October 1764* was published by Thomas Nelson and Sons Ltd in 1961.

18 'Proximus huic, longo sed proximus intervallo Insequitur Salius' says the poet of the first two competitors, Nisus and Salius, in the race on the sands near Anchises' grave (*Æneid*, v, 320).

27 recent memorials—The only memorial of Genoa's deliverance which G mentions in his journal is the statue of the duke of Richelieu (see *Journey*, p. 80, n. 3). Perhaps there was some confusion in his memory between the events of 1746-1748 and those of 1528 (see *Ibid.*, p. 79, n. 4).

Page 134

2 lessons of Italian—see *Journal A*, p. 10.

3 learned native—see *Journey*, p. 120.

7 For Sir Horace Man, see *Ibid.*, p. 119, n. 5. 'conversations' is the Italian word 'conversazioni' meaning 'evening assemblies'; the English form was usual in the 18th century and even later (see *N.E.D.*).

26 a last review—see *Journey*, pp. 236-251.

31 boy-king—Ferdinand IV (1751-1825).

32 For Sir William Hamilton (1730-1803), envoy to the court of Naples from 1764 to 1800, see *D.N.B.*

39 Lambertini—Pope Benedict XIV (1740-1758).
Ganganelli—Pope Clement XIV (1769-1773).

Page 135

4 paradox of Montesquieu—'J'ai resté plus d'un an en Italie où je n'ai vu que le débris de cette ancienne Italie, si fameuse autrefois. Quoique tout le monde habite les villes, elles sont entièrement désertes et dépeuplées.' (*Lettres persanes*, cxvii.) In ch. xvii of *Considérations*, to which Emerson refers here, Montesquieu describes the desertion of Italy which followed the transfer of the capital from Rome to Constantinople, a description which is irrelevant to this line.

9 Venice—For G's impressions on the spot, see *Letters*, i, p. 193.

17 often been debated—See, *e.g.*, Hurd's dialogues *On the Uses of Foreign Travel* in his *Moral and Political Dialogues* (1763).

Page 136

26-30 This passage, composed in January 1790 (see *above*, p. xxiii), was altered in several respects when, some months later, G came to rewrite it: he suppressed the statement that 'the place and moment of conception' were recorded in his journal; he changed his remembering himself 'musing in the Church of the Zoccolanti' into 'musing on the Capitol'; he inverted the order of the whole sentence so as to increase its dramatic interest; realizing that it might leave the reader in doubt as to whether the Church and the Temple of Jupiter were, or were not, one and the same building, he removed the possibility of any hesitation by taking himself out of the Church; lastly, he replaced the matter-of-fact 'close of the evening' by the emotional 'gloom of the evening'. And thus the passage became in fragment D:

> 'It was on the fifteenth of October, in the gloom of evening, as I sat musing on the Capitol, while the barefooted fryars were chanting their litanies in the temple of Jupiter, that I conceived the first thought of my history.'

This new version, however, did not satisfy him when, a very few weeks later, he once again rewrote it: he had not really succeeded in clearly bringing out the close connection he felt there was between the office in the Church of the bare-footed friars, symbol of Christianity, and the 'ruins of the Capitol', witnesses of the decline and fall of Rome. The contrast was enough in itself to create an impression of 'gloom', and the emotional word could be dropped. So the third version runs:

'It was at Rome, on the fifteenth of October, 1764, as I sat musing amidst the ruins of the Capitol while the barefooted fryars were singing Vespers in the temple of Jupiter, that the idea of writing the decline and fall of the City first started to my mind.'

Lord Sheffield's substitution of the last (E) version for the former ones was justified from a literary point of view, for it is the result of an elaboration due to the writer's urge to make the important passage as dramatic and significant as he could. But such an urge may have entailed some disregard for the actual facts. Where did G really sit musing on the fateful evening? The 'ruins of the Capitol', he had only seen in his imagination, for, in 1764, the Capitol was already what it now is. To what extent is the famous sentence fact, to what extent imagination?

26 in my journal—G's journal of his journey to Rome ends on a few lines written on Tuesday, 2 October 1764, which is no doubt why he suppressed the reference to it in his first version. He did not go on with it. The remaining blank pages he used later on, in December, to start a kind of catalogue of what he had found of especial interest in the Eternal City; he never completed this catalogue (see *Journey*, p. xi). William Guise, who was visiting Rome with G, went on writing his own journal to the end of the month: according to him, their guide, Bryers, took them to the Capitol on the 6th ('At ten o'clock this morning, Mr Gibbon, Mr Ponsonby, and myself, attended by our Antiquarian, Mr Byers, set out together . . . Tri [Triumphal] Arch of Septimus Severus . . . remains of the Temple of Concord . . . Capitol . . . Circ Maximus . . . Constantines arch'); on the 8th ('Mr Byers took us this morning to see the Tarpeian Rock . . . Circus Maximus . . .'); on the 9th ('Equestrian statue of Marcus Aurelius—Cap. Museum: pictures'); on the 10th ('Capitol, arch of Titus, Temple of the Sun and Moon. Temple of Peace'); the 12th ('We returned this Morning to the Capitol to see the statues &c that are kept in the wing on the right hand') and on the 13th ('Second visit to the statues . . . ancient plan of Rome'). On the 15th, 'being wet weather this Morning' they went to see the collection of Mr Jenkins, an English painter living in Rome (on him, see *D.N.B.*). It may be surmised of course that, after leaving Jenkins, the rain having stopped, G returned once more to the Capitol by himself, Guise declining to accompany him to a place they had already seen so often.

Page 137

15 chearful submission—see *Letters*, i, pp. 195-196.

20 casual lodging—For G's lodgings in London from 1765 to 1770, see *Ibid.*, iii, p. 388.

28 Horace invites his friend Maecenas to come to him in the country, for-

getting for a while 'fumum, et opes, strepitumque Romae' (*Ode* xxix of L.III, 12).

31 Sir Thomas Worsley, Lieutenant-Colonel of the South Hants Militia, died 23 September 1768 (*Letters*, iii, p. 455).

Page 138

4 Peaceful subordination—the looseness of subordination in time of peace.

20 res angusta domi—Juvenal, *Satirae*, iii, 165: Haud facile emergunt, quorum virtutibus obstat Res angusta domi.

29 Deyverdun was attracted to England by the hope of finding there some suitable employment, and by a natural curiosity to see a new country, which reasons for coming over from Germany were strengthened by the expectation of soon seeing G returned from his travels.

Page 139

2 Clarke—G had probably first met Godfrey Bagnoll Clarke (see *Letters*, iii, 403) at Rome, but their acquaintance only ripened into friendship in 1772. Clarke fell ill in September and died in December 1774.

6 Roman club—In a note to *Misc. Wks*, i, p. 200 Lord Sheffield gave a list of the members of the 'Roman Club'.

Page 140

26 domestic disorders—See *Letters*, i, pp. 402-407, Appendix III, 'The Financial Affairs of Edward Gibbon II'.

Page 141

6 association of the three peasants—G dates it 1307; see his *Introduction à l'histoire générale de la république des Suisses* in *Misc. Wks*, iii, pp. 260-265.

7 plenitude—After the conquest or occupation of several districts south of the Alps (1500-1512), the conquest by Berne of the Pays de Vaud (1536), and the admission in 1513 of Appenzell as thirteenth member of the Confederation, Switzerland had attained the limits which it preserved until the end of the 18th century.

10 but in a field of Battle—G did not believe in the story of Tell, a mere legend in his eyes; see his *Introduction, Ibid.*, pp. 265-266.

12 trophies—In his tour of Switzerland, in 1755, G had seen in various places actual trophies of the wars waged by the Swiss (see *Misc. Gibb.*, pp. 18, 38, 61, 64), but he appears to use the word 'trophy' here in the unusual sense of 'glorious victories'.

16 The present editor has not been more successful in tracing to its source this Latin quotation than Hill (see his preface, p. xxi). At the request

of Professor Jean Béranger, of Lausanne University, the collections of the *Thesaurus Linguae Latinae* and of the *Mittellateinisches Wörterbuch*, both at Munich, have been thoroughly examined, but in vain. The *Thesaurus'* General Redaktor, Dr W. Eihlers, gave the result of the researches in these words: '. . . es handelt sich um kein Zitat aus lateinischer Literatur vor dem Jahre 600 n.Chr . . .Wir haben keine Vorstellung, woher das Zitat stammt und in welchem Zusammenhang es begegnet.'

25-30 See in G. von Wyss, *Geschichte der Historiographie in der Schweiz* (Zurich 1895) notices on Diebold Schilling (*c.* 1436-*c.* 1486), pp. 135-137—Aegidius Tschudi (1505-1572), pp. 196-202—Johann Jakob Lauffer (1688-1734), pp. 302-303—Johann Jakob Leu (1689-1768), pp. 274-275).

25 he translated—Deyverdun's translations fill five large copy-books which are now in the *Archives cantonales vaudoises* at Lausanne.

Page 142

3 to the flames—To this Lord Sheffield added in 1796 the following footnote: 'He neglected to burn them. He left at Sheffield-Place the introduction, or first book, in forty-three pages folio, written in a very small hands, besides a considerable number of notes. If Mr Gibbon had not declared his judgment, perhaps Mr Hume's opinion, expressed in the letter in the last note, might have justified the publication of it.' When preparing the 2nd ed. of *Misc. Wks*, Sheffield decided to include the *Introduction* in the third vol. and accordingly changed the end of his footnote into: 'Mr Hume's opinion . . . perhaps may justify the publication of it.' What Lord Sheffield found among the papers G had left at Sheffield-Place, before leaving for L. in 1783, was not an *Introduction* as he entitled it, but all G had written of the *History of the Swiss*, its first two chapters, the 43 folio pages he had submitted to the judgment of Hume through Deyverdun with a letter dated 4 October 1767 in which he wrote: 'If you advise me to burn what I have already wrote, I shall immediately execute your sentence with a full persuasion that it is just' (*Letters*, i, p. 218-219). Three weeks later, on 24 October, Hume returned the manuscript with a letter saying he had 'perused it with great pleasure and satisfaction', though regretting that the author should not have used his 'native tongue', and ending 'On the whole, your History, in my opinion, is written with spirit and judgement; and I exhort you very earnestly to continue it' (*Misc. Wks*, i, 204-205). To this, G replied at once: '. . . when I have finished the work, which your kind approbation encourages me to pursue, I will endeavour to put it into an English dress: at the risque perhaps of appearing a foreigner to my own countrymen, and of betraying myself to foreigners for an Englishman' (*Letters*, i, p. 222). In spite of Hume's encouragement, G left his manu-

script as Hume had seen it, and put it aside, probably conscious that he had made a mistake to write it in French. But he did not deliver it 'to the flames'. When writing his *Memoirs*, he either forgot that, though he had offered to destroy it if Hume did not approve of it, he had not done so after Hume had exhorted him to go on with it, or perhaps thought that his burning a manuscript which had cost him a lot of trouble would add a dramatic touch to his *Memoirs*.

31 According to the *Royal Kalendar* for the year 1767, p. 113, Deyverdun was a clerk in the Northern Department whence he was transferred, according to the *Court and City Register* for 1769, p. 109, to the Southern Department of the secretary of state's offices. Hume had been asked by General Conway, Secretary of State, to be Under-Secretary, and acted as such for two years from February 1767.

Page 143

8 Lord Sheffield rightly corrected G's Lyttleton. G's review is of the first vol. of the *History of Henry II*, which was published in 1767.

13 *The New Bath Guide. . . . A Series of Poetical Epistles*, which was praised for its humour by Walpole and Gray, and had immediate success, was the work of Christopher Anstey (1724-1805); it was published in 1766. Deyverdun's prose translation of extended passages was meant to give some idea of the original.

22 two associates—In the latter part of his article on *Edward Gibbon and Georges Deyverdun, collaborators in the Mémoires littéraires de la Grande Bretagne* (Publications of the Modern Language Association of America [P.M.L.A.], xvii (1932), pp. 1028-1049), V. P. Helming has endeavoured to ascertain the respective shares, not only of the two collaborators, but of G. L. Scott from whom G had solicited 'three or four abstracts every year of the best Philosophical works that appear during that interval' (*Letters*, i, p. 221).

30 more reputation than emolument—The publishers of vol. i, Becket and De Hondt (who had published G's *Essai* in 1761), refused to assume the risk of publishing vol. ii, no doubt because vol. i had not sold well enough. The publishers of vol. ii were Heydinger and Elmsley, but the editors had offered to pay for the paper, the printing and the advertising. The 2nd vol. sold no better than the first and Deyverdun, who appears to have been responsible for the financial arrangements, was still owing the publishers a sum of £18 when he left England. (See the fragments of a letter from the minister of the Swiss Church in London, A. Bugnion, to Deyverdun who was then in Paris with his pupil, published in translation by Meredith Read, *op. cit.*, ii, p. 32.)

36 dedication—'Au Comte de Chesterfield . . . Milord, S'il est en Angleterre un Seigneur qui s'est distingué comme Homme de Lettres, &

comme Homme d'Etat: qui a su joindre les agréments d'un peuple aimable & léger aux qualités d'une Nation plus solide, qui réunit enfin les vertus aux talens; c'est à ce Seigneur qu'un Etranger libre doit rendre un hommage qu'il refuse toujours à la seule grandeur. Permettez-moi donc, Milord, que j'ose vous présenter cette Partie d'un ouvrage honoré de votre approbation. Je suis, avec un profond respect, Milord, Votre très-humble & très-obéissant Serviteur, Georges Deyverdun Londres, le 12ᵉ Avril, 1769.'

37 reserved the author—See the end of A. Bugnion's letter to Deyverdun in M. Read, *loc. cit.*

Page 144

1 a reply to Mr Walpole—Walpole's *Historic Doubts on the Life and Reign of King Richard the Third* (1760), an attempt to exonerate Richard III of the crimes with which posterity had charged his memory, provoked several answers. One of these was published as article i in vol. ii of the *Mémoires littéraires*. After several pages in which Walpole's arguments are criticized, the author concludes: 'Les argumens de M. Walpole nous avoient ébloui °sans nous convaincre. Les réflexions suivantes nous ont ramené au sentiment général; elles sont de M. Hume, qui nous les a communiquées avec la permission d'en enrichir nos Mémoires.' The review ends with Hume's sixteen critical observations. Who the reviewer was is in question. Though in this passage of his *Memoirs*, G does not say that he was the author, Lord Sheffield declared in the 'Advertisement' to the 2nd ed. of *Misc. Wks*: 'This Article is mentioned by Mr Gibbon in his Journal and Memoirs as written by him', an assertion which is doubly wrong, as the *Memoirs* do not say so, and G's journals end with his arrival at Rome in 1764. On the strength of his mistaken statement, Sheffield included the article in *Misc. Wks*, iii, pp. 331-349, where Hume's 'Réflexions' begin on p. 341. As G says here, Hume 'shaped his reflections into the form of a note' to the 1773 ed. of his *History of England*, iii, p. 451. The refutation of Walpole's *Historic Doubts* which was published in the *Mémoires littéraires* is the work of an historian familiar with English history and can only be ascribed to G. If for the wrong reasons, Sheffield was right to include it in *Misc. Wks*.

5 lately deceased—See *above* n. to l. 31 of p. 137.

7 Some time after—in May 1772 (*Letters*, i, p. 313).

30 a singular chapter—*Divine Legation* (1737-1741), Book ii, Section 4.

Page 145

5 servile flatterers—G's own *note 20* (which has not been included in *Gibbon's Notes to Chapter VII*, pp. 166 ff. *below*, as has been explained

in the Preface, pp. xxxi-xxxii), may be given here: 'Our litterary Sylla was encompassed with a guard of Flatterers and slaves ready to execute every sentence of proscription which his arrogance had pronounced. The assassination of Jortin by Dr Hurd, now Bishop of Worcester (see the Delicacy of friendship), is a base and malignant act, which cannot be erazed by time or expiated by *secret* penance' (MS *f* 98 – M 304). In 1755, Dr John Jortin (for him, see *D.N.B.*) had published *Six Dissertations on Various Subjects* in the last of which, an essay *On the State of the Dead as described by Homer and Virgil*, he opposed Warburton's interpretation of *Æneid VI*. For this he was malignantly attacked by Hurd in a treatise entitled *On the Delicacy of Friendship: A Seventh Dissertation addressed to the Author of the Sixth.* (See A. W. Evans, *Warburton*, 1932, ch. xi.)

6 exalting—G ends his *Critical Observations* with a paragraph turning to ridicule Hurd's praise of Warburton for uniting 'the severe sense of ARISTOTLE with the sublime imagination of LONGINUS.' (*Misc. Wks*, iv, p. 509.)

12 Dr Lowth—see notes to p. 47 above.

31 Vetabo . . .—G's quotation of Horace (*Odes*, III, ii, 26) is given in full in *Critical Observations* (*Misc. Wks*, iv, pp. 503-504).

Page 146

1 Heyne's reference to Gibbon is in his *Excursus X (ad Librum VI) Descensus ad inferos an ex initiis Eleusiniis sit adumbratus*. See his Virgil, ed. quarta (1832), vol. II, pp. 1022-1023.

3 William Hayley attacked Warburton in his *Essay on Epic Poetry in five Epistles to the Rev. Mr. Mason*:

> That subtle Pedant's . . . Presumptive pride,
> Whose bloated page, with arrogance replete,
> Imputes to Virgil his own dark conceit:
> And from the tortur'd Poet dares to draw
> That latent sense, which Horace never saw . . . (242-246)

To this poem Hayley added elaborate notes; in his note V, he gave of the *Critical Observations* a summary, from whose beginning G drew his quotations.

12 justify—In the same note V, Hayley wrote: 'Professor Heyne, the late accurate and accomplished Editor of Virgil, has mentioned it [G's short essay] with the honour it deserved. He remarks, indeed, that the author has censured the learned Prelate with some little acrimony . . . But what lover of poetry, unbiassed by personal connection, can speak of War-

burton without some marks of indignation?' Three copies of Hayley's *Poems* were in G's library at L.

16 to my esteem—In his E *note 25*, G judged *The Divine Legation* 'a monument, already crumbling into dust, of the vigour and weakness of the human mind. But some Episodes of the work, on the Greek philosophy, the hieroglyphics of Egypt, etc., are entitled to the praise of learning, imagination, and discernment' (MS *f* 98 – M *305*).

18 To the testimonies of Heyne and Hayley given here (in C), G added when writing E (MS *f* 88ᵛ – M *305*) that of Samuel Parr (1747-1825; on him, see *D.N.B.*) which he quoted in his *note 24*. Under the title of *Tracts, by Warburton and a Warburtonian not admitted into the collections of their respective Works*, Parr attacked, rather meanly, the famous critic and his devoted champion, Richard Hurd, by giving an edition of those tracts of theirs which the editors of their Works had omitted on account of the harm they had done and would continue to do to their authors' reputation, and by making his purpose clear in two prefaces. In the preface to Hurd's *On the Delicacy of Friendship* and *Letter to Dr Thomas Leland*, Parr had written, p. 192, 'In regard to the sixth Book of the Æneid, I have always admired the Ingenuity of Warburton's Hypothesis. I have, in the Course of my own Reading, frequently examined his Quotations. I have never assented to his Conclusions. I applaud Dr Jortin for speaking of Warburton's interpretation in Terms of measured Praise, and I consider it as completely refuted in a most clear, elegant, and decisive work of criticism; which could not, indeed, derive authority from the greatest name, but in which the greatest name might with propriety have been affixed.' In his *note 24*, G quoted the latter part of this passage from 'as completely refuted . . .'. The two footnotes in M *283*, wrongly ascribed to Lord Sheffield are in fact G's own *notes 24* and *25* to E, rightly printed as such by M, p. *305*.

22 the Journal—the *Mémoires littéraires*.

33 Augustan history—collection of biographies of the Roman emperors from Hadrian to Carinus, the work of the so-called Scriptores Historiae Augustae.

Page 147

6 At Bentinck Street, G had in his library two edns of the *Histoire des empereurs*, namely those of Brussels 1707 in 5 vols 12⁰ and of Paris 1720 in 6 vols 4⁰, as well as the *Mémoires pour servir à l'histoire ecclésiastique des six premiers siècles*, Brussels 1706, 10 vols 12⁰. For Sébastien Le Nain de Tillemont (1637-1698), see *B.U.* and Sainte-Beuve, *Port-Royal*, iv.

11 Muratori—At Bentinck Street and L., G had on his shelves Muratori's

Annali d' Italia, Milano 1753-1756, 18 vols 8⁰, and *Antiquitates Italicae medii Aevi*, Milano 1738-1742, 6 vols f⁰. For Ludovico Antonio Muratori (1672-1750), see encyclopaedias, *B.U.*, etc.

12 Sigonius—Besides Sigonio's *Historiarum de regno Italiae libri XV* which was among his books at Bentinck Street in the early 1575 ed., G had both in London and at L. the most complete ed. of Sigonio's *Opera*, Milano 1732-1737, 6 vols f⁰. For Carlo Sigonio (Carolus Sigonius) (1520-1584), see the same.

13 Maffei—G had in his library, at Bentinck Street and L., Maffei's *Istoria diplomatica*, 1727 f⁰. For Francisco Scipione marchese di Maffei (1675-1755), see the same.

Baronius—For Cesare Baronio (1538-1607), see the same. His *Annales ecclesiasticae*, 12 vols f⁰, 1588-1607, was in G's library at L. in the 2nd ed., 1622-1627.

Pagi—For Antoine Pagi (1624-1699), see *B.U.* His critical notes on Baronio's *Annales: Critica historico-chronologica in universos annales ecclesiasticos Baronii*, 4 vols f⁰ 1727, as well as his *Breviarum historico-chronologico criticum* of the Popes' *Gesta* and the Councils' *Acta*. 3 vols 4⁰ 1717, were in G's library at Bentinck Street and L.

17 The original ed., Lyons 1665, of *Codex Theodosium, cum perpetuis commentariis J. Gothefredi* was in G's library at Bentinck Street and L. For Jacques Godefroy (1587-1652), see *B.U.*

30 Lardner—For Nathaniel Lardner (1684-1768), see *D.N.B.* His *Large collection of ancient Jewish and heathen testimonies to the truth of the Christian Religion*, 4 vols London 1764-1767, was in G's library at Bentinck Street and L.

38 conversation—in the sense of commerce, society (the last example cited by *N.E.D.* is dated 1770).

Page 148

4 wise maxim—Pliny, *Epistles*, VII, ix, 15: 'Aiunt enim multum legendum esse non multa.'—Quintilian, X, i, 59: 'Multa quam magis multorum lectione formanda mens.'

14 break the line—'line' in the sense of 'rule, standard of life or practice' is given as obsolete and rare by *N.E.D.*

Page 149

10 Horace, *Epodon Liber*, ii, 1-4.

18 first mortgage—£10,000 raised in 1758 (*Letters*, i, p. 405, V).

20 interest on the £10,000 borrowed on mortgage—allowance due to G himself (see p. 90 above).

24 obsolete law-suits—see *Letters*, i, p. 404, I.

28 additional mortgage—£7000 raised in 1764, see *Ibid.*, V.

31 reluctant delays—see *Ibid.*, pp. 234, 235, 239, 240.

33 Tacitus, *Historiae*, iii, 54.

38 the tenth—G's father died on the 12th (*Letters*, i, p. 263).

Page 150

14 all the duties—'Dans toute sa maladie, je ne me suis jamais absenté de Beriton un seul jour, à peine ai je quitté sa Chambre un seul instant: tout, jusqu'à mes lectures, a été interrompû, et je goûte la triste consolation d'avoir rempli mes devoirs de fils, jusqu'au moment où ils ont cessé.' (G to Deyverdun, *Ibid.*, p. 267.)

Page 152

20 reluctance—See *Ibid.*, p. 340.

24 tenant—For G's first tenant, a man called Winton, see *Ibid.*, passim (ref. to *Index*, iii, p. 455). Buriton was in Winton's hands from 1772 to 1778; he appears to have neglected his work as a farmer and let the estate run down.

30 Lenborough—see *Ibid.*, i, p. 312, n. 2.

35 worthless fellow—An army contractor of Oxfordshire, Lovegrove by name; for him see *Ibid.*, *passim* (ref. to *Index*, iii, p. 431).
three years—Lovegrove promised, early in June 1773 (see *Ibid.*, i, p. 367), to buy the Lenborough estate but then raised various difficulties until, in October 1776, 'the long and troublesome business' was 'broke off' (see *Ibid.*, ii, p. 118).

Page 153

3 fifteen years—The Lenborough estate was at last sold at the end of 1783 (see *Ibid.*, p. 382), nearly twelve years after it had been first advertised, on 25 April 1772. But G probably reckons fifteen years from 1769 when, with the help of James Scott and Stanier Porten, he drew up a scheme for putting an end to his father's financial difficulties (see *Ibid.*, i, p. 406).

6 delicious—The Gibbon share in the New River Co. was valued at £8000 in 1721 (see *Ibid.*, p. 403). It was no doubt worth more in 1771.

13 enjoyment of life—G of course refers to his father's enjoyment of life.

23 heirs of my choice—When G wrote this, in 1789, he had already chosen for his heir John Eliot, the younger son of his cousin Katharine Elliston, Lady Eliot (see the *Will of Edward Gibbon made in 1788* in *M.*, pp. 420-424). But, by his last will of 1791, he left the bulk of his property to the

children of his uncle, Sir Stanier Porten, who had died in June 1789, 'the most indigent and the most deserving of my relations' (see *Letters*, iii, p. 215).

Page 154

6 my father's decease—See above, n. to l. 38 of p. 149.

29 domestic—*i.e.* in my own house.

Page 156

7 first reigns—*D.F.*, ch. iv-vi.

9 Feeling very ill, Hume decided in April 1776, against the advice of his doctor, to try the Bath waters. He left Edinburgh on 21 April, travelled 'by slow Journies' and reached London on Wednesday, 1 May. There he stayed four full days, and left for Bath on the 6th. Owing to the deplorable state of his health, he is unlikely to have let his London friends know of his passage. But he wanted to meet his publisher, Strahan, and wrote him a brief note before leaving Scotland: 'My Body sets out tomorrow by Post for London, but whether it shall arrive there is somewhat uncertain . . . I bring up my philosophical Pieces corrected, which will be safe, whether I dye by the Road or not.' Now Strahan was the publisher of *D.F.*, and through him G may have heard that Hume was to be in London, and may have tried to meet him, not on the Thursday when Hume 'saw nobody' but the famous physician Sir John Pringle, an old friend, whose medical advice he desired, but perhaps on the Friday, when he says he saw some 'little Company' (see the *Letters of David Hume*, ed. by J. Y. Greig, Oxford 1932, ii, p. 309 ff.). It may be thought somewhat surprising, not perhaps that Hume did not refer to G's visit in his letter to Strahan of 8 June, but surely that G himself did not mention it in his letter of 7 May to Deyverdun in which he quotes from Hume's letter to him of 18 March (see *Letters*, ii, p. 106).

18 For Lord Eliot, see *Ibid.*, iii, pp. 410-411.

27 Horace, *Ars Poetica*, i, 82.

Page 157

4 Peter Elmsley was the publisher of G's *Observations on the Æneid*. For G's letters and various references to him, see *Letters*, iii, 411-412.

5 very easy terms—see *Bibliography*, pp. 44-45.
For G's relations with Thomas Cadell, his publisher, and the Strahans, see *Letters*, iii, 398 and 450.

13 stinted—Cadell himself had proposed an edition of 750 copies (see *Ibid.*, ii, p. 30), but G preferred it to be limited to 500, because, as he wrote to Deyverdun, 'je voulois pressentir le goût du public' (*Ibid.*, p. 105).

22 deduced—*N.E.D.* does not list G's somewhat peculiar use, here and elsewhere, of 'deduce' in the sense of 'pursue from age to age' (cf. above, p. 122, 'deduce a chain of revolutions'); his meaning here is: 'starting from the last period of classical reading, the age of the Antonines, which was also the age of Tacitus, Juvenal and the younger Pliny, my narrative follows the vicissitudes of the Roman empire.'

32 second edition—The 2nd ed. of 1500 copies was published in June 1776, and the 3rd, of 1000, in May 1777.

34 pyrates—Vol. i was twice reprinted, but in two volumes, at Dublin, in 1776, and again in 1777: see *Bibliography*, pp. 101, 106-109.

37 profane—the only 'barking' to be heard at this early date came from members of the clergy.

Page 158

6 Dr Robertson's opinion of *D.F.* was first expressed in a letter, dated 15 March 1776, to W. Strahan (see *Letters*, ii, p. 106, n.). Strahan communicated it to G who copied part of it for his own benefit (*Add. MSS 34886, f 63*), and copied the first sentences of his copy in his letter to Deyverdun of 7 May. Lord Sheffield published G's copy (*Misc. Wks*, ii, Nº LXXVII). About a year later, on 5 June 1777, Robertson wrote to G himself a letter beginning 'I have desired Mr Strahan to take the liberty of sending you a copy of the History of America, which I hope you will do me the honour of accepting, as a testimony of my gratitude for the instruction which I have received from your writings ...' (*Ibid.*, Nº CIX). For G's letter of thanks, see *Letters*, ii, pp. 152-154.

12 The Neckers were in London from the latter part of April to the end of May.

32 my old friend—see *above*, p. 127 and *Misc. Gibb.*, p. 98.

Page 159

5 For Dr John Hunter (1718-1783), professor of anatomy at the Royal Academy, see *D.N.B.* G daily attended Hunter's lectures from the end of January to the end of April 1777: 'bones and guts from two to four' (*Letters*, ii, p. 140).

6 For Bryan Higgins (?1737-1820) who had opened a school of practical chemistry in Soho in 1774, see *D.N.B.*

10 track me in their own snow—Dryden used the same phrase: 'He was not only a professed imitator of Horace, but a learned of all the others: you track him everywhere in their snow.' *Essay on Dramatic Poesy*, Ker's ed. of *Dryden's Essays*, i, p. 43.

11 Arian controversy—*D.F.*, ch. xxi.

14 age of Constantine—*Ibid.*, ch. xvii-xx.

16 six months—from 10 May to the end of October.

34 he two invidious Chapters—xv and xvi.

Page 160

2 clamorous—'When I delivered to the world the First Volume . . . in which I had been obliged to connect the progress of Christianity with the civil state and revolutions of the Roman Empire, I could not be ignorant that the result of my inquiries might offend the interest of some and the opinions of others. If the whole work was favourably received by the public, I had the more reason to expect that this obnoxious part would provoke the zeal of those who consider themselves as the Watchmen of the Holy City. These expectations were not disappointed; and a fruitful crop of Answers, Apologies, Remarks, Examinations, &c. sprung up with all convenient speed.' (*Vindication, &c., Misc. Wks*, iv, p. 517.) For an examination of all the early attacks on G's ch. xv-xvi, see the first four ch. of S. T. McCloy's *Gibbon's Antagonism to Christianity*, London, 1933.

7 (34)—For G's own *notes* (reference numbers in round brackets) 34 to 41, see below, pp. 170-173.

14 Apthorpe—For The Rev. East Apthorpe, of Boston (Massachusetts), his career and his *Letters on the Prevalence of Christianity before its Civil Establishment, with Observations on a late History of the Decline and Fall of the Roman Empire* (1777), see McCloy, *op. cit.*, pp. 107-113. For his *Observations on a late History*, see also G's *Vindication*, pp. 596-597. As a reward for his publication, Apthorpe received from Archbishop Cornwallis the rectory of St Mary-le-Bow, London. For all the other critics of ch. xv-xvi mentioned by G, see *D.N.B.*

29 May—G sent his draft of the *Mémoire Justificatif* to Lord Weymouth with a covering letter dated 10 August 1779 (see *Letters*, ii, p. 224), but he cannot have started work on it before mid-July; his dating in E must be due to what Miss Norton calls 'an error of memory' (*Bibliography*, p. 26).

31 Chancellor—Edward, 1st baron Thurlow (1731-1808) was Lord Chancellor from June 1778 to April 1783.

32 Weymouth—Thomas Thynne, 3rd Viscount Weymouth (1734-1795), was secretary of state from 1775 to 1779; he was created 1st Marquis of Bath in 1789.

34 Stormont—David Murray, Viscount Stormont (1727-1796), was ambassador at the court of Versailles from August 1772 to March 1778: he became 2nd Earl Mansfield on the death of his uncle in 1792.

31 At the request—For the circumstances that led to G composing an answer to the French manifesto, 'Exposé des Motifs de la Conduite du Roi de France', see *Bibliography*, pp. 22-27.

Page 161

1 The *Mémoire Justificatif pour servir de réponse à l'Exposé de la Cour de France*, published in October 1779, was reprinted in *Misc. Wks*, v, pp. 1-34.

11 Wedderburne—For Alexander Wedderburn (1733-1805) see *D.N.B.*: Attorney General in 1778, Lord Chief Justice in 1780 when he was created Baron Loughborough. (See *Letters*, ii, p. 219.)

24 Provoked—Fox, for instance, is said to have been the author of this skit:

King George in a fright
Lest Gibbon should write
The story of Britain's disgrace,
Thought no means more sure
His pen to secure
Than to give the historian a place.

But his caution is vain,
'Tis the curse of his reign
That his projects should never succeed;
Tho' he wrote not a line,
Yet a cause of decline
In our author's example we read.

His book well describes
How corruption and bribes
O'erthrew the great empire of Rome;
And his writings declare
A degeneracy there,
Which his conduct exhibits at home.

(*Notes and Queries*, 1st Series, viii, p. 312)

27 never . . . enlisted—See *Letters*, ii, p. 219.

33 Dunning—For John Dunning M.P. (1731-1783) see *D.N.B.* His celebrated motion was passed on 6 April 1780.

Page 162

1 American—Lord George Germaine (1716-1785), secretary of state for the American colonies from November 1775, had been President of the Board of Trade from 1775 to 1779.

8 flames of London—The Gordon riots of 2-11 June 1780, so called from their instigator, Lord George Gordon.

28 bigotted advocate of Popes and monks—Thus, presumably, does G refer
to Travis who, in his 2nd letter, after declaring 'I mean now to establish
the authenticity of the verse itself (1 John, v. 7) by testimonies of
different kinds', quotes Laurentius Valla (c. 1406-1457), Nicolaus of
Lyra (1265-1349), St Thomas, St Bernard, Walafrid Strabo, and many
other medieval scholars, but neither Erasmus nor any later exegetist, and
to their evidence joins the testimony of councils.

29 turned over—even the bigots of Oxford would know how to deal with
him.

Page 163

4 testimonies of applause—by Robertson, Adam Smith, Lord Hardwicke,
Mme Necker. See their letters in *Misc. Wks*, ii, Nᵒˢ CXLVIII, CXLIX,
CLII, CLIII.

12 French translation—For it, see *Bibliography*, pp. 120-121.

34 surrendered—on 20 March 1892: 'Lord North is no more. This day . . .
he gave solemn notice that the whole administration was dissolved, and
the House has adjourned . . .' (*Letters*, ii, p. 292).

Page 164

9 my first engagement—'As I have ventured, perhaps too hastily, to
commit to the press a work, which, in every sense of the word, deserves
the epithet of imperfect, I consider myself as contracting an engagement
to finish, most probably in a second volume, the first of these memorable
periods from the Antonines to the subversion of the Western Empire
about the beginning of the 6th century . . . With regard to the subsequent
periods, though I may entertain some hopes, I dare not presume to give
any assurances.' (Preface to *D.F.*, i, dated 'Feb. 1. 1776'.)

12-13 summer lodgings—For a few weeks from July to September 1781, G
rented a house at Brighton, 'a small pleasant house', with 'a full prospect
of the sea' (*Letters*, ii, pp. 271, 273). For September-October 1782, a
friend lent him at Hampton Court 'a ready furnished House close to the
Palace, and opening by a private door into the Royal garden which is
maintained for my use but not at my expense. The air and exercise, good
roads and neighbourhood, . . . adapt this new scene very much to my
wishes' (*Ibid.*, p. 306). He was there again in May-August 1783.

20 preface of a new edition—For a new 4to ed. of vols i-iii (vol. i of which
was alone published in 1782, vols ii and iii only coming out in 1787), G
added to the original Preface, which he kept, a postscript dated 'March 1,
1781' in which he declared that 'The entire History, which is now published, of the Decline and Fall of the Roman Empire in the West' dis-
charges all his 'engagements with the Public', but added: 'Perhaps
their favourable opinion may encourage me to prosecute a work, which,

however laborious it may seem, is the most agreeable occupation of my leisure hours.' This postscript is followed in its turn by an additional postscript, dated March 1, 1782: 'An author easily persuades himself that the public opinion is still favourable to his labours; and I have now embraced the serious resolution of proceeding to the last period of my original design, and of the Roman Empire, the taking of Constantinople by the Turks . . .'

23 Agathias (c. 536-582), Greek poet and historian, wrote the history of his own times, beginning from where Procopius ended; he is the chief authority for the middle years of the 6th century.

27 abstract of the Civil law—D.F., ch. xliv.

33-35 The new Administration formed at the end of March 1782, with Rockingham at its head, Shelburne for colonial affairs, and Fox for foreign affairs, had assumed the tasks of carrying out the financial reforms advocated by Burke and of restoring the peace with France and America. It more or less accomplished the former but found itself divided on the question of what kind of independence to grant America, Fox being for a total unconditional one, while Shelburne wanted it to be restricted to domestic affairs. When Fox realized that the majority of his colleagues supported Shelburne, he resigned. Thereupon Rockingham died (1 July 1782) and Shelburne was appointed to succeed him. His plans for American independence and the restoration of the peace were laid before the House in February 1783 and met with strong opposition. Fox and North then entered into an alliance to bring Shelburne down. At the end of the month, Shelburne was defeated and a new ministry was formed in April with Fox and North as secretaries of state; it concluded the peace in September.

Page 165

1 the great antagonists—Fox had first taken office in 1770 under North, but was dismissed in 1774 by the King who had come to regard him as a 'Young Man' who 'has so thoroughly cast off every principle of common honour and honesty that he must become as contemptible as he is odious'. His dismissal, together with his growing sympathy for the cause of American independence, made him 'turn patriot', as G put it (Letters, i, p. 309). Henceforth he was in the House of Commons one of the leaders of the opposition to North's policy, criticizing, denouncing it with untiring energy and often assailing North himself with unmeasured invectives.

Page 166

17 Elliston—See n. to p. 20, l. 9.

20 Hymenæal feast—Mallet's 'pleasing little composition', as G describes it, is the poem entitled Cupid and Hymen or the Wedding-Day, from

which G quotes the invitation addressed to his widowed father (see *above*, p. 35). Mallet married his second wife, Lucy Elstob, on 7 October 1742 (see Hill's ed. of Johnson's *Lives*, iii, p. 409); the ninth anniversary of their marriage must have been in 1751 when Catherine Elliston (1735-1804) was sixteen, and not in 1750, as G thought.

Page 167

1 Teague—a nickname for an Irishman (earliest example in *N.E.D.*, 1644; latest, 1884).

5 cit—short for citizen, contemptuously applied to a townsman, a shop-keeper (*N.E.D.*).

15 soon—Catherine Elliston married Edward Craggs Eliot in 1756, some five years after Mallet had written his verses about her. On Edward C. Eliot (1727-1804) and his family, see *Letters*, iii, p. 410.

23 Copying Hume's Letter, G made four minor mistakes, three of which Sheffield corrected (see *above*, p. 168, textual notes), probably by referring to the original, but he did not correct the first: Hume had written 'with a great deal of avidity' and not merely 'with avidity'. Neither G nor his first editor, of course, thought of respecting Hume's punctuation and use (really abuse) of capitals. See *The Letters of David Hume*, ed. cit., ii, pp. 309-311.

Page 169

1 By omitting 'still', Sheffield was correcting, not G's copy, but Hume.

12 an unknown Critic—The author of the *Supplément à la Manière d'écrire l'histoire* was Paul Philippe Gudin de la Brenellerie (1758-1812), for whom, see *B.U.* His *Supplément à la Manière d'écrire l'histoire*, Kehl 1784, is essentially a survey of the achievements of ancient and modern historians, meant as a severe criticism of the ungenerous treatment they had received from Mably in his *De la manière d'écrire l'histoire* (1782).

15 Countess of Froulay—unidentified, not mentioned in L. Séché, *Les Derniers Jansénistes*, Paris 1891.

Page 170

7 For Gabriel Bonnot de Mably, known as l'Abbé de Mably (1709-1785) see *B.U.* He was Condillac's younger brother and the author of fourteen, chiefly historical, works.

8 The *Eloge historique de l'Abbé de Mably*, par M. l'Abbé Brizard, fills pp. 1-120 of the 1st vol. of Mably's *Œuvres complètes*, Lyon 1796, and ends on a *Notice des ouvrages . . . de Mably par ordre chronologique*. Gabriel Brizard (d. 1793) published some of his works under the name of *Abbé Brizard*, but was not an abbé.

16-17 Of Voltaire, Mably says, 'il n'est qu'un fou'; of Hume 'qu' il nefait que des réflexions communes . . . par ignorance . . . par paresse ou lenteur d'esprit', of Robertson's *Introduction to The History of Charles V*, that it is 'un ouvrage croqué, rien d'approfondi'.

19 G's *note 33*—G's first quotation of *De la manière d'écrire l'histoire* is preceded by 'Un lecteur raisonnable exige qu'une narration soit rapide, & veut cependant que rien ne soit oublié, de ce qui doit la rendre très-claire & très-intelligible. Le principal art consiste donc à préparer le lecteur aux événemens qu'on va mettre sous ses yeux.' and is followed by 'Rien ne doit m'arrêter dans un récit, & il faut être clair, c'est la première loi de tout historien; mais il faut l'être avec art pour ne pas me rebuter . . .'.

23 another passage—'Le second moyen pour plaire, c'est de rendre votre narration rapide. On n'y réussira pas en mutilant, pour ainsi dire, les faits . . . Ne négligez aucune des circonstances propres à me faire connaître la nature d'un événement . . .; mais disposez-les si sagement qu'elles ne s'embarrassent point les unes les autres. Vous voyez des historiens, par exemple M. *Guibbon*, qui s'empêtrent dans leur sujet, ne savent ni l'entamer ni le finir, se tournent, pour ainsi dire, toujours sur eux-mêmes.'

24 I am indebted—After his report of the discussion between Mably and Gibbon, which took place in 1777, Gubin devotes several pages (128-134) to a warm eulogy of *D.F.*, too long to be quoted.

26 As to Hayley, G's reference is to the 2nd vol. of the 6 vol. ed. of Hayley's *Poems and Plays*, London, 1785, which was in his library at L. On pp. 261-263, in the course of the notes he added to his own poem, *An Essay on History*, Hayley thus replies to Mably's strictures on *D.F.*:

'The French language, so fertile in miscellaneous criticism, affords us many works that relate to Historical composition: the most extraordinary of these, is a very late publication by the Abbé Mably, "De la Maniere d'ecrire l'Histoire". As this insolent and dogmatical Author has grossly insulted our country, by vilifying our most eminent writers of History, I had thoughts of chastising his presumption by a full display of his various absurdities; but as this unpleasant office has been in some measure performed by one of his own countrymen, under the title of a Supplement to his Work, I shall only make a few remarks on the illiberal terms in which he speaks of my friend Mr Gibbon.

'As the Abbé has only read a translated extract from the accomplished Historian, he certainly could not be a competent judge of the spirit and beauty of his immortal work. No matter: he had a private pique against the Author, and was therefore determined to decry his composition. In the blindness and precipitancy that usually belong to base anger, he attributes the defect of dullness to a Book, more universally read than any modern performance of equal magnitude.

'The Abbé talks loudly of the literary virtues that become an Historian: but he seems to have forgot that there are literary vices, which may render even a learned and ingenious critic contemptible. No productions of the press are more disgraceful to literature, than those in which a dissertation on any art is made the vehicle of personal malignity: yet, as this is the most plausible and insinuating method of giving vent to malice, it is, perhaps, the most common. In the end, however, this species of literary slander defeats its own purpose; for, if the envious are pleased to echo it for a time, to more candid and generous readers it endears the merit it traduces. They lament the hard destiny of superior talents; and recollect, with a sigh of affectionate indignation, the just and spirited remark of Monsieur D'Alembert, "Que les grands Genies sont toujours déchirés par des gens, qui ne sont pas digne de les lire!" '

28 *A Vindication*—G's answer to the attacks of Davis (*Misc. Wks*, iv, pp. 575-595), Watson (pp. 598-602), Chelsum and Randolph (pp. 602-643), the anonymous author (Francis Eyre) of 'A few Remarks' (pp. 643-657), was published on 14 January 1779, a 2nd ed. following at the end of February.

33 Davis—Henry E. Davis, B.A., of Balliol College (1756-1784) published in 1778 *An Examination of the Fifteenth and Sixteenth Chapters of Mr. Gibbon's History of the Decline and Fall of the Roman Empire. In which his view of the Christian Religion is shewn to be founded on the Misrepresentation of the Authors he cites: and Numerous Instances of his Inaccuracy and Plagiarism are produced*. On Davis's *Examination*, see McCloy, *op. cit.*, pp. 64-67.

Chelsum—Rev. James Chelsum, D.D. (?1740-1801) launched the first attack on G in an anonymous pamphlet published in October 1776 and re-issued in a 2nd, greatly augmented ed., in 1778. It was simply entitled *Remarks on the Two Last Chapters of Mr. Gibbon's History*. McCloy describes it as 'a sort of loose collection of a multitude of choppy paragraphs' and analyses it at length (pp. 56-67); G called it 'very illiberal' (*Letters*, ii, p. 120), 'choleric' and 'dull' (*Ibid.*, p. 129).

Page 171

1 Watson—For Richard Watson (1737-1816) see *D.N.B.* He sent G a copy of his *Apology for Christianity in a Series of Letters Addressed to Edward Gibbon, Esq.* and G thanked him for 'the liberal treatment which he has received from so candid an adversary' (*Letters*, ii, p. 119). For his *Apology* see McCloy, *op. cit.*, pp. 94-104.

4 clear his Theological character—Watson's praise of G and Voltaire for their service to the cause of tolerance shows him to have been the very opposite of a bigot; see McCloy's quotation from the *Apology*: *op. cit.*, pp. 98-99.

6 Chemical Essays—Watson, who had been professor of Chemistry and had not given up the study of that science after he had been appointed professor of Divinity, published in 1781-1782 three volumes of *Chemical Essays* which G had in his library at L. He was made Bishop of Llandaff by Shelburne in 1782 as a reward for his opposition to North's American policy, not for his *Apology*.

9 For Rev. Henry Taylor (1711-1785), rector of Crawley (Hants), see *D.N.B.* and *Letters*, ii, p. 244. As an Arian, Taylor regarded the Church as having deviated from the true doctrine when the Council of Nice condemned Arianism. For his *Thoughts on the Nature of the Grand Apostasy, with Reflections on the Fifteenth Chapter of Mr. Gibbon's History*, 1781, see McCloy, *op. cit.*, pp. 116-120.

15 For Joseph Milner (1744-1797), see *D.N.B.* 'He was an ardent disciple of the rising evangelical school.' G calls him 'Methodist'. His *Gibbon's Account of Christianity Considered: together with some Strictures upon Hume's Dialogues concerning Natural Religion* was published in 1781; for his critical remarks on G, see McCloy, *op. cit.*, pp. 122-127.

23 two gauntlets—The 2nd vol. of Priestley's *History of the Corruption of Christianity* ends on a 'General Conclusion' in two parts, Part I 'containing Considerations addressed to Unbelievers, and especially to Mr Gibbon' who refuses to admit that Christianity is of divine institution— and Part II 'Containing Considerations addressed to the Advocates for the present Civil Establishments of Christianity, and especially Bishop Hurd' who as a champion of the Trinitarian dogma, believes too much.

38 Jean Astruc (1684-1766), successively professor at the medical faculties of Toulouse, Montpellier and Paris, was the author of numerous works mentioned in *B.U.*, where, however, no mention is made of *La structure du coeur*, which was vainly sought in the Bibliothèque nationale (Paris) and elsewhere.

Page 172

1 continues—Priestley resumed his attack on Gibbon in his *Letters to a Philosophical Unbeliever* (Birmingham 1787), Part II 'Containing a State of the Evidence of Revealed Religion, with Animadversions on the two last Chapters of the first Volume of Mr. Gibbon's History*. For Priestley's *Animadversions*, see his *Letter* XVI, pp. 199-231.

3 *my* replies—In his first letters to Priestley, G had repeatedly refused to be drawn into controversy with him. See *Letters*, ii, pp. 320, 322, 324. He had probably heard that a complaint about his refusal had been published in Priestley's journal, *Theological Repository*, in 1788, and took the opportunity of this note to reassert it.

Socinian—As a Unitarian, Priestley could be charged with holding Socinian, anti-Trinitarian views.

5 Horsley—For Samuel Horsley (1733-1806), Bishop of St David's (1788) and later of Rochester, see *D.N.B.* As archdeacon of St Albans he had made himself conspicuous as a champion of the doctrine of the Trinity against Priestley, who had denied that it was held by the early Christian Church. In this controversy Horsley proved superior to his adversary in learning and polemical ability.

sedition—Priestley was a member of the Revolution Society stigmatized by Burke in the opening pages of his *Reflections on the French Revolution*. Burke quotes a passage from the *History of the Corruptions of Christianity* that shows its author as a 'trumpet of sedition': 'A man amongst them of great authority, and certainly of great talents, speaking of a supposed alliance between church and state, says, "perhaps *we must wait for the fall of the civil powers* before this most unnatural alliance be broken. Calamitous no doubt will that time be. But what convulsion in the political world ought to be a subject of lamentation, if it be attended with so desirable an effect?" ' (*Reflections . . .* , ed. Phillips, pp. 57-58).

7 For David Dalrymple, Scottish lawyer and historian (1726-1792), see *D.N.B.* Made a judge in 1761, he took the title of Lord Hailes. He was appointed a lord of Session (lord of justiciary) in 1776. As a historian, he published *Annals of Scotland* in 1776-1779, and *Remains of Christian Antiquity*, 4 vols, in 1776-1783. The latter are full of critical notes on Gibbon which, together with others, scattered in various publications, he collected into a thick 4⁰ vol. entitled *An Inquiry into the Secondary causes which Mr Gibbon has assigned for the rapid growth of Christianity* Edinburgh and London, 1786.

16 For Joseph White, Oxford professor of Arabic (1745-1814), see *D.N.B.* White delivered his famous Bampton lectures, entitled *A Comparison of Mahometism and Christianity in their History, their Evidence, and their Effects*, at St Mary's in 1784; they were published in the following year: *Sermons preached before the University of Oxford in the Year 1784 at the Lecture founded by the Rev. John Bampton, M.A. . . . by Joseph White, Fellow of Wadham College, and Laudian Professor of Arabic.*

19 In the preparation of his Bampton Lectures, White had required the service of two paid and secret collaborators, Rev. Samuel Badcock being one of them. Four years later, in 1788, Badcock told in a conversation the story of his collaboration, and died soon after. One of his hearers, Rev. R. B. Gabriel, hastened to buy from Badcock's sister all the private papers he had left, promising her to help her to obtain the payment of the sum which her brother had pretended White was still owing him. He tried to redeem his promise under threat of making public the true story of the Bampton Lectures. White denied owing anything and Gabriel published his *Facts relating to the Rev. Dr White's Bampton Lectures*

which contained White's private letters to Badcock. In one of these letters, of 8 January 1784, White had entrusted to his collaborator the task of writing a few pages showing that 'there were such apparently insuperable obstacles to Christianity that it would have been impossible for it ever to have succeeded without the divine interposition', and thus opposing G's thesis of the natural causes that accounted for the spread of the new religion, and White added 'The part where we encounter Gibbon, ought to be brilliant; and the conclusion of the whole must be animated and grand' (Gabriel, *Facts* . . ., pp. 28-30). White answered Gabriel in *A Statement of Dr White's Literary Obligations to the late Rev. Mr. Samuel Badcock* . . . published at Oxford in 1790, in which he also reproduced his letter to his collaborator of 8 January 1784 and declared 'For the . . . part of the sermon relating to Mr Gibbon's five causes . . . and the recapitulation of the principal topics discussed in the two sermons, Mr Badcock had no share.' (The editor is indebted to M. M. Baridon, of Dijon University, for a copy of Badcock's private letter.) For the story of the Bampton Lectures, see also *D.N.B.* under Badcock and White.

20 Edwards—G had not read Dr Edwards's sermon itself. What he quotes of it are passages from the review published in the *Monthly Review* for October 1790 under the title *The Jewish and Heathen Rejection of the Christian Miracles. Preached before the University of Cambridge, March 7, 1790, By Thomas Edwards, LL.D.* Here are the opening lines of the review: 'The able and sensible writer of this discourse thinks it necessary to awaken, in the minds of his clerical brethren, apprehension . . . and calls on them to provide against the attacks which are daily made on the entire fabric of Christianity itself. He particularly solicits their attention to the objections which have been revived by the celebrated historian of the Roman empire inserted in the body of a work which can only perish with the language itself. . . .' In what follows, the reviewer says Dr Edwards calls G a 'formidable adversary'.

Page 173

8 controversy &c—G summed up in a mere '&c' the last words of the reviewer: 'but darts forth the envenomed shafts of sarcastic ridicule . . . he approaches not, like a Goliath, to call forth a champion, but to insult and triumph over his vanquished enemies.'

10 Beaumarchais—G's reference is to the ed. of Beaumarchais's *Œuvres* published in Paris in 1780 in 5 vols 8vo, which ed. was in his library at L.; vol. iii contains *Observations sur le Mémoire Justificatif de la Cour de Londres.* As proof of the help that the French government constantly gave to the American rebels, G had adduced in his *Mémoire* the many vessels that were known to sail from the French ports with war equip-

ment as, for example, 'les neuf gros vaisseaux équipés et frêtés par le Sieur de Beaumarchais et ses associés. . . . L'Hippopotame, appartenant au Sieur Beaumarchais doit avoir à son bord quatorze mille fusils, et beaucoup de munition de guerre, pour l'usage des rebelles' (*Misc. Wks*, v, pp. 18-19). In his *Observations*, Beaumarchais explains that, far from helping the Americans, the French government did all it could to hamper trade between French merchants and the rebels, as he, Beaumarchais, knew to his cost (pp. 321-347). But this fact Lord Stormont never mentioned in his reports to his government: 'Lorsque le Vicomte de Stormont résidoit à Paris, & qu'il s'y débitoit un mensonge politique, une fausse nouvelle un peu fâcheuse pour les Américains . . . le mot des Députés du Congrès, interrogés par tout le monde, étoit constamment: Ne croyez pas cela, Monsieur, *c'est du Stormont tout pur*. Eh bien! Lecteur, on en peut dire autant du Mémoire justificatif; *c'est du Stormont tout pur*, au style près, qui, bien qu'un peu traînant dans la traduction, ne manqueroit pas de graces, ni la logique de justesse, si l'Ecrivain n'oublioit pas sans cesse que le Lord Stormont en a fourni les données . . .' (p. 347).

16 the assertion—'Mon âme est ainsi composée: dans les plus grands maux, elle cherche avec soin, pour se consoler, le peu de bien qui s'y rencontre. Ainsi pendant que mes efforts avoient si peu de fruit en Amérique . . . & moi, triste jouet des événemens, seul, privé de repos . . . desséché d'insomnie et de chagrins . . . Mais mon courage renaissoit, quand je pensois qu'un grand peuple alloit bientôt offrir une douce & libre retraite à tous les persécutés de l'Europe; que ma patrie seroit vengée de l'abaissement auquel on l'avoit soumise en fixant par le Traité de 1763, le petit nombre des vaisseaux qu'on daignoit encore lui souffrir . . .' (*Observations*, p. 334).

18 Choiseul's letter complaining of Beaumarchais's 'daring falsehood' and a copy of the government's decree ordering the suppression of his pamphlet are in the archives of the French Foreign Office (*Bibliography*, p. 32, n. 3).

19 G's reference is presumably to the original ed. in pamphlet form of the speech by which, on 13 March 1780, Burke introduced his bills for economic reform and in particular for abolishing sinecure places. There was in his library at L. an artificial vol. of Burke's 'Political tracts and speeches' 1769-1780, which may have contained it.

22-25 After the clause for abolishing the Board of Trade had been opposed by the then First Lord, Mr Eden, Burke 'thanked the hon. gentleman for his historical account of the origin and utility of the B. of T.; he was ready to accept that, but not his 2'300 volumes which he begged to be excused from taking; he would not look into one of them. They would serve, however, as a monument, under which both he and his clause might be buried, and form a funeral pile for them as large as one of the pyramids of Egypt' (Cobbett's *Parliamentary History*, xxi, pp. 235-236).

27 The Italian translation to which G refers is the second one, 'tradotta dell' inglese', published at Pisa in 9 vols from 1779 to 1786, and containing the first 3 vols of *D.F.*, that is, all that had appeared by 1786. Early in 1779 there had previously been published at 'Losanna' a translation in 3 vols in 8⁰ of G's first vol., chapters i-xvi, made, not from the English original, but from the French version of le Clerc de Septchênes. A copy of this rare ed. was recently acquired by the Lausanne University Library. See *Bibliography*, pp. 144 ff.

30 five letters—vol. V, pp. 363-435: *Riflessioni sopra il tomo V. e VI . . . divise in III. Lettere dirette ai sigg. Foothead e Kirk inglesi catollici*; Vol. VII, pp. 301-379: *Riflessioni sopra il tomo VII . . . divise in II Lettere*. See *Ibid*.

Page 174

5 critical Essay—Vol. III contains G's ch. xiv-xvi, followed, after a separate title-page, by *Saggio di confutazione de due capi XV e XVI di Gibbon spettanti all'esame del Cristianesimo* in 147 pp. paged separately. See *Ibid*.

8 Spedalieri, Niccolò, *Confutazione dell'esame del cristianismo fatto dal sig. Eduardo Gibbon*, Roma 1784, 2 vols. See *Ibid.*, p. 238.

13 Travis—For Rev. George Travis, archdeacon of Chester (1741-1797), see *D.N.B.* His attack on G first appeared in *The Gentleman's Magazine* for June, July and November 1782 in three letters signed 'T' which he later published under his full name, with two more letters, as *Letters to Edward Gibbon, Esq. . . . in defence of the authenticity of the seventh verse of the fifth chapter of the first epistle of St John*, Chester, 1784. Though, since Erasmus, the authenticity of 1 John, v, 7 had been doubted by many scholars, it was still considered by Anglican orthodoxy as genuine and a main support for the dogma of the Trinity. G had called it 'a fraud' in a note to ch. xlvii of *D.F.* (*Ev. Lib. ed.*, v, p. 9, n. 1) which aroused the ire and indignation of the worthy archdeacon.

15 Porson—For Richard Porson (1759-1808), see *D.N.B.* Porson, then a fellow of Trinity College, Cambridge, still unknown, but who was to be recognized as the best Greek scholar of his time, came to G's rescue: in the same *Gentleman's Magazine*, from October 1788 to March 1790, he published a series of letters, signed 'Cantabrigiensis', which he collected, adding seven more, in a vol. published in London in 1790.

23 spurious—1 John, v, 7 is now admitted by all Protestant theologians to

be a spurious verse. It has at last disappeared from the 1952 Revised Standard Version of the Bible.

27 For Thomas Newton, Bishop of Bristol (1704-1782), see *D.N.B.* In *Some Account of the Author's Life, written by himself but a very few days before his death*, which was prefixed to the posthumous ed. of his *Works* (1782, 3 vol. 4to, 2nd ed. 1787, 6 vols 8vo), Bishop Newton, writing of himself in the third person, tells how he had read G's *History* and found it 'a prolix and tedious performance, his matter uninteresting, and his style affected' and adds: 'The Bishop's reading the whole was a greater compliment to the work than was paid to it by two of the most eminent of his brethren for their learning and station. The one entered upon it, but was soon wearied, and laid it aside in disgust. The other returned it upon the bookseller's hands . . . .'

32 charge—In the same page, Newton had accused G of 'making a false quotation' of Dr Burnet's treatise *De statu mortuorum* in a note to his ch. xxviii (*Ev. Lib. ed.*, iii, p. 144) and had exclaimed: 'Who would not from hence infer, that Dr Burnet was an advocate for the sleep and insensible existence of the soul after death? Whereas his doctrine is directly the contrary.' By quoting Burnet's Latin, G shows his note to have been perfectly justified and the Bishop utterly mistaken.

Page 175

12 The passage to which Louis XVI objected was in G's concluding observations of ch. xxxviii (*Ev. Lib. ed.*, iv, p. 109): 'Europe is now divided into twelve powerful . . . kingdoms . . . the chances of royal and ministerial talents are multiplied, at least, with the number of its rulers; and a Julian, or Semiramis, may reign in the North, while Arcadius and Honorius again slumber on the thrones of the House of Bourbon'. Since the 1789 ed. of vol. iii, the passage ends 'the thrones of the South'.

16 late King—See *Preface*, p. xxvii, n. 2.

19 If the concluding observations to ch. xxxviii were really written before Louis XVI ascended the throne (1774), they must have preceded by many years the actual writing of vol. iii.

Page 176

8 several English—Deyverdun was travelling tutor to Richard Worsley, born 1751, son of G's Lieutenant-Colonel (1769-1770); Philip Stanhope, b. 1755, godson and adopted heir of the 4th earl of Chesterfield (1772-1774); George Brodrick, 4th viscount Middleton, b. 1754 (May-October 1774); Alexander Hume, b. 1758, younger brother of Sir Abraham Hume, M.P. for Petersfield (1775-1779).

11 my first letter—of Mai 20, 1783 ('first' after a silence of five years), (*Letters*, ii, pp. 326-330).

12 immediate answer—Deyverdun's answer, written 10 June, reached G on the 21st (*Misc. Wks*, ii, pp. 280-289).

24 my Journey—G recorded the successive stages of his journey on a note found among his papers and now in B.M. (*Add. MSS 34882, f 254*): 'Sittingbourne September 15—Dover 16—Boulogne 17—St Omer 18—Douay 19—St Quentin 20—Rheims 21—St Dizier 22—Langres 23 —Besançon 24—Pontarlier 25—La Sarraz 26. Arrived at L. in the morning of September 27.'

26 less than three months—The Fox-North Administration, formed in April 1783, lasted until mid-December and thus was dissolved 'less than three months' after G's arrival at L.

hidden rocks—What these hidden rocks were G, now living abroad, may never have known: the coalition was brought down by the action of the King himself (J. Stephen Watson, *The Reign of George III* (*Oxford History of England*, xii), 1960, pp. 266-267.

32 seven years—These last pages of E were written early in 1791.

Page 177

13 a more regular settlement—On arriving at L., G found he could not settle at La Grotte until the following spring when he and Deyverdun would 'enter on a larger and more regular establishment' (*Letters*, ii, pp. 375, 390). In the meantime they rented 'a convenient ready furnished apartment' in the lower part of the rue de Bourg.

21 dissolution—Parliament was dissolved on 25 March 1784.

32 I began—G and his friend left their winter quarters early in May (*Ibid.*, p. 406).

Page 178

26 Dr Tissot—For Samuel-Auguste Tissot (1728-1797), see E. Olivier, *Médecine et Santé dans le Pays de Vaud au XVIIIe Siècle*, Lausanne 1939, ii, pp. 1060-1062.

Page 179

10 abstract—*D.F.*, ch. xlvii.

Page 180

19 or at least five—Remembering what he had written earlier (see *above*, pp. 155-156) of the composition of his first vol., G felt he could not say, of his first vol., that 'the first rough manuscript had been sent to the press'.

24 July 29—date of G's departure from L. on his return journey to England which took him ten days. He reached London on 7 August, saw his printer and publisher and went on to Sheffield Place on the 17th (*Add. MSS 34882, ff 254-255*).

32 Holroyd had entered Parliament in 1780 as member for Coventry, but
had lost his seat in the general election of 1784; he had been Lieutenant-
Colonel of the 22nd regiment of Dragoons from 1779 to January 1783
when he resigned from the army; he was created Baron Sheffield in 1780,
and earl of Sheffield much later, in 1816.

Page 181

6 Downing Street—Lord Sheffield's town-house. G had deposited there
that part of his library which he had not removed to L. in 1783; he
packed it in 1788: 'the casing of my books is a prodigious operation'
(*Letters*, iii, p. 109).

13 the minister—William Pitt was head of the administration since 1784.
In his capacity as First Lord of the Treasury and Chancellor of the Ex-
chequer, he succeeded in restoring the country's finances after the
American war.

18 For G's first and last visits to Lord North during his stay in England,
see *Letters*, iii, pp. 72, 123.

20 my public tribute—In G's *Preface* to vol. iv of *D.F.*, dated 1 May 1788:
'Were I ambitious of any other Patron than the Public, I would inscribe
this work to a Statesman, who, in a long, a stormy, and at length an unfortunate administration, had many political opponents, almost without
a personal enemy, who has retained, in his fall from power, many faithful
and disinterested friends, and who, under the pressure of severe in-
firmity, enjoys the lively vigour of his mind, and the fidelity of his incomparable temper. Lord North will permit me to express the feelings
of friendship in the language of truth: but even truth and friendship
should be silent, if he still dispensed the favour of the crown.'

27 compliment—Reporting Sheridan's speech in the House on 13 July 1788
in support of Warren Hastings's impeachment, the *Morning Chronicle*
of the 14th wrote that the orator had charged the late governor of India
with crimes that 'were unparalleled in atrociousness, and that nothing
equal in criminality was to be traced, either in ancient or modern history,
in the correct periods of Tacitus or the luminous pages of Gibbon'. G
was present and, on the same day, informed Sheffield that 'Sheridan had
surpassed himself' and paid 'a compliment much admired to a certain
historian of your acquaintance'. (*Letters*, iii, pp. 108-109.)

in the presence of the English nation—See Macaulay's essay on *Warren
Hastings, ad finem*.

Page 182

2 Assises de Jerusalem—G's attention to the *Assises de Jerusalem* was
roused by his seeing the Italian translation in the Biblioteca Magliab-
bechiana at Florence in 1764; see *Journey*, pp. 212-213: 'Collection des
Loix du Royaume de Jérusalem qui sont passées dans le Royaume de

Chypre sous la Maison de Lusignan et qui paroissent s'y être conservées sous le Gouvernement des Venetiens. Ce livre est en Italien et ne peut être par conséquent qu'une traduction.' The book which he 'procured' in 1787 in London was the French original; see *D.F.*, ch. lviii (*Ev. Lib. ed.*, vi, p. 89, nn. 1 and 4).

3 Ramusius—Paolo Ramusio (1532-1700) turned into Latin Villehardouin's *Conquête de Constantinople*, 'enriching his narrative with Greek and Latin materials' as G says in *D.F.*, ch. lx, last note. The book was published at Venice in 1635 as *De bello Constantinopolitano*, which G abbreviated into C.Pano.

Greek acts—In a note to his ch. lxvi (*Ev. Lib. ed.*, vi, p. 376, n. 3) G does not mention specially the 'Greek acts' of the Synod of Florence among the sources of his 'account of the councils of Basil, Ferrara, and Florence'. He merely says: 'I have consulted the original acts which fill the 17th and 18th tomes of the edition of Venice,' *viz.* the *Collectio regia* published in Paris in 1715, and enlarged by N. Coletus, Venice 1728-1732.

4 *Statuta almae Urbis Romae Auctoritate S.D.N. Gregorii . . . reformata et edita* (*D.F.*, ch. lxx, n. 95; *Ev. Lib. ed.*, vi, p. 539, n. 1).

15 compliment—Cadell had it printed as a four-page 4to pamphlet; he sent a copy to Mme de Sévery at L. which is now in the *Archives cantonales vaudoises*; though very poor poetry, the first and the four last stanzas may be quoted (for the full text, see *Misc. Wks*, i, pp. 260-261):

Occasional Stanzas,
Read after the dinner at Mr Cadell's
May 8, 1788
Being the day of the publication of the
Three last volumes of Mr Gibbon's History
And his birthday.

Genii of England and of *Rome*!
In mutual Triumph here assume
The Honors, each may claim!
This social Scene with Smiles survey!
And consecrate the festive day
To Friendship and to Fame!
. . . . .

Lo! sacred to the *Roman* Name,
And rais'd, like Rome's immortal Fame,
By Genius and by Toil,
The splendid Work is crown'd Today,
On which Oblivion ne'er shall pray,
Nor Envy make her Spoil!

England, exult and view not now
With jealous Glance each Nation's Brow,
    Where Hist'ry's Palm has spread!
In every Path of liberal Art,
Thy Sons to prime Distinction start,
    And no Superior dread.

Science for Thee a *Newton* rais'd;
For thy renown a *Shakespeare* blaz'd,
    Lord of the Drama's Sphere!
In different Fields to equal Praise
See Hist'ry now thy Gibbon raise
    To shine without a Peer!

Eager to honour living Worth,
And bless To-day the double Birth,
    That proudest Joy may claim,
Let artless Truth this Homage pay,
And consecrate the festive Day
    To Friendship and to Fame!

19 For the first 4to ed. of vols iv-vi, 3,000 copies issued on 8 May, see *Bibliography,* pp. 62-63.

20 The first 8vo ed. of vols iv-vi, published in April 1790, was followed in December 1791 by an 8vo ed. of the entire *History* in twelve vols, sold at £3 the set (see *Ibid.,* pp. 95 and 105, No. 38).

34 Irish pyrates—See *Ibid.,* pp. 94, 101, 106-109.

Page 183

1 For the Basle ed., see *Ibid.,* pp. 98, 102, 109-112.

8 announced—'I shall soon visit the banks of the lake of Lausanne which I have known and loved from my early youth. Under a mild government, amidst a beauteous landskip, in a life of leisure and independence, and among a people of easy and elegant manners, I have enjoyed, and may again hope to enjoy, the varied pleasures of retirement and society. But I shall ever glory in the name and character of an Englishman. I am proud of my birth in a free and enlightened country, and the approbation of that country is the best and most honourable reward for my labours' (Preface to vol. iv dated: from Downing Street May 1, 1788).

22 At Tunbridge—G left London on 17 July and went to Sheffield Place. On the 19th, he went to Tunbridge Wells accompanied by his friends who stayed the night with him. On the 20th he said good-bye and with Wilhelm de Sévery proceeded to Dover. They crossed on the 21st, lay at Calais, left it on the 22nd and arrived at L. early on the 30th (*Add. MSS 34882,* f 255).

25 introduced to the English world—For Wilhelm de Sévery's stay in
England, see M. et Mme William de Sévery, *La Vie de Société dans le
pays de Vaud à la fin du dix-huitième siècle*, 2 vols, Lausanne and Paris,
1912, ii, ch. iii.

Page 184

11 interval—pause, interruption.

30 respectable family—the Charrière de Sévery: Salomon (1724-1793),
Catherine, née de Chandieu (1741-1796), their son Wilhelm (1767-
1858) and their daughter Angletine (1770-1848). On their relations
with G see M. et Mme de Sévery, *op. cit.*, ii, ch. I (Edward Gibbon) and
II (Le genre de vie de Gibbon à Lausanne).

Page 185

19 above 250 years—The Pays de Vaud was part of the possessions of the
dukes of Savoy until 1536, when it was conquered by the republic of
Bern.

Page 186

16 Horace, *Epistolarum*, I, i, 60-61.

32 superfluous health—Pope, *Essay on Man*, III, 3.

34 animal machine—Although 'machine' was 'applied to the human and
animal frame' as early as 1602 (*N.E.D.*, 4 c.) G may be indebted,
perhaps unconsciously, to J. de la Mettrie (1709-1775) whose famous
work *L'Homme machine* appeared in 1748, and was translated into
English in 1750.

37 about the age of forty—G was actually 35 when, early in December
1772, 'a horrid Monster ycleped the Gout' (*Letters*, i, p. 352) made
him a first visit.

Page 187

15 By her will, G's aunt Hester left him her Sussex estate with a sum of
£1,000, reduced by codicil to £100. The rest of her property went to
the family of William Law.

16 jointure—From 1779, Mrs Gibbon received from her step-son £300 a
year in two half-yearly payments at Midsummer and Christmas.

Page 188

32 Fontenelle—Fontenelle's opinion that 'l'âge où il avait été le plus
heureux était de cinquante-cinq à soixante-quinze ans' was recorded by
Buffon: 'Quelqu'un demandoit au philosophe Fontenelle, âgé de quatre-
vingt-quinze ans, quelles étoient les vingt années de sa vie qu'il re-

grettoit le plus; il répondit qu'il regrettoit peu de chose, que néanmoins l'âge où il avoit été le plus heureux étoit de cinquante-cinq à soixante-quinze ans; il fit cet aveu de bonne foi, & il prouva son dire par des vérités sensibles et consolantes. A cinquante-cinq ans la fortune est établie, la réputation faite, la considération obtenue, l'état de la vie fixe, les prétentions évanouies ou remplies, les projets avortés ou mûris, la plupart des passions calmées ou du moins refroidies, la carrière à peu près remplie pour les travaux que chaque homme doit à la société . . .' Buffon, *Histoire naturelle*, Collection complette des œuvres, 45 vols in-12, Paris 1769-85, xi (Supplément), 'Addition à l'article de la Vieillesse et de la Mort', pp. 146-147.

Page 190

1 G first mentions the Neckers' arrival at L. at the end of a letter to his step-mother of 2 June 1784 (*Letters*, ii, p. 413). That he saw them 'frequently' in the following months is evident from various passages in his letters (*Ibid.*, iii, pp. 2, 9, 10-11, 17).

2 country-house—For a description of the 'château de Beaulieu' which Necker rented for the summer, a fairly large house, which was new in 1784, see P. Kohler, *Madame de Staël et la Suisse*, Lausanne 1916, pp. 63-64.
composed—Necker spent the summer at L. partly no doubt because the Château de Coppet which he had just bought was in need of repairs, but essentially because he had made arrangements with the publisher Grasset and the 'Société typographique' for the printing and publication of his 3 vol. treatise *De l'administration des finances de la France*, which he had written at Paris since his resignation in 1781. He may have done some revision before taking his manuscript to the printer, but his time at L. was mostly spent in correcting his proofs. The book came out in December 1784.

9 Prince Henry of Prussia (1726-1802), 3rd son of Frederick-William I, King of Prussia. Frederick II, the eldest son, having no heir, it had been arranged that, after him, the crown would pass to the second son, Augustus-William, and his descendants. Augustus-William died in 1757; his son became heir presumptive and, at the death of Frederick II, ascended the throne as a matter of course, and reigned as Frederick-William II. Born in 1744, he was forty-two when his reign began, and had a son of eighteen. Prince Henry had therefore no chance of ever reigning. But according to the author of *Histoire secrette de la Cour de Berlin*, Prince Henry was not reconciled to seeing his nephew on the throne and having no influence himself on public affairs: 'Le prince ne se farde plus sur sa position' mais 'clabaudant déjà, disant que le pays est perdu . . . il acheve par l'intempérance de sa langue . . . de se perdre

dans l'esprit du Roi . . . il quittera, si on le lui permet, ce pays où il n'a pas un ami, ni une créature, si ce n'est dans le subalterne le plus abject; il quittera ce pays; ou il deviendra fou; ou il mourra; voilà mon pronostic.'—'Le prince Henri . . . se promet tôt ou tard une grande influence . . . c'est un mélange d'exaltation & de rodomontades, de présomption et d'anxiétés, un flux de paroles sans rien de positif . . . il est difficile de conclure s'il se trompe, ou s'il veut tromper: s'il soutient le procès de son amour-propre, ou s'il se repait d'illusions . . .' (*Histoire secrette*, i, p. 84, lettre du 5 Septembre 1786). 'Le prince Henri se regarde comme écarté . . . Il est persuadé, ou croit être persuadé, que la foule innombrable de sottises qui résultera de son éloignement, (car dans son opinion, sans lui le pays est perdu) fera recourir à son expérience, à ses talens', mais 'très-probablement il sera mort avant qu'on ait eu le temps de s'apercevoir qu'on a besoin de lui . . . Il vient passer quatre mois à Berlin, comme un martyr, dit-il, afin qu'on ne puisse pas dire qu'il a déserté la chose publique; ensuite de quoi . . . le lac de Genève, la France seront ses asyles. Il en trouvera facilement partout pour les consolations de son choix, aujourd'hui qu'il peut rester des heures entières à jouer au colin-maillard, ou la main-chaude, chez les plus insipides comédiennes, telles que n'en offriroient point nos plus mauvaises villes de province' (*Ibid.*, ii, p. 15, lettre du 24 Octobre 1786). For Prince Henri's distinguished military career see *B.U.* under 'Henri'. *Histoire secrette de la Cour de Berlin ou Correspondance d'un voyageur françois, depuis le cinq Juillet 1786 jusqu'au dix-neuf Janvier 1787, Ouvrage posthume*, 3 vols, s.l., 1789. Though published anonymously and as after its author's death, it was almost at once known to be by young Mirabeau whom Vergennes, Louis XVI's minister for foreign affairs, had sent to the court of Prussia on a secret mission (see H. Welschinger, *La mission secrète de Mirabeau à Berlin*, Paris, 1900). G had first written 'malice of Mirabeau', but as he regarded Mirabeau as one of the leaders of the Revolution which he hated and feared, he corrected 'Mirabeau' into 'a Demon'.

15 Fox's visit to G was on 18-19 September 1788; see *Letters*, iii, pp. 127 and 132.

20 Arriving in Hades, Heracles is recognized by Diogenes the Cynic to whom he says that he is only part of himself, his mortal part, the son of Alcmene and Amphytrion, whilst his immortal part, Zeus' true son, is now in Olympus with his father and all the other gods; an explanation which rouses the philosopher's laughter and derision.

Page 191

1 At the Synods of Ephesus (431) and Chalcedon (451) the dogma of the Incarnation—Christ one person but two natures—was finally fixed. See *D.F.*, ch. xlvii.

4 Prideaux—For Humphrey Prideaux, D.D. (1648-1724), see *D.N.B.* In his library at L. G had a copy of the 1718 ed. of Prideaux's *The True Nature of Imposture fully Displayed in the Life of Mahomet*, London, 1697.

9 apprehensive—'. . . my purpose was to give an account, first of the Controversies which miserably divided those Eastern Churches, and then of that grievous Calamity and Ruin which hapned to them thereupon through that deluge of *Mahometan* Tyranny and Delusion . . . I hoped that perchance by laying open before the Contending Parties here among us what mischief those Eastern Churches suffered . . . through that dismal Ruin which was by their divisions brought upon them, I might awaken them . . . to think of those things which might tend to their peace . . . But when I had made my Collections and gone a great way in putting my last hand to the Composure, those Disturbances that hapned about the Doctrine of the Holy Trinity among us, gave me a reflection which put a stop to my pen, and made me resolve to surcease the whole Work. For perceiving what advantage the unwary stirring of this Controversy did give the *Atheist*, the Deist, and the Socinian, for the advancing of their Impieties . . . I durst not, considering the Subject of the Book, venture it abroad in so wanton and lewd an Age . . . and therefore I rather chose totally to suppress my labours, than run the hazard in their publication of doing more hurt than good thereby. Only that part which relates to the life of Mahomet . . . I have here published' (Prideaux, *op. cit.*, ed. 1697, *To the Reader*, xiv-xviii).

15 Après Constantin,' says Mably, 'Vous ne trouverez plus que quelques princes qui méritent d'être connus, & l'histoire ne doit s'occuper alors que des barbares qui détruisirent bientôt le nom romain.'

18 Ovid, *Metamorphoses*, iv, 428.

21 For Nicolas-Edme Restif de la Bretonne (1734-1806) see *B.U.*, which merely says that 'Rétif composait souvent des passages entiers sans copie, et ces morceaux étaient à son avis, les meilleurs, les mieux écrits, les mieux pensés'. He was not only a prolific writer, but a printer by trade, owning at one time his own printing-house.

Page 192

11 1784—Lord Sheffield's *Observations . . . Ireland* was first published in 1785. In the MS, it looks as though G had meant to correct his 4 into 5, but he hesitated.

20 Managers' box—See in Macaulay's essay on *Warren Hastings* his pages on the proceedings in Parliament, and in particular the paragraph on the managers, the conductors of the impeachment: '. . . the box in which the managers stood contained an array of speakers such as perhaps had not

appeared together since the great age of Athenian eloquence. . . . '. For the full list of the managers, headed by the names of Burke, Fox and Sheridan, any one of whom may have invited G to come and sit in their midst, see G. B. Malleson's *Life of Warren Hastings*, London 1896, p. 467. For a contemporary print showing Westminster Hall as it was fitted up for the proceedings, in which the managers' box appears as a bench long enough to sit a dozen gentlemen, see A. Mervyn Davies's *Warren Hastings*, London 1935, p. 484. (For these two references, the editor is indebted to Sir Gavin de Beer.)

27 Hayley published his *Essay on History in three Epistles to Edward Gibbon, Esq.* in 1780.

29 Thanked me in verse—For Hayley's *Sonnet to Edward Gibbon on the Publication of his Second and Third Volumes* see *Misc. Wks*, i, pp. 261-262.

Page 193

1 For the *Invitation*, see *Ibid.*, pp. 262-263.

9 The most naked tale—Joseph Warton devoted thirty-five pages (311-347) of his *Essay on the Genius and Writings of Pope* to the *Epistle of Eloisa to Abelard*. Coming to l. 90, Warton is content to say: 'Next she describes their unparalleled happiness in the full and free enjoyment of their loves . . .', but quotes ll. 100-105 which refer to Abelard's castration: 'A naked lover, bound and bleeding lies!' on which he comments: 'It was difficult to mention this catastrophe with any dignity and grace; in which there is still something *indelicate*, notwithstanding all the dexterity and management of our poet, in speaking of so untoward a circumstance. I know not where castration is the chief cause of distress, in any other poem, except . . . in one of Catullus, where Atys . . . inflicts this punishment on himself.' Warton may thus be said to have told the story of the celebrated lovers, in paraphrasing and quoting Pope, if not explicitly, plainly enough to be what G calls a 'naked tale'. G himself was content to allude to the 'famous and unfortunate Abelard . . . the lover of Eloisa', who is mentioned in *D.F.* once only as the master of Arnold of Brescia (ch. lxix, *Ev. Lib. ed.*, vi, p. 471), and left it to Joseph Warton, headmaster of Winchester, to tell what might have been 'the most naked tale' in his history, had he chosen to tell it himself.

12 My English text is chaste—See, for instance, in ch. xl, the pages devoted to 'the famous Theodora' (*Ev. Lib. ed.*, iv, pp. 153 ff.) and G's notes in which he referred to his Greek and Latin sources and quoted in particular Procopius' plain-spoken testimony, but in the author's own Greek.

14 Boileau's *Art Poétique*, II, 175.

21-22 praise . . . acid—'An impartial judge, I think, must allow that Mr Gibbon's History is one of the ablest performances of its kind that has ever appeared. His industry is indefatigable; his accuracy scrupulous; his reading, which indeed is sometimes ostentatiously displayed, immense; his attention always awake; his memory retentive; his style emphatic and expressive; his periods harmonious. His reflections are often just and profound; he pleads eloquently for the rights of mankind, and the duty of toleration; nor does his humanity ever slumber, unless when women are ravished or the Christians persecuted.' Though Porson sees 'nothing wrong in Mr Gibbon's attack on Christianity', he blames him, in the following paragraph, 'for carrying on the attack in an insidious manner and with improper weapons.' He then adds some fully justified strictures on the style of *D.F.*, regards as 'a less pardonable fault that rage for indecency which pervades the whole work, but especially the last volumes', and ends: 'But these few faults make no considerable abatement in my general esteem. Notwithstanding all its particular defects, I greatly admire the whole; as I should admire a beautiful face in the author, though it was tarnished with a few freckles; or as I should admire an elegant person and address, though they were blemished with a little affectation' (R. Porson, *Letters to Mr Archdeacon Travis, in answer to his Defence of the three Heavenly Witnesses, 1 John v. 7*, London, 1790, pp. xxviii-xxxi).

26 Meuselius—For Johann Georg Meusel (1743-1820), professor of history first at Erfurt, then at Erlangen Universities, see *Allgemeine Deutsche Biographie*. He was the third editor of B. G. Struve's *Bibliotheca Historica*: Bibliotheca Historica Aucta a C. G. Budero, nunc vero a I. G. Meuselio ita digesta, amplificata et emendata, ut paene novum opus videri possit, 11 vols, Lipsiae, 1782-1804.

Page 194

16-24 For the French, Italian and German translations of *D.F.*, see *Bibliography*, ch. XI and XII.

Page 195

1-4 Swift's Imitation of *The Sixth Satire of Horace's Second Book*, first published in 1727, opens on these lines:

> I've often wish'd that I had clear
> for life, six hundred pounds a year,
> A handsome House to lodge a Friend,
> A River at my garden's end,
> A Terras-walk, and half a Rood
> Of Land, set out to plant a Wood.
> Well, now I have all this and more,
> I ask not to increase my store;
> But here a Grievance seems to lie,
> All this is mine but till I die.

Remembering Swift's lines, Pope wrote in *The Second Satire of the Second Book of Horace Paraphrased*, which he published in 1734,

> My lands are sold, my Father's house is gone;
> I'll hire another's, is not that my own,
> And yours, my friends? thro' whose free-opening gate
> None comes too early, none departs too late
>
> . . . . .
>
> 'Pray Heav'n it last (cries Swift)—
> 'I wish to God this house had been your own:
> 'Pity! to build, without a son or wife
> 'Why, you'll enjoy it only all your life.'—
> Well, if the Use be mine, can it concern one
> Whether the Name belong to Pope or Vernon?
> What's Property? dear Swift! you see it alter
> From you to me, from me to Peter Walter. . . .

18 'La moitié du genere humain périt avant l'âge de huit ans un mois, c'est-à-dire avant que le corps soit développé, et avant que l'âme se manifeste par la raison' (Buffon, *Des probabilités de la durée de la Vie* in *Œuvres*, Paris 1836, iv, pp. 293-332, *Histoire naturelle*, ed. 1777, Supplément iv, p. 161).

Page 196

6 this proud sentiment—In ch. i of Book XIII of *Tom Jones*, Fielding calls on the 'fair, gentle maid, the happy nymph' who inspired Homer, Virgil and Milton, to come and fill his 'ravished fancy with the hopes of charming ages yet to come. Foretel me that some tender maid, whose grandmother is yet unborn, hereafter, when, under the fictitious name of Sophia, she reads the real worth which once existed in my Charlotte, shall from her sympathetic breast send forth the heaving sigh. Do thou teach me not only to foresee, but to enjoy, nay, even to feed on future praise. Comfort me by a solemn assurance, that when the little parlour in which I sit at this instant shall be reduced to a worse furnished box, I shall be read with honour by those who never knew nor saw me, and whom I shall never know nor see.'

10-14 'Après y avoir réfléchi, j'ai pensé que de toutes les probabilités morales possibles, celle qui affecte le plus l'homme en général, c'est la crainte de la mort, et j'ai senti dès lors que toute crainte, ou toute espérance dont la probabilité serait égale à celle qui produit la crainte de la mort, peut dans le moral être prise pour l'unité à laquelle on doit rapporter la mesure des autres craintes . . . Je cherche donc quelle est réellement la probabilité qu'un homme qui se porte bien, et qui par conséquent n'a nulle crainte de la mort, meure néanmoins dans les vingt-quatre heures. . . . En consultant les tables de mortalité, je vois qu'on en peut déduire qu'il n'y a que 10,189 à parier contre 1 qu'un homme de cinquante-six ans vivra plus d'un jour. Or comme tout homme de cet âge, où la raison a acquis toute sa maturité et l'expérience toute sa force, n'a néanmoins nulle crainte de la mort dans les vingt-quatre heures, quoiqu'il n'y ait que 10,189 à parier contre 1 qu'il ne mourra pas dans ce court lapse de temps; j'en conclus que toute probabilité égale ou plus petite, doit être regardée comme nulle, et que toute crainte ou toute espérance qui se trouve au-dessous de dix mille ne doit ne nous affecter, ni même nous occuper un seul instant le coeur ou la tête' (Buffon, *op. cit.*, p. 56).

12 or rises above—This is a mere slip on G's part: Buffon speaks of 'a chance that falls below (plus petite) or *does not rise above* (égale) ten thousand to one'.

30 Strait is the way—St Matthew, vii, 14: 'strait is the gate, and narrow is the way, which leadeth unto life, and few there be that find it.'

Index

Printed in Great Britain by
Robert Cunningham & Sons Ltd., Alva

Bound by Thomas Nelson (Printers) Ltd.,
London and Edinburgh